# SUN SIGN BOOK

Copyright ©1993 Llewellyn Publications
All rights reserved

Printed in the United States of America
Typography is property of Llewellyn Worldwide, Ltd.

ISBN: 0-87542-911-4

**Cover Design:** Christopher Wells

**Forecasts:** Gloria Star

**Contributing Writers:**
Tom Bridges, Barbara Everett,
Ninah Kessler, Ralph Pestka,
Vince Ploscik, Jeraldine Saunders,
Noel Tyl, Jude C. Williams

**Editor:** Connie Hill


Published by
LLEWELLYN WORLDWIDE, LTD.
P.O. Box 64383-911
St. Paul, MN 55164-0383

# 1994

### DECEMBER 1993
| S | M | T | W | T | F | S |
|---|---|---|---|---|---|---|
|   |   |   | 1 | 2 | 3 | 4 |
| 5 | 6 | 7 | 8 | 9 | 10 | 11 |
| 12 | 13 | 14 | 15 | 16 | 17 | 18 |
| 19 | 20 | 21 | 22 | 23 | 24 | 25 |
| 26 | 27 | 28 | 29 | 30 | 31 |   |

### JANUARY 1994
| S | M | T | W | T | F | S |
|---|---|---|---|---|---|---|
|   |   |   |   |   |   | 1 |
| 2 | 3 | 4 | 5 | 6 | 7 | 8 |
| 9 | 10 | 11 | 12 | 13 | 14 | 15 |
| 16 | 17 | 18 | 19 | 20 | 21 | 22 |
| 23 | 24 | 25 | 26 | 27 | 28 | 29 |
| 30 | 31 |   |   |   |   |   |

### FEBRUARY 1994
| S | M | T | W | T | F | S |
|---|---|---|---|---|---|---|
|   |   | 1 | 2 | 3 | 4 | 5 |
| 6 | 7 | 8 | 9 | 10 | 11 | 12 |
| 13 | 14 | 15 | 16 | 17 | 18 | 19 |
| 20 | 21 | 22 | 23 | 24 | 25 | 26 |
| 27 | 28 |   |   |   |   |   |

### MARCH 1994
| S | M | T | W | T | F | S |
|---|---|---|---|---|---|---|
|   |   | 1 | 2 | 3 | 4 | 5 |
| 6 | 7 | 8 | 9 | 10 | 11 | 12 |
| 13 | 14 | 15 | 16 | 17 | 18 | 19 |
| 20 | 21 | 22 | 23 | 24 | 25 | 26 |
| 27 | 28 | 29 | 30 | 31 |   |   |

### APRIL 1994
| S | M | T | W | T | F | S |
|---|---|---|---|---|---|---|
|   |   |   |   |   | 1 | 2 |
| 3 | 4 | 5 | 6 | 7 | 8 | 9 |
| 10 | 11 | 12 | 13 | 14 | 15 | 16 |
| 17 | 18 | 19 | 20 | 21 | 22 | 23 |
| 24 | 25 | 26 | 27 | 28 | 29 | 30 |

### MAY 1994
| S | M | T | W | T | F | S |
|---|---|---|---|---|---|---|
| 1 | 2 | 3 | 4 | 5 | 6 | 7 |
| 8 | 9 | 10 | 11 | 12 | 13 | 14 |
| 15 | 16 | 17 | 18 | 19 | 20 | 21 |
| 22 | 23 | 24 | 25 | 26 | 27 | 28 |
| 29 | 30 | 31 |   |   |   |   |

### JUNE 1994
| S | M | T | W | T | F | S |
|---|---|---|---|---|---|---|
|   |   |   | 1 | 2 | 3 | 4 |
| 5 | 6 | 7 | 8 | 9 | 10 | 11 |
| 12 | 13 | 14 | 15 | 16 | 17 | 18 |
| 19 | 20 | 21 | 22 | 23 | 24 | 25 |
| 26 | 27 | 28 | 29 | 30 |   |   |

### JULY 1994
| S | M | T | W | T | F | S |
|---|---|---|---|---|---|---|
|   |   |   |   |   | 1 | 2 |
| 3 | 4 | 5 | 6 | 7 | 8 | 9 |
| 10 | 11 | 12 | 13 | 14 | 15 | 16 |
| 17 | 18 | 19 | 20 | 21 | 22 | 23 |
| 24 | 25 | 26 | 27 | 28 | 29 | 30 |
| 31 |   |   |   |   |   |   |

### AUGUST 1994
| S | M | T | W | T | F | S |
|---|---|---|---|---|---|---|
|   | 1 | 2 | 3 | 4 | 5 | 6 |
| 7 | 8 | 9 | 10 | 11 | 12 | 13 |
| 14 | 15 | 16 | 17 | 18 | 19 | 20 |
| 21 | 22 | 23 | 24 | 25 | 26 | 27 |
| 28 | 29 | 30 | 31 |   |   |   |

### SEPTEMBER 1994
| S | M | T | W | T | F | S |
|---|---|---|---|---|---|---|
|   |   |   |   | 1 | 2 | 3 |
| 4 | 5 | 6 | 7 | 8 | 9 | 10 |
| 11 | 12 | 13 | 14 | 15 | 16 | 17 |
| 18 | 19 | 20 | 21 | 22 | 23 | 24 |
| 25 | 26 | 27 | 28 | 29 | 30 |   |

### OCTOBER 1994
| S | M | T | W | T | F | S |
|---|---|---|---|---|---|---|
|   |   |   |   |   |   | 1 |
| 2 | 3 | 4 | 5 | 6 | 7 | 8 |
| 9 | 10 | 11 | 12 | 13 | 14 | 15 |
| 16 | 17 | 18 | 19 | 20 | 21 | 22 |
| 23 | 24 | 25 | 26 | 27 | 28 | 29 |
| 30 | 31 |   |   |   |   |   |

### NOVEMBER 1994
| S | M | T | W | T | F | S |
|---|---|---|---|---|---|---|
|   |   | 1 | 2 | 3 | 4 | 5 |
| 6 | 7 | 8 | 9 | 10 | 11 | 12 |
| 13 | 14 | 15 | 16 | 17 | 18 | 19 |
| 20 | 21 | 22 | 23 | 24 | 25 | 26 |
| 27 | 28 | 29 | 30 |   |   |   |

### DECEMBER 1994
| S | M | T | W | T | F | S |
|---|---|---|---|---|---|---|
|   |   |   |   | 1 | 2 | 3 |
| 4 | 5 | 6 | 7 | 8 | 9 | 10 |
| 11 | 12 | 13 | 14 | 15 | 16 | 17 |
| 18 | 19 | 20 | 21 | 22 | 23 | 24 |
| 25 | 26 | 27 | 28 | 29 | 30 | 31 |

### JANUARY 1995
| S | M | T | W | T | F | S |
|---|---|---|---|---|---|---|
| 1 | 2 | 3 | 4 | 5 | 6 | 7 |
| 8 | 9 | 10 | 11 | 12 | 13 | 14 |
| 15 | 16 | 17 | 18 | 19 | 20 | 21 |
| 22 | 23 | 24 | 25 | 26 | 27 | 28 |
| 29 | 30 | 31 |   |   |   |   |

### FEBRUARY 1995
| S | M | T | W | T | F | S |
|---|---|---|---|---|---|---|
|   |   |   | 1 | 2 | 3 | 4 |
| 5 | 6 | 7 | 8 | 9 | 10 | 11 |
| 12 | 13 | 14 | 15 | 16 | 17 | 18 |
| 19 | 20 | 21 | 22 | 23 | 24 | 25 |
| 26 | 27 | 28 |   |   |   |   |

# TABLE OF CONTENTS

**Gloria Star**

The sign descriptions, yearly and monthly horoscopes for Sun Signs 1994 are all written by Gloria Star. A professional astrologer for 20 years, she is an internationally renowned author and teacher. In addition to writing the *Sun Sign Book* for Llewellyn since 1990, she is the author of *Optimum Child: Developing Your Child's Fullest Potential through Astrology* (Llewellyn 1987), and a contributing author of *Houses: Power Places in the Horoscope* and *How to Manage the Astrology of Crisis* (Llewellyn 1990, 1993).

Gloria is active in the astrological community, serving on the faculty of the United Astrology Congress (UAC) since its inception in 1986, and has lectured for groups and conferences throughout North America. She is a member of the Advisory Board for the National Council for Geocosmic Research (NCGR) and has served on the Steering Committee for the Association for Astrological Networking (AFAN) She is also the editor of the AFAN Newsletter. She makes her home in the shoreline township of Clinton, Connecticut with her husband and son.

# NEW CONCEPTS
# FOR THE SIGNS OF THE ZODIAC

| Aries | ♈ | The Initiator |
| Taurus | ♉ | The Maintainer |
| Gemini | ♊ | The Questioner |
| Cancer | ♋ | The Nurturer |
| Leo | ♌ | The Loyalist |
| Virgo | ♍ | The Modifier |
| Libra | ♎ | The Judge |
| Scorpio | ♏ | The Catalyst |
| Sagittarius | ♐ | The Adventurer |
| Capricorn | ♑ | The Pragmatist |
| Aquarius | ♒ | The Reformer |
| Pisces | ♓ | The Visionary |

# New Concepts for the Signs of the Zodiac

The signs of the zodiac represent characteristics and traits which indicate how energy operates within our lives. The signs tell the story of human evolution and development, and are all necessary to form the continuum of whole life experience. In fact, within your own personal astrological chart, all twelve signs are indicated!

Although the traditional metaphors for the twelve signs (e.g. "Aries, The Ram") are always functional, these alternative concepts for each of the twelve signs are indicative of the gradual unfolding of the human spirit.

**Aries. The Initiator,** is the first sign of the zodiac and encompasses the primary concept of getting things started. This fiery ignition and bright beginning can prove to be the thrust necessary for new life. But The Initiator can also appear before a situation is ready for new change and create disruption!

**Taurus. The Maintainer,** sustains what Aries has begun and brings stability and focus into the picture. Yet there can also be a tendency to try to maintain something in its current state without allowing for new growth!

**Gemini. The Questioner,** seeks to determine if alternatives are possible—and offers diversity to the processes Taurus has brought into stability. Yet questioning can also lead to distraction, subsequently scattering energy and diffusing focus.

**Cancer. The Nurturer,** provides the qualities necessary for growth and security and encourages a deepening awareness of the emotional needs. Yet this same nurturance can stifle individuation if it becomes smothering.

**Leo. The Loyalist,** directs and centralizes the experiences Cancer feeds. This quality is powerfully targeted toward self-awareness, but can be short sighted. Hence,

The Loyalist can hold steadfastly to a viewpoint or feelings which inhibit new experiences.

**Virgo. The Modifier,** analyzes the situations Leo brings to light and determines possibilities for change. Even though this change may be in the name of improvement, it can lead to dissatisfaction with the self if not directed in harmony with higher needs.

**Libra. The Judge,** is constantly comparing everything to be sure that a certain level of rightness and perfection is presented. However, The Judge can present possibilities which are harsh and seem to be cold or without feeling.

**Scorpio. The Catalyst,** steps into the play of life to provide the quality of alchemical transformation. The Catalyst can stir the brew just enough to create a healing potion, or may get things going to such a powerful extent that they boil out of control.

**Sagittarius. The Adventurer,** moves away from Scorpio's dimension to seek what lies beyond the horizon. The Adventurer continually looks for possibilities which answer the ultimate questions, but may forget the pathway back home.

**Capricorn. The Pragmatist,** attempts to put everything into its rightful place and find ways to make life work out "right." Although The Pragmatist can teach lessons of practicality and determination, when short-sighted, can become highly self-righteous.

**Aquarius. The Reformer,** looks for ways to take what Capricorn has built and bring it up to date. Yet there is also a tendency to scrap the original in favor of a new plan which may not have the stable foundation necessary to operate effectively.

**Pisces. The Visionary,** brings mysticism and imagination and challenges the soul to move into the realm beyond the physical plane into what might be. The visionary can pierce the veil, returning enlightened to the physical world. The challenge is to avoid getting lost within the illusion of an alternate reality.

# How To Benefit Most From Sun Sign Astrology

**Gloria Star**

Astrology is a complex system used to clarify your identity and your needs. The Sun, Moon, and each of the planets symbolize many levels of need and energy expression. The Sun symbolizes the ego self, the individual drive to be noticed as a significant being. Each sign of the zodiac represents a set of characteristics and traits which modify the energy of the Sun, Moon, and planets, adding color to the personality. Your Sun Sign is only one factor among many which describes who you are, but it is a powerful one!

The horoscopes in the following section are based upon the sign the Sun was in at the time of your birth. Although we can examine a number of your needs and life situations from this information, there are many other factors which a professional astrologer would explore to help you guide your life. If you would like more information to accompany the guidelines in this book, you might appreciate the personalized, more detailed information you'll receive from a competent professional astrologer.

I've described the year's major challenges and opportunities for every Sun sign in the "Year Ahead" section. The first part of the section applies to all individuals born under the influence of the sign. In addition, I've included information for specific birth dates that will help you understand the inner process of change you'll be experiencing during 1994. The cycles described in this section illustrate your fundamental themes for the year ahead. Consider these ideas as underlying principles that will be present throughout the entire year. These cycles comprise your major challenges and opportunities relating to your personal identity. Blend these ideas with the information you find in the monthly forecast section for your Sun Sign and Ascendant.

To best use the information in the monthly forecasts, you'll want to determine your Ascendant or rising sign. If you don't know your Ascendant, the Ascendant Tables (following this description) will help you determine your rising sign. They are most accurate for those born in the Western Hemisphere between 60-130 degrees longitude (e.g. the Continental United States). Once you've figured out your Ascending Sign, you'll know two significant factors in your astrological chart. Read the monthly forecast sections for both your Sun and Ascendant to gain the most useful information.

Your "Rewarding and Challenging Days" sections indicate times when you'll feel more centered ("Rewarding") or out of balance ("Challenging"). The Rewarding Days are not the only times you can perform well, but you're likely to feel better integrated! These days support your expression of individual identity. During the Challenging Days, take some extra time to center yourself by meditating or using other techniques which help you feel more objective.

These guidelines, although highly useful, cannot incorporate all the factors influencing your current life situation. However, you can use this information as a form of objective awareness about the way the current cycles are affecting you at an ego level. Realize that the power of astrology is even more useful when you have a complete chart and professional guidance.

During the entire year of 1994, we are incorporating many of the changes which began during the Uranus-Neptune conjunction of 1993. Although the intensity of this cycle is diminishing, we are collectively continuing to experience the need to examine our values and life choices. The themes for 1994 involve getting in touch with ourselves at the emotional level and acknowledging our real worth. As we learn to accept and acknowledge our personal emotional needs, we can begin to step away from many of the attitudes and behaviors which are based upon a fear of loss. As individuals, we are each charged to create a safe place for ourselves spiritually, emotionally, and physically. By choosing to use your heightened sensibilities to become a more complete person, you move further onto the path of positive self-realization. Your personal evolutionary choices do make a significant difference, not only for yourself, but for all of humanity. Have a superb year!

Gloria Star

*Horus non numero nisi serenas*

Count only the Sunny Hours

Your Ascendant is the following if your time of birth was:

| If your Sun Sign is: | 6 to 8 am | 8 to 10 am | 10 am to Noon | Noon to 2 pm | 2 to 4 pm | 4 to 6 pm |
|---|---|---|---|---|---|---|
| Aries | Taurus | Gemini | Cancer | Leo | Virgo | Libra |
| Taurus | Gemini | Cancer | Leo | Virgo | Libra | Scorpio |
| Gemini | Cancer | Leo | Virgo | Libra | Scorpio | Sagittarius |
| Cancer | Leo | Virgo | Libra | Scorpio | Sagittarius | Capricorn |
| Leo | Virgo | Libra | Scorpio | Sagittarius | Capricorn | Aquarius |
| Virgo | Libra | Scorpio | Sagittarius | Capricorn | Aquarius | Pisces |
| Libra | Scorpio | Sagittarius | Capricorn | Aquarius | Pisces | Aries |
| Scorpio | Sagittarius | Capricorn | Aquarius | Pisces | Aries | Taurus |
| Sagittarius | Capricorn | Aquarius | Pisces | Aries | Taurus | Gemini |
| Capricorn | Aquarius | Pisces | Aries | Taurus | Gemini | Cancer |
| Aquarius | Pisces | Aries | Taurus | Gemini | Cancer | Leo |
| Pisces | Aries | Taurus | Gemini | Cancer | Leo | Virgo |

| If your Sun Sign is: | 6 to 8 pm | 8 to 10 pm | 10 pm to Midnight | Midnight to 2 am | 2 to 4 am | 4 to 6 am |
| --- | --- | --- | --- | --- | --- | --- |
| Aries | Scorpio | Sagittarius | Capricorn | Aquarius | Pisces | Aries |
| Taurus | Sagittarius | Capricorn | Aquarius | Pisces | Aries | Taurus |
| Gemini | Capricorn | Aquarius | Pisces | Aries | Taurus | Gemini |
| Cancer | Aquarius | Pisces | Aries | Taurus | Gemini | Cancer |
| Leo | Pisces | Aries | Taurus | Gemini | Cancer | Leo |
| Virgo | Aries | Taurus | Gemini | Cancer | Leo | Virgo |
| Libra | Taurus | Gemini | Cancer | Leo | Virgo | Libra |
| Scorpio | Gemini | Cancer | Leo | Virgo | Libra | Scorpio |
| Sagittarius | Cancer | Leo | Virgo | Libra | Scorpio | Sagittarius |
| Capricorn | Leo | Virgo | Libra | Scorpio | Sagittarius | Capricorn |
| Aquarius | Virgo | Libra | Scorpio | Sagittarius | Capricorn | Aquarius |
| Pisces | Libra | Scorpio | Sagittarius | Capricorn | Aquarius | Pisces |

1. Find your Sun Sign (left column);
2. Determine correct approximate time of birth column;
3. Line up your Sun Sign with birth time to find ascendant.

# PLANETARY ASSOCIATIONS

**Sun:** Authority figures, favors, advancement, health, success, display, drama, promotion, fun, matters related toleeoand the 5th House.

**Moon:** Short trips, women, children, the public, domestic concerns, emotions, fluids, matters related to Cancer and the 4th House.

**Mercury:** Communications, correspondence, phone calls, computers, messages, education, students, travel, merchants, editing, writing, advertising, signing contracts, siblings, neighbors, kin, matters related to Gemini, Virgo, and the 3rd and 6th Houses.

**Venus:** Affection, relationships, partnerships, alliances, grace, beauty, harmony, luxury, love, art, music, so cial activity, marriage, decorating, cosmetics, gifts, income, matters related to Taurus, Libra, and the 2nd and 7th Houses.

**Mars:** Strife, aggression, sex, physical energy, muscu-lar activity, guns, tools, metals, cutting, surgery, police, soldiers, combat, confrontation, matters related to Aries, Scorpio, and the 1st and 8th Houses.

**Jupiter:** Publishing, college education, long-distance travel, foreign interests, religion, philosophy, forecasting, broadcasting, publicity, expansion, luck, growth, sports, horses, the Law, matters related to Sagittarius, Pisces, and 9th and 12th House issues.

**Saturn:** Structure, reality, the laws of society, limits, ob-stacles, tests, hard work, endurance, real estate, dentists, bones, teeth, matters related to Capricorn, Aquarius, and the 10th and 11th Houses.

**Uranus:** Astrology, the New Age, technology, comput-ers, modern gadgets, lecturing, advising, counseling, in-ventions, reforms, electricity, new methods, originality, matters related to Aquarius and the 11th House.

**Neptune:** Mysticism, music, creative imagination, dance, illusion, sacrifice, service, oil, chemicals, paint, drugs, anesthesia, sleep, religious experience, matters related to Pisces and the 12th House.

**Pluto:** Probing, penetration, goods of the dead, investi-ation, insurance, taxes, others' money, loans, the masses, he underworld, transformation, death, matters related to Scorpio and the 8th House.

14

# SUN SIGN
# FORECASTS

## for

## 1994

| Sign | Glyph | Dates | Ruler | Element | Quality | Nature |
|------|-------|-------|-------|---------|---------|--------|
| Aries | ♈ | Mar 21–Apr 20 | Mars | Fire | Cardinal | Barren |
| Taurus | ♉ | Apr 20–May 21 | Venus | Earth | Fixed | Semi-Fruitful |
| Gemini | ♊ | May 21–June 22 | Mercury | Air | Mutable | Barren |
| Cancer | ♋ | June 22–July 23 | Moon | Water | Cardinal | Fruitful |
| Leo | ♌ | July 23–Aug 23 | Sun | Fire | Fixed | Barren |
| Virgo | ♍ | Aug 23–Sept 23 | Mercury | Earth | Mutable | Barren |
| Libra | ♎ | Sept 23–Oct 23 | Venus | Air | Cardinal | Semi-Fruitful |
| Scorpio | ♏ | Oct 23–Nov 22 | Pluto | Water | Fixed | Fruitful |
| Sagittarius | ♐ | Nov 22–Dec 22 | Jupiter | Fire | Mutable | Barren |
| Capricorn | ♑ | Dec 22–Jan 21 | Saturn | Earth | Cardinal | Semi-Fruitful |
| Aquarius | ♒ | Jan 21–Feb 20 | Uranus | Air | Fixed | Barren |
| Pisces | ♓ | Feb 20–Mar 21 | Neptune | Water | Mutable | Fruitful |

# ♈ ARIES ♈
## The Ram

### March 21 to April 20

**Element:** Fire

**Quality:** Cardinal

**Polarity:** Masculine/Yang

**Planetary Ruler:** Mars

**Meditation:** "I actively pursue the fulfillment of my destiny"

**Gemstone:** Diamond

**Power Stones:** Ruby, carnelian, bloodstone

**Key Phrase:** "I am"

**Glyph:** Ram's head

**Anatomy:** Head and face

**Colors:** Red and white

**Animal:** Ram

**Myths/Legends:** Jason & the Golden Fleece, Artemis

**House Association:** 1st

**Opposite Sign:** Libra

**Flower:** Geranium

**Key Word:** Initiative

**Positive Expression:**
  Courageous
  Exuberant
  Innovative
  Assertive
  Intrepid
  Daring
  Self-reliant
  Exciting
  Inspiring
  Energetic
  Incisive

**Misuse of Energy:**
  Combative
  Blunt
  Impatient
  Rash
  Reckless
  Abrasive
  Incomplete
  Belligerent
  Careless
  Childish

# ♈ ARIES ♈

## Your Ego's Strengths and Weaknesses

You're always on the move, ready to take on new challenges and blaze a path toward your desires. Through the energy of your ruling planet, Mars, you express your natural courage and strong physical drive to make things happen. It's not your style to wait for the right time—you invented the phrase, "Go for it!"

While you're pioneering new territories and instigating new activities, you can be the inspiration for those who lack the courage to take the lead. And even though you can use your powerful drive to get where you're heading, others may experience your exuberant energy as abrasive. By becoming more aware of the effect your actions and words can have upon others, you can avoid negative confrontation and instead inspire more admiration and success.

You possess an ability to continually create new ideas and options for yourself, and can move forward when others see no way out. Your exuberance sets you apart from the apathetic crowd who would be content with the status quo. But remember to take time to enjoy your creations, and to revitalize yourself before you reach a point of complete exhaustion. Through your excitement for life you can remain ever-young and continue to create an exceptional reality.

## Your Career Development

A career needs to keep you busy and active, and you may decide to pursue an option which keeps you both mentally alert and physically challenged. You can sell anything, and may prefer a job which gives you plenty of independence and room to try new ideas. Your sharp intellect is well-suited to a career in medicine or politics. Or you might prefer a physically demanding career in athletics, coaching, fire-fighting, dancing, police work or the military. Occupations in the travel industry, beauty and hair-design, jewelry-making, auto mechanics or design, metalworking, masonry, or welding can be appealing.

## Your Approach to Romance

For you, the enticement of romance is its challenge and the joy of conquest. If you're interested, it's more likely you will be the pursuer, since waiting for the other person to act may try your patience! But watch your passion—since it can overwhelm the shy types. For any relationship to become long-term, you'll need to feel positive support for your own self-expression. Your ideal mate will enjoy your playfulness and desire to expose the reaches of the unexplored!

Although you might be stimulated by a relationship with another Aries, the heat of passion can be too intense unless you give yourselves some time apart. With the other fire signs—Leo and Sagittarius—you may feel an easy camaraderie. Leo is a joy, but can become upset if your loyalty fails. And with Sagittarius, your flirtatious antics meet good humor and high adventure.

The appeal of Taurus is their sensuality, but you may grow impatient with their slower pace. Gemini's diversity is highly appealing, and you'll both enjoy your battles of wits. The protectiveness of Cancer is great when it comes to support at home, but you may run into trouble if you don't show up on time! Virgo may have strong appeal and can be an excellent working partner, but you may feel pressured by their expectations.

Your provocative opposite sign, Libra, can be your perfect partner, but you may feel that you never quite measure up to their demands for perfection. An intense relationship with Scorpio definitely lights your fire, but your flame may wane if they try to overpower you. Capricorn may provide intrigue, but you can feel put off by all those rules and commitments. There may be a natural ease with independent Aquarius, whose friendship and support give you plenty of room to grow. And with Pisces, you can forgive a sense of not quite knowing where you stand, since you may feel a deep sense of friendship and bonding.

## Your Use of Power

Your greatest feeling of power emerges when you're beginning something new and your engine is at full throttle! With your natural leadership abilities, you can be a strong motivator of others or an independent operator capable of making your own way alone. When activity ceases and everyone else has run out of steam or reached a blockade, you're the one with the power to get things moving again. But in many circumstances, maintaining power means heavy responsibility, which is not your cup of tea!

By watching a tendency to become domineering or selfish when faced with difficulties or challenges, you can avoid the backlash of uncooperative behavior from others. And there is that tendency to "accidentally" run rough-shod over another, leaving trauma or hurt feelings in your wake. By becoming more aware of the effect your actions have upon the others in your world, you can avoid increased difficulties in both personal and professional relationships.

You can be the lighthouse in the storm, ever-shining when others have lost their way. Your path is that of self-knowledge, which can only come from exploring both the outside world and the inner path to your True Self.

## Famous Aries

Dana Carvey, Sandra Day O'Connor, Percy Faith, Albert Gore, Jr., Jan Hammer, Conchata Ferrell, Joel Grey, Alec Guinness, Marilu Henner, Elton John, Cloris Leachman, Henry Mancini, Eddie Murphy, Debbie Reynolds, Florenz Ziegfeld.

# THE YEAR AHEAD FOR ARIES

Your most intensive feeling this year may be one of a need to complete those unfinished projects. It's as though you're standing at the tip of the iceberg, knowing there's a new direction, but not quite certain of all the exact details. The expansion of last year may have left you feeling that there was just not enough time to get everything done, but now you can concentrate more on the specifics and make some adjustments.

While Saturn begins its transit of your Solar 12th House, you may also be experiencing the release of many situations from your past which are no longer relevant. Look for a stronger incorporation of the spiritual in your everyday life, bringing the spiritual element into a practical focus. This is a maturing phase, and you're reviewing both accomplishments and failures. It may be time to let go of the people and situations which have supported you in the past, especially if it's time to stand on your own. But the temptation to keep using those outworn crutches can overwhelm you through the emergence of old fears. Examine fears to discover their source, and then marshal your courage to deal with them directly. You'll be tossing those cumbersome crutches in no time!

Jupiter's transit in Scorpio lasts until December 9, and can encourage your growth in areas that are not entirely comfortable, but which are necessary. It's time to look beneath the surface and deal with many of the underlying issues that have blocked your progress in the past. You may find that there are many people who are both willing and capable of helping you reach your goals. In fact, by cooperatively utilizing the resources and energy of others, you may find that you can each accomplish more than you could as individuals. This is an excellent time to improve your health through greater attention to your own attitudes toward your physical needs. And it's also an important year for improvement in your personal relationships—a time when a deeper level of intimacy can bring the type of connection you've avoided out of fear or self-doubt. You may find that the barriers blocking your needs for a deepening of intimacy are finally ready to fall away.

Spiritually, 1994 is a year of addressing your needs to understand the experiences of healing and transformation. It's time to embrace your own worth, and open to a deeper sense of love and compassion. While the Solar Eclipses in May and November emphasize issues of self-worth, you may also find yourself taking a closer look at your attitudes toward the material side of life. You can be *both* spiritually aware and financially successful! Take a good look at the level of your attachment to the things you own and the people you love. There may be contrasts you hadn't seen before. With Chiron traveling through your Solar 6th House, you may also find a renewed interest in self-improvement. Even your work can become a form of positive therapy! Replenish your sense of passion and compassion through exercising greater care and concern for others and for yourself.

**If your birthday occurred from March 21–April 3, you may be feeling an underlying sense of apprehension while Saturn transits in semi-sextile to your Sun.** This can be a time of strong success, but you have to be willing to take on the responsibilities and to maintain the focus necessary to achieve your goals. If you feel you've dropped the ball, this cycle offers the opportunity to try again. Giving way to hesitation can undermine your confidence if you don't deal directly with the root cause. Get clear about your motivations, and discover the reasons behind your drive (or lack of it!). Many times, the discouraging voice inside your head comes from old fears or anxieties incorporated at a earlier age. Certainly it's important to be honest with yourself and realistic about your life circumstances, but you must also realize the power of your own drive and mental ingenuity. If you uncover some inner messages which have brought you self-sabotage in the past, now's the time to eliminate those messages and replace them with self-confidence and courage to accomplish your dreams.

**If you were born between March 22–26, you are experiencing a subtle influence from Neptune transiting in quintile to your Sun.** This energy can help to provide you with the creative imagination to tap into your finer talents and gifts. If you're feeling creatively blocked, begin to work with your dreams to help unlock your creative drive. Creative visualization works very effectively during this cycle, since this an energy that can open the gateways to your ability to manifest those hopes which are in harmony with your highest needs.

**For those born between March 23–28, Uranus is transiting in quintile to your Sun,** bringing a subtle impulse to break out of the bondage that has thwarted some of your natural aptitudes. To work most effectively with this energy, take time to connect with your inner center. Then, allow your mind to be open to new ideas and more freely flowing directions for those ideas. This is an excellent cycle to begin fine-tuning a special talent or experimenting with a new approach to your life.

**If you were born between April 4–8, this is an excellent time to stabilize the new directions you began during the last two years.** Your sense of self should be in good shape, and others may be seeing more consistency in your efforts. It may be tempting to fall back into the old patterns you've rebelled against since the beginning of this decade. Before you retreat, be sure of your motivations. If you feel you've given way to illusions that have no basis in reality, this is an excellent time to incorporate what you've learned and return to your "real" self. But make sure that you avoid the ruts left in your path from your earlier revolution!

**You're feeling the imaginative and mystical influence of Neptune transiting in square aspect to your Sun if you were born between April 9–13.** Although you may have been highly motivated to achieve particular ideals in the past, this cycle draws your attention to another side of reality. This can be a time of spiritual initiation and blending with your Higher Self, and you may be drawn to a more idealistic lifestyle. But you can also fall into the trap of self-deceit if you fail to maintain contact with your true self. You may feel a stronger need to help others who are suffering, although you can become the victim if you are drawn into unhealthy situations. For creative and artistic endeavors, the energy of Neptune helps you blend with the elements of life that are beyond the physical plane. Bringing what you feel inside into a physical manifestation can be challenging. Your drive may be less intense than usual, since much of your energy draws you deep within instead of stimulating your assertiveness. To maintain a strong level of physical vitality, avoid substances which drain energy. Remain conscious that your body's physical needs require paying some attention to your health, and you'll avoid the physically draining side of this transit.

The explosive, changeable energy of Uranus squares your Sun this year if you were born between April 10–16. This cycle stimulates the sudden and unexpected, and you may feel that each day brings a different reality. Since you're also feeling influence from Neptune's transit, you may feel somewhat out-of-touch with your needs. But you're also ready to drop the shackles that inhibit your self-expression. Relationships frequently undergo powerful changes during this cycle, especially those which have been highly influential in shaping your sense of self. Although there's a tendency to be directly rebellious, you may also find that others are acting rebelliously toward you! If this is the case, take a good look inside yourself. You may be ignoring a strong urge to make significant changes. To avoid the negative side of this cycle, maintain a more consistent quality of mindfulness. Listen to your own intuitive voice. If you maintain a close contact with yourself during such an intensive time of change, your breakthroughs can be more productive and less disruptive.

If you were born from April 14–20, you're feeling the intensive pull of Pluto transiting in quincunx to your Sun. You may feel that your efforts are constantly bogged down with complications, and can find yourself confronting some unfinished emotional issues. The essence of this cycle involves a deepening of your real power. Situations which connect you with influential and powerful individuals may be uncomfortable, but you can also see a new strength emerging from yourself. Self-doubt needs to vanish in the face of restored faith in yourself. This is the perfect time to get to the core of physical problems, but you'll need to take a holistic approach to have the most effective results. Your individual work in reshaping your own attitudes toward yourself is as effective as any medicine. Focus carefully on your goals early in the year while Saturn sextiles your Sun. Then, use Pluto's energy to help clear away the crusty debris that may be hiding that part of you which is like a priceless gem. It's your time to become whole.

## Tools to Make a Difference

Throughout this year you're finding ways to get back to the more basic elements of yourself. You can also make significant improvements in the world around you by becoming more aware of the best ways to restore, reuse and recycle. This not only applies to the *things* you're utlizing, but also to your own personal expenditure of energy.

In your career, find ways to incorporate innovative technology and better forms of communication. Attend motivational workshops, or, if you're so inclined, offer them to others! If you're "sick of work," make sure your feelings don't manifest as physical ailments by addressing the real issues you have with your job. It may be time for either a change of job or a change of attitude!

As with every Sun Sign, you are naturally attuned to particular colors and vibrational forms. The red and white which represent Aries energy are high-energy colors. Whether wearing or using your colors in your environment, you'll find that red is a stimulating color, while white radiates a quality of purity and protection. In meditations, work with breathing techniques to bring energy into balance. Focus on the color pink as you inhale, allowing this color to penetrate every cell in your body. When working with crystals or stones, use your power stones—diamonds, carnelian, rubies and bloodstone—to amplify your natural passion and inner strength.

To avoid carrying excessive tension in your face and neck, take time each day to concentrate on stretching the muscles in the back, neck, and arms, and remember to preface and end each of your physical exercise sessions with some stretching.

## Affirmation for the Year

"I am an initiator of creative change and healing."

## ACTION TABLES FOR ARIES

These dates reflect the best (but not the only) times for success and ease in these activities according to your Sun Sign.

| | |
|---|---|
| **Change Residence** | May 28–July 1; July 10–Aug. 2 |
| **Request a Raise** | Apr. 11 |
| **Begin a Course of Study** | June 9; Dec. 3 |
| **Visit a Doctor** | Feb. 1–20; Mar. 18–Apr. 8; Aug. 18–Sep. 3 |
| **Start a Diet** | Jan. 2–3, 29–30; Feb. 25–26; Mar. 25–26; Apr. 21–22; May 18–20; June 15–16; July 12–13; Aug. 8–9; Sep. 5–6; Oct. 2–3, 29–30; Nov. 26–27; Dec. 23–24 |
| **Begin a Romance** | Aug. 7 |
| **Join a Club** | Feb. 10 |
| **Seek Employment** | Jan. 1–13; Aug. 18–Sep. 3; Dec. 19–31 |
| **Take a Vacation** | Jan. 8–9; Feb. 4–5; Mar. 3–5, 31–Apr. 1, 27–28; May 25–26; June 21–22; July 18–19; Aug. 15–16; Sep. 11–12; Oct. 8–9; Nov. 4–5; Dec. 2–3, 29–30 |
| **Change Your Wardrobe** | Aug. 3–17 |
| **End a Relationship** | Mar. 27 |
| **Seek Professional Advice** | Jan. 4–5, 31; Feb. 1, 27–28; Mar. 27–28; Apr. 23–24; May 21–22; June 17–18; July 14–15; Aug. 10–11; Sep. 7–8; Oct. 4–5, 31, Nov. 1, 28–29; Dec. 25–26 |
| **Have a Makeover** | April 11–12 |
| **Obtain a Loan** | Jan. 6–7; Feb. 2–3; Mar. 1–2, 29–30; Apr. 25–26; May 23–24; June 19–20; July 16–17; Aug. 12–13; Sep. 9–10; Oct. 6–7; Nov. 3–4, 30; Dec. 1, 27–28 |

## PRIMARY FOCUS

You're definitely making significant progress in your job, and need to take assertive action. But watch a tendency toward unintentional abrasiveness—you could step on the wrong toes!

## HEALTH AND FITNESS

Keep the stress monster at bay by balancing time for work, exercise and relaxation, especially mid-month. Get a massage on the 30th.

## ROMANCE AND RELATIONSHIPS

A flirtation at work can be the real thing, but it could also mean trouble. Instead of jumping directly into the fires of passion from the 4th–19th, try to move with reasonable caution. This could be a dangerous liaison! If you're already involved with someone, get out of routine and experiment with more playful options. Romance runs more smoothly after the 19th, when communication improves from all sides. Connect with friends after the 14th, and plan a party for the Full Moon on the 27th. Of course, it could be a party for two.

## FINANCE AND CAREER

Your drive to succeed is stronger than ever, and you may receive that recognition you've craved. But if you're unprepared or have been slacking off on the job, the recognition could be uncomfortable! Do your homework and instigate a fresh approach to your career challenges with the New Moon on the 11th. Old debts could also haunt you early in the month. Seek financial counsel to help you sort out the details on the 24th.

## OPPORTUNITY OF THE MONTH

Although you may feel driven toward your goals from the 1st, you'll have better success in reaching them between the 11th–27th.

**Rewarding Days:** 8, 9, 12, 13, 17, 18, 22, 23, 27, 28
**Challenging Days:** 2, 3, 4, 7, 10, 11, 24, 25, 31

## AFFIRMATION FOR THE MONTH:
"I am aware of the effect of my actions."

## PRIMARY FOCUS

Active participation in making dreams a reality adds to your success now. Team efforts can provide positive rewards and recognition for leadership abilities.

## HEALTH AND FITNESS

Participate in a fitness class, get back to your workout routines, or join in your favorite team sport to increase your vitality. A retreat after the 13th could be highly beneficial.

## ROMANCE AND RELATIONSHIPS

A disagreement with a friend from the 6th–11th can create havoc unless you deal honestly with the underlying issues. This is an excellent time to uncover the truth and clarify both their motives, and your own. Differences about the most effective way to approach intimacy can thwart your love life mid-month. You may find that you're constantly pushing the wrong buttons. To avoid increasing conflict, take time to really listen to one another instead of placing blame. Watch for the hidden agenda during the Full Moon on the 25th.

## FINANCE AND CAREER

Careful investigation of the source of investments is necessary to avoid losing ground financially. Disputes over jointly held resources may surface near the time of the New Moon on the 10th. A resolution may be slow, since Mercury begins its retrograde cycle on the 11th, leading to miscommunication or delays. Follow up on all important paperwork, and be sure you understand the facts before presenting documents to your boss.

## OPPORTUNITY OF THE MONTH

Research uncovers the truth from the 8th–12th, but you may be unable to convince the right person until the 23rd!

**Rewarding Days:** 4, 5, 9, 14, 15, 19, 24
**Challenging Days:** 2, 3, 6, 7, 10, 21, 22, 27

## AFFIRMATION FOR THE MONTH
"I am honest with myself and others."

## PRIMARY FOCUS

Slow down and focus on the necessities, leaving the extraneous elements on a lower priority. You have the resources to get what you need, but your "wants" may have to wait a while.

## HEALTH AND FITNESS

Concentrate on creating a sense of inner calm and a feeling of harmony and balance. Pushing beyond your limits from the 11th–19th can take a high toll. Indulge your need for pampering on the 18th.

## ROMANCE AND RELATIONSHIPS

Although your love life may improve once Venus enters Aries on the 8th, you still may have to deal with the resurfacing of an old flame. If you're only experiencing the memory of love gone by, take time to get in touch with your real feelings and make sure you've reached a sense of closure. A sudden attraction from the 22nd–28th looks promising, but be sure you're both available! The Full Moon on the 27th highlights partnerships or the desire for one. Mend some fences. You need the relief.

## FINANCE AND CAREER

Once Mercury moves into direct motion on the 5th progress may be slow, but at least it's progress. Long-standing financial disputes may finally be complete by the 19th, giving you room to consider a new investment strategy. But watch the tendency toward impulsive spending from the 28th–31st, since you may be overlooking a costly detail. Careful cooperation with others from the New Moon on the 12th until the end of the month can assure career success.

## OPPORTUNITY OF THE MONTH

Schedule an important meeting or presentation on the 13th or 14th; be ready to launch a project on the 23rd.

**Rewarding Days:** 4, 13, 18, 19, 23, 24, 31
**Challenging Days:** 2, 6, 7, 20, 21, 27, 28

## AFFIRMATION FOR THE MONTH
"I listen to my intuitive voice."

29

## PRIMARY FOCUS

Finally, breakthroughs allow you to do what you do best—take the lead! Use this time to set up effective communications in all areas—professional and personal.

## HEALTH AND FITNESS

You may feel more like tackling challenges as Mars moves into Aries on the 14th. Until then, take plenty of time to rest and rejuvenate. You'll be glad you did.

## ROMANCE AND RELATIONSHIPS

If you've been waiting for the right time to approach the object of your desires, the New Moon in Aries on the 10th signals a cycle of reaching out. Even though you may feel like exploding onto the scene, a graceful rhythm and slow beginning leave you more opportunity to savor the experience. Stay in touch from the 10th–25th, and watch a tendency to appear too vague or confusing on the 22nd and 23rd. A short trip or romantic rendezvous from the 27th–29th can be just the thing to turn the tide.

## FINANCE AND CAREER

Your financial judgment may be more sound, but there are still opportunities to get in over your head the week of the 17th. Take advantage of another's generosity or seek out fellow investors from the 10th–13th. Just be sure you know what's expected in return. Presentations, business travel or meetings fare well from the 11th–20th, but an unexpected interruption can cause problems from the 23rd–25th. Any financial disputes are amplified during the Full Moon on the 25th, so try to limit your involvement where possible.

## OPPORTUNITY OF THE MONTH

You can shine on the 10th, so choose your focus and give it your best shot!

**Rewarding Days:** 1, 4, 9, 10, 14, 15, 19, 27, 28
**Challenging Days:** 2, 3, 5, 12, 16, 17, 24, 30

### AFFIRMATION FOR THE MONTH
"I act with courage and compassion."

### PRIMARY FOCUS

You're going places, and, in your inimitable style, moving quickly into the next phase of your path toward success. A careful look at finances helps to keep you from getting in over your head.

### HEALTH AND FITNESS

Mars continues its transit in Aries, and can boost your energy, but pace yourself to avoid burning out too quickly. Avoid extreme risks from the 13th–21st.

### ROMANCE AND RELATIONSHIPS

Favorable communication enhances romance. Your overtures are well-received, but you may be sending mixed signals. To be sure your actions aren't misinterpreted, pay special attention to your lover's response. Secrecy or deception can work against you midmonth, whether you're the perpetrator or intended victim. Your words during the time of Lunar Eclipse on the 24th can have a powerful impact—think before you speak. This is also an excellent time to reconnect with siblings to clear the air.

### FINANCE AND CAREER

Money issues may seem intensive during the Solar Eclipse on the 10th, and extra attention to finances can bring everything back into order. Eliminate and avoid the accrual of debt to maintain the freedom you need. Network with influential individuals to spur progress in career, but guard your battle plans from undermining influences from the 12th–17th. Business travel can also produce exceptional results from the 9th–27th.

### OPPORTUNITY OF THE MONTH

Make a quick adjustment to sudden changes on the 17th and 18th in order to take advantage of a possible weakness in the competition.

**Rewarding Days:** 2, 3, 6, 7, 11, 16, 25, 29
**Challenging Days:** 1, 10, 14, 15, 21, 22, 27, 28

### AFFIRMATION FOR THE MONTH
"I take time to replenish my energy."

## PRIMARY FOCUS

Old obligations from the past can get in the way of progress unless you deal with them directly and honestly.

## HEALTH AND FITNESS

Work toward gradually building your physical stamina and endurance, but remember to stay flexible! Pay attention to your diet, avoiding indulgence in excessive sweets.

## ROMANCE AND RELATIONSHIPS

Family relationships can be nerve-racking and may even interfere with your love life. Listen carefully to your own inner voice and get clear about how you really feel before you deal directly with these outside influences. An infatuation from the 6th–14th may be totally unfounded, and you seem especially vulnerable near the New Moon on the 9th. Avoid the tendency to get into manipulative games, when power struggles can negatively effect your sexual relationship. Find ways to bring more playfulness into your life, but be sure not to force the issue from the 26th–29th.

## FINANCE AND CAREER

Emotion can get in the way of clear thinking and objectivity, especially once Mercury turns retrograde on the 12th. Joint financial ventures are highly pressurized after the 12th with disagreement reaching a peak with the Full Moon on the 23rd. Stress a creative approach to the problem on the 21st and 22nd, and encourage cooperative efforts to help equalize power struggles. Intensity continues to build after the 24th. Stay cool.

## OPPORTUNITY OF THE MONTH

Seek others' support on the 20th, and present your ideas to authorities on the 21st. Success is possible despite delays.

**Rewarding Days:** 2, 3, 8, 12, 21, 22, 25, 30
**Challenging Days:** 4, 6, 10, 11, 17, 18, 23, 24

## AFFIRMATION FOR THE MONTH
"I am safe and secure."

## PRIMARY FOCUS

Expand your efforts to make contact, building a network of support in your career and a sense of connection to your community.

## HEALTH AND FITNESS

Increased physical activity helps you keep a more even balance this month, but you're also in a good position to refine your image. Fitness activities may spur the beginning of a friendship.

## ROMANCE AND RELATIONSHIPS

Contacts which have fallen by the wayside are more easily renewed from the 1st–9th. Continue working out issues that may have blocked an intimate relationship. Love may be thwarted by hidden fears the week of the 3rd, and you may find yourself responding to your partner inappropriately. Try to avoid a tendency to dominate every situation the week of the 17th. Improvements in family relationships are promising after the New Moon on the 8th, but breaking out of your rut can cause confusion with your parents or family during the Full Moon on the 22nd.

## FINANCE AND CAREER

Follow-up unfinished business until Mercury leaves its retrograde on the 6th. New avenues open more readily after the 8th, but you may confront a blockade within the system from the 17th–22nd. Concentrate on harmonious working relationships, but keep the existing hierarchy intact. Restructuring works better next month. Investors are conservatively agreeable after the 19th.

## OPPORTUNITY OF THE MONTH

Finishing an important project on the 5th and 6th can draw positive attention and recognition your way.

**Rewarding Days:** 5, 6, 10, 18, 19, 23, 27, 28
**Challenging Days:** 1, 3, 7, 8, 14, 15, 20, 21, 25

## AFFIRMATION FOR THE MONTH
"My words are inspired by Divine wisdom."

## PRIMARY FOCUS

Greater satisfaction results from a positive shift in attitude. Relationships take a front seat.

## HEALTH AND FITNESS

Recreation activities bring an easy improvement to your fitness level. Even if your competitive urge wanes, you can still enjoy yourself!

## ROMANCE AND RELATIONSHIPS

Partnerships improve through increasing harmony after the 8th. You may feel more positively about commitment, realizing that you can still be free to be yourself. The New Moon on the 7th spurs fresh energy for a new love or greater enjoyment in an existing relationship. But watch your flirtations after the 28th, when you may create havoc by sending the wrong signals. If you're feeling too penned in by your partner the week of the 14th, you may just need a short time alone. Friends provide a good sounding board before the Full Moon on the 21st, but you're on your own after that.

## FINANCE AND CAREER

Business travel produces excellent results, but you may need to stay closer to home after the 16th when there are plenty of fires burning nearby! Reevaluate roles in working partnerships the week of the 7th, but be alert to power struggles with others after the 15th. These can be resolved by getting to the core issues and work behind the scene after the 22nd. Avoid speculation after the 27th unless you've thoroughly investigated the situation.

## OPPORTUNITY OF THE MONTH

The 6th–12th marks a powerful time for forward progress involving your personal and professional relationships.

**Rewarding Days:** 1, 2, 6, 7, 15, 19, 24, 29
**Challenging Days:** 4, 10, 11, 17, 18, 22, 24, 31

## AFFIRMATION FOR THE MONTH
"I am creating harmony and joy."

## PRIMARY FOCUS

You may feel that you're working all the time—even at home. Others may seem to make impossible demands on your time. Give yourself some space to let off steam!

## HEALTH AND FITNESS

It's tempting to run in high gear all month, but pacing yourself is crucial. Deliberately slow down after the 18th.

## ROMANCE AND RELATIONSHIPS

If turmoil at home results from conflict with your family, you can deal most effectively from the 1st–11th. After that time, it's easy to fall into argumentative or confusing battles that lead nowhere. However, partnerships fare better, with your increased appreciation for one another leading to deepening intimacy. Plan to spend some time alone or with someone you trust during the Full Moon on the 19th. There's a tendency to deceive yourself after the 18th, so be sure you're actually in touch with your real feelings. Running away just complicates matters.

## FINANCE AND CAREER

Concentrate on improving work relationships after the New Moon on the 5th. Dialogue with employees or co-workers fares best from the 5th–13th, but open conflict or jealous undermining can ensue from the 17th–22nd. Avoid weakening your position by immediately clarifying any confusing or incorrect information. Keep spending within reasonable limits this month. It's easy to blow your budget on things you don't really need.

## OPPORTUNITY OF THE MONTH

Listen carefully to the needs of others on the 7th. You may find the key to avoiding unnecessary conflict.

**Rewarding Days:** 2, 3, 11, 12, 15, 20, 25, 30
**Challenging Days:** 1, 7, 8, 13, 14, 21, 27, 28

## AFFIRMATION FOR THE MONTH

"I am courageous in the face of challenge."

## PRIMARY FOCUS

Even though your impatience may get the best of you, this is a great time to uncover and clear away unfinished business (of all types).

## HEALTH AND FITNESS

Assessment of chronic physical ailments now can provide the answers for more complete healing and rejuvenation.

## ROMANCE AND RELATIONSHIPS

Instead of blaming the other person for the ailments of a relationship, take a look in the mirror. Although you may be dissatisfied, perhaps you're the one who's short-changing yourself! The New Moon on the 4th marks a good time to initiate the actions which will uncover the love that's been buried beneath the debris of everyday hassles. If you discover there's nothing there, then its time to say good-bye. Use the Full Moon on the 19th to objectively evaluate your progress. And remember—it all begins with you!

## FINANCE AND CAREER

Close scrutiny of your finances may be alarmingly revealing. To evaluate your options, use the retrograde of Mercury from the 9th–30th to get a grip on the situation. This is a good time to research information your investors need to make their final decision. Promises made on the 28th are hopeful, even if you do feel an undermining of that support from the resurfacing of an old problem on the 29th. Keep your eye on the larger picture.

## OPPORTUNITY OF THE MONTH

The Full Moon in Aries on the 19th emphasizes both your strengths and weaknesses. Situations which expose your vulnerability may bring positive results!

**Rewarding Days:** 8, 9, 12, 13, 17, 18, 22, 23, 27
**Challenging Days:** 4, 5, 10, 11, 15, 20, 25, 26, 31

## AFFIRMATION FOR THE MONTH
"I am aware of my inner needs."

## PRIMARY FOCUS

Love relationships continue to be emphasized. The essence of this time involves expressing a true creative spirit and the emanation of pure love from the center of your self.

## HEALTH AND FITNESS

Powerful healing can occur only if you reach the core of a problem. Conscious directing of positive energy turns the tide.

## ROMANCE AND RELATIONSHIPS

Relationship issues intensify during the Solar Eclipse on the 3rd. Experience the power of connecting to the Source, and a need to share that feeling with the one you love. The love emerging now can have a transformational effect on every aspect of your life. Whether you're alone or deeply involved with another, you're finally experiencing the best ways to love yourself. Allow a deeper understanding of your sexual needs to emerge. You're experiencing a rebirth, and may finally remove much unneeded guilt.

## FINANCE AND CAREER

Getting rid of inventory that is dead weight frees up space for future expansion. Creative ideas need a place to express themselves, and may lead to a new level of success. Benefit from the financial resources of others gives you a boost, but be sure you're willing to pay the price before you make an agreement. The Moon's Eclipse on the 18th can amplify financial disputes. Try to avoid accelerating any conflict over taxes.

## OPPORTUNITY OF THE MONTH

Friendly advice on the 9th or 10th may inspire the new direction you've sought. Stay involved, since a low profile might inhibit an opportunity.

**Rewarding Days:** 5, 6, 9, 10, 13, 14, 18, 23, 24
**Challenging Days:** 1, 2, 7, 8, 12, 21, 22, 28, 29

## AFFIRMATION FOR THE MONTH
"I am confident about my creative abilities."

## PRIMARY FOCUS

Broaden your horizons and take advantage of a climate of expansion. Travel and educational pursuits are rewarding.

## HEALTH AND FITNESS

Getting back to nature feels good in every respect now. Concentrate on creating a well-rounded program of health and fitness. Accelerate your pace gradually to avoid strain.

## ROMANCE AND RELATIONSHIPS

A change of scenery can improve your love life or may even offer the possibility of meeting an intriguing individual. Watch for power plays in your relationship from the 1st–12th, and remain aware of your own desire to be in control of the situation. The New Moon on the 2nd can accelerate changes that have been brewing beneath the surface. The hope of the Full Moon on the 17th may be undermined by unrealistic expectations. Be sure you know where you stand before jumping into final plans.

## FINANCE AND CAREER

This can be a complex period of negotiations, but you still can come out ahead if you stay aware of the vulnerabilities in the situation you're promoting. Presentations and conferences bring positive results on the 2nd, 3rd, 11th, and 12th. There's a battle between conservative and experimental factions late in the month, and you'll need to satisfy both to gain the cooperation and support required. Don't underestimate your competition this month!

## OPPORTUNITY OF THE MONTH

Miracles are possible, but they may occur in the face of explosive change on the 2nd and 3rd.

**Rewarding Days:** 2, 3, 6, 7, 11, 12, 16, 21, 22, 30
**Challenging Days:** 1, 4, 5, 14, 18, 19, 25, 26, 31

## AFFIRMATION FOR THE MONTH
"I have faith in myself."

# TAURUS
## The Bull

### April 20 to May 21

**Element:** Earth

**Quality:** Fixed

**Polarity:** Feminine/Yin

**Planetary Ruler:** Venus

**Meditation:** "I am the steward of my environment"

**Gemstone:** Emerald

**Power Stones:** Diamond, rose quartz, topaz, blue lace agate

**Key Phrase:** "I have"

**Glyph:** Bull's head

**Anatomy:** Neck and throat

**Color:** Green

**Animal:** Cattle

**Myths/Legends:** Ceriddwen, Osiris & Isis, Bull of Minos

**House Association:** 2nd

**Opposite Sign:** Scorpio

**Flower:** Violet

**Key Word:** Conservation

**Positive Expression:**
Focused
Calm
Persistent
Prosperous
Stable
Loving
Steadfast
Substantial
Enduring

**Misuse of Energy:**
Obstinate
Lethargic
Unyielding
Avaricious
Greedy
Possessive
Covetous
Materialistic

# ♉ TAURUS ♉

## Your Ego's Strengths and Weaknesses

Your focused drive toward stability can be easily expressed in your accumulation of material and financial security. But you are driven by the desire to experience and express the depths of love. Your stable energy allows you to weather the storms of life and emerge intact, while your unfaltering devotion toward maintaining security is a haven for those you love.

The expression of beauty in all forms, especially those which occur naturally, draws your interest. You may need an outlet for expressing your own artistry, but at the least, you'll enjoy associating with artistically gifted people. You're ruled by the planet Venus, whose energy emanates as the expression of love and emotion. The appreciation of quality and durability are also Taurean traits you'll seek out in every aspect of your life. Even though life brings many changes, you're not always happy about them, since the possibility of losing resources or time can threaten your security.

If you do feel threatened, you can become stubbornly resistant to cooperation with others. In fact, you can even act against your own best interests in order to simply hold onto what you possess. Your tendency toward possessiveness or excessive materialism may result from feeling that you are what you have. By building emotional safeguards, you'll discover that you can more easily let go and allow change when it's necessary.

You're learning to express steadfastness in a world of change without falling into a rut, mastering your own sense of values. As you develop ways to release unnecessary attachments, you make room for even more love to flow into your life.

## Your Career Development

Consistent growth and a stable base are strong requirements for your career choices. You can recognize a reliable opportunity and have the ability to build a solid financial future, and you don't mind working hard if it leads to reward. You have a good sense of structure, and might enjoy working with your hands. These can be applied in the building industry, furniture construction, or architectural design. Landscape design, gardening, farming, and ranching give you a chance to stay connected to your element, the Earth.

Banking, real estate, and investment are appealing areas. Or, you may be an accomplished sculptor, potter, or singer. You can be an encouraging counselor or teacher, in both business and professional areas. Your love for food might stimulate you to own or work in a restaurant, bakery, or grocery store. The beauty industry (including clothing design, sales, or manufacturing), cosmetic industry, or hairdressing can provide satisfying outlets for your desire to remain creative.

## Your Approach to Romance

You're looking for commitment and seek the loyalty from others you are willing to express to them. You can be tender, yet strong, in your physical expression of love and have a sensuality that is well-suited to romance. Your love for home and family may prompt you to seek out a mate with similar values.

You're looking for a love that endures the test of time, but you can also become highly possessive of those you love. To avoid disappointments, watch your tenacity toward trying to keep the status quo instead of allowing the natural changes which occur through the years. Generally comfortable with other earth signs—Taurus, Virgo, and Capricorn—your feelings of harmony and ease of expression promote trust. The sense of steadfast commitment from another Taurean can be highly appreciated. Virgo's understanding of your need for comfort and Capricorn's assurance of your financial stability are also highly appealing to you.

The attraction you feel to Aries may be short-lived, and Gemini's versatility challenges you to become more adaptable. Cancer, who may share your desire for home and family, could create an easy contentment. Competitive ego conflicts could arise with Leo, although you may find their loyalty and drama appealing. Libra's charm entices, but their indecisiveness can drive you nuts.

Your polar opposite, Scorpio, stimulates your passionate side and can match your possessiveness. And you can enjoy the generosity of Sagittarius, but may worry when you'll next see one another. You can be baffled by the detachment of Aquarius, and feel that you don't get enough personal attention. And with Pisces, you can share the fantasy of romance, together building a place for your dreams to come alive.

## Your Use of Power

Your power often comes through building a fortress of strength which no threat can penetrate. This is actually a feeling you can build within yourself, but you may find that you're also drawn to surround yourself with strong material resources, a loyal company or dedicated family. You generate power through maintaining your assets.

If you're feeling threatened, you can abuse your power through greed or excessive possessiveness. And you can stand in the way of your own progress when you refuse to change when it's necessary. Learning to let go is not easy for you.

One of the best ways to conserve and utilize what you have around you is through acknowledging your understanding of the resources of Mother Earth. Developing an attitude of sharing can bring greater reward than you might have dreamed. By accepting the value of the people around you, you may feel the kinship that knows no boundaries. You're capable of assuring a positive future for your children and future generations through the conservation and replenishing of Earth's riches. This can be your strongest expression of an endless love which endures beyond time.

## Famous Taurus

Burt Bacharach, Candice Bergen, Valerie Bertinelli, Frank Capra, Sheena Easton, Ella Fitzgerald, Billy Joel, George Lucas, Zubin Mehta, Michelle Pfeiffer, Harry S Truman, Rudolph Valentino, Orson Welles, Stevie Wonder

# THE YEAR AHEAD FOR TAURUS

Your growing social base offers you an opportunity to interact with more people, and can bring rewards through dealing with the public. Nineteen ninety-four can be a year of positive growth without the sense of restriction that you have felt in the past few years. By building on your knowledge and experience from the past, you can stand on a firm foundation while broadening your horizons. Relationships play an important role this year, with both friends and partners offering a more promising level of support.

The mirror of relationships, especially close partnerships, can provide a positive source of feedback and encourage you to reach beyond your old set of limitations. Until December 9, Jupiter transits in Scorpio opposing your Sun sign and highlighting your Solar 7th House. This cycle works at an inner level to help you gain a more profound sense of your needs in relationships. However, you may feel a strong contrast from what you see in others versus what you feel from within. Expectations can become a block if you place too much emphasis upon them. Although this period is often accompanied by increasing support from a partner, just as important is an increase in your ability to *accept* this level of support. The essence of this cycle is an increasing sense of your own wholeness, and you'll do yourself a disservice by feeling that this is determined by the presence of another in your life. Too much emphasis placed on others will only lead to disappointment.

The Jupiter cycle gains emphasis from the Solar Eclipses in Taurus and Scorpio this year. Eclipse cycles generally indicate areas in our lives which require accentuation in some way, and the accompanying transit of Jupiter adds to this punctuation. You may find more life experiences acting as symbols to illustrate deeper meaning. Take the time to reflect upon what's happening around you and how you fit into the scene. This is a cycle of integration and can be a time of profound self-realization. But you're also releasing many elements of the past through this energy, especially those which have become artificial in their meaning.

43

Saturn finally leaves the square to your Sun this year and moves into a supportive sextile aspect. There's still work to be done, but it may not feel quite as limiting or over-burdening. All Taureans will feel the energy of this transit sometime during the next two years. You can utilize this energy to strengthen the positive rewards from your career, but there are also greater sensibilities in your feeling of accomplishment in areas of personal growth and self-awareness.

The exact conjunction of Uranus and Neptune in Capricorn has ended, but these two planets continue to travel closely together in their orbit. This change lessens the intensity of the cycle, but there will still be a feeling of major changes in the collective elements of society. Human evolution follows a slow course, and although the conjunction of these two planets has historically coincided with events that have turned the tide, the adjustments to these changes are not always immediately forthcoming. If you know your chart, continue to watch the effect of these transiting planets in the astrological house they're influencing. The Solar chart (in which your Sun is placed on the Ascendant) shows Uranus and Neptune continuing through your 9th House. The most profound effects of these energies will occur in your philosophical outlook on life. Both an increased sensitivity to your spiritual needs and a revolutionary change in your belief systems are likely to occur as these planets continue their impact.

Nineteen ninety-four marks the last full year Pluto will continue its transit in Scorpio. The eliminatory quality of this cycle will gradually diminish in its effect upon your ego after next year. But until then, there is still likely to be a feeling of foreboding that may accompany your life. The world as you knew it has definitely changed in the last decade, and it's had a definitive impact on your personal growth and development. Continue to work toward eliminating the attitudes and circumstances that inhibit your growth. Chiron has moved into Virgo, and is emphasizing your need to become more acutely aware of the healing effect of your creative self-expression. And you do have the ability to create your own life! This can be a year of breakthrough.

**For Taureans born from April 20–22,** the influence of Pluto transiting in quincunx to your Sun is beginning. Keep a careful eye on physical needs, since this can be a time when your vitality is not quite up to par. Changes which upset your routine need to be countered with appropriate shifts that allow time for you to take care of yourself. You may need to make a new assessment of nutritional needs, since the different stresses you're experiencing now may require a new level of nutritional support. In your work, be sure you're clear about your motivation and the way you deal with changes in the system. This can be a time to clear away the blocks to your success, when you make final adjustments that allow you to feel more confident about your life choices.

**If you were born from April 20–May 5, you're feeling the impact of Saturn's transit in sextile to your Sun.** Your primary responsibilities can be much more accommodating to your needs during this cycle. This is a good time to take on leadership or positions of greater authority and not be overwhelmed. Relationships with family can improve, and you may find that your ways of dealing with family issues are more objective and less dependent. Use the energy of this cycle to bring a greater feeling of stability and focus. It's easier to clear out what you no longer need, to dust away the excess from your life and enjoy in full measure the security you deserve.

**For those born from May 6–14, this is a year of emphasis upon increased personal awareness and the achievement of balance and harmony.** The Solar Eclipses are strongly influencing your Sun this year, and you may finally gain clarity and insight into your most troubling dilemmas. Use this energy to underscore the difference between what you need for yourself and what others demand from you. You may find that the one with the greatest (and perhaps most unreasonable) expectation is yourself. Often these cycles bring increased recognition, and you may finally attain a cherished goal. But the real impact of this attainment may be understanding why you were driven toward the goal in the first place. You can use this time to become more accepting of yourself and more honest about your needs and desires.

**If you were born from May 11–16, you're feeling an increased sensitivity amplified through Neptune's transit in trine to your Sun.** Creative or artistic pursuits may have an especially rapturous effect upon your life. Even if you're not involved in personal expressions of artistry as a profession, you may find that you're enjoying feeling more in tune to the process of life itself. And you can use this cycle to soften many of the harsh elements of reality. From a spiritual standpoint, you're feeling a more powerful sense of your inner self. Your need to become involved in doing something to make a difference in the quality of life can be expressed many ways during this phase. Just be sure to know the charities you're drawn to support. In relationships, you may become more attuned to the spiritual bonding between yourself and others. This is an excellent time to see the light in other people and to work toward developing the most intimate levels of personal contact. In essence, you're becoming closer to yourself, and can make every aspect of your life your meditation.

**Uranus is transiting in trine to your Sun if you were born between May 12–18.** This can be a cycle of awakening, and certainly gives you the opportunity to make changes. Instead of a disruptive revolution, you can manifest a breakthrough in areas you've longed to pursue. Travel and education can be especially rewarding. If you're interested in writing, this cycle encourages publication, but may also offer opportunities in broadcasting. It's your turn to experiment with levels of self-expression you'd only dared dream about in the past, and this time, you can actually get a taste of that dream.

**Be prepared to strip away the unnecessary elements from your life if you were born between May 16–21.** Pluto has finally reached its opposition to your Sun, and you may be faced with some of the most far-reaching changes you've experienced thus far. Although some of these changes may come from others, your reactions may lead you to take a closer look inside. This is an excellent time to work with a counselor and to finally heal much of the old pain you've been carrying with you. In digging into your past, you may uncover things you'd been hiding from yourself. Whether physical or emotional, the issues you're facing are about regaining your own power. You are, after all, a survivor. Now's the time to go beyond survival and into a more promising and fulfilling sense of your true destiny.

## Tools to Make a Difference

Your natural affinity with the continual growing processes of life may stimulate you to get back to nature in some way. While the world continues to evolve, you can take pride in the fact that you're working to make the most of all your resources. In this way, you're never without what you need. If you've not done it before, make a commitment this year to avoid wasting or discarding what can still be useful.

Becoming more involved with a group of friends, or getting in touch with your community in more effective ways may offer a level of support you've denied yourself for too long. You are likely to have something special to offer, especially if the focus is on the best ways to attain growth or harmony with the environmental or economic climates.

If you need to recharge yourself, take advantage of your own responsiveness to nature. You may feel an easy attunement to trees and plants, and can benefit from daily contact with living things. Make the process of food preparation an enjoyable one, reminding yourself that your energy is drawn not only from the physical foods you're putting into your body, but also from the love you feel when you're creating the meal. You may be especially attuned to the power of stones or crystals, and can surround yourself with your power stones—emeralds, diamonds, topaz, or rose quartz—to help stabilize and clear the energy around you.

The most positive energy expression for change and growth comes from within. Try to maintain a constant awareness of the slowly evolving changes that are part of the earth and all the creatures who share her abundance.

## Affirmation for the Year

"I am filled with the love that flows from
the Source of All Life."

## ACTION TABLES FOR TAURUS

These dates reflect the best (but not the only) times for success and ease in these activities according to your Sun Sign.

| | |
|---|---|
| **Change Residence** | Aug. 3–17 |
| **Request a Raise** | May 10 |
| **Begin a Course of Study** | Jan. 11, July 8 |
| **Visit a Doctor** | Apr. 9–25, Sep. 4–27, Oct. 19–Nov. 9 |
| **Start a Diet** | Jan. 4–5, 31; Feb. 27–28; Mar. 27–28; Apr. 23–24; May 21–22; June 17–18; July 14–15; Aug. 10–11; Sep. 7–8; Oct. 4–5, 31; Nov. 1, 28–29; Dec. 25–26 |
| **Begin a Romance** | Sep. 5 |
| **Join a Club** | March 12–13 |
| **Seek Employment** | Feb. 21–Mar. 17; Sep. 4–26, Oct. 19–Nov. 9 |
| **Take a Vacation** | Jan. 10–11; Feb. 6–7; Mar. 6–7; Apr. 2–3, 29–30; May 26–28; June 23–24; July 20–21; Aug. 17–18; Sep. 13–14; Oct. 10–11; Nov. 7–8; Dec. 4–5, 31 |
| **Change Your Wardrobe** | Aug. 18–Sep. 3 |
| **End a Relationship** | April 25–26 |
| **Seek Professional Advice** | Jan. 6–7; Feb. 2–3; Mar. 1–2, 29–30; Apr. 25–26; May 23–24; June 19–20; July 16–17; Aug. 12–13; Sep. 9–10; Oct. 6–7; Nov. 3–4, 30; Dec. 1, 27–28 |
| **Have a Makeover** | May 10 |
| **Obtain a Loan** | Jan. 8–9; Feb. 4–5; Mar. 15–17; Apr. 11–13; May 9–10; June 5–6; July 2–3, 30–31; Aug. 26–27; Sep. 11–12; Oct. 8–9; Nov. 5–6; Dec. 2–3, 30 |

## PRIMARY FOCUS

You're in a good position to stabilize your opportunities in the face of reorganization or change. Education or travel provide positive challenges.

## HEALTH AND FITNESS

Building physical strength and stamina enhances your emotional stability. Get involved in sports. At least stand up and cheer!

## ROMANCE AND RELATIONSHIPS

Meeting someone whose ideas and opinions are harmonious with your own is favorable from the 1st–14th. The New Moon on the 11th can be highly romantic, and you may feel a greater willingness to take chances. A careful second look at the situation the week of the 16th may provide a different viewpoint. If you're still convinced that your feelings haven't changed by the Full Moon on the 27th, you may be ready to confront your fears about your own worthiness of love. Parents can be antagonistic in their attitudes about your life choices after the 20th. You don't have to bite back.

## FINANCE AND CAREER

Business travel can be just the ticket for advancement through the 15th. Presentations, conferences or workshops bring positive results through the 18th, and are especially effective on the 10th and 11th. A change in plans from the 13th–17th doesn't have to eliminate your possibilities of progress, and can work to your benefit if you're willing to incorporate something new. Avoid arguments with your boss on the 30th and 31st.

## OPPORTUNITY OF THE MONTH

Use the confidence and optimism you're feeling from the 10th–12th to take the lead. It's time to expand options.

**Rewarding Days:** 2, 3, 10, 11, 15, 20, 21, 25, 29
**Challenging Days:** 6, 7, 12, 13, 18, 27, 28, 30

## AFFIRMATION FOR THE MONTH
"I have confidence in myself and in my future."

### PRIMARY FOCUS
Your drive to succeed in your career is sharpened and may have you burning the candle at both ends. Watch a tendency toward aggravating the very people you're trying to impress!

### HEALTH AND FITNESS
Stress levels increase. Avoid wearing down by staying physically active and also allowing yourself time to catch your breath.

### ROMANCE AND RELATIONSHIPS
You're not likely to respond well to others who try to manipulate or control you this month. Even though you might not enjoy it, standing up for yourself is healthy. But if you're the one who's painted yourself into a corner, don't be surprised if you feel resistance on the part of the other person! Your love relationship can be complicated by conflicts with career, either yours or theirs. Use the increasing flexibility on the few days prior to the Full Moon on the 25th to talk it over. Stay open.

### FINANCE AND CAREER
Opportunities for career advancement are promising, but may require you to put forth more effort. Pacing yourself is easier through the 9th. Mercury begins its retrograde on the 11th, and a period of delays and static energy can frustrate your plans for expansion from the 17th–22nd. Contracts signed now may carry heavier obligations than anticipated. Be alert to a difference of opinion over finances from the 10th–12th and the 23rd–28th. Think before you speak on the 22nd and 23rd.

### OPPORTUNITY OF THE MONTH
You're in a good position to complete a transaction that's ready for closure on the 7th or 8th.

**Rewarding Days:** 6, 7, 11, 12, 16, 17, 21, 26
**Challenging Days:** 2, 3, 5, 9, 10, 23, 24

### AFFIRMATION FOR THE MONTH
"I have great satisfaction in my work."

## PRIMARY FOCUS

Career progress results from direct assertive energy on your part. Stand your ground on important issues. Consensus is much more profitable.

## HEALTH AND FITNESS

Stress can drain vitality early this month, but pressure cools after the 19th. Sound nutritional support and reasonable physical activity levels help you maintain balance.

## ROMANCE AND RELATIONSHIPS

Conflicts in career can undermine your effectiveness in your personal relationships until after the New Moon on the 12th. You may also be dealing with family pressure, and can feel trapped by the expectations of others unless you continue to concentrate on a broader perspective. Your needs and opinions are important and deserve acknowledgment. Use the perspective gained from supportive advice from a friend to step into a new direction on the 15th. An extended weekend with your sweetheart can turn the tide on the 19th–22nd.

## FINANCE AND CAREER

Power struggles with authorities can seem beyond your control until after the 7th. Mercury's retrograde until the 5th can create costly delays. Follow-through and attention to details makes the difference. Watch for complex negotiations to reach a critical point on the 16th when a well-prepared argument emerges victorious, but poor work stalls progress. Attend to complaints at work before the Full Moon on the 27th.

## OPPORTUNITY OF THE MONTH

An easier flow of your creative energy can bring healing into a relationship or give you a boost in career on the 25th and 26th.

**Rewarding Days:** 6, 7, 10, 11, 12, 15, 16, 21, 25, 26
**Challenging Days:** 1, 2, 8, 9, 14, 23, 24, 29, 30

## AFFIRMATION FOR THE MONTH
"I am powerful without overpowering."

### PRIMARY FOCUS

Financial progress can be soured by a frustration with an ethical problem or a difference in beliefs. Your faith in yourself is confirmed by the end of the month, so keep up the momentum!

### HEALTH AND FITNESS

Team sports can help you maintain a high level of energy, but allow for extra rest and relaxation after the 15th.

### ROMANCE AND RELATIONSHIPS

Time spent with friends through the 13th can help you create an excellent platform for personal growth. However, a period of introspective analysis during the New Moon on the 10th can inspire a new direction. Relationships can be complex during the latter half of the month, and you're likely to see some old patterns infiltrating your current relationship. Use the energy of the Full Moon on the 25th to emphasize emotional healing and strengthening of your intimate partnership.

### FINANCE AND CAREER

Convincing others that your plan is valid can meet with positive results through the 8th, but there can be a delay in their responsiveness after that time. Legal proceedings are likely to stall, but behind-the-scenes negotiations work to relieve the pressure on the 10th–11th. Your partner's resources can make the difference after the 25th, when joint ventures prove highly lucrative and may promise long-term success. Contracts signed on the 29th and 30th are reasons for celebration.

### OPPORTUNITY OF THE MONTH

Plan activities that are personally gratifying on the 12th and 13th. The results can be a far-reaching boost in confidence.

**Rewarding Days:** 2, 3, 7, 8, 12, 13, 17, 21, 22, 29
**Challenging Days:** 1, 4, 5, 9, 10, 19, 20, 25, 26

### AFFIRMATION FOR THE MONTH
"I am loving, gentle and kind."

### PRIMARY FOCUS

An inner restlessness can disrupt your sense of optimism. This is the time to make contacts that will lead to a network of support over the next few months.

### HEALTH AND FITNESS

Attend to the needs of your nervous system by supplying adequate B-vitamins and allowing reasonable periods of rest.

### ROMANCE AND RELATIONSHIPS

Take advantage of Mercury transiting in Taurus until the 9th to talk about your personal needs. The Solar Eclipse in Taurus on the 10th may bring a different perspective concerning your intimate ties. Issues that originate from early family imprints can be more easily resolved now. You may also find that you've drifted away from a friendship which is no longer pertinent, and trust with friends is definitely worth examining mid-month. Distraction from a secret or fanciful love can undermine the reality of your current relationship from the 13th–20th. Infatuation can be hazardous!

### FINANCE AND CAREER

Look into your financial records from the 9th–27th to be sure you're aware of all the details, since a mistake now could be costly later. The Lunar Eclipse on the 24th underlines the need to have a clear overview of your finances, and may stimulate a much needed resolution of tax or debt problems. You're in a strong position to negotiate and to progress in career from the 25th–31st. Your sense of the conservative may be your key to success.

### OPPORTUNITY OF THE MONTH

Dig into the past on the 9th to get to the core of emotional issues and to uncover the mystery of your motivations.

**Rewarding Days:** 4, 5, 9, 10, 14, 15, 19, 27, 31
**Challenging Days:** 1, 2, 8, 16, 17, 21, 22, 23, 29

### AFFIRMATION FOR THE MONTH
"I am at peace with myself."

### PRIMARY FOCUS

Mercury's retrograde after the 12th can work to your benefit if you take time to get back in touch and establish a firm connection to those who are important to your professional growth.

### HEALTH AND FITNESS

It's easy to burn the candle at both ends while Mars transits in Taurus all month. A massage on the 10th, 11th, 16th, or 23rd can aid release of blocked tension and help you feel more flexible.

### ROMANCE AND RELATIONSHIPS

Time away from routine can bring the vitality back into a tired relationship or may kindle a new love. An imaginative turn of events during the New Moon on the 9th stimulates a dialogue which explores your innermost secrets. Honesty with yourself is crucial, since it's the best way to avoid falling into deception. Digging up old skeletons from the past could be therapeutic near the Full Moon on the 23rd, but seek out the support of a counselor if you feel you're lacking objectivity.

### FINANCE AND CAREER

Progressive action on the career front comes from your willingness to take an assertive position instead of falling behind. Creative or artistic pursuits fare beautifully through the 14th, and may provoke the expression of your finest work. Seek outside advice on financial contracts or offers from the 7th–12th or the 25th–28th, since there may be factors at work hidden from incomplete scrutiny.

### OPPORTUNITY OF THE MONTH

Express yourself! Tremendous progress is yours on the 1st, 5th, and 6th.

**Rewarding Days:** 1, 5, 6, 10, 11, 15, 16, 23, 24, 28
**Challenging Days:** 3, 12, 13, 19, 20, 25, 26

### AFFIRMATION FOR THE MONTH
"My creative energy flows from
the Source of Divine Love."

### PRIMARY FOCUS
Your expanding professional network helps to solve financial dilemmas and provides needed clarification. Stay connected.

### HEALTH AND FITNESS
Gradual building of stamina and endurance pays off, since your increased fitness level gives you more energy. Avoid the temptation to engage in too much of a good time the week of the 24th.

### ROMANCE AND RELATIONSHIPS
Romance is definitely in the air after the 11th, when your drive to express feelings is stronger and your desire to indulge in sensual pleasures can be intensified. Anticipation grows with the New Moon on the 8th, when you're ready for a refreshing change in your love life. Travel can introduce someone new, or may provide a different perspective on your relationship. The Full Moon on the 22nd encourages sharing of ideas and a look toward the more spiritual elements in your relationships.

### FINANCE AND CAREER
A misunderstanding about financial details can create confusion from the 2nd–7th, but should be cleared up by the 11th. Contracts and agreements progress with greater ease after Mercury moves into direct motion on the 6th, but you're still cautioned to use your best judgment with expenditures; there's a tendency toward impulsive purchases all month. Emotions can cloud your judgment from the 23rd–31st, so seek out objective opinions. You're in control of negotiations the 16th–22nd.

### OPPORTUNITY OF THE MONTH
Sound advice on the 21st steers you into an exciting direction.

**Rewarding Days:** 2, 3, 7, 8, 12, 13, 21, 25, 26, 30, 31
**Challenging Days:** 1, 10, 11, 16, 17, 23, 24

### AFFIRMATION FOR THE MONTH
"I respect my intuitive voice."

### PRIMARY FOCUS

Home and family need special attention. Search for ways to bring more enjoyment into personal life after the 18th.

### HEALTH AND FITNESS

There's a tendency to scatter your energy, which could lead to feeling exhausted unless you maintain a balance between work and personal needs. Emotional stress can undermine your effectiveness.

### ROMANCE AND RELATIONSHIPS

Differing opinions between yourself and your parents can open the door to better understanding on the 7th, the day of the New Moon. This may also be a time when you're taking steps to create a personal environment which will foster greater security. Be alert to power plays in personal relationships from the 13th–16th, when words can either wound or heal. Romance is most promising from the 26th–31st, when your favorite pleasures set the pace for memorable intimate encounters.

### FINANCE AND CAREER

Taking time to make improvements in your work environment may even increase your productivity. Concentrate both on the place and the people involved in your work. Weigh your words carefully from the 11th–17th, since you may leave yourself open to attack later on by alienating the wrong person. By the time of the Full Moon on the 21st, you're likely to gain a stronger level of recognition from your superiors. Be sure your work is impeccable. Presentations or conferences fare nicely on the 26th, 27th, and 31st.

### OPPORTUNITY OF THE MONTH

Contrast and conflict can bring positive changes. Break away from the unacceptable on the 18th.

**Rewarding Days:** 4, 5, 8, 17, 18, 21, 22, 26, 27, 31
**Challenging Days:** 2, 6, 7, 12, 13, 14, 19, 20

### AFFIRMATION FOR THE MONTH
"I am open to creative change."

## PRIMARY FOCUS
Keeping the more conservative elements of your life happy while heading into new territory can be difficult. Try to familiarize yourself with your new surroundings before you leap.

## HEALTH AND FITNESS
Increased activity levels help take the edge off a heightened mental energy now. Choose a careful pace after the 18th, and watch out for the other guy to avoid unwelcome surprises.

## ROMANCE AND RELATIONSHIPS
Improving your love life can also mean taking inventory of your true feelings. If you're honestly not interested, why are you putting forth so much energy?! But if you are ready to become a more complete partner, this is the time to integrate your needs so that you're both happy. From the New Moon on the 5th until the Full Moon on the 19th you're in an excellent position to deal with the status quo. After that, there's change in the air, and you can be distracted by unreliable fantasies or infatuation.

## FINANCE AND CAREER
Business travel can be both profitable and enjoyable. If you're investigating the competition, be sure you have all the facts. Calling their bluff after the 18th may put you in a powerful position, but you must be sure of the facts to avoid embarrassment. Creative pursuits respond well to new directions from the 21st–24th. Everything is more stabilized after the 27th.

## OPPORTUNITY OF THE MONTH
Innovations within the existing structure supply an opening for you on the 14th, but change feels more secure on the 23rd.

**Rewarding Days:** 1, 5, 6, 13, 14, 18, 19, 22, 23, 28
**Challenging Days:** 2, 3, 9, 10, 15, 16, 30

## AFFIRMATION FOR THE MONTH
"My words are inspired by truth."

## PRIMARY FOCUS

Your partner can be demanding, and you may have doubts about your real feelings. Give yourself time to reevaluate, and eliminate attitudes that can inhibit the level of intimacy you desire.

## HEALTH AND FITNESS

Suppression of your feelings can create physical distress. Negative emotions need release in order to avoid a block in your physical vitality. Good health involves inner harmony.

## ROMANCE AND RELATIONSHIPS

Before you decide that you can't handle the pressure from everyone else, take a look at your own expectations. You may be suffering from the disappointing realization that life is not as you had hoped. Repairing an existing relationship after the New Moon on the 4th may work out nicely, but you need to be honest with yourself about your old resentments to avoid recreating the same situation. Discrepancies between yours and your partner's success can be at the root of your discontent.

## FINANCE AND CAREER

Your response to the socializing required by your job can make the difference between the success and failure of your business venture. Build momentum by encouraging others to take part and share their enthusiasm from the 4th–8th. But watch for a build-up of friction after Mercury turns retrograde on the 9th. Any important communication, negotiation of contracts, or new business contacts made after the 23rd can be flawed. Research can save your hide and your pocketbook.

## OPPORTUNITY OF THE MONTH

Finalize old business on the 2nd and 3rd.

**Rewarding Days:** 2, 3, 10, 11, 15, 20, 21, 25, 30
**Challenging Days:** 1, 6, 7, 9, 12, 13, 18, 25, 26

## AFFIRMATION FOR THE MONTH
"I release my expectations."

## PRIMARY FOCUS

The Solar Eclipse on the 3rd may enhance your awareness of the conflicts existing within yourself about your relationships. It's time to look into the mirror to clarify the real dilemmas.

## HEALTH AND FITNESS

You can break out of much of the stress that's been inhibiting your sense of vitality, but you may have to change a few habits. This is a great time to reverse the tide and begin healing.

## ROMANCE AND RELATIONSHIPS

With the level of emotional change you're feeling, any relationship can be under the microscope now. You can now uncover many old wounds that have inhibited the fulfillment of your needs. Looking to another person as your salvation can be an indicator that you're ignoring your own power. During the Lunar Eclipse in Taurus on the 18th, take an honest look at things from your past which need to be eliminated. It's time to plow through the past and prepare for a bountiful harvest of love.

## FINANCE AND CAREER

Careful investigation of contracts and investments from the 1st–6th can help you avoid future loss. Use this month to clear out inventory that is draining or to eliminate those activities producing negative or insufficient results. Your past career success can be the launching pad for new endeavors. Mend fences the week of the 13th.

## OPPORTUNITY OF THE MONTH

Meetings on the 7th can produce surprisingly positive results. You're also in a good position to finalize agreements on the 16th.

**Rewarding Days:** 7, 8, 11, 16, 17, 21, 22, 26, 27
**Challenging Days:** 3, 4, 9, 10, 15, 23, 24, 30

## AFFIRMATION FOR THE MONTH
"I have the power to release the attachments
which inhibit my growth."

### PRIMARY FOCUS

Explosive changes early in the month open a path to more creative options. Maintain your concentration during times of intensity.

### HEALTH AND FITNESS

The way you handle stress now is a large factor in determining your physical status. Spend extra time on flexibility and relaxation in your exercise routine.

### ROMANCE AND RELATIONSHIPS

Your partner may be experiencing major upheavals which can affect your attitude toward the relationship. If you're just beginning a relationship, you may find that you're gaining more than you had first realized. The New Moon on the 2nd is accompanied by a powerful conjunction of Jupiter and Pluto, and can stimulate a deepening of your feelings, both positive and negative. Stability in your own feelings after the 11th can generate a more reliable response from others.

### FINANCE AND CAREER

Financial matters become more marked, and you'll definitely need to take more vigorous steps to bring about the stability you require. The energy during the Full Moon on the 17th can help you draw a contrast between the necessary and the frivolous. The emotional issues around money are amplified now, and can be the source of conflict with others who share your financial circumstance. Promise only what you can deliver!

### OPPORTUNITY OF THE MONTH

The time for a dramatic statement about changing your life occurs on the 2nd. Make the most of it by knowing your own limits.

**Rewarding Days:** 4, 5, 9, 13, 19, 23, 24, 31
**Challenging Days:** 1, 2, 3, 6, 7, 21, 22, 26, 27, 28

### AFFIRMATION FOR THE MONTH
"I am connected to the Power from
the Source of All Life."

# ⚹ GEMINI ⚹
## The Twins

### May 21 to June 22

**Element:** Air

**Quality:** Mutable

**Polarity:** Masculine/Yang

**Planetary Ruler:** Mercury

**Meditation:** "My mind is linked to The Source"

**Gemstone:** Agate

**Power Stones:** Herkimer diamond, Alexandrite, Celestite, Aquamarine

**Glyph:** Pillars of Duality

**Key Phrase:** "I think"

**Anatomy:** Hands, arms, shoulder, lungs, nervous system

**Colors:** Orange & yellow

**Animal:** Monkeys, talking birds, flying insects

**Myths/Legends:** Castor and Pollux, Peter Pan

**House Association:** 3rd

**Opposite Sign:** Sagittarius

**Flower:** Lily of the Valley

**Key Word:** Versatility

**Positive Expression:**
Articulate
Clever
Skillful
Inquisitive
Perspicacious
Rational
Sophisticated
Flexible
Perceptive
Incisive

**Misuse of Energy:**
Gossipy
Prankish
Unsettled
Erratic
Nervous
Distant
Frivolous

# ♊ GEMINI ♊

## Your Ego's Strengths and Weaknesses

Your insatiable curiosity leads to a life filled with great diversity. In order to avoid the unthinkable state of boredom, you may go out of your way to create change. Your youthful aura (regardless of your age) springs from your eagerness to embrace new ideas.

A natural negotiator, your knack for bringing the right people together at the right time can be a strong asset. People from many backgrounds and all walks of life are attracted to your debonair attitude and strong communicative abilities. Your love of travel, literature, and intelligent ideas keeps you informed and gives you a distinctly cosmopolitan air.

It's not unusual for you to have several projects going on at once, which can scatter your energy. This juggling act may keep your life interesting, but can be frustrating to others who are uncertain as to your level of commitment. Your changeability can baffle those who are not accustomed to your multiple-track mind!

Your planetary ruler is Mercury, the energy of communication. This correspondence places a high priority on mental function. Your keen and intuitive mind can help develop your trademark ingenuity. Although you may be well-acquainted with the premise, "What you think, you become," you may need to remind yourself that your mind can be both healer and slayer.

## Your Career Development

Unless your career path is mentally challenging, you probably won't be interested. Concentration on developing your communication skills can enhance your natural ability to relate to others. You'll perform better if your life is continually opening to new pathways, or if your job is highly diversified.

Public speaking, writing, advertising, public relations, and broadcasting are all positive expressions for you. Your fascination with the mind may lead you to a career in teaching or counseling. The performing arts (including clowning, pantomime, and juggling) can be a good arena for your wit and charm. Or you can use your manual dexterity in drafting, dentistry, carving, design, secretarial, or musical pursuits. Highly technological areas can present the right opportunity to work with your mind and hands together.

## Your Approach to Romance

The opportunity to share your ideas with others may be your impetus for relationships. Your sociability provides plenty of options for partners, but you're only interested in those who appreciate freedom and independence as much as you do! Intellectual repartee can be highly arousing for you. But it's important to remember that you tend to use ideas and abstractions as a diversion or shield to avoid dealing with or expressing your deeper feelings. You may feel that it's safer to stay in your head!

Your polar opposite, Sagittarius, may be highly attractive, but there can be a battle if one of you tries to be domineering! Another Gemini is likely to bring excitement, but you can become overly distracted by one another unless you keep your personal boundaries in tact. Attraction to others in your element, Air, can be comfortable, and you'll feel you always have something to talk about! Libra's sense of refinement and artistry is alluring. And Aquarius' unique approach to life is a breath of fresh air.

Aries' assertive exuberance is invigorating. And although you find great appeal in Taurus' sensuality, you may find the pace of the relationship too slow. The emotional sensitivity of Cancer can be comforting, but you may resist their attempts to take care of you. Leo's flare for a good time can be truly heavenly.

Although you find Virgo thought-provoking, you're likely to be restless. Scorpio's intense emotionality is definitely engaging, although baffling, and you may have a power struggle with Capricorn's level of control. You're intrigued, although occasionally confused, by Pisces' imaginative sensibilities.

## Your Use of Power

With a clear awareness of the power of the mind, you can be provoked to show your best qualities in circumstances which require knowledge and strong ideas. Your liveliness can be contagious, drawing people from a wide array of cultures, incorporating an awareness of many facets of human experience. When a situation calls for a quick solution, you can dazzle them all!

In an age when technology and communication are important, you can move into positions of influence. However, others will lose confidence in your abilities if you fail to keep your priorities in focus. Since projecting an air of superficiality can undermine your power, keep your desires to have constant diversity within reasonable control.

You identify with the eager spontaneity of the young, and can encourage and inspire young people to manifest their own dreams and hopes. Use the power of communication to bridge differences between divergent factions. Celebrate and nurture the continual growth of new ideas. You're here to soar through life, and are keenly attuned to the whisper of Divine Intelligence. Through opening your mind to greater truth you are uplifted, and the spirit of humanity flies with you.

## Famous Geminis

Jim Belushi, James Brown, Dixie Carter, Mario Cuomo, Bob Dylan, Louis Gossett, Jr., Bob Hope, Waylon Jennings, John F. Kennedy, Jerry Mathers, LeRoy Neiman, Stevie Nicks, Igor Stravinski, Jessica Tandy, Al Unser

# THE YEAR AHEAD FOR GEMINI

Your reputation this year can be altered by a willingness to take on additional responsibilities without over-extending yourself. It's time to stabilize your career path and clarify your professional image. Although you may find that you're spending more and more time working, you can gain more from your professional experience through fostering an attitude of optimism and hope for the future. This is a year of making adjustments, and some of those may entail redefining your duties in a way that allows room for both stability and expansion.

Jupiter's transit in Scorpio this year emphasizes your Solar 6th House, providing an opportunity to improve physical health through a more positive attitude about your body's needs. There is a temptation to push your body beyond its limits. Because of that, you'll do yourself a favor if you concentrate on building increased stamina and resistance through physical activity. It's also easy to overindulge in those sweet things which create problems for the body. If you want to make strides in well-being, you'll need a well-rounded program, concentrating on self-improvement. Mental focus is a crucial factor in the success of these endeavors.

The Solar Eclipses in Taurus (May 10) and Scorpio (November 3) add to the emphasis of Jupiter's cycle, and underline the need to become more aware of your inner self. By dedicating more time to inner awareness, you can begin to feel more connected to life's natural rhythms and to your own intuitive flow. This can stimulate improvement in your creative expression and increase your tie to humanity's collective unconscious. You may also feel prompted to spend more time in charitable efforts, or at least support a special interest which fosters positive improvements in the lives of others. It's neces-sary to take a careful look at your feelings toward the work you've chosen, and to make changes that will pro-mote greater harmony.

You're likely to experience Saturn's entry into Pisces this year as a slow-down in your constant motion. If you've been scattering energy, this is the cycle to stop, reconsider and begin again with a narrower focus.

Becoming easily distracted may seem more like a nuisance than a joy during this next two years, but you can still continue to diversify. The difference comes from changing priorities, and making room to stabilize. Your load may feel heavier, prompting you to look at the amount of unnecessary garbage you've piled onto your life. It's easy to see only the negative side of situations during this cycle, and to feel that the limitations around you are some type of punishment. Instead of taking a defensive view, concentrate more on clarifying the things that really make a difference. Making changes often requires some level of loss, and you may have tried to keep all those plates spinning. If that line of plates has become exceedingly long, you have some serious reconsideration ahead of you!

Uranus and Neptune are no longer in exact conjunction, but are still traveling in extremely close proximity to one another. Revolutionary changes continue around you, especially in the area of finance. Instead of trying to make the old theories work, look at the results of the changes. Use your easy adaptability to create new options and new paths for your future. Pluto's cycle in Scorpio is almost complete, and you may be finally getting to the core of many of your own issues. At the social level, it's quite likely that you'll see things which lead you to believe that we're moving backward, but that motion does not have to continue. Perhaps it's time to deal directly with the present moment and to allow a different perspective on the past.

If you were born from May 21–June 4, you're feeling the full power of Saturn's transit square to your Sun. Although there's a tendency to feel strapped into a straight-jacket, once you stop struggling you may realize that you've just gotten tangled in the debris of unfinished business! This is definitely a time to slow your pace and make a careful assessment of your current position. If you find that you're perfectly happy, then this can be a period of self-confirmation. But if you find that you're still caught in situations that aren't working, you have to take the responsibility to change them. Another aspect of this cycle involves the necessity of taking a definitive stand and setting honest priorities for yourself. Parents or authority figures can seem excessively critical. Your sense of control over your own destiny is up for review. If you've been allowing others to influence your motivations too strongly, then it's time to shift gears and drive for yourself. Also watch your own tendency to become too controlling of others, who may not cooperate with your new set of rules. By all means keep your sense of humor. After all, it's only a test!

**Geminis born from May 25–June 16 are experiencing Chiron's transit square to their Sun.** The effects of the cycle are often felt at a subtle level, with perspective on the situation coming after the cycle is complete. Sharpen your attunement, since you're now making a careful assessment of your connection to your own sense of life purpose. You may need to break away from family traditions in order to set your feet on the path most suitable for you. But you also need to acknowledge your roots, and recognize that you cannot totally eliminate the influence of earlier life. The key is in ceasing to allow that influence to block your growth, and to use it instead as the basis for a new level of self-understanding.

**If you were born from June 10–16 you're subdued by the fog of Neptune's cycle transiting in quincunx to your Sun.** Even though this can be a period of increased imagination and creativity, you may not always feel you have enough energy to make your dreams a reality. Make your health a top priority, since allowing a situation to go unexplored can lead to problems later. Of course, it's also easy to forget about your physical needs during this time, since expanding consciousness may take you into the intangible planes of reality. It's easier to let go of past creative blockages and surrender to those images which inspire you. But you'll be happier with the outcome of those creative efforts if you also attend to life's practical necessities.

**Uranus is transiting in quincunx to your Sun if you were born from June 11–18, stimulating some surprising changes.** There's a temptation to just throw away all those circumstances that seem to be in the way of independent self-expression. However, burning bridges may not be necessary. The important thing is to cross those bridges and gain a greater sense of your identity. Inconsistency on your part may create a loss of support from others now. Even if you do need to move in new directions, your willingness to communicate with those who share your life can make the difference between a lonely pursuit of your goals or a deeper level of unconditional support. Change for its own sake profits little during this cycle, but changes made to allow your passage into a more unique quality of self-affirmation produce the effect of real freedom.

You're feeling the energy of Pluto transiting in quincunx to your Sun if you were born from June 16–22. This is one of the most powerful cycles of personal growth, but it brings a strong sense of dissatisfaction with the status quo. Evaluating your life circumstances may provide you with insight, but you're ready to clear away all that outworn stuff standing in the way of your progress. The only problem is that some of these things are likely to be necessary supports during your period of change! You may find that renovation and renewal work better than starting anew. You just have to peel away the layers until you get to the good stuff!

## Tools to Make a Difference

Your watchword this year could be "Finish what you start!" Simply scattering your energy in all directions may not offer the same level of satisfaction it has provided in the past. You're in the midst of refocusing and redefining your priorities. This is a good time to work with a personal journal or diary. Not only is it a good idea to write about your observations and feelings, but your review and contemplation of that writing can be highly illuminating. You may find that you'll make all those adjustments in your life more easily if you have a sense of your feelings about them!

Develop your communication skills. Joining a special interest group may give you the chance to share your perspectives about a subject you enjoy. If you feel uncomfortable in public speaking, this is a good cycle to get to the core of your fears and deal with them directly. A Toastmasters group can be just the answer to getting over your uncertainty and offer a chance to familiarize yourself with one of your developing gifts.

You might enjoy learning about hypnosis techniques, and can definitely benefit from learning the basics of neurolinguistic programming. After all, one of the things you're here to learn about is the true nature of communication. If you feel you're not being heard, make sure you're also listening! This is especially true in situations with authority figures. Rather than just assuming that all those rules are meant to inhibit your progress, take a more careful look at what they really say. If you need to be part of making changes in the system, you must first learn how it operates!

From a physical perspective, this can be a trying time for many Geminis. Using positive affirmations about yourself and your health can help you work on the mental side of fitness. But you also may need to increase your actual physical activity level. Yoga, Tai Chi, or martial arts can offer the type of body awareness that will help you be more in touch with your physical body. And the discipline and focus can help to improve your concentration. You might also enjoying combining breathing techniques with different forms of visualization to help you manifest some of those ideas that need to be more rooted in reality.

Take good care of your hands. In fact, you can obtain a strong benefit from using the accupressure points in the hands to help balance your entire body. You can frequently find guidelines to these pressure points from holistic health manuals, or cards with the information in your local metaphysical book store or health food outlet.

Remember the power of your words and thoughts, and take some extra time to focus on inner peace and prosperity. There are many levels of prosperity. See and feel yourself experiencing growth and abundance in your ideas, your relationships, your career, your personal health and your spiritual awareness.

### Affirmation for the Year

"My mind is clear, my thoughts are pure,
and I am One with my Higher Self."

# ACTION TABLES FOR GEMINI

These dates reflect the best (but not the only) times for success and ease in these activities according to your Sun Sign.

| | |
|---|---|
| Change Residence | Aug. 17–Sep. 3 |
| Request a Raise | June 9–10 |
| Begin a Course of Study | Feb. 10–11; Aug. 7–8 |
| Visit a Doctor | Apr. 25–May 8; Sep. 27–Oct. 19; Nov. 10–30 |
| Start a Diet | Jan. 6–7; Feb. 2–3; Mar. 1–2, 29–30; Apr. 25–26; May 23–24; June 19–20; July 16–17; Aug. 12–13; Sep. 9–10; Oct. 6–7; Nov. 3–4, 30; Dec. 1, 27–28 |
| Begin a Romance | Oct. 4–5 |
| Join a Club | April 10–11 |
| Seek Employment | Feb. 1–20; Mar. 18–Apr. 8; Sept. 27–Oct. 18; Nov. 10–29 |
| Take a Vacation | Jan. 12–13; Feb. 9–10; Mar. 8–9; Apr. 4–5; May 1–3, 29–30; June 25–26; July 23–24; Aug. 19–20; Sep. 15–16; Oct. 12–14; Nov. 9–10; Dec. 6–7 |
| Change Your Wardrobe | Sep. 4–26; Oct. 19–Nov. 9 |
| End a Relationship | May 24–25 |
| Seek Professional Advice | Jan. 8–9; Feb. 4–5; Mar. 3–5, 31; Apr. 1, 27–28; May 25–26; June 21–22; July 18–19; Aug. 15–16; Sep. 11–12; Oct. 8–9; Nov. 5–6; Dec. 2–3, 29–30 |
| Have a Makeover | June 9–10 |
| Obtain a Loan | Jan. 10–11; Feb. 6–8; Mar. 6–7; Apr. 2–3, 29–30; May 27–28; June 23–24; July 21–22; Aug. 17–18; Sep. 13–14; Oct. 10–11; Nov. 7–8; Dec. 4–5, 31 |

## PRIMARY FOCUS

As the beneficiary of another's support, you can take risks you could not afford alone. Restore something of value now.

## HEALTH AND FITNESS

Now's the time to get to the core of any physical discomforts and work to eliminate or deal directly with the cause.

## ROMANCE AND RELATIONSHIPS

An existing love relationship deepens, or a new love can take you into areas you've rarely, if ever, explored. Use the energy of the New Moon on the 11th to enjoy sensual pleasures. If you get into uncomfortable territory, it could be that you've gone beyond words and into that sense of the unspeakable. Honesty is imperative! Take time to appreciate nature and the wonder of life's cyclical changes. Distractions the week of the 16th can interfere with a long-standing commitment, but you're able to clarify the situation before the Full Moon on the 27th, when you come back to your senses.

## FINANCE AND CAREER

You're in there with the power brokers and need to trust your own powers of persuasion to get you through that feeling of uncertainty. Just because circumstances are changing, you don't have to feel that you're being pushed out into the cold. Avoid highly speculative ventures from the 8th–22nd, when you're tempted to trust before you've tested an individual or situation. Travel, conferences, or workshops after the 15th inspire success.

## OPPORTUNITY OF THE MONTH

Your ability to act in the midst of sudden changes can stimulate important options on the 22nd and 23rd.

**Rewarding Days:** 4, 5, 12, 13, 17, 18, 22, 23, 27, 31
**Challenging Days:** 2, 3, 8, 9, 11, 15, 16, 29, 30

## AFFIRMATION FOR THE MONTH:
"My life is filled with abundant possibilities."

## PRIMARY FOCUS

Reaching into new territory is promising and profitable, but you need to take time to investigate before your final decision.

## HEALTH AND FITNESS

A sense of increased vitality and energy stimulates greater activity. Action taken now brings vast improvements in your health.

## ROMANCE AND RELATIONSHIPS

Traveling with your partner may seem like a good idea, but you may squabble over fundamental differences in preferences the week of the 6th. It's probably better to be in an environment you know well. Others may misinterpret your actions, although you "meant well." Instead of wondering what went wrong, make a special effort to start over with a more clear understanding after the New Moon on the 10th. Following a few adjustments the week of the 13th, you're in a good position to solidify your commitment by the Full Moon on the 25th.

## FINANCE AND CAREER

The word coming down from superiors and authorities may not be exactly what you wanted to hear—you could feel you've just experienced a set-back. Jumping to the wrong conclusion can be costly, so take time to learn about the expectations and possibilities of the situation. Use Mercury's retrograde after the 11th to review and consider necessary adjustments. Delays can actually work to your benefit. Just budget your time wisely.

## OPPORTUNITY OF THE MONTH

Clear out closets, desks, and drawers, and make space for something new this month. Look for a bright note on the 24th.

**Rewarding Days:** 1, 9, 10, 14, 19, 20, 23, 24, 28
**Challenging Days:** 3, 4, 5, 11, 12, 18, 25, 26

## AFFIRMATION FOR THE MONTH:
"I am flexible in the face of change."

## PRIMARY FOCUS

To avoid the extra pressure around work, take time out
with friends and get involved in some activities that help
you feel more a part of your community.

## HEALTH AND FITNESS

Complex circumstances early in the month can take the
wind out of your sails. Pace yourself, and remain aware
that everyday stress can be limited by allowing time out
to break the tension.

## ROMANCE AND RELATIONSHIPS

Family, especially parents, may expect a lot from you
now. By handling their demands in a way that still
allows you to express yourself, you'll avoid much of the
frustration. If you feel that work is taking too much personal time, realign priorities. Set a goal for change with
the New Moon on the 12th, realizing that it may take a
while for everything to fall into place. You're in a
romantically playful mood during the Full Moon on the
27th, and need space to exercise some of your fantasies!

## FINANCE AND CAREER

Contract negotiations may reach a snag thru the 6th, so
step back and reevaluate. The conservative faction
asserts strong pressure now, and success without their
support can be limited. Instead of swimming upstream
the week of the 6th, listen to suggestions and incorporate
change in your program. Greater flexibility emerges after
the 18th. Investments and expenditures the week of the
20th should be scrutinized for details.

## OPPORTUNITY OF THE MONTH

Talk about your real needs and feelings on the 18th,
when you're more likely to be open to supportive com-
mentary.

**Rewarding Days:** 8, 9, 13, 18, 19, 23, 24, 27, 28
**Challenging Days:** 2, 3, 4, 5, 10, 11, 25, 26, 31

## AFFIRMATION FOR THE MONTH:
"I am an effective communicator."

# ♊ GEMINI/APRIL ♊

### PRIMARY FOCUS
You're still pushing hard in your career, but there's more room for creative energy to emerge. Still, it may seem you're moving two steps forward, one step back.

### HEALTH AND FITNESS
Time to exercise can vanish early this month, but team sports or group fitness activities look promising after the 15th.

### ROMANCE AND RELATIONSHIPS
Your reluctance to show how you feel can be a drawback in a new romance. Even though fantasizing is safer, you need to test your fantasies against reality. The energy of the New Moon encourages support from a friend, but you still have to deal with the situation. Complications in your love life the week of the 17th can arise if you're not being honest or if the other person keeps side-stepping the issues. Spend some time alone to balance and reflect during the Full Moon on the 25th.

### FINANCE AND CAREER
It's tempting to take an argumentative stance with your ideas until the 9th, and you may have to defend your position. But stirring unnecessary confrontation with authorities or superiors can result in costly alienation. Work out details from the New Moon on the 10th until the 19th. Jealousy from co-workers or employees can undermine your position from the 21st–24th. If you've been making improvements in your work, they pay off now and help to calm stormy situations with others.

### OPPORTUNITY OF THE MONTH
Your alliance with the most successful team draws positive attention your way on the 19th and 20th.

**Rewarding Days:** 4, 5, 9, 10, 14, 15, 19, 20, 23, 24
**Challenging Days:** 1, 3, 6, 7, 18, 21, 22, 27, 28

### AFFIRMATION FOR THE MONTH:
"I am cooperative and helpful in
stressful circumstances."

### PRIMARY FOCUS

Use your most shining attributes now to insure the realization of your hopes and dreams. Get involved!

### HEALTH AND FITNESS

Sharpen your competitive edge by setting strong fitness goals for yourself. It's time to overcome feelings of lethargy by taking charge of your physical and emotional well-being.

### ROMANCE AND RELATIONSHIPS

Take advantage of Venus transiting in Gemini through the 20th by stabilizing your own self-esteem. You can be more attractive to others, but there's a tendency to sabotage positive experiences now because an episode that left you hurt in the past. An existing relationship may be tested from the 1st–7th, and can show great improvements through positive communication on the 11th and 12th. Time alone to reflect on the past can be illuminating during the Sun's Eclipse on the 10th. But prepare to deal with the demands of others by the time of the Lunar Eclipse on 24th.

### FINANCE AND CAREER

By taking time for adequate preparation you can be quite convincing in business discussions mid-month. But the more conservative forces are likely to criticize your future plans if you've shown yourself to be unreliable in the past. Succeeding in high-risk options is more likely from the 14th–25th if your presentation is well-supported by the facts. Take extra care where loans or borrowed resources are concerned on the 26th and 27th.

### OPPORTUNITY OF THE MONTH

Progressive steps from the 11th–17th can improve both your standing and your finances.

**Rewarding Days:** 2, 3, 6, 11, 12, 16, 17, 21, 29, 30
**Challenging Days:** 4, 5, 10, 18, 19, 20, 25, 26, 31

### AFFIRMATION FOR THE MONTH:
"I am filled with love and joy!"

## PRIMARY FOCUS

Review of your finances now helps you avoid disappointments in the future. Read the fine print before signing contracts—it's easy to overlook an obligation you hadn't anticipated.

## HEALTH AND FITNESS

Stress on the job can escalate now, leading to fatigue and sluggish energy. Take time to relax and release tension so you can maintain your course of action without falling behind.

## ROMANCE AND RELATIONSHIPS

It can be frustrating to deal with the needs of others now, since you may feel more inclined to take care of yourself first. Concentrate on self-fulfillment, and take an honest look at your relationships. A refreshed perspective during the New Moon in Gemini on the 9th can inspire greater clarity in the communication of your needs and desires. A romantic getaway from the 17th–19th or the 25th–26th can inspire a positive exchange of energy and revitalize the love in your love.

## FINANCE AND CAREER

It may seem that you're under scrutiny in every aspect of your career. Perhaps you have your own doubts about your choices! This is an excellent time for self-analysis in your work. Careful scrutiny of your finances and financial plans at work can expose weak links during Mercury's retrograde after the 12th. Be sure you've taken care of old debts, or they're likely to haunt you during the Full Moon on the 23rd!

## OPPORTUNITY OF THE MONTH

Slow down this month. Speeding too quickly can lead to inaccurate conclusions and cost you precious resources.

**Rewarding Days:** 3, 8, 9, 12, 13, 17, 18, 25, 26
**Challenging Days:** 1, 6, 7, 15, 16, 20, 21, 22, 30

### AFFIRMATION FOR THE MONTH:
"I am awake and alive!"

## PRIMARY FOCUS

Instead of worrying about what's *not* happening, take a careful look at the best way to use your available resources. You can make progress only if you stay focused on the present.

## HEALTH AND FITNESS

It's tempting to overextend yourself in order to compensate for what seems to be a lack of time. Keep a reasonable pace to avoid burn-out while Mars transits in Gemini from July 3rd–Aug. 16th.

## ROMANCE AND RELATIONSHIPS

If you've been allowing your fantasies to go too far, reality is likely to slap you in the face the week of the 3rd. Become more aware of the emotional sensitivity of others and concentrate on spending true quality time with your family after the 11th to help alleviate complaints of your lack of availability near the time of the Full Moon on the 22nd. New romance may be far from your thoughts, and time alone can stimulate an imaginative opportunity.

## FINANCE AND CAREER

Networking proves successful from the 1st–10th, but be sure you understand their motivations if they offer their assistance. Concentrate on completing an important project from the 18th–22nd, since you can create delays by scattering your energy. Reviews by your superiors may focus more on your weak points after mid-month, so be sure you have a clear understanding of their expectations before requesting advancement.

## OPPORTUNITY OF THE MONTH

You're in your best form the week of the 3rd, when you can recapture a position or opportunity which appeared to be lost.

**Rewarding Days:** 1, 5, 6, 10, 11, 14, 15, 23, 24, 27, 28
**Challenging Days:** 2, 3, 12, 13, 17, 19, 20, 25, 26

## AFFIRMATION FOR THE MONTH:
"I carefully consider my thoughts."

## PRIMARY FOCUS

Improvements are easier now, when your attitudes are more easily focused upon enjoying your challenges instead of feeling confined by them.

## HEALTH AND FITNESS

Take pleasure in favorite recreational activities, and take time to get out in the beauty of nature this month. This is a time of renewal and revitalization for you.

## ROMANCE AND RELATIONSHIPS

More playful circumstances can stimulate your romantic nature and may lead to great improvements in your love life. The New Moon on the 7th helps open your mind to more fruitful possibilities and stimulates your communicative abilities. Share your creative talents, since this can be the most enticing vehicle for attracting the love you desire. Integrating the spiritual and inspirational into your intimate relationships is positively empowering during the Full Moon on the 21st.

## FINANCE AND CAREER

Travel, workshops, or seminars can provide excellent opportunities for career advancement. But be sure you've taken care of business close to home from the 14th–17th, when a jealous or disgruntled employee or co-worker can create trouble. Joint investments need careful scrutiny through the 16th. But after that time, watch your own tendency toward frivolous or impulsive spending. Review finances on the 30th–31st.

## OPPORTUNITY OF THE MONTH

Your talents shine brightly on the 11th. Use this time to make your best impression and start things moving in the right direction.

**Rewarding Days:** 1, 2, 3, 6, 7, 10, 11, 19, 20, 29, 30
**Challenging Days:** 4, 8, 9, 14, 15, 16, 21, 22

## AFFIRMATION FOR THE MONTH:
"My creative ideas are manifesting as
abundance and prosperity."

## PRIMARY FOCUS

Even though work seems to consume much of your time, an improvement in your attitude helps lighten the load. Use your ability to see all sides when you're faced with conflicts.

## HEALTH AND FITNESS

Instead of adding to your stress levels, find enjoyable ways to release tension. Incorporating grace and artistry into your workout can bring greater inner peace.

## ROMANCE AND RELATIONSHIPS

Familial or parental relationships bring you face to face with old emotional issues near the New Moon on the 5th. Sharing resources can bring out the worst in others, and may tempt you to disassociate from the process. Take a close look at your feelings of self-worth, and use this time to break away from meaningless values and to release unnecessary attachments. An honest appraisal of your emotional stability can encourage progress on all fronts during the Full Moon on the 19th.

## FINANCE AND CAREER

Financial frustrations mount, and can create hair-raising dilemmas the week of the 18th. Your strongest vulnerability arises when you're tempted to jump into the unknown totally unprepared. Safeguard your position by showing a willingness to change while harmonizing with the expectations necessary to secure your career advancement. Alienating others can be costly, and only you can determine if the cost is worthwhile.

## OPPORTUNITY OF THE MONTH

After the dust settles you can begin to stabilize on the 25th and 26th. Unfortunately there's still more work to do!

**Rewarding Days:** 2, 3, 7, 15, 16, 25, 26, 30
**Challenging Days:** 1, 5, 6, 11, 12, 14, 17, 18, 19

## AFFIRMATION FOR THE MONTH:
"My efforts shine in the face of challenge."

### PRIMARY FOCUS

Increasing your outreach through specialized forms of communication, concentrated travel, and improvement in your skills brings you closer to realizing your goals.

### HEALTH AND FITNESS

Concern over health matters may stimulate your solicitation of several opinions about improving your sense of well-being. Highly strenuous activities need careful monitoring the 13th–16th.

### ROMANCE AND RELATIONSHIPS

Instead of retreating, set your aim on mending an existing relationship. It's easy to allow misunderstandings to escalate into battles, but you're in an excellent position to turn the tide. The New Moon on the 4th can lead to refreshing change. If you're still uncertain about your best course of action, advice from a close friend near the Full Moon on the 19th can give you a more workable perspective. A fascinating individual may only be part of a passing infatuation from the 23rd–31st, so cool your jets!

### FINANCE AND CAREER

Mercury's retrograde from the 9th–30th can help you get to the bottom of work-related disputes, but you may also uncover some details that lead to changes you hadn't anticipated. Instead of assuming that significant contacts have been made, take care to follow through the week of the 9th, and allow time for delays through the 20th. Artistic or creative ventures bring success after the 23rd, but payment for your services might be postponed.

### OPPORTUNITY OF THE MONTH

An opening for expansive and imaginative efforts arises on the 28th. Have your documentation ready.

**Rewarding Days:** 1, 4, 5, 12, 13, 17, 18, 22, 23, 27, 28
**Challenging Days:** 2, 3, 8, 9, 15, 16, 29, 30

### AFFIRMATION FOR THE MONTH:
"I deserve love and prosperity."

### PRIMARY FOCUS

Honest personal appraisal can lead to positive self-improvement. This is also an excellent time to praise the efforts of others and strengthen cooperative ventures.

### HEALTH AND FITNESS

Gradually increasing your activity level helps to alleviate much work-related stress. A change in your environment can go a long way in helping to improve your perspectives now.

### ROMANCE AND RELATIONSHIPS

It's easy to use a new relationship as a distraction from your life pressures early in the month. The Solar Eclipse on the 3rd can bring an enhanced awareness of your own emotional and sexual needs, and may stimulate fulfillment in your intimate relationship. But you may also find yourself shrinking away from intimacy if you don't trust the level of commitment. By the Lunar Eclipse on the 18th, you may be more inclined to take a break and look more deeply into your own inner blocks.

### FINANCE AND CAREER

Business travel, conferences, workshops, or presentations stimulate your career from the 1st–11th, and can provide a foundation for long-term growth. Supportive individuals may need more encouragement from you now, so avoid focusing only on your own demands. A power struggle can arise after the 26th, when competitive forces seem to offer greater incentives. Research and strong preparation are your best insurance.

### OPPORTUNITY OF THE MONTH

Take time to discover your own forms of self-sabotage on the 17th and 18th, when insight provides positive inspiration.

**Rewarding Days:** 1. 9. 10, 14, 15, 18 19, 20, 24, 28
**Challenging Days:** 3, 4, 5, 11, 12, 13, 26, 27

### AFFIRMATION FOR THE MONTH:
"I speak words of truth and inspiration."

## PRIMARY FOCUS

Watch your communication, since you may feel that your own words are being used against you. When clarifying your position, remember that honesty is an absolute requirement for success now.

## HEALTH AND FITNESS

Pressures mount early in the month and your time may be consumed by all those irons in the fire. Take deliberate steps to slow your pace.

## ROMANCE AND RELATIONSHIPS

Conflicts arising from different viewpoints can escalate out of control through the 11th. The New Moon on the 2nd highlights partnerships, but you may not be inclined to resolve differences or reach conclusions before the Full Moon in Gemini on the 17th. You may feel family pressures growing from the 12th–23rd, and need to avoid trying to satisfy everyone but yourself! Have a serious talk with your partner on the 17th–18th. Resolutions don't have to come overnight.

## FINANCE AND CAREER

Jealousy can stimulate others to attack your position in favor of their own concerns early in the month. Seek allies through communicative interaction from the 1st–19th. You can actually improve your situation by using conflict to eliminate the rotten deception at the core. Once everything is brought to the surface, you have ample room to advance after the 16th. But if you allow a hidden agenda to continue, you'll lose ground.

## OPPORTUNITY OF THE MONTH

Take steps to expand your base of operations on the 16th and 17th. But be sure you're on a firm foundation before you proceed.

**Rewarding Days:** 6, 7, 11, 12, 16, 17, 21, 22, 26
**Challenging Days:** 2, 3, 8, 9, 10, 23, 24, 29, 30

## AFFIRMATION FOR THE MONTH:

"I carefully consider the needs and opinions of others."

# CANCER
## The Crab

### June 22 to July 23

**Element:** Water

**Quality:** Mutable

**Polarity:** Feminine/Yin

**Planetary Ruler:** Moon

**Meditation:** "I am aware of my inner feelings"

**Gemstone:** Pearl

**Power Stones:** Moonstone, chrysocolla

**Glyph:** Breast or crab claws

**Key Phrase:** "I feel"

**Anatomy:** Stomach, breasts

**Colors:** Silver, pearl, white

**Animal:** Crustaceans, cows, chickens

**Myths/Legends:** Hecate, Asherah, Hercules and the Crab

**House Association:** 4th

**Opposite Sign:** Capricorn

**Flower:** Larkspur

**Key Word:** Receptivity

**Positive Expression:**

Tenacious
Protective
Nurturing
Patriotic
Sympathetic
Tenderhearted
Maternal
Intuitive
Sensitive
Concerned

**Misuse of Energy:**

Smothering
Defensive
Insecure
Suspicious
Moody
Anxious
Brooding
Crabby
Manipulative
Isolationistic

# ♋ CANCER ♋

## Your Ego's Strengths and Weaknesses

Your delight in fostering the growth necessary to sustain vitality stems from your natural ability to nurture and support life. You can be tireless in your aid if a child or family member needs support. Even others in the work place are likely to look to you for comfort and understanding.

You are naturally attuned to the energy of the Moon, which represents the quality of cyclical change. Home is important, with your surroundings reflecting an atmosphere of comfort and ease. But you're also drawn to create an air of warm security wherever you may be. You may have an easy ability in cooking, crafts, and gardening and enjoy sharing these talents with others.

Your psychic attunement is a natural extension of your strong feeling nature, although sometimes you may tend to project your own needs onto someone else. Use your enhanced sensitivity to give you an indication of when you've reached too deeply into another person's boundaries. Allow your reverence for the past to emerge as part of your inner security, instead of insulating yourself from change or positive new growth.

Sustaining your connection to the essence of the Divine Feminine comes from your awareness of both your own inner rhythms and the innate rhythm of the life process. To keep this energy flowing smoothly, you need only learn the lesson of the cycles—"for everything there is a season."

## Your Career Development

Develop your special awareness of the energy around you to assure your career success. With your ability to hold onto your assets and possessions, you may become quite wealthy and influential. Working in the restaurant business, hotel industry, home furnishings, antiques, or real estate businesses may be enjoyable and lucrative for you. Teaching may feel natural for you, and you might also enjoy history, anthropology, or archaeology.

A patriotic support of your nation or community may lead you to pursue a political career. Any position of prominence can be suitable, and your aptitude for influencing others can assist your climb up the ladder.

Your desire to care for others can be expressed in the medical field or in the counseling professions. Personnel management and social work can be good choices. Or you may prefer to use your enviable green thumb in landscaping or the floral industry.

## Your Approach to Romance

The comfort of a supportive partner and devoted family are part of your sense of personal fulfillment. You need a love that will mature through caring for one another and devotion to similar ideals. You can be a first-class cuddler, and need a partner who appreciates your sensuality. Since you tend to feel everything that's going on, you might find it difficult to keep positive boundaries in a relationship. But you don't have to be responsible for the happiness of the one you love! And remember to watch your own tendency to withdraw when you're feeling hurt, instead of seeking the comfort and closeness you crave.

You may be magnetically drawn to your polar opposite, Capricorn, whose persistent and steadfast drive help you build greater security. And it can be easier to get along with the other water signs—Cancer, Scorpio and Pisces. With another Cancerian you may devote much of your energy toward developing a strong home and family life. Scorpio encourages your deeper passions and can facilitate your creativity while Pisces' mystical imagination inspires you to reach beyond your limits.

Aries is attractive, but you can get scorched! You're safe with Taurus, whose support helps you maintain a sense of hope. Gemini brings wit and fun, but really might not appreciate being mothered all the time. And although Leo loves the attention you offer, they might not give back in kind.

Virgo's understanding can provide a good platform for your free self-expression. But Libra can seem too detached and throw you off-balance. Sagittarius requires some adjustment on your part, since you may be getting comfortable just about they time they're ready to leave! Intimate surroundings may not fit with Aquarius, who, for you, is a more reliable confidante than lover.

## Your Use of Power

You feel most powerful when you know you can take care of not only today, but that you're prepared for that inevitable "rainy day!" Your own emotional nature can provide a positive environment for your personal growth while encouraging the growth of others, building a powerful foundation for long-term stability. Your energy may provide a haven in the storm, ingratiating others and offering you a wide range of influence.

You might find that your most powerful position is within your family. But in a business, you can also create a feeling of family, forging a network of devoted individuals who share a common goal. You tend to allow the traditions from the past to inhibit your power, unless you can find a way to reshape the traditions within the new framework of current trends. Your most profound sense of power emerges when you feel secure and know that you and those you love are sheltered from harm and have an opportunity for future growth. In order to stay strong, you must maintain an open awareness of your own needs and continue to find ways to remain connected to the Source which constantly fills and sustains you.

## Famous Cancers

Dan Akroyd, Ingmar Bergman, Mel Brooks, John Chancellor, Bill Cosby, David Dinkins, Dianne Feinstein, Ann Landers, Greg LeMond, Cheech Marin, Thurgood Marshall, H. Ross Perot, Carlos Santayana, Richard Simmons, Pinchas Zukerman

# THE YEAR AHEAD FOR CANCER

Although you're continuing to make wide-ranging changes, the opportunities to expand your influence are balanced with a strong sense of personal stability during 1994. While humanity continues to reshape many philosophical and political attitudes, you may be searching for a safe place to rest and reevaluate your own positions. Some of your best possibilities arise from a quickening of your personal creativity, which can make a significant difference in the level of your success throughout the year.

Friends may play an important part, even in the context of your career. It's important to look at the people you've included in your circle of friends and associates, since you may find some of these relationships inappropriate following the changes you've made in the past. All relationships continue to provide an excellent backdrop for your personal growth, and you may feel that you're challenged to change many of your expectations of others. This begins with a look at your own expectations for yourself, since holding the mirror up to someone else rarely reflects your own personal truth.

The eclipses during this year emphasize your need to develop your self-expression through intimate relationships, personal creativity, and sharing of unconditional love. You're challenged to look toward your hopes for the future without losing track of the sanctity of the present. Of course, you're always interested in finding the best ways to incorporate what you've experienced in the past with the path you're currently following, and this cycle is no exception. But you may find, after introspection and deeper consideration of your future plans, that you need to let go of some elements of your past in order to move into the full light of the present. Not only are you taking a closer look at the larger picture, but you're also discovering how readily you can allow others to give their energy and support to you. Loving involves a flow of energy, with the release of giving and the opening of acceptance. It's time to feel that flow in its fullest measure in every aspect of your life.

Jupiter's transit in Scorpio works in supportive trine to your Sun this year, and encourages an improved sense of optimism. You're in the midst of a period of enhanced creative inspiration and may feel more open about sharing your talents with the rest of the world. Self-promotion or finding the right person to act as your agent can easily expand your possibilities for success. If you're oriented toward family and children, you may find that they provide some of your most precious moments this year. In fact, this is a great time to add to your family or to support the development of your children's talents. An element of self-indulgence often accompanies this cycle, and it's important to keep your priorities in order to avoid wasting your energy or resources.

Saturn enters Pisces at the end of January, and will be transiting through your Solar 9th House until 1996. The timing of the exact trine to your Sun is determined by your specific birth date and time, but you'll still feel the support of this cycle throughout the next two years. You must make choices under this influence, but you may find that the choices are less disturbing than those you've faced in the past. This cycle represents a period of personal integration and a strengthened self-concept and can be the stabilizing force which allows you to carry your personal responsibilities more easily. If you are willing to be held accountable for your own efforts, you can find this a rewarding period with greater advancement and more profound influence in your community or work situation. During the year, build a bridge between the mundane and Divine aspects of your life, and feel more profoundly connected to the functioning of the Universal Laws.

**If you were born from June 22–July 6, you're experiencing the support and discipline of Saturn transiting in trine to your Sun.** You can use this cycle to take bold steps in your business or career, but you may also choose to focus on the learning or teaching aspects of your work. If you've been wanting to finish educational requirements, this can be the right time to complete them. Or you might choose to teach or write, sharing the knowledge you've gained while enhancing your own understanding. To reach the level of mastery you hope to achieve during this time, you may need to eliminate circumstances, attitudes, or relationships that are stifling your success. Chapters naturally come to a close in preparation for the things that are yet to unfold. You may feel a certain measure of self-satisfaction if you've accomplished what you set out to do. But if you still have another task ahead, then you need to use this cycle to clear away the unfinished elements.

If you were born from June 30–July 4, you're in an especially powerful period this year when Jupiter and Saturn's transits are forming a Grand Trine with your Sun. Many factors in life may finally integrate to provide you with an opportunity to take significant steps to stabilize your career or to finally clarify your life path. Not only do you benefit from the self-discipline and clarity of Saturn's influence, but you're capable of reaching beyond the experiences of your past and into a broader form of self-expression. Travel may be an excellent outlet for the utilization of these energies, but you can also find tremendous reward in improving your life close to home. Your growth is more balanced with your ability to control and focus your energy, when you feel that you're in the right place at the right time. It's time to trust yourself and move confidently forward toward achieving a strong sense of self-realization.

If your birth occurred from June 24–July 18, you're feeling a need to identify your life purpose more clearly while Chiron transits in sextile to your Sun. Your everyday relationships can have a profound effect, and you may find teachers in the most unexpected situations. You're also discovering both the healing and wounding effects of your words or the word of others. Learning to communicate with greater clarity and intent requires a more highly developed sense of inner awareness, and you may feel challenged to avoid speaking when you know you can do more harm than good!

For Cancerians born from July 13–18, Neptune is transiting in exact opposition to your Sun this year. Your sense of compassion grows during this cycle, and you'll also feel more imaginative. Although the spiritual aspects of your life may seem more real than the tangible during this cycle, what is actually changing is your openness to the other levels of existence. It's easy to believe that the only reality is that which exists on the physical plane, but your intuitive awareness has always taken you beyond this limited viewpoint. With the expansion of consciousness which can occur during this cycle, you're more likely to embrace the spiritual and abandon the physical! There's danger in either extreme, since life involves a synthesis of many levels of reality. If your self-concept is fairly strong, then the influence of Neptune can be a tremendous enhancement to your creativity and psychic sensitivity. But if you've been undermining your stability through self-destructive behaviors or attitudes, then this cycle can tempt you to disengage from yourself rather than integrating. Addictive behaviors are easily amplified during this phase, as are addictive relationships. To avoid the more negative qualities of this cycle, it's important to stay in touch with your true center. You can emerge from this period with an awareness that you've experienced a true initiation, and may finally know the true meaning of compassion for yourself and for others.

**Uranus is transiting in opposition to your Sun if you were born from July 14–19,** helping you break away from the outworn elements of your life and become more positively independent. It's time to express your true individuality without feeling the restraint of those barriers which have previously inhibited you. Your attachment to the past may finally give way to trying something new (maybe even without the guilt!). Relationships are frequently the primary source of change during this cycle, but you may also feel that your entire life is undergoing a revolutionary shift. Your impetus is to become free and more self-expressive, and you may simply need to be more open about your needs with a partner rather than just walking away from the partnership. Any stifling behaviors or attitudes are definitely up for review now, and you have the chance to finally break away, but watch for enticements that are simply breaking up the status quo. Remind yourself that all your changes need to be in harmony with your highest needs, check your parachute, and then jump!

**If you were born from July 18–23** you're feeling the energy of Pluto trine to your Sun. One of the more powerful results of this transit is the restoration and healing you can create through a healthy examination of your life. You're likely to experience the healing power of love in your life, and can now see the evidence of positive forms of self-transformation. You may experience a unification of your family, or may simply feel more awareness of your ability to give of yourself. This can be a period of true self-acceptance and a sense of unity with Divine Love.

## Tools to Make a Difference

Even though many of your changes may be prompted by shifting circumstances, you can be the initiator of change more often than not. One of your best arenas for personal growth is within your intimate relationships– lover, partner, and family—which provide an excellent level of feedback and support. Arrange time in your life for family meetings or time to sit down with your partner and express your joy in sharing life together.

Some of the cycles you're experiencing this year can stimulate a level of detachment, and you'll need to find ways to stay in touch with your spiritual and emotional center. Without this connection, you may find that it's more difficult to separate your own inner voice from the needs and emotions of others, a process which can be jamming your intuitive airwaves. Each morning, before you begin your busy day of interaction and activity, take some time to quiet your mind and create a feeling of peace and tranquility. With each breath, feel yourself in touch with the natural rhythm of the Universe, with the heartbeat of Divine Mother. When you're ready to begin your day, you can then start in step with your own energy in harmony with that of The Source.

## Affirmation for the Year

"I feel at peace with the natural changes which
are flowing through my life."

## ACTION TABLES FOR CANCER

These dates reflect the best (but not the only) times for success and ease in these activities according to your Sun Sign.

| | |
|---|---|
| **Change Residence** | Sep. 4–26; Oct. 19–Nov. 9 |
| **Request a Raise** | July 8 |
| **Begin a Course of Study** | Mar. 4; Sep. 5 |
| **Visit a Doctor** | May 10–28; July 3–9; Nov. 30–Dec. 18 |
| **Start a Diet** | Jan. 8–9; Feb. 4–5: Mar. 3–5, 31–Apr. 1, 27–28; May 25–26; June 21–22; July 18–19; Aug. 15–16; Sep. 11–12; Oct. 8–9; Nov. 4–6; Dec. 2–3, 29–30 |
| **Begin a Romance** | Nov. 3–4 |
| **Join a Club** | May 10–11 |
| **Seek Employment** | Apr. 9–25; Nov. 30–Dec. 18 |
| **Take a Vacation** | Jan. 15–16; Feb. 11–12; Mar. 10–11; Apr. 6–8; May 4–5, 31–June 1, 27–29 July 25–26; Aug. 21–22; Sep. 17–19; Oct. 15–16; Nov. 11–12; Dec. 8–10 |
| **Change Your Wardrobe** | Sep. 27–Oct. 18; Nov 10–29 |
| **End a Relationship** | July 21–22 |
| **Seek Professional Advice** | Jan. 10–11; Feb. 6–8; Mar. 6–7; Apr. 2–3, 29–30; May 27–28; June 27–29; July 21–22; Aug. 17–18; Sep. 13–14; Oct. 10–11; Nov. 7–8; Dec. 4–5, 31 |
| **Have a Makeover** | July 8–9 |
| **Obtain a Loan** | Jan. 12–13; Feb. 9–10; Mar 8–9; Apr. 4–5; May 1–3, 29–30; June 25–26; July 23–24; Aug. 19–20; Sep. 15–16; Oct. 12–13; Nov. 9–10; Dec. 6–7 |

## PRIMARY FOCUS

Maintaining a balance between your own priorities and demands from others can be a challenge, but you're in a position to make sure everyone else does their part to help!

## HEALTH AND FITNESS

To keep your energy level strong, be sure you maintain a regular schedule of fitness activities. Add extra nourishment for your nervous system (B-vitamins and minerals) from the 10th–22nd.

## ROMANCE AND RELATIONSHIPS

Discontent within your partnership can prompt a straight-forward look at your issues during the New Moon on the 11th. Start with your own attitudes before you point any fingers! Honestly express your true needs and feelings, even if you do feel vulnerable, since by the time of the Full Moon on the 27th you can use vulnerability as an excuse to hide from your honest desires. Reach out on the 25th, 29th, or 30th.

## FINANCE AND CAREER

Arguments over finances can be more the norm than agreements. Sketchy details and incomplete facts complicate the picture from the 8th–17th. There's a good window for signing contracts from the 2nd–6th, but if you're uncertain, wait until your questions are satisfied. Clear up details and organize facts concerning loans or taxes after the 15th. Use reasonable caution in making credit purchases, since it's easy to overspend.

## OPPORTUNITY OF THE MONTH

To improve your outlook and fulfill your needs, take greater responsibility for your feelings by acknowledging them.

**Rewarding Days:** 2, 3, 6, 7, 15, 20, 21, 25, 26, 29
**Challenging Days:** 4, 5, 10, 11, 13, 17, 18, 31

## AFFIRMATION FOR THE MONTH
"Divine Love is my constant companion."

### PRIMARY FOCUS

An excellent time to actively seek the support of others, this is a great month for fund-raising or courting investors. Travel can provide positive long-term results.

### HEALTH AND FITNESS

Getting to the core physical discomforts can provide lasting relief. A holistic approach works best now, since simply relieving symptoms won't satisfy your deeper needs.

### ROMANCE AND RELATIONSHIPS

To experience the level of bonding you're hoping to achieve in your intimate relationship, you're seeking not only physical closeness by spiritual union. Your willingness to get beyond your old issues about your sexual needs opens a new doorway at the New Moon on the 10th. A more profound level of trust can emerge now. If you're looking, a new relationship can result from travel or sharing an inspirational experience. Don't be surprised if you feel that you've met before!

### FINANCE AND CAREER

Even though Mercury is retrograding after the 11th you can still make tremendous progress in your career. Presentations, workshops or conferences give you a chance to show your best attributes the week of the 13th. Go back over financial details after the 22nd, when professional advice offers important insights. Negotiations, contracts or legal dealings can prove rewarding from the 21st–26th. Business travel keeps avenues open during this time.

### OPPORTUNITY OF THE MONTH

The days surrounding the Full Moon on the 25th can bring remarkable results. Allow time to celebrate.

**Rewarding Days:** 2, 3, 11, 12, 16, 21, 22, 25, 26
**Challenging Days:** 1, 6, 7, 13, 14, 15, 27, 28

### AFFIRMATION FOR THE MONTH
"I am inspired by a higher truth."

### PRIMARY FOCUS

Increasing your knowledge through classes, workshops or travel can stabilize your career opportunities. Now is the time to take a position of leadership.

### HEALTH AND FITNESS

Join or organize sports or fitness activities that inspire you to increase your stamina and build your physical agility. Set up a routine that fits into and supports your lifestyle.

### ROMANCE AND RELATIONSHIPS

To connect with an intriguing individual or add inspiration and joy to an existing relationship, get involved in experiences that broaden your horizons. Travel and education are excellent options now, but you might also benefit from a spiritual retreat or participation in incentive-building activities. Take steps to begin to open your horizons for personal growth on the 12th, and you'll see tremendous improvements in your relationships. The need to honestly evaluate your family's needs takes precedence on the 27th.

### FINANCE AND CAREER

Review your finances from the 1st–5th before signing important contracts or reaching final agreements. The New Moon on the 12th marks a good time to get moving on delayed plans or to launch a new project. Advertising and other outreach programs fare beautifully this month, and can be highly significant the week of the 13th. Writing, public speaking, and political involvement are to your advantage.

### OPPORTUNITY OF THE MONTH

Appeals made on the 20th–21st can lead to mutual understanding and firm agreements, the 25th and 29th.

**Rewarding Days:** 1, 2, 10, 11, 12, 16, 20, 21, 22, 25, 26, 29
**Challenging Days:** 5, 6, 7, 18, 19, 27, 28

### AFFIRMATION FOR THE MONTH
"My plans are inspired by Divine Guidance."

### PRIMARY FOCUS

Even though you're getting more from your career, you can still benefit from setting goals that offer even greater rewards.

### HEALTH AND FITNESS

Until the 10th you may feel pretty balanced, but friction at work after the 14th may increase your stress levels. Keep fitness a high priority to avoid burn-out.

### ROMANCE AND RELATIONSHIPS

Sharing a spiritually inspiring experience brings a lift to your love-life through the 13th. Even though pressures from the outside world can dampen your spirit on the 9th, your faith in yourself can overcome any feelings of despair. Spend time with a special friend from the 11th–13th, when your alliance can bring mutual support. Familial conflicts on the 17th may lead to misunderstandings the following week, and can escalate during the Full Moon on the 25th. Look for a common goal to unite your efforts from the 24th–28th.

### FINANCE AND CAREER

Your drive to succeed can forge positive bonds with co-workers and superiors alike early this month. Confusing policies issued now need to be clarified in order to take advantage of the tremendous growth possible by the 28th. Supporting and inspiring others can improve work circumstances while advancing your own standing. Take extra care with finances from the 20th–24th, when it's easy to overlook critical details. Read the fine print before you sign!

### OPPORTUNITY OF THE MONTH

Powerful allies contacted on the 7th–8th can be responsible for opening doors to long-term success.

**Rewarding Days:** 7, 8, 12, 13, 17, 18, 21, 22, 25, 26, 28
**Challenging Days:** 2, 3, 9, 10, 14, 23, 24, 29, 20

### AFFIRMATION FOR THE MONTH
"I feel joy today and hope for the future."

### PRIMARY FOCUS

Concentration on your primary goals is a strong impetus, but you need to watch for a tendency to "accidentally" offend the wrong person. Stay aware of what's happening around you!

### HEALTH AND FITNESS

It can be difficult to strike an even pace, and disruptions in your regular schedule can throw you off balance. Be especially kind to your body the 16th–20th.

### ROMANCE AND RELATIONSHIPS

The Sun's Eclipse on the 10th draws your focus to your larger life directions, and can stimulate a greater sense of clarity about your ability to maintain an unconditional quality in your personal relationships. Jealousy can strike even a solid friendship, and you need to know your own weak points in this regard. Resolutions by the Lunar Eclipse on the 24th leave room for both your differences and similarities. Romance fares best after the 23rd, but watch for the surfacing of your own vulnerabilities on the 27th.

### FINANCE AND CAREER

The competition can feel fierce, and you need to watch for dirty tricks the week of the 15th. However, you can also be the perpetrator of a hoax in order to keep your own foot in the door. Be sure your goal is worth the cost of your efforts. You can definitely move forward, and may not have to fight as fiercely as you had assumed. Target reaching a consensus the week of the 22nd, but be prepared for changes on the 27th.

### OPPORTUNITY OF THE MONTH

While maintaining a position of strength, listen to your intuitive voice on the 5th and 14th.

**Rewarding Days:** 4, 5, 9, 10, 14, 15, 19, 23, 31
**Challenging Days:** 1, 2, 6, 7, 21, 22, 23, 27, 28

### AFFIRMATION FOR THE MONTH
"I feel the power of sharing love."

### PRIMARY FOCUS

Careful attention to your intuitive voice can help you avoid costly delays and frustrating circumstances. A creative approach to everyday situations inspires greater enjoyment.

### HEALTH AND FITNESS

Join in a team sport, or get into a fitness class with a friend. Your stamina and energy are consistently strong, and it's a great time to stabilize your health.

### ROMANCE AND RELATIONSHIPS

Along with a promising turn in your love life, you're also gaining more self-admiration. Communication of your deeper feelings may feel less threatening, and can lead to increasing your commitment in an intimate relationship. Bring romance back into your life from the 5th–14th, but more with care in a new situation, since it's easy to project an unrealistic image on your partner. Expectations of yourself and your partner intensify during the Full Moon on the 23rd, and this time is excellent for renewing your vows.

### FINANCE AND CAREER

Even though Mercury begins a retrograde cycle on the 12th, you can still make career progress. To strengthen your influence, get back in touch with established clients or renew old alliances. It's easy to lose valuable items or make costly mistakes in your finances from the 8th–13th, so take security precautions. Get preparatory work in order during the New Moon on the 9th, and be ready to talk specifics from the 22nd–29th.

### OPPORTUNITY OF THE MONTH

Building your reputation puts you in an excellent position for recognition on the 1st, 6th, 28th, and 29th.

**Rewarding Days:** 1, 5, 6, 10, 11, 15, 19, 20, 28, 29
**Challenging Days:** 2, 3, 12, 17, 18, 23, 24, 26

### AFFIRMATION FOR THE MONTH
"I feel safe and secure."

### PRIMARY FOCUS

Deal directly with your own attitudes about your life situation. Getting to the core of your anxieties opens the way for greater stability and more spontaneous fulfillment of your needs.

### HEALTH AND FITNESS

Give yourself some extra time to kick back and relax from the 1st–10th. Reshaping your attitudes about yourself and concentration on "inner" fitness forms the basis for more sound physical health.

### ROMANCE AND RELATIONSHIPS

The New Moon in Cancer on the 8th can help to awaken the positive elements of your relationship. Whether you're stabilizing a commitment or leaving an old situation, it's important to clarify your own needs. Make an extra effort to reach out to those you love after the 12th and share your more cherished pleasures on the 16th and 17th. As the Full Moon on the 22nd approaches, be prepared to mend fences. Concentrate on achieving balance and equanimity.

### FINANCE AND CAREER

You may have to go back to the drawing board until the 11th, so try not to rush situations that are not ready to move forward. Negotiations and presentations are positively received on the 12th and 13th, and you're in a good position to nudge things along on the 25th and 26th. Money matters can be sticky from the 3rd–7th, when you may have to give way in order to reach an agreement. Forward motion begins after the 17th, when most barriers are finally out of the way!

### OPPORTUNITY OF THE MONTH

Exercise your strongest talent on the 16th and 17th to assure the response you desire from others.

**Rewarding Days:** 3, 7, 8, 9, 12, 13, 16, 17, 25, 26, 30
**Challenging Days:** 1, 2, 6, 14, 15, 20, 21, 22, 27, 28

### AFFIRMATION FOR THE MONTH
"I am responsible for my own happiness."

### PRIMARY FOCUS

Make the best use of your resources to assure the success and recognition you deserve. An increased sense of self-assurance emerges after the 21st.

### HEALTH AND FITNESS

Gently increasing your activity level helps you maintain stamina. Pushing too hard could lead to feeling strung-out. Try relaxing herbal tea in the evenings.

### ROMANCE AND RELATIONSHIPS

Exploring the undercurrents of a love relationship can expose the possibilities of transformational changes for each of you early this month. Take time to remove yourselves from the daily pressures in a special rendezvous after the 18th. Squabbles over finances or different values can be a clue to hidden insecurities about self-esteem leading up to the Full Moon in the early morning of the 21st. After the dust settles, take time to really look at your issues; you may find clues to resolving core problems.

### FINANCE AND CAREER

Review your financial records and outline proposals from the 3rd–17th. Improving your career options and strengthening your professional alliances can lead to your much-deserved advancement after the 20th. However, you should be on the alert for possible sabotage from the 27th–31st, when trusting the wrong person can be costly. These are good days to discover the true loyalty of your friends or professional allies. Share your generosity only where it is honestly appreciated!

### OPPORTUNITY OF THE MONTH

Rewards for your creativity are forthcoming on the 27th and 31st.

**Rewarding Days:** 4, 5, 8, 9, 13, 14, 21, 22, 26, 27, 31
**Challenging Days:** 2, 10, 11, 17, 18, 19, 24, 25

### AFFIRMATION FOR THE MONTH
"My life is filled with abundance in all things!"

### PRIMARY FOCUS

Home and family bring the most profound rewards this month, when romantic or playful activities highlight your favorite pastimes. Children can play an important role now.

### HEALTH AND FITNESS

Measuring your pace is critical, since you can allow yourself to feel overwhelmed by trying to please everyone at the same time. Put yourself on your priority list.

### ROMANCE AND RELATIONSHIPS

Contact with siblings proves positive from the 1st–6th, allowing you all to follow a more open direction after the New Moon on the 5th. Romantic contacts build in intensity while Venus transits your Solar 5th House, and can be especially positive at the Full Moon on the 19th. If you have children, sharing their creative activities brings a special joy this month. Give your imagination room to express itself after the 18th. But know that the person in your dreams can be quite different in reality!

### FINANCE AND CAREER

Redecorating your work environment can help increase productivity, but you may change your mind about the details before it's all over! Use plans and models to help reach a final decision. Financial negotiations and investments can bring surprising results from the 18th–22nd, so allow extra time for the changes that can occur. Contracts or legal agreements on the 23rd–24th may have unfortunate loopholes. Search for them.

### OPPORTUNITY OF THE MONTH

An emotional involvement gains momentum after the 23rd, and can develop into a lasting commitment.

**Rewarding Days:** 1, 5, 9, 10, 18, 19, 22, 23, 27, 28, 29
**Challenging Days:** 3, 7, 8, 13, 14, 15, 20, 21

### AFFIRMATION FOR THE MONTH
"My heart is full. I am in love with life!"

### PRIMARY FOCUS

A period of review and reevaluation of your relationships and personal worth offers insight which can lead to more security.

### HEALTH AND FITNESS

Concentrate on building stamina and endurance, but remember to include stretching and flexibility as part of your routine. Inactivity now can actually decrease your vitality levels.

### ROMANCE AND RELATIONSHIPS

You're more inclined to share your feelings of love with others now, but are watching to see if your efforts are worthwhile. New love or more openness in an ongoing relationship moves swiftly after the New Moon on the 4th, when you're most comfortable in intimate surroundings. Questioning the motivations of others and examining your own intentions reveals the truth on the 15th–16th. Family values and tradition need to be consided in your decisions near the Full Moon on the 19th.

### FINANCE AND CAREER

Creative pursuits gain momentum and can lead to your recognition and financial success now. Working in concert with others is most beneficial through the 16th, but ego conflicts over shared resources can arise on the 12th–13th. Whenever possible, try the most imaginative solutions to problems. Mercury's retrograde from the 9th–30th can resurrect past circumstances you thought to be settled.

### OPPORTUNITY OF THE MONTH

Take bold steps to secure recognition for your efforts or the efforts of those you love on the 6th and7th.

**Rewarding Days:** 2, 3, 6, 7, 15, 16, 20, 25, 26, 30
**Challenging Days:** 4, 5, 10, 11, 14, 17, 18, 31

### AFFIRMATION FOR THE MONTH
"My life is filled with abundance."

### PRIMARY FOCUS

Emphasis on your love relationships, including those with children and family, brings opportunities for exceptional joy.

### HEALTH AND FITNESS

It's easy to overindulge in all the sweet things, and you may not feel like disciplining yourself. Rather than restriction, consider the option of moderation!

### ROMANCE AND RELATIONSHIPS

Questioning and reconsidering deeper feelings continues, but you can still enjoy many precious moments with loved ones. An intimate love relationship needs careful examination, though, since you can now break away from old patterns of response and experience a more profound love. The Solar Eclipse on the 3rd brings an awakening of feelings you had thought were lost, and can cause you to risk sharing your dreams. From the Lunar Eclipse on the 18th until the 30th, you can finally release those pesky old ghosts from the past.

### FINANCE AND CAREER

Investments show growth, although risky speculation may have you on the edge of your seat. Analysis of finances can reveal weak points, and you'll see benefits from eliminating unproductive things, focusing on those which show promise. Watch for new opportunities on the 7th and be ready to act before the Lunar Eclipse on the 18th. After the 20th, power struggles can ensue, and you need to stand firmly in your position.

### OPPORTUNITY OF THE MONTH

Allowing your ethics to guide you on the 11th–12th, you can determine your real friends and allies. Join with them on the 17th.

**Rewarding Days:** 3, 4, 11, 12, 16, 17, 21, 22, 26, 30
**Challenging Days:** 1, 2, 7, 8, 9, 13, 14, 15, 28, 29

### AFFIRMATION FOR THE MONTH
"I respect my intuitive guidance."

### PRIMARY FOCUS

Even though your work schedule can intensify, your originality can make a notable difference in your products. Avoid taking responsibility for others.

### HEALTH AND FITNESS

Learn better ways to keep yourself fit; you still have to take care of physical needs despite your busy schedule. Information is an excellent form of self-defense.

### ROMANCE AND RELATIONSHIPS

If your expectations have been too high, you may feel that you're at the crash and burn stage of a love affair. Be realistic if you're stepping into new situations on the 2nd, since the New Moon is accompanied by a cycle of amplified anticipation. Stop the suspense by avoiding the complex options and concentrating on the simple approach. Stabilization of emotional turmoil is most likely from the 7th–10th. Allow your passion to cool a bit during the Full Moon on the 17th.

### FINANCE AND CAREER

Avoid feeling overwhelmed with obligations by careful consideration before you agree to increase your workload. Advancement of your position is possible, and it's easy to give the impression that you're willing to go beyond the call of duty. Mistakes made the 1st–8th seem larger than life. Speculation is best avoided during this time, when you can be inclined to exceed your limit. You're in a more reasonable mood after the 23rd.

### OPPORTUNITY OF THE MONTH

A friend or business ally is an excellent source of support and advice from the 13th-15th. Return the favor on the 18th.

**Rewarding Days:** 1, 8, 9, 13, 14, 15, 18, 19, 23, 24, 28
**Challenging Days:** 2, 4, 5, 6, 11, 12, 25, 26, 31

### AFFIRMATION FOR THE MONTH
"I am willing to accept assistance and
support when I need it."

# LEO
## The Lion
### July 23 to August 23

**Element:** Fire

**Quality:** Fixed

**Polarity:** Masculine/Yang

**Planetary Ruler:** The Sun

**Meditation:** "Self glows with Light from the Source"

**Gemstone:** Ruby

**Power Stones:** Topaz, Sardonyx

**Key Phrase:** "I will"

**Glyph:** Lion's tail

**Anatomy:** Heart, upper back, sides

**Colors:** Gold

**Animal:** Lions, large cats

**Myths/Legends:** Apollo, Isis, Helius

**House Association:** 5th

**Opposite Sign:** Aquarius

**Flower:** Marigold

**Key Word:** Magnetism

**Positive Expression:**
Loyal
Creative
Regal
Dramatic
Bold
Honorable
Benevolent
Self-confident
Dynamic
Elegant

**Misuse of Energy:**
Egocentric
Arrogant
Domineering
Pompous
Insolent
Ostentatious
Chauvinistic
Selfish
Dictatorial

# ♌ LEO ♌

## Your Ego's Strengths and Weaknesses

Although you may have many talents, it's your warmth and radiance that people remember. Your dynamic and dramatic self-expression can act as a guide to those who need leadership, or you can stand alone in the spotlight when your opportunity comes along. It seems natural for you to be the center of attention, much like the Sun, your ruler, is at the center of our own planetary system.

You may be presented with a broad scope of opportunities for self-expression, and need ample room for your legendary creativity and playfulness. You can be regal or flamboyant, polished or garish, but at all times possess a loving and benevolent nature which draws others to you. If you're feeling unappreciated, you can lash out and become insolent or demanding. It can be difficult for you to share the limelight; you can act outrageously dejected.

When you see evidence of loyalty from those you love, you can sparkle! And your big-hearted generosity easily extends to those individuals and circumstances to which you're committed. Honor ranks high in your priorities. You can be a capable champion, and have plenty of courage to stand firm when the going gets tough. But when this need is misplaced you can become excessively proud and stubborn. Positively using your intrinsic magnetic energy to create your life on your own terms imbues you with confidence. By placing your ego at the disposal of your higher nature, you can create a true monument to Divine Power.

## Your Career Development

Positions of leadership and authority are perfect for your natural abilities. It can be highly important to receive recognition for your achievements. As Chairman of the Board, C.E.O. or Union President, you can excel when you reach the top. You might function well as a foreman or supervisor, and can be a great promoter. You can also be an inspiring teacher, and can engender a sense of self-importance in others.

In the performing arts you may excel as an actor, musician, or model. You can also be a highly effective producer or director. Since you like to be in places where others are enjoying themselves, you might successfully develop businesses such as restaurants, clubs, amusements, or theaters. Politics may also be a choice, but you might prefer to promote and direct a candidate rather than becoming one!

## Your Approach to Romance

You can be lavish with your affection, and love special attention in an intimate atmosphere. Whether you're in elegant or humble surroundings, romance with you can be a royal experience. Once you've extended your love to another, your eternal loyalty can make it difficult if a relationship ends. But when you do find the right partner, you can keep your love alive by rekindling warm romance on a regular basis.

Active relationships keep your fiery energy alive, and you may be most excited in relationships with other fire signs. Aries are spontaneously attractive, but you may wonder if they're loyal. Sagittarius' sense of adventure harmonizes with your desire to play. And with another Leo the heat can be intense, but you each need your own time in the limelight.

Taurus attracts, but you may not enjoy feeling like their possession. Gemini's wit and intelligence stimulates your imagination, and you can be excellent travelling companions. While the nurturance of Cancer feels comforting, they may not light your fire. Inspired by Virgo's attention to perfection, you might be more comfortable as friends.

You're enticed with Libra's refined beauty and charm, and with Scorpio you enjoy sensual delights but can feel choked by the intensity. Although Capricorn may be good for business, romance can be strained. Your attraction to your opposite, Aquarius, can tug at your heart strings, but it can mean trouble. And Pisces woos you into an alternative reality which can be distracting if you lose your bearings!

## Your Use of Power

Just as the Sun stimulates and sustains our life force, you are closely connected to the Power of Life. You're eager to tap into this energy and shine as brightly as possible, and may be fueled by the recognition and acknowledgment you gain from others. You're most comfortable when you're radiating that power to others through leadership, inspiration, or authority.

Whether at home or at work, you can be a benevolent ruler. Those around you feel safe and comforted by your magnetism, and you can inspire them to follow their own special talents. But you can be dictatorial, stealing power from others to maintain your own, if you're too far out of control. Watch the effect you have upon others as a positive guideline to your ability to wield power. Remember that you can become self-absorbed to the extent that the efforts and needs of others may not be as noticeable to you as they once were.

Your path is not always an easy one, since you may feel that your only ally is often the will of The Creator. By maintaining a communion with this power, your own light can shine as a beacon of hope and love.

## Famous Leos

Ian Anderson, Neil Armstrong, Rosalynn Carter, Fidel Castro, Julia Child, Bill Clinton, Garrison Keillor, Norman Lear, Carroll O'Connor, Annie Oakley, Maxfield Parrish, Robert Redford, Gene Roddenberry, Arnold Schwarzenegger, Malcom-Jamal Warner

# THE YEAR AHEAD FOR LEO

This is the year to make room for greater emphasis in your personal and spiritual growth. You're challenged to trim away excesses from your ego, while maintaining a strong sense of self. Even though your attitudes toward your work are changing, you may still have a need to fine-tune your approach in order to experience the rewards you desire.

Jupiter's transit in Scorpio until December 9th can stimulate a heightened interest in your home and family. This can be a good time to incorporate a sense of openness in your home environment, and you may feel that you need more space. It's tempting to move into a dwelling that offers more room, but take care to avoid overextending your budget! Before you pack up and move, try eliminating excessive clutter and use your imagination. You may be able to accomplish your aims through simpler (and possibly less expensive!) pursuits. This cycle also brings an incentive to reach beyond your current life circumstances, and you can respond with a sense of buoyancy and optimism that leads to accelerated personal growth. But it's also tempting to reach beyond your limits through self-indulgence and excess. Although moderation can be a difficult choice this year, it's your best option toward avoiding getting in over your head!

The Solar Eclipses this year also add emphasis to your need to balance personal and professional aims. If the pendulum swings widely toward one direction, you are likely to see the opposite polarity demanding just as much of your time and energy. However, your need to create a secure foundation is a primary motivation, and can easily be applied to each of these areas. You may feel a greater responsibility emerging which can actually bring a stabilizing, rather than an undermining, effect. It may be time to step out of the limelight for a while, giving yourself time to create and enjoy that foundation. Before you accept that committee appointment or extra assignment, be sure you feel absolutely sure that you're capable of meeting the obligations involved. If you have doubts, it's probably a good idea to postpone those extra duties in favor of spending more time on the things already on your busy agenda.

Chiron's travels during 1994 accentuate your self-esteem. The utilization of your resources, whether material, physical, or spiritual, can be a good indicator of any holes in your self-worth. You can actually create a more substantial financial situation, but you'll probably find that you can't afford the pressure of feeling that you've wasted any of your resources. Pay attention to time obligations, since your time is also a highly valuable resource.

**If you were born from July 22–August 6 you're feeling some frustration all year while Saturn transits in quincunx to your Sun.** This cycle brings a series of adjustments, and can prove to be quite irritating if you've become too self-absorbed. But the strong point of this time is that you're learning more about yourself and the way you interface with the world. You can strengthen your position in your career by listening more carefully to the expectations of others. If you feel that you're not being compensated adequately for your efforts, you could be basing your own expectations on circumstances which do not actually exist. Exploration and research can prove quite illuminating—since you may actually uncover the reasons for the shortfall. With your own finances, be sure you're paying adequate attention to keeping your indebtedness to a minimum. If you're seeking investment or support from others, you may have to make a few changes before they're willing to go along with your ideas. This is also a great time to expose your hidden fears and deal with them directly by confronting their validity. You may find that you're no longer vulnerable, and can experience a new level of personal freedom. In health issues, investigate any problems which arise, since adaptations made now can help you avoid more critical issues later. You may feel more susceptible to the negative effects of stress, and can benefit from deliberately dealing with any stressful circumstances. Ignoring problems now will only add to their burden. You're moving toward a period of powerful opportunity within the next two years, and need to make room for those changes. Fine-tuning now will help to place you in just the right position to take advantage of those changes later.

**For Leo's born from August 7–11, no cycles of intense challenge are facing you at an ego level.** You can establish a stronger base now, and may find less personal conflict during this time. Allow yourself to become more aware of the impact your actions have upon the world around you. Take time to reaffirm your own power.

**If you were born from August 12–17, you're feeling the subtle force of Neptune transiting in quincunx to your Sun.** You may find yourself drawn more toward the spiritual elements of life, and can use this year as a time of deeper personal reflection and the development of greater mindfulness. Many aspects of your life can shift toward more imaginative forms of expression. Any creative activity can be enhanced, and this is an especially good time to work with photography, film or visual imagery. Music can become more meaningful, and can influence your consciousness more easily. Consequently, take special care to expose yourself to music that takes you into a psychological space which is both comfortable and inspiring. Since you're more easily attracted to intangible elements, you may feel inspired to spend some extra time in spiritual service or an involvement in charitable activities. When dealing with relationships, be aware that you can tend to be enchanted by aspects that may not be what they seem. Take your time before plunging into the unknown, since both people and circumstances can be hard to analyze. Most deception which occurs during this cycle is likely to be the result of unconscious projection, but you can become the victim of others if you fail to follow your best judgement. If you're filled with doubts you cannot fully explain, take time to center your energy before you proceed. You may just be out of focus! By staying in contact with your Higher Self, you'll avoid many of the pitfalls inherent in this period. In caring for your physical health, you may become more sensitive to both environmental and dietary elements which had not caused problems in the past. Once again, increased mindfulness on your part can help to alleviate what could become a period of lowered vitality. If you find that an environmental change or change in diet creates a loss of energy, spend some time analyzing the situation before you duplicate or enhance it in some way. Simplification can help you avoid many of the pitfalls of this period.

**If your birth occurred from August 13 to 19, you're experiencing the influence of Uranus transiting in quincunx to your Sun.** This cycle can throw you into a tailspin before you know it, especially if you give in to every distraction this period can present. There are likely to be surprising changes which offer an opportunity to try something completely different, but it's not the best time to burn all your bridges. More often than not, you're likely to cross those bridges several times before you decide on your pathway. This is a period of experimentation, and is an excellent time to develop a fresh approach to your job. Even if you decide to continue on the same career path, you may feel your attitudes toward your work shifting in significant ways. Many times, these cycles are accompanied by a need to adjust to new technological advances. Inconsistency is more the norm than predictability, and you'll enjoy this period more by keeping an open mind! This is a great time to clear out closets, garages, and attics, since you're needing to eliminate the clutter that's been in the way of your progress. Continuing to drag around in circumstances or relationships which are in need of revision can be highly frustrating as well, since you're ready to feel more inner freedom. Airing your grievances can be helpful, but be sure you're really getting to the core issues and not just dancing around them. Physically, you may find it difficult to rest unless you're effectively using your nervous energy. Staying active is crucial, and you may also need to increase your intake of foods high in B-vitamins in order to maintain a consistent vitality.

**For Leos born from August 17–23, personal transformation through conscious change occurs while Pluto is transiting in a square aspect to your Sun.** You're experiencing a period of increased intensity, and may feel compelled to leave behind aspects of your life that have been inhibiting your growth. This is an excellent time to work with a therapist, since old issues can be more readily extracted. Relationships with parents may need closer scrutiny as you struggle to break free of your past. You may also question the validity of your career choices, and can experience major changes within your work environment. The key factor involves your willingness to release those things which are no longer part of your positive self-expression. Avoiding these changes can lead to a tendency to repress your feelings, which can result in physical problems later. But this is also a time to bring healing into your life on all levels by addressing the necessary changes and incorporating them into your existence.

### Tools to Make a Difference

To experience the most positive aspects of the cycles during 1994, you'll need to allow time for your inner self, instead of just dealing with the external circumstances. Bring a greater mindfulness to your life experiences by allowing time for reflection or meditation. Take some time each day to get back in touch with what you're really feeling, and make a conscious effort to connect with your inner and higher self.

Your health may need special attention this year, and it's probably a good time to concentrate on clearing your physical system. A heart-healthy diet is critical for you, since your heart and circulatory system are likely to be the victims of excessive stress in your life. Many of the physically stressful cycles you've experienced in the last few years are coming to a close this year, and positive changes incorporated now can add years of increased vitality.

Use your increased spiritual awareness in every aspect of your life. Feel your own energy connected to the Source of All Life, allowing this power to flow into everything you do and say. Your life is indeed a golden opportunity, and this is the time to fine-tune yourself in harmony with your higher needs.

### Affirmation for the Year

"My will is guided by Divine Love and Power."

## ACTION TABLES FOR LEO

These dates reflect the best (but not the only) times for success and ease in these activities according to your Sun Sign.

| | |
|---|---|
| **Change Residence** | Sep. 27–Oct. 18; Nov. 10–29 |
| **Request a Raise** | Aug. 7–8 |
| **Begin a Course of Study** | Apr. 11–12; Oct. 5–6 |
| **Visit a Doctor** | Jan. 1–13; June 28–July 2; July 10–Aug. 2; Dec. 19–31 |
| **Start a Diet** | Jan. 10–11; Feb. 7–8; Mar. 6–7; Apr. 2–3, 29–30; May 27–28; June 23–24; July 21–22; Aug. 17–18; Sep. 13–4; Oct. 10–11; Nov. 7–8; Dec. 4–5, 31 |
| **Begin a Romance** | Dec. 2–3 |
| **Join a Club** | June 9–10 |
| **Seek Employment** | Jan. 1–13; Apr. 26–May 9; Dec. 19–31 |
| **Take a Vacation** | Jan. 17–18; Feb. 13–14; Mar. 13–14; Apr. 9–10; May 6–7; June 2–4, 30–July 1, 27–29; Aug. 24–25; Sep. 20–21; Oct. 17–18; Nov. 13–15; Dec. 11–12 |
| **Change Your Wardrobe** | Nov. 30–Dec. 18 |
| **End a Relationship** | Aug. 21–22 |
| **Seek Professional Advice** | Jan. 12–13; Feb. 9–10; Mar. 8–9; Apr. 4–5; May 1–2, 29–30; June 25–26; July 23–24; Aug. 19–20; Sep. 15–16; Oct. 12–13; Nov. 9–10; Dec. 6–7 |
| **Have a Makeover** | Aug. 7–8 |
| **Obtain a Loan** | Jan. 15–16; Feb. 11–12; Mar. 10–12; Apr. 7–8; May 4–5, 31–June 1, 27–29; July 25–26; Aug. 21–22; Sep. 18–19; Oct. 15–16; Nov. 11–12; Dec. 8–9 |

### PRIMARY FOCUS

Increase your efficiency by adjusting your schedule to accommodate projects which produce positive results. Eliminating circumstances that drain your energy frees your creativity.

### HEALTH AND FITNESS

A critical examination of your lifestyle reveals necessary changes that improve your ability to cope with stress. Take time to get to the core of physical complaints.

### ROMANCE AND RELATIONSHIPS

Although work requires more attention early in the month, your partnership needs a balanced portion of your time after the 15th. Family expectations are high, and can get in the way of decisions between you and your partner. The ghosts of old emotional trauma offer an opportunity to heal the past, but you may be tempted to retreat into yourself. Open communication with loved ones after the 15th helps you avoid escalating unfounded fears near the time of the Full Moon on the 27th.

### FINANCE AND CAREER

Improve an established tradition by adding an imaginative change after the New Moon on the 11th. Co-workers or those under your supervision may be counting on your leadership to make a difference. If you're indifferent to or unaware of others' discontent you can leave yourself open to deception or undermining of your position. Curb spending until after the 20th. Wait for the dust to settle before speculative investing.

### OPPORTUNITY OF THE MONTH

Be sure you've done your homework to avoid feeling exposed or embarrassed, instead of being prepared for the Leo Full Moon on the 27th.

**Rewarding Days:** 4, 5, 8, 9, 17, 18, 27, 28, 31
**Challenging Days:** 6, 7, 11, 12, 13, 14, 20, 21

### AFFIRMATION FOR THE MONTH
"I am healthy, strong, and powerful."

### PRIMARY FOCUS

An urge to compete can stimulate behavior that others perceive as too aggressive or offensive. Be aware of their responses, and gauge your actions accordingly.

### HEALTH AND FITNESS

Channel your energy toward increasing activity levels, but avoid pushing beyond your limits. Build flexibility to avoid injury.

### ROMANCE AND RELATIONSHIPS

Feelings of disappointment can be the result of unrealistic expectations within your intimate relationship. You may also have some problems allowing yourself to receive the generosity of others, and you can tend toward excessive generosity through the 13th. Explore your true feelings during the New Moon on the 10th, since you may be doing things for the wrong reasons! A need to plunge into deeper levels of intimacy after the 13th can lead to greater satisfaction in your love life by the time of the Full Moon on the 25th.

### FINANCE AND CAREER

Cooperative ventures may reach a stalemate mid-month, but may not have to be abandoned. Evaluate the reasons for delays, working patiently to overcome the inertia generated by a slow-down in your progress. Mercury's retrograde on the 11th can signal a time to emphasize research before you take action, instead of getting caught in red tape later. Power struggles over joint ventures can sabotage efforts from the 22nd–28th.

### OPPORTUNITY OF THE MONTH

Careful consideration or review of partnerships illuminates a novel direction on the 10th, the day of the New Moon.

**Rewarding Days:** 1, 4, 5, 14, 15, 20, 23, 24
**Challenging Days:** 2, 3, 7, 8, 9, 10, 16, 17, 19

### AFFIRMATION FOR THE MONTH
"I am clearly aware of my Higher Self."

### PRIMARY FOCUS
Look beneath the surface to locate solutions and avoid losing valuable time. Appearances can deceive.

### HEALTH AND FITNESS
Frustrations in personal and professional realms can send your stress level through the roof. Instead of forcing yourself, ease off and take a more relaxed pace. Compulsion can be your enemy now.

### ROMANCE AND RELATIONSHIPS
Deception or unresolved past issues may finally be out in the open, giving you an opportunity to clarify your feelings and take more satisfying action. Talk over your fears about intimacy with a trusted advisor on the 12th, and look for ways to move into a truly gratifying relationship. You're likely to feel more inclined to communicate your desires to your sweetheart by the Full Moon on the 27th. Plan a short get-away from daily pressures sometime between the 23rd–29th.

### FINANCE AND CAREER
Selfish greed on the part of others can block progress from the 1st–6th. Seek an alliance with a more supportive investor or partner from the 13th–20th. But be aware that only conservative actions are likely to bring positive results! Proposals during the week of the 20th should be enthusiastically received, but you may be most successful by completing transactions previously begun. Avoid speculation from the 27th–31st, since important facts may be omitted or overlooked.

### OPPORTUNITY OF THE MONTH
Inspiring individuals offer new ideas on the 13th. Listen carefully, and find ways to incorporate your new understanding.

**Rewarding Days:** 3, 4, 13, 14, 18, 19, 23, 24, 27, 31
**Challenging Days:** 1, 2, 7, 8, 9, 15, 16, 17, 29, 30

### AFFIRMATION FOR THE MONTH
"I gladly release unnecessary attachments."

### PRIMARY FOCUS
Working out solutions to financial dilemmas early in the month gives you room to expand options after the 15th. High stakes speculation is still a questionable risk!

### HEALTH AND FITNESS
Aggressive action which targets the core of any physical distress proves successful. Ignoring a problem only aggravates it.

### ROMANCE AND RELATIONSHIPS
Disagreements over the most satisfying way to achieve a deeper level of intimacy in your love relationship may reach a stand-off by the 9th. The New Moon on the 10th indicates a period of reaching toward a mutual understanding through integrating your spiritual and emotional needs. Travel brings excitement and the potential for a stimulating encounter from the 10th–21st. Matters at home take priority with the Full Moon on the 25th, but you should still have time for a romantic interlude on the 27th and 28th.

### FINANCE AND CAREER
Conservative factions can override your more creative options from the 4th–9th, when necessity stands in the way of imagination. By incorporating expansion into the framework of reasonable possibility, you'll impress your superiors and stymie the competition. Watch out for unexpected expenses on the 12th and 13th, and make sure you're prepared for interruptions in your plans from the 21st–26th.

### OPPORTUNITY OF THE MONTH
Schedule meetings or presentations with influential individuals on the 19th and 20th. Sharing your vision can inspire support boosting you toward your goals.

**Rewarding Days:** 1, 9, 14, 15, 19, 20, 23, 27, 28
**Challenging Days:** 3, 4, 5, 5, 12, 13, 25, 26 30

### AFFIRMATION FOR THE MONTH
"I am guided by truth and inspired by love."

### PRIMARY FOCUS
A question of trust can arise and may undermine your sense of confidence in leadership. Align yourself with personal truth and moral honor to avoid eroding your self-confidence.

### HEALTH AND FITNESS
Team sports and group fitness activities offer satisfying opportunities to improve your vitality. Take extra care in high risk situations from the 13th–21st.

### ROMANCE AND RELATIONSHIPS
Concentrate on developing a friendship or sharing time with others of like mind. Even in an intimate relationship you may feel a need to remove some negative restraints. Near the Solar Eclipse on the 10th, allow time to reflect on your early life to illuminate any early disappointments that may have undermined your self-esteem. This healing awareness can allow more room for intimacy. Share special experiences with those you cherish during the Lunar Eclipse on the 24th.

### FINANCE AND CAREER
Business travel, conferences, workshops or classes which improve your skills can build great rewards. Presentations fare nicely from the 7th–12th. Be cautious when sharing your plans the week of the 15th, when you can be the victim of deceptive tactics or unscrupulous individuals. If you require more time to complete documentation and research, it may work to your benefit. Begin long-term negotiations the week of the 22nd.

### OPPORTUNITY OF THE MONTH
Get involved in inspirational or educational activities on the 6th and 7th. You may also find others seeking your advice!

**Rewarding Days:** 6, 7, 11, 12, 16, 21, 25, 26
**Challenging Days:** 1, 2, 4, 9, 10, 15, 23, 24, 29

### AFFIRMATION FOR THE MONTH
"My will is in harmony with my Highest Needs."

### PRIMARY FOCUS

Avoid the temptation to forge ahead unless you have adequate support and resources. You may unknowingly invite challenges from others who are threatened by your actions or attitudes.

### HEALTH AND FITNESS

Build greater physical well-being with a more positive attitude. Short-term satisfaction will seem woefully inadequate by the Full Moon on the 23rd.

### ROMANCE AND RELATIONSHIPS

From the 1st–12th, you may feel a desire to escape the pressure of an existing relationship, only to discover later that your denial has cost you precious time and energy. Candid conversation near the time of the New Moon on the 9th helps to reveal the true nature of your relationship. Once Venus moves into Leo on the 15th, it can be easier to express your feelings. Share your favorite pastime with your sweetheart or your children on the 21st or 22nd, when playtime is second-nature.

### FINANCE AND CAREER

You may be tempted to ignore signals that things aren't quite correct the week of the 5th, but will do yourself a favor by looking into any suspicious areas. Progress can seem to go in circles for a while! Mercury enters a retrograde cycle from June 12th–July 6th, when thorough investigation of an ongoing project or proposal currently under consideration can reveal the source of instability. Watch for power struggles after the 26th.

### OPPORTUNITY OF THE MONTH

Follow-up on important communication the 17th and 18th. Your interest and concern can lead to a powerful alliance.

**Rewarding Days:** 3, 8, 13, 14, 17, 21, 22, 30
**Challenging Days:** 1, 5, 6, 11, 19, 20, 25, 26

### AFFIRMATION FOR THE MONTH
"I trust my intuitive guidance."

### PRIMARY FOCUS

Direct affirmative energy toward goals. If you're dissatisfied, create a more positively challenging direction. Get involved with community projects mid-month.

### HEALTH AND FITNESS

Balancing your schedule to allow for recreation and relaxation help you maintain your energy. Develop an efficient system which truly supports your lifestyle.

### ROMANCE AND RELATIONSHIPS

Mending a relationship torn apart by misunderstanding brings you even closer the week of the 3rd. However, if it's time to bring a relationship to a close, you can break your attachment and move into untried territory after the New Moon on the 8th. Developing a friendship may be your most comfortable option if you can't completely say good-bye. Be sure you're not giving in to pressure from your family which is counter-productive for yourself! Your personal needs may be quite different from their expectations.

### FINANCE AND CAREER

It's a good idea to know your competitors, since ignoring their presence can be damaging to your reputation. Discontent from those under your supervision can reach a boiling point during the Full Moon on the 22nd, when it's important to know the extent of your personal responsibility. Self-restraint in spending from the 17th–23rd can help you avoid squabbles over jointly held resources on the 19th and 20th.

### OPPORTUNITY OF THE MONTH

Unfinished business from May 26th–29th can finally be completed from the 3rd–9th. (This may be personal business!)

**Rewarding Days:** 1, 5, 6, 10, 14, 19, 27, 28
**Challenging Days:** 2, 3, 11, 16, 17, 23, 24, 30, 31

### AFFIRMATION FOR THE MONTH
"I am open to new ideas."

### PRIMARY FOCUS

You're in the groove of success and can finally see forward progress. Take every opportunity to network and make sure you're given credit where credit is due!

### HEALTH AND FITNESS

Your vitality is strengthened, but it's still important to maintain your health regimen. Travel or recreation gives you a boost of energy through the 14th.

### ROMANCE AND RELATIONSHIPS

It seems natural to dissolve those barriers which have blocked effective communication of your emotions, making this a great time to initiate a new relationship or refresh an existing commitment, especially during the New Moon in Leo on the 7th. If you're open to a new love now, you're most likely to meet someone while enjoying your favorite activities. After the 7th, contact with a sibling can establish a supportive link, although you may have different opinions about family issues! Partnership or commitment needs careful consideration during the Full Moon on the 21st.

### FINANCE AND CAREER

Your time in the spotlight has its greatest effect from the 3rd–20th, and on the 29th and 30th. Your words may be easily misconstrued from the 13th–16th when you may overlook some critical details, so double-check for clarity. Although you may be inspired by brilliance, actualizing your vision may have surprising consequences. Take care to protect your valuables from the 26th–28th, when higher priorities can distract you.

### OPPORTUNITY OF THE MONTH

Reach out toward the familiar on the 10th and 11th, and you're likely to discover an untapped resource.

**Rewarding Days:** 1, 2, 6, 7, 10, 11, 15, 24, 29
**Challenging Days:** 5, 12, 13, 14, 19, 20, 26, 27

### AFFIRMATION FOR THE MONTH
"My life is a creative work in progress."

### PRIMARY FOCUS

You may feel a need for more time alone to collect your thoughts and revitalize your energy. Spreading yourself too thin now will sap your enthusiasm.

### HEALTH AND FITNESS

Incorporate a period of meditation or contemplation into your daily routine. Inner awareness has a tremendous healing effect.

### ROMANCE AND RELATIONSHIPS

A brief get-away with your sweetheart sometime from the 1st–6th can give you just the chance you've needed to speak your heart's desires. After that time, you're most inclined to share romance at home in your most comfortable surroundings. Regardless of your "commitment" situation, you're primed to focus more attention on your home environment after the 7th. Sexual or monetary disputes are likely to escalate near the time of the Full Moon on the 19th. The waters calm after the 23rd.

### FINANCE AND CAREER

If you're considering asking for a raise or negotiating fees for services, you may underestimate your worth. Take a clear look at the situation during the New Moon on the 5th. Work behind the scenes in preparation for launching a new project moves smoothly until the 17th, when you may encounter a lack of cooperation from others and/or mechanical problems which create frustrating delays. Forward momentum resumes on the 25th.

### OPPORTUNITY OF THE MONTH

Instead of fighting against yourself, allow time to develop an inspirational idea on the 7th. The perspective can be impelling.

**Rewarding Days:** 3, 4, 7, 8, 11, 12, 20, 21, 25, 30
**Challenging Days:** 1, 9, 10, 15, 16, 17, 22, 23, 24

### AFFIRMATION FOR THE MONTH
"I am aware of my true inner feelings."

### PRIMARY FOCUS

Although your intention may be to start things in forward motion, you're likely to run into some resistance from previously unfinished business.

### HEALTH AND FITNESS

High stress, especially in the personal arena, can block physical vitality. Satisfy your need for emotional stability, and physical energy will flow more readily.

### ROMANCE AND RELATIONSHIPS

Home and family are high priorities, and your responsibilities in this area can seem larger than life. Before surrendering to the feeling of being overwhelmed, tackle one issue at a time. You're ready for instantaneous satisfaction, and the reality may be slower than your ability to conceptualize it! Talk over solutions on the 4th and 5th, and be ready to reach for new horizons by the Full Moon on the 19th. There's room for everyone, but you have to safeguard against trying to keep them all happy at once.

### FINANCE AND CAREER

If the flame of your productivity burns out of control early in the month, you may have to make serious reconsiderations and adjustments once Mercury turns retrograde on the 9th. It's easy to try to burn the candle at both ends from the 8th–15th, and you may be accused of dictatorial behavior by those with no sense of humor. Listen to your advisors and work toward achieving a balance from the 22nd–29th. Mercury turns direct on the 30th. Pray for rain.

### OPPORTUNITY OF THE MONTH

Use that network you've been building to provide assistance and support you need on the 22nd and 23rd.

**Rewarding Days:** 1, 4, 8, 9, 17, 18, 22, 23, 27, 28
**Challenging Days:** 6, 7, 11, 12, 13, 14, 20, 21

### AFFIRMATION FOR THE MONTH
"My heart is filled with love and hope."

### PRIMARY FOCUS

You're feeling the need to bring greater intimacy and emotional security to your relationships, but may get caught in a family feud. Avoid your tendency to try to control the outcome.

### HEALTH AND FITNESS

Increase your vitality by staying active, but be aware of your tendency to push yourself too hard. Choose your competition wisely, since you can get in over your head.

### ROMANCE AND RELATIONSHIPS

You may be in the midst of inner conflict, which can result in volatile experiences in your personal and family relationships. Give yourself time to reflect upon the experiences from your past which have brought joy into your life during the Solar Eclipse on the 3rd. Use this cycle to incorporate experiences which magnify your sense of personal stability. Anticipation and expectation in an intimate relationship can cause tremendous trouble, when open communication is more productive.

### FINANCE AND CAREER

Take advantage of travel or arrange business conferences and presentations from the 1st–9th. The time's right to bring your plans forward and build a positive supportive network in the process. The temptation to blow your budget can overcome your common sense after the 14th. Pay extra attention to the demands of authorities near the Lunar Eclipse on the 18th, since you may feel you ought to be a "law unto yourself!"

### OPPORTUNITY OF THE MONTH

Generate enthusiasm in those whose support you value by sharing your creative talents on the 5th.

**Rewarding Days:** 1, 5, 13, 14, 19, 24, 25, 28
**Challenging Days:** 3, 4, 7, 9, 10, 16, 17, 30

### AFFIRMATION FOR THE MONTH
"I am motivated by a loving spirit."

## PRIMARY FOCUS

You can be at the height of success now, especially if you've concentrated on balance. But things can quickly get out of control if your ego gets in the way!

## HEALTH AND FITNESS

Through the 12th you're likely to feel that your life is much like a marathon. Keep your energy strong by pacing yourself and giving extra attention to the nutritional substance of your diet.

## ROMANCE AND RELATIONSHIPS

The roller-coaster of love can get wild and crazy early in the month. A new love relationship beginning on the 2nd offers tremendous promise, but you may also have to overcome a few barriers before you can enjoy the experience. An existing partnership needs more time for play, when simplicity may the most exciting and satisfying option. Time spent with friends near the Full Moon on the 17th brings each closer to understanding the potential and worth of your association.

## FINANCE AND CAREER

Enjoy the accolades, accepting success with grace and charm. You're in a superb position to bring others into your field of influence during the month, but can shine especially brightly on the 2nd, 3rd, 12th, 16th, 21st, and 39th. However, you can lose your ability to set limits for yourself (including spending) from the 5th–9th, when demands from others may seem to tempt you to go beyond your means and lose valuable support.

## OPPORTUNITY OF THE MONTH

Use the power of Jupiter and Pluto conjuncting on the 2nd to help you reach into a powerful new dimension of success.

**Rewarding Days:** 2, 3, 11, 12, 16, 17, 21, 22, 26, 29, 30
**Challenging Days:** 5, 6, 7, 13, 14, 27, 28

## AFFIRMATION FOR THE MONTH
"Life is a grand adventure!"

♍ **VIRGO**  ♍
**The Virgin**

## August 23 to September 23

**Element:** Earth

**Quality:** Mutable

**Polarity:** Feminine/Yin

**Planetary Ruler:** Mercury

**Meditation:** "I experience love through service"

**Gemstone:** Sapphire

**Power Stones:** Rhodochrosite, peridot, amazonite

**Colors:** Taupe, blue-gray

**Key Phrase:** "I analyze"

**Glyph:** Greek symbol for "virgin"

**Anatomy:** Abdomen, intestines, gall bladder, duodenum, pancreas

**Animal:** Domesticated animals

**Myths/Legends:** Demeter, Astraea, Hygeia

**House Association:** 6th

**Opposite Sign:** Pisces

**Flower:** Pansy

**Key Word:** Perfection

**Positive Expression:**

Efficient
Helpful
Conscientious
Precise
Humble
Methodical
Practical
Meticulous
Discriminating

**Misuse of Energy:**

Tedious
Intolerant
Self-deprecating
Hypercritical
Superficial
Nervous
Skeptical
Hypochondriacal

# ♍ VIRGO ♍

## Your Ego's Strengths and Weaknesses

As the efficiency expert of the zodiac, you're always searching for ways achieve a high level of personal perfection. Learning may be one of your passions, and you truly appreciate quality. You can develop keen observational skills, putting your discriminatory powers to the task of staying "on track." You love to share what you know, and have a knack for guiding and teaching others.

Contrary to popular opinion, Virgos are not always neatness freaks. But you do appreciate organization, and you definitely have a critical eye. If you do apply your attention to detail to your environment, you'll have at least one closet, drawer, or basket around to catch all the "surplus." (Of course, you're the first to notice when someone else is a complete slob!) Learning to apply your critical powers to include those things you appreciate about a person or situation will help you avoid the reputation of nitpicking. You can be an easy companion, and will operate most effectively if others will allow you to do things your own way.

Your quest for expertise and excellence may lead you into intellectual pursuits or studies which can isolate you from the world-at-large. But your spiritual lesson draws you to find ways to develop your own expertise within the world while allowing others to follow their own pathways.

## Your Career Development

You're happiest at the end of the day when you feel you've accomplished something, and will flourish best in a career which challenges your mind and allows you an opportunity to improve yourself. Writing, speaking, or teaching can provide outlets for your desire to share your knowledge. Service-oriented fields such as social work, dental hygiene, or medicine may also draw your interest. Or you may find a fascinating career in dietetics or herbology. Use your natural planning abilities in administration, accounting, systems analysis, secretarial service, office management, or research. Scientific fields can be satisfying.

Since you're particular about the way you like things done, consider the possibility of running your own business. Occupations which require adept manual dexterity can be rewarding. Most crafts-oriented fields, detail work in the building industry, drafting, design, or graphic arts can be good choices. You may actually develop more than one career throughout your lifetime, and can probably juggle more than one job at a time. Whatever your choices, you can be counted on to do your best.

## Your Approach to Romance

You definitely have an ideal mate, and may have developed a long list of qualifications before you allow a relationship to reach the romantic stage. Your sensuality may be one of your best-kept secrets, and once you've opened the door to intimacy, your loving touch can be magical. A relationship that offers ample room for positive growth will inspire your commitment, and you'll blossom in an atmosphere of acceptance and trust.

Like all earth signs (Taurus, Virgo, and Capricorn), you're willing to take your time if a relationship seems worthwhile. With another Virgo, you may find it easy to be yourself, and will have a mutual understanding about keeping all that grumbling to yourselves. Taurus can feel stabilizing, and you can easily appreciate that earthy sensuality. You may be one of the few who truly appreciate Capricorn's dry wit, and can even enjoy a special playfulness once you've developed mutual trust.

Aries' frolicking about can excite you, but may distract you from your focus. Although you enjoy Gemini's intellectual curiosity and levity, you can be confounded by their changeability. With Cancer, you may feel both a strong friendship and a powerful physical bond. Leo's warmth and drama can be the stuff of your most romantic dreams, but you may feel more comfortable as friends. With Libra, you can be objective and open, but have to continually clarify where you stand with one another.

You can feel thoroughly satisfied sharing the depth of passion you experience with Scorpio. Talking over tea or sharing your favorite pleasures with Sagittarius can be truly exciting, even if you don't see much of one another. With Aquarius, there can be fireworks and spiritual strength, but you may feel left out in the world when you're ready to settle into a sweet caress. Your zodiacal opposite, Pisces, may feel like a soulmate, but you may have difficulty relating on the same plane of awareness.

## Your Use of Power

Even though you may not seek power for its own sake, you're drawn to the idea of influencing others and changing the course of events. You see the power of the mind as primary, and make honest use of information and wisdom. Since you tend to make things appear effortless, others may not recognize the breadth of power you possess. But you can enjoy the fact that you've fine-lytuned your skills and abilities and need to learn to give yourself praise for a job well done.

Be careful of your motivation if you're drawn into fields of ministry or service since you can become caught in the quagmire of co-dependent circumstances. You can help others help themselves if you find healthy ways to both give and receive. You may discover that you're compelled to call attention to mankind's inhumanity to other life forms or to ourselves, and may have the power to speak or act in their stead. Learn to use the power of service to help improve the quality of life and to bring a higher quality to your own existence.

## Famous Virgos

Nell Carter, Jane Curtin, Faith Ford, Paul Harvey, Jeremy Irons, Michael Keaton, Branford Marsalis, Bob Newhart, Roger Tory Peterson, Joe Regalbuto, Lily Tomlin, Peter Ueberroth

# THE YEAR AHEAD FOR VIRGO

Throughout the year you'll experience both opportunities to express your talents and abilities and tests of your willpower and endurance. Maintaining a balance can be a tricky proposition, since you may feel strongly drawn in one direction or another. By staying strongly focused on your higher needs and keeping your priorities aligned with your spiritual nature, you'll find that even the most ordinary experiences have an extraordinary effect. Now's the time to remind yourself of your priorities, and to make an agreement to carry those responsibilities which truly belong to you.

With Jupiter transiting through your Solar 3rd House in Scorpio, you're likely to feel a bit restless, and may need to get outside your regular routine more than usual. Travel can be more satisfying, even trips close to home. Your mind is ready to absorb more information, with your hunger for knowledge drawing you into all sorts of learning experiences. If you're involved in writing or communicating, these fields show tremendous promise, giving you a chance to advance in your career. You can also benefit through sharing your knowledge with others or attending conferences or workshops, but watch a tendency to be distracted by too many options, and choose the most beneficial. This cycle encourages a higher level of personal confidence and inspires greater courage to risk sharing your ideas with others.

The Solar Eclipses this year also amplify your need to expand your understanding and provide an element of increasing spiritual awareness. Search for the areas in which you may have been drawn away from Truth, and find ways to incorporate a higher level of understanding. Your spiritual life can become more readily incorporated into your daily activities now if you allow this emerging awareness to penetrate your consciousness. But you may have to allow some of your old belief systems to drop away in favor of the discovery of truth.

The separating conjunction of Uranus and Neptune in Capricorn continues to stimulate your creativity in surprising ways. And you have an excellent cycle for opening to your more playful nature. But you may feel a bit more inhibited now, since Saturn is traveling in Pisces for the next two years, in opposition to your Sun Sign. This force can actually be a stabilizing factor, but you do have to make choices about which things in your life are necessary and which are simply taking up space.

Chiron's transit in Virgo also has a particularly influential effect this year, bringing you more closely in contact with your true nature and helping you determine choices that align more positively with your feeling of purpose. But you can also fall into the rut of old patterns if you're not allowing your full awareness to guide your actions and decisions.

For **Virgos born from August 23–September 5, the restrictions influenced by Saturn's transit in opposition to your Sun may create a feeling of frustration.** But you can also use this cycle to determine the best course of action and to lay a sturdy foundation for future growth. Now's the time to clean out those closets, basements, and attics. You might also take a look at your relationships to determine the validity of your involvement and honesty of your interaction with one another. Power struggles can arise, and may bring issues to the surface that have been simmering for a long time. Your critical eye can go haywire, with very little escaping your scrutiny—including yourself! To avoid alienating those you would like to draw closer, take the time to observe the areas in which you feel dissatisfaction. Are you projecting your own self-recriminations onto your environment or relationships? You may be unconsciously directing negative energy to others, when you actually need to do some personal, internal clearing. But be careful, since it's easy to find all the things you *don't* like and overlook those things about yourself which deserve your own personal pat-on-the-back. Allow your sense of responsibility to extend into those areas which will bring stability and improvement to your life. And while you're at it, give back some of those responsibilities you've been carrying for others. Part of gaining control over your own life may involve eliminating the need to be everybody's helper! On the physical side, be alert to any problems and take time to investigate their root causes. You can actually improve your physical health now, but ignoring problems can drive you into a cycle of chronic disease. At work, make an effort to carefully evaluate your circumstances. If you're unhappy, discover what you can do to change things. You may have to buckle down and get to work on some projects which are not your favorites, but which will help stabilize your job security. You may feel a need to continue your education or improve your skills in some way, and can even be given the opportunity to teach or train others. The one thing you can be sure of this year is that you'll definitely feel acquainted with "necessity!" But that doesn't have to stop your forward progress!

**If you were born from August 26–September 17, you're experiencing the conjunction of Chiron to your Sun.** This can be a clarifying cycle, but you may also find yourself becoming more aware of your limitations and assets. Your life path may seem more focused now, and you may discover new keys to your inner self. This can be a period of healing, and your physical health needs to be given a high priority. There can be a reopening of an early wound or weakness, and you may feel more physically or psychically vulnerable. Instead of allowing that vulnerability to work against you, use this enhanced awareness to create a deep healing and rejuvenation. Make the changes in your life which will more effectively support your needs as a whole, healthy person.

**Increased sensitivity on all levels accompanies Neptune's transit in trine to your Sun if you were born from September 12–17.** This transit can stimulate a remarkably creative period, and is quite helpful if you're engaged in any form of artistic expression. The more subtle vibrations penetrate your consciousness more readily now, and can bring a more profound spiritual influence into your life. Seek ways to stay with the natural ebb and flow instead of pushing upstream. Attune your consciousness to that of your higher self, surrendering to Divine Guidance in all things. This is a cycle of forgiveness and illumination, initiating you into a more compassionate form of relating to yourself and others. The spiritual can be part of your every thought and movement, instead of a separate form of reality. It's easier to release the past, to allow room for a more peaceful existence. You may feel a lack of motivation under Neptune's influence, and need to maintain your central focus in order to avoid getting lost in the fog of illusion. But generally, this cycle is welcome and, when used effectively, can help you create a rewarding experience of inner peace, as well as the opportunity to extend that experience to the world around you.

**For those born from September 13–19, this year may prove to be more exciting than you had anticipated!** Uranus is transiting in trine to your Sun, opening the way for a more free form of self-expression. You may finally be able to create that individualized path without the resistance you've experienced in the past. And unlike the disruptive changes of 1986 and 1987, those innovations occurring now may feel more comfortable and natural. If there's something holding you back, discover what it is and release your attachment. This is a cycle of change, discovery, innovation, and experimentation. It's not a time to move backward! You're likely to discover the ways you've blocked your own progress, but you may also find circumstances around you which are no longer supporting your personal growth. In either case, your cooperative release of those things you've outgrown will speed your progress now.

**If you were born from September 18–23, you're feeling a deeper connection to your sense of Self while Pluto travels in sextile to your Sun this year.** A sense of personal power can emerge, providing you with an opportunity to create and manifest in ways you had only conceptualized before. Many of the changes in the world around you may have produced unfamiliar and unusual circumstances, but you can more easily incorporate those changes into your life than you could in the past. You may be sought after to share your expertise or understanding in your field, giving you an opportunity to carve out a more secure path. It's time to apply the knowledge you've gained through your personal experience and rescue your own life! Allow yourself to feel the healing power of this cycle by removing the blockades to your progress and surging forward with confidence into a brighter day.

## Tools to Make a Difference

Most of the cycles affecting your Sun this year involve the types of changes which can bring healing on every level into your life. By cooperating with these transformative and illuminating changes you can maneuver through them more effectively. Use your mind in the best possible ways now —turn your thinking toward what can be instead of what is not. Become an agent of hope by developing an honest level of optimism.

Physical disciplines can be highly rewarding this year. The balance and harmony developed through the practice of yoga, Tai Chi, martial arts, or dance can be extended into your entire sense of Being. Apply your discriminating nature to your diet by choosing foods which add vitality, instead of those which simply satisfy a few cravings. Evaluate your nutritional needs in the context of your current life situation. You can make your body a finely-tuned instrument of your consciousness.

This year and next year challenge you to become a master of your own destiny, and part of that mastery may include sharing your knowledge or understanding with others. Whether you're in the position of student or teacher, you can carve a meaningful place for yourself. Seek out learning or teaching opportunities, particularly in the fields of human relations, metaphysical studies, or artistic expression. Create positive tests for yourself and others.

Focus your mind on images which bring a sense of joy. During your visualizations, see yourself as part of a circle. Dance, whirling around the circle in harmony with the rhythm around you. Feel the energy of the dance moving through your body, carrying your mind to a place of laughter and harmony. Once the dancing has ceased, and the circle has broken, step away with the awareness that there is joy around you if you only look for it. Throughout the day, be open to these joyful moments and drink them into your consciousness.

## Affirmation for the Year

"I am aware of the significance of my words
and actions."

# ACTION TABLES FOR VIRGO

These dates reflect the best (but not the only) times for success and ease in these activities according to your Sun Sign.

| | |
|---|---|
| **Change Residence** | Nov. 30–Dec. 18 |
| **Request a Raise** | Sept. 5–6 |
| **Begin a Course of Study** | May 10, Nov. 3 |
| **Visit a Doctor** | Jan. 14–31; Aug. 3– 17 |
| **Start a Diet** | Jan. 12–13; Feb. 9–10; Mar. 8–9; Apr. 4–5; May 1–2, 29–30; June 25–26; July 23–24; Aug. 19–20; Sep. 15–16; Oct. 12–14; Nov. 9–10; Dec. 6–7 |
| **Begin a Romance** | Jan. 11–12 |
| **Join a Club** | July 8–9 |
| **Seek Employment** | Jan. 14–31; May 10–27 |
| **Take a Vacation** | Jan. 20–21; Feb. 16–17; Mar. 15–17; Apr. 12–13; May 9–10; June 5–7; July 2–4, 30–31; Aug. 26–27; Sep. 22–24; Oct. 20–21; Nov. 16–17; Dec. 13–15 |
| **Change Your Wardrobe** | Jan. 1–13; Dec. 19–31 |
| **End a Relationship** | Sep. 19 |
| **Seek Professional Advice** | Jan. 15–Mar. 10–12; Apr. 7–8; May 4–5, 31– June 1, 27–29; July 25–26; Aug. 21–22; Sep. 18–19; Oct. 15–16; Nov. 11–12; Dec. 8–10 |
| **Have a Makeover** | Sep. 5–6 |
| **Obtain a Loan** | Jan. 17–18; Feb. 13–15; Mar. 13–14; Apr. 9–10; May 6–7; June 2–4, 30; July 1, 27–28; Aug. 24–25; Sep. 20–1; Oct. 17–18; Nov. 13–14; Dec. 11–12 |

### PRIMARY FOCUS

Resolve to give your creative genius free rein this month, even if it interrupts your schedule. Wouldn't it be a hoot if you enjoyed your work for a change?!

### HEALTH AND FITNESS

Take time for recreation in early January to revitalize and inspire yourself. After the 20th, gather information about the best ways to keep yourself healthy and put it immediately to use.

### ROMANCE AND RELATIONSHIPS

Breathe life back into an existing relationship by taking time to enjoy the company of the one you love. From the 6th–11th you're in an excellent position to create memorable experiences together. During the New Moon on the 11th you're ready to unleash your more playful side. Partnerships need extra attention on the 15th–16th, especially since your work may be more demanding during the following week. And you may feel a need for some time alone with your favorite book or project during the Full Moon on the 27th.

### FINANCE AND CAREER

Changes in organizational structure may give you an opportunity to take advantage of an opening from the 1st–12th. You can be highly influential in bringing about positive changes through your work from the 16th–26th, but need to be aware of the extra responsibilities which could be involved. Speculative ventures or investments pay off early this month, and a successful option may surface on the 20th–21st. Act quickly.

### OPPORTUNITY OF THE MONTH

The chaos which can paralyze others opens doors for you on the 2nd, 3rd, 11th and 20th. Be prepared to move forward!

**Rewarding Days:** 2, 3, 6, 7, 10, 11, 20, 21, 25, 26, 29, 30
**Challenging Days:** 8, 9, 15, 16, 18, 22, 23

### AFFIRMATION FOR THE MONTH
"I trust my creative inspiration."

### PRIMARY FOCUS

Demands from others can get in the way of your independent functioning, but with an adjustment in attitude, you can actually use this to your advantage.

### HEALTH AND FITNESS

The temptation to fret or worry too much over details can quickly drain your vitality. Keep your priorities in order, and take time out for exercise, reflection and balancing.

### ROMANCE AND RELATIONSHIPS

If you've been avoiding commitment, now's the time to discover why. Your fears may be unfounded, but need closer, more honest scrutiny. An existing partnership can be the source of friction if your priorities have placed outside activities or work ahead of the relationship. Even if you're tempted to run for the hills you may not get very far if you've ignored your real needs. The Full Moon in Virgo on the 25th stirs a chance to finally bring everything back into focus, but you may have to take the first step.

### FINANCE AND CAREER

Your attempts to improve your working conditions may reach an impasse once Mercury turns retrograde on the 11th. Don't expect much forward progress, since the conservative forces are hard at work trying to maintain the status quo. Only by satisfying your immediate needs will you feel successful, since speculation or experimentation now seems to involve too much red tape. You might as well get to work on that overdue project and clear out those files.

### OPPORTUNITY OF THE MONTH

Extra attention to the finer points of your work will save much time and effort, but don't expect perfection!

**Rewarding Days:** 2, 3, 6, 7, 16, 17, 21, 22, 25, 26
**Challenging Days:** 1, 4, 5, 9, 10, 11, 12, 19, 20

### AFFIRMATION FOR THE MONTH
"My life is in balance and harmony."

### PRIMARY FOCUS

Your busy social calendar may leave little flexible time, but your interaction with others can pay off through enhancing contacts within your community.

### HEALTH AND FITNESS

Developing a positive attitude improves your overall health. However, it's easy to put your needs behind the demands and needs of others. Keep your priorities intact and take care of yourself, too!

### ROMANCE AND RELATIONSHIPS

Any increasing frustrations in your intimate relationship are likely to center around differences in your sexual needs. Instead of feeling hurt or unfulfilled, talk about your concerns with your partner. Avoid getting caught in battles of control after the New Moon on the 12th, when you may both want to be in charge. You're ready for some diversity in your love life after the 20th, and need to find ways to enliven your relationship by the Full Moon on the 27th. Your passion needs a playful, yet meaningful, focus.

### FINANCE AND CAREER

Evaluate your working conditions and take an active role in making improvements early this month. Competition can be discouraging if you fail to put forth your best efforts the week of the 13th, when hidden agendas work against your best interests. Curb impulsive spending after the 26th, when you may be enticed by surface features, only to find that the quality isn't up to your standards.

### OPPORTUNITY OF THE MONTH

Let others know how much you value their presence in your life by offering positive support and helpful assistance on the 26th.

**Rewarding Days:** 1, 2, 6, 7, 16, 20, 25, 26, 29
**Challenging Days:** 3, 4, 5, 9, 11, 12, 13, 18, 19, 31

### AFFIRMATION FOR THE MONTH
"My life is filled with love."

### PRIMARY FOCUS

Even though you're still busy meeting all those demands on your time, you're seeing good results and can feel your horizons broadening. Concentrate on creating stable finances this month.

### HEALTH AND FITNESS

Channel competitive drive into physical activity, setting fitness goals and increasing your stamina. Check your tendency to push beyond your limits through the 13th.

### ROMANCE AND RELATIONSHIPS

Anger with your partner can actually bring healing into your relationship if you work with your feelings instead of trying to stifle them. This energy also promotes clear, direct communication. If you're single, you'll feel more confident about pursuing your interest in someone after the New Moon on the 10th. Romantic inclinations are especially potent from the 6th–13th and the 16th–22nd. You may even risk indulging in some of your fantasies during the Full Moon on the 25th!

### FINANCE AND CAREER

Clarify the reasons for expenditures which involve joint finances or investors from the 10th–25th, when viewpoints and priorities may differ. Seek out creative agreements from the 20th–26th, when you may find a new direction for your resources. Meetings, conferences, and presentations bring successful results the 2nd–26th, and are especially effective after the 22nd. Teaching or facilitating others gives you a chance to shine.

### OPPORTUNITY OF THE MONTH

Increase your span of professional influence on the 25th and 26th, when your pragmatic approach brings powerful results.

**Rewarding Days:** 2, 3, 12, 13, 17, 18, 21, 22, 25, 26, 30
**Challenging Days:** 4, 6, 7, 8, 14, 15, 27, 28

### AFFIRMATION FOR THE MONTH
"I am flexible in the face of change."

### PRIMARY FOCUS

Use your most creative energy to highlight a fresh path toward success and career advancement. But watch your tendency to run rough-shod over the wrong toes!

### HEALTH AND FITNESS

By dealing directly with any physical problems, you can quickly eliminate them at their source. Healing on all levels can be achieved, but you have to cooperate!

### ROMANCE AND RELATIONSHIPS

You're eager to keep things moving in your love life, with a strong urge to connect at a spiritual and philosophical level driving you toward deeper intimacy. During the Solar Eclipse on the 10th take time to reflect on the larger truth of your life, clarifying your own sense of spiritual direction. Any differences with your partner can bring a greater understanding and acceptance, and do not have to create a breech in your relationship. Family issues are likely to erupt during the Moon's Eclipse on the 24th.

### FINANCE AND CAREER

Some friction between the more conventional factions and your sense of creative adventure may lead you to question your career choice. These can accelerate from the 14th–24th, when your eagerness needs to be balanced by adequate preparation and reasonable caution. Speculative spending can also be too risky during this time. If possible, take action or sign contracts from the 23rd–27th. But be sure to read the fine print!

### OPPORTUNITY OF THE MONTH

Work toward achieving important agreements on the 23rd, when your innovative ideas are incorporated within a practice approach.

**Rewarding Days:** 9, 10, 14, 15, 18, 19, 23, 27
**Challenging Days:** 2, 4, 5, 11, 12, 21, 25, 26, 31

### AFFIRMATION FOR THE MONTH
"Divine Love is my source of strength and power."

## PRIMARY FOCUS

Designing a plan and setting goals can provide a positive direction for your energy. Travel, education or teaching may also play a positive role this month.

## HEALTH AND FITNESS

Increase your activity level now, concentrating on building strength and flexibility. A group fitness class or team sport offer positive outlets for your energy.

## ROMANCE AND RELATIONSHIPS

Traveling with your sweetheart is most pleasant from the 5th–11th, although you could also enjoy a long weekend at your special hide-away the 17th–20th. These are good dates to meet someone new, if you're looking, and mark periods of easier communicability when you may feel like trying something completely different. However, Mercury's retrograde cycle from the 12th–30th can complicate matters if your expectations are too high! Spend extra time with friends, especially during the Full Moon on the 23rd.

## FINANCE AND CAREER

Negotiations fare well, but may take a bit longer than you'd anticipated. However, things are not coming to a screeching halt, they just run into surprising circumstances, especially from the 8th–14th. The New Moon on the 9th may herald a period of tension with your superiors or authorities, and you may feel a new direction emerging. Take time to get back in touch with those who've been influential in your career from the 17th–24th.

## OPPORTUNITY OF THE MONTH

Your willingness to try a new direction from the 5th–13th can set you on a new and exciting path of self-expression.

**Rewarding Days:** 5, 6, 10, 11, 15, 16, 19, 20, 23
**Challenging Days:** 3, 4, 8, 9, 18, 21, 22, 28, 29

## AFFIRMATION FOR THE MONTH
"I am a creative and confident person."

## PRIMARY FOCUS

Involvement with community activities or special interest groups offers an opportunity to share your knowledge and expertise and build your reputation. Political action has positive results.

## HEALTH AND FITNESS

Stress levels at work can drain your physical vitality unless you take time to rejuvenate. You're strongest from the 13th–20th.

## ROMANCE AND RELATIONSHIPS

Your unspoken desires can undermine an intimate relationship from the 1st–9th. By staying aware of your feelings and sharing your needs, you can, instead, create a more sensitive blending between yourself and your partner. Concentrate on self-acceptance on the 8th and 9th in order to create greater harmony with others. Venus moves into Virgo on the 11th, initiating a time of more positive interaction and promoting a period of greater self-esteem. An afternoon of passion during the Full Moon on the 22nd can be quite satisfying.

## FINANCE AND CAREER

Be alert to rumblings behind-the-scenes from the 3rd–8th, when shifts in power can create significant changes. Others may take a defensive posture if you're too pushy mid-month, so be aware of your self-presentation. From the 11th–23rd you can be strongly influential and advance your position, but only if you have a strong grasp on the long-term effects of your actions. Be skeptical of investment options from the 28th–30th.

## OPPORTUNITY OF THE MONTH

Set plans in motion from the 8th–13th, and remember to keep your sense of humor the week of the 17th!

**Rewarding Days:** 3, 4, 7, 8, 12, 13, 16, 17, 20, 21, 30
**Challenging Days:** 1, 5, 6, 15, 18, 19, 23, 25, 26, 27

## AFFIRMATION FOR THE MONTH
"My mind is clear and open to new ideas."

### PRIMARY FOCUS
Expansive growth is possible, but you must equalize it with a firm grasp of your limitations. Seek out advice from experts in your field, and incorporate that knowledge into your future plans.

### HEALTH AND FITNESS
Although a hectic pace keeps you on your toes, your ability to keep things in balance is improving. Conscious breathing exercises can make a difference in your mental alertness through the 17th.

### ROMANCE AND RELATIONSHIPS
Conflicts between personal and professional demands can cause some heartache early this month. Take time to contemplate and regroup on the 6th or 7th, when a little self-indulgence can be revitalizing. A change of scenery on the 13th improves your outlook, but romance fares best after the 17th. Reconfirmation of vows or a promise of long-term commitment can be positively sobering and bring remarkable results after the 26th. Enjoy the support of friends during this time, when unity brings strength.

### FINANCE AND CAREER
Stepping into a position of greater influence or achieving recognition seems inevitable, but you still may not feel you can relax your attention to details. Make the move to improve your circumstances after the 17th. Communication, travel and presentations can bring lucrative results from the 21st–31st, but keep careful watch on your finances after the 28th.

### OPPORTUNITY OF THE MONTH
Choosing the right associates on the 22nd and 26th can place each of you in a stronger position by the end of the month.

**Rewarding Days:** 4, 5, 8, 9, 13, 17, 18, 26, 27, 31
**Challenging Days:** 1, 2, 7, 15, 16, 21, 22, 29

### AFFIRMATION FOR THE MONTH
"I am a good judge of character."

### PRIMARY FOCUS

Take bold steps to improve career options and manifest positive changes in your environment. Get involved, build a supportive network, make a difference!

### HEALTH AND FITNESS

Your eager participation in fitness brings immediate results, and may also introduce you to a special friend. You can actually generate more energy now by staying active.

### ROMANCE AND RELATIONSHIPS

Initiate a dialogue to improve an existing relationship or get a new connection off to a good start. The New Moon in Virgo on the 5th can inaugurate a cycle of energetic interaction which brings to the surface any unfinished business and allows you to reach positive levels of consensus. Sharing travel can be rewarding after the 8th, and can bring you in contact with an intriguing individual if you're open to a new relationship. But an inappropriate flirtation causes trouble near the Full Moon on the 19th.

### FINANCE AND CAREER

Your financial picture brightens now, but it's easy to overlook important details or surrender to impulsive spending from the 18th–24th. Business contacts bring exciting results after the 5th, but can get bogged down in red tape on the 12th and your energy can be diverted by interruptions on the 18th–20th. However, if you stay on track, this can be a highly successful month for most presentations, negotiations and political action.

### OPPORTUNITY OF THE MONTH

Networking and cooperative efforts are rewarding all month; schedule something special for the 5th, 6th, or 9th.

**Rewarding Days:** 1, 5, 6, 9, 10, 13, 22, 23, 28
**Challenging Days:** 3, 11, 12, 17, 18, 19, 25, 26

### AFFIRMATION FOR THE MONTH
"My life is filled with abundant joy!"

## PRIMARY FOCUS

With Mercury and Venus both entering retrograde cycles this month, you may feel like you're continually cleaning out closets and reviewing what you thought to be finished. Guess again!

## HEALTH AND FITNESS

Getting in touch with your mind/body connection is crucial to maintain the energy you desire. Improve inner fitness through meditation. Become more aware of your body's responses.

## ROMANCE AND RELATIONSHIPS

Your expectations can get you in trouble through the 13th, so be alert to your real feelings. Relationships from the past can surface now, and may cause some difficulty in your current life situation. It's crucial that you take an honest approach to your feelings, since this is a superb time to reach closure where it was previously avoided. Disputes over joint finances on the 18th–19th (Full Moon), can be indicative of deeper issues about intimacy and satisfaction. Clear communication helps you climb out of that sticky situation after the 24th.

## FINANCE AND CAREER

Take a good look at your business policies, inventory and personnel relations. Initiate a plan of action on the 4th. Circumstances that aren't working need reconsideration after the 9th, and may not improve dramatically until after the 30th. Be especially careful in financial dealings from the 15th–19th, when quick decisions can bring long-lasting responsibilities.

## OPPORTUNITY OF THE MONTH

Make major decisions on the 2nd or 3rd, then wait until after the 30th to agree on other long-term commitments.

**Rewarding Days:** 2, 3, 6, 7, 10, 20, 29, 30
**Challenging Days:** 5, 8, 9, 13, 15, 16, 22, 23

## AFFIRMATION FOR THE MONTH
"I listen to my intuitive voice."

146

## PRIMARY FOCUS

Sharing your ideas with others helps define your expertise and may offer an opportunity for recognition or advancement in your career. Get involved in learning or sharpening your skills.

## HEALTH AND FITNESS

With so much mental energy driving you, it's easy to lose physical vitality. Foods or supplements which keep your B-vitamin level strong will help you stay alert and feel less fatigued.

## ROMANCE AND RELATIONSHIPS

The love you're seeking may be right in your own backyard! To strengthen an ongoing relationship, begin an honest dialogue with one another after the 3rd, and take time to explore the underlying causes of your concerns from the 13th–22nd. Ignoring deeper feelings or not exploring your fears can lead to explosive disagreements later. Sharing an inspirational experience can open the way for deeper bonds near the time of the Lunar Eclipse on the 18th.

## FINANCE AND CAREER

Stay closely in touch with budgetary concerns from the 1st–8th, when you can easily overlook an important obligation. Your eagerness to impress others with your ideas can tempt you to exaggerate possibilities after the 18th. Strong awareness of the reality of a situation will better prepare you to take on increased responsibilities without being taken advantage of from the 20th–30th. Impulsive spending or investing can be too costly.

## OPPORTUNITY OF THE MONTH

Open your mind and thoughts during the Solar Eclipse on the 3rd, when an inspiration to move into a new direction can occur.

**Rewarding Days:** 1 3, 7, 8, 16, 17, 21, 26, 27, 30
**Challenging Days:** 4, 5, 6, 11, 12, 18, 19, 25

## AFFIRMATION FOR THE MONTH
"My thoughts are pure, my words are true."

## PRIMARY FOCUS

Stay on track during the New Moon on the 2nd, when a Jupiter–Pluto conjunction emphasizes the probability of pushing your outer limits. Used harmoniously, this cycle can accelerate your progress.

## HEALTH AND FITNESS

Avoid burn-out by taking breaks in your routine to relax and rejuvenate. Don't worry, the momentum will keep you going!

## ROMANCE AND RELATIONSHIPS

Family relationships take first priority, and can be a source of strong support early in the month. A fresh look at traditions on the 2nd may prompt you to begin a new approach that fits your current circumstances. However, a conflict can loom out of control after the 16th, when you're in no mood to be pushed into a corner! A period of quiet harmony can improve close family ties and intimate relationships from the 23rd–28th. Consider short excursions close to home after the 27th.

## FINANCE AND CAREER

Make sure you are in agreement or at least have reached an understanding with your superiors before you proceed with large projects; once things are set in motion, they may be difficult to stop from the 2nd–23rd. Your own sense of discipline and focus can add sanity to a situation gone out of control, and others may seek your counsel after the 5th. Take care with choices that involve partners, since you may be in over your head!

## OPPORTUNITY OF THE MONTH

This is a time of power for you, but as long as you've explored the details, you should be able to take advantage of it.

**Rewarding Days:** 1, 4, 5, 13, 14, 19, 23, 24, 28
**Challenging Days:** 2, 3, 8, 9, 16, 17, 22, 29, 30

## AFFIRMATION FOR THE MONTH
"I honor my personal limitations
and know my boundaries."

# LIBRA
# The Scales

## September 23 to October 23

**Element:** Air

**Quality:** Cardinal

**Polarity:** Masculine/Yang

**Planetary Ruler:** Venus

**Meditation:** "Creating beauty and harmony"

**Gemstone:** Opal

**Power Stones:** Tourmaline, kunzite, blue lace agate

**Glyph:** Scales, Setting Sun

**Key Phrase:** "I balance"

**Anatomy:** Kidneys, adrenals, lower back, appendix

**Colors:** Blue, pastels

**Animal:** Brightly plumed birds

**Myths/Legends:** Hera, Venus, Cinderella

**House Association:** 7th

**Opposite Sign:** Aries

**Flower:** Rose

**Key Word:** Harmony

**Positive Expression:**
Gracious
Diplomatic
Artistic
Sociable
Considerate
Impartial
Refined
Agreeable
Logical

**Misuse of Energy:**
Conceited
Placating
Unreliable
Argumentative
Inconsiderate
Distant
Indecisive
Critical

# ♎ LIBRA ♎

## Your Ego's Strengths and Weaknesses

Charming and elegant, your easy grace and agreeable manner make you a welcome addition in most situations. Your objectivity and ability to see both sides of an issue come to the rescue when a situation calls for a diplomatic solution or mediation. You may be viewed as highly artistic by others, since your refined taste is apparent in everything you do.

It's important to you that you present yourself in the best possible manner, although you may not like excessive shows of opulence. Everything is relative for you, and you need to keep a perspective on the whole picture to avoid getting thrown out of balance. In relationships, preserving your equilibrium can be difficult, since your search for high ideals of perfection in yourself and others can make you feel off-center.

Your experience of the true Libra conflict is likely to involve learning to maintain a strong sense of yourself in the midst of relating to the world around you. Rather than placing another person or their situation at odds with your circumstances, set goals involving your personal needs. By concentrating on your inner partner you can more easily preserve a sense of harmony with your Higher Self.

## Your Career Development

You add a touch of class to any career, and may feel most at home with a career in the arts. You may choose to develop your own artistry, or represent and maintain the arts and literature of others through museums, galleries, or conservatories. A career in the fashion or beauty industry might also be enjoyable.

Your ability to see and enhance the strengths of others can help you in areas such as image consulting and counseling, but can also be expressed in more dramatic arenas such as costume or set design. With natural public relations ability, you might enjoy personnel management or advertising. Relationship counseling would be a logical choice, although you could also be an effective attorney or judge.

## Your Approach to Romance

You clearly love to be around other people and may yearn for that perfect fairy-tale relationship. Because those ideals are not always met, you may have a list of stories to share about your conquests and losses. You can become the quintessential partner, but can also vacillate between absolute involvement and cool detachment. Remind yourself that you will not lose part of yourself if you lose a partner!

A safe and beautiful atmosphere can enhance your mood for love-making, and you can thoroughly enjoy the physical aspects of an intimate relationship. You may feel most at home with other air signs—Gemini, Aquarius or Libra, since a meeting of the minds is one of your prerequisites for involvement. You can enjoy a fabulous companionship with Gemini, whose mental agility delights you. Aquarius' unique approach tickles your fancy and feeds your creativity. The understanding you feel with another Libran can be highly amicable, but occasionally unstable.

Your magnetic attraction to Aries, your opposite, can be exciting, but frequently one-sided! With Taurus you share a love for the aesthetic element, but may not like the underlying agenda of control issues. With Cancer you may feel trapped by their smothering form of nurturance. Leo's passion for life inflames your own passionate desires, but Virgo's grounding practicality may not feel especially romantic to you.

Scorpio's intensity can overtake you like a tidal wave, and you can become inexplicably intertwined. With Sagittarius, you can enjoy sharing life's grand adventure and may enjoy travelling together. Capricorn's attraction can be powerful, but may lead to tense open conflict. The high emotionality of Pisces, which may at first seem uncomfortable, can be just what you're looking for when you're in the mood for a romantic interlude.

## Your Use of Power

You may prefer to ignore the idea that you want power, but once you understand the idea you may discover you have more than you thought! Your power results from your ability to use a logical, impartial approach to any circumstance, rather than allowing your emotions to get in your way. This approach can make you appear distant, and you can deliberately project an icy exterior when you're hurt.

The ideals you seek in yourself you also search for in the world around you. But your tendency to compare yourself and your life situation with others can undermine your power. Know what you want for yourself, and allow yourself to feel positively about these desires and needs. Establish strong boundaries and begin to use your power to create life on your own terms, sharing yourself as a whole person with the world around you.

With your awareness of your environment and the people within it, you can inspire improvement and change where it's needed. You can offer hope that change is possible by demonstrating the other side of an option. When you're allowing the energy which flows through you from the Source to center and empower you, you'll find that your outer life reflects a more stable, balanced reality. You can then blend the perfect colors and textures which become a beautiful portrait of your life.

## Famous Librans

Julie Andrews, Art Buchwald, Michael Crichton, Jeff Goldblum, Bryant Gumbel, Jesse Helms, Angela Lansbury, Ralph Lauren, Martina Navratilova, William Rehnquist, Sting, Tanya Tucker, Tim Robbins, Ben Vereen

# THE YEAR AHEAD FOR LIBRA

Simple solutions may not be forthcoming during 1994, but you're definitely in the perfect position to work toward improving your life circumstances. Career and job standing require careful scrutiny, since you may not be happy with the situations you've chosen in the past. Even though you might not need to move into a completely new situation, you are likely to feel that improvements are well within your grasp. The first place to start is within yourself, by taking an honest look at your attitudes and the way you're using your resources. With a few adjustments, you can streamline, simplify, and make room for more of the things you truly value.

You're experiencing the effect of Jupiter travelling through your Solar 2nd House, and may actually have greater financial or material resources available to you. But there's a trick to it—the temptation to overspend and overextend is tremendous. The real opportunity this year involves finding the most effective way to use your resources so that they grow, rather than diminish. This begins with an improving understanding of your own worth and self-esteem, since you are your own best asset! Listen to your own internal messages, and search for ways to accept and support your needs. If you've been feeling that you're not getting what you want out of life, can you uncover the elements of your psyche which are blocking your path? You're ready to embrace yourself as a whole and powerful being, but cannot if you undermine your worth by wasting your precious resources.

The Solar Eclipses this year are also pointing to a need to emphasize your self-esteem and your emotional attachments. You may actually be holding onto a person, thing, or circumstance that you've outgrown. Now you have a chance to really understand the key to those situations where your old co-dependent behaviors and attitudes have been so costly. You may feel that there are some definite spiritual lessons involved in your increased awareness, and these have their own rewards. You're finding out about another layer of intimacy and can improve your ability to open to your partner. But more importantly, you can become more honestly intimate with your inner self.

Changes continue to occur in the world, and although Uranus and Neptune are no longer exactly conjunct, they are still traveling in tandem! Change for change's sake may not get you anywhere now, but those changes which free you from the negative elements of your past and give you a boost in your personal security may feel miraculous. One of the most important guidelines during this period of accelerated growth involves knowing your own limitations.

**If you were born from September 23–October 7 you're feeling the brunt of Saturn's disciplinary energy in quincunx to your Sun.** This cycle brings a greater awareness of your life circumstances, and can provide the impetus for self-improvement. However, this is not a comfortable awareness, and frequently leads to a period of discontent. Take a good look at the elements of your life which feel controlling (including the part of you that can be excessively controlling). Sometimes, governmental changes or shifts in the hierarchy at work provide levels of control which feel stifling, and you may be able to make some adjustments of your own to overcome the blocks and become more productive. It's also easy to feel that you're being held accountable for things which actually belong to someone else. To avoid getting saddled with those monkeys, give them back to the people who are truly responsible for them. And if they refuse to carry their own burdens, resist the temptation to pick them up—otherwise you really will get stuck! On the physical level, this is your year to take your health seriously, even if you don't feel too excited about it. The tendency during this cycle is to put your physical needs low on your priority list. But you'll do yourself a favor by examining your lifestyle and making those adjustments in diet, exercise, and rest which will keep your vitality at the highest level.

**If you were born from October 3–9, you're feeling some friction from Pluto transiting in semisquare to your Sun.** There is a great deal of invigorating energy to be gleaned throughout this cycle, but you'll have to dig deep to find it! Those desires which have lain buried in the recesses of your heart and mind can be brought to the surface and addressed candidly. Perhaps you're ready to allow your creativity to move in a different direction, or you may discover a better way to express your ideas and needs. Now you can address your fears by discovering their origins and dealing with them directly. Outside changes are likely to occur and divert the direction of your goals somewhat, but you can still attain the growth you desire. Work with this energy to reach the core of many of your hidden issues and gain more profound control over your life direction. Any problems of a physical nature need to be thoroughly examined, and you can uncover the nucleus of some troubling issues. During this cycle of healing, allow yourself to participate as a primary healer of your own body by filling yourself with the power of love.

For Librans born from October 10–12, the slower-moving planets are not presenting any challenging aspects this year. Many of these changes you made during 1991 and 1992 are now bearing fruit, and you are probably feeling more at ease with yourself. You may need to take a careful look at your personal relationships, especially an intimate one, since there are likely to be some things you've taken for granted. Allow some extra time during the spring and summer to express your gratitude and understanding to your partner.

You may be feeling a bit confused about your sense of identity if you were born from October 13–18. Neptune's transit is square to your Sun, providing you with a more transcendent vision of reality. It takes a while to get used to this new dimension, and you may be drawn into situations which are not quite what they seem. Although this can be quite helpful in artistic and creative expression, this energy brings some liabilities to your dealings in the more mundane fields of life experience. You're more likely to see what you wish, rather than seeing things as they are. (Although this is arguable, since you're actually seeing the inner view of many people. However, they may not ever express that aspect of themselves!) The problem with this cycle is the illusion it can bring. You're definitely ready to do something that has spiritual value, and may seek to gain more intimate contact with an alternative reality. Concentrate on forgiving your past and opening to a more compassionate view of yourself and the world. Avoid the temptation to rescue others, and look instead for possibilities which will allow you to help someone help themselves. This initiation prepares you for life filled with greater sensitivity and expanded consciousness.

**For Librans born from October 14–20, life may feel like an experimental roller-coaster.** You're experiencing the influence of Uranus square your Sun, a period of unpredictability and change. Many of these changes can be welcome, like finally eliminating those factors from your life that have been dragging you down. But some of the changes can throw you off-balance, especially those you hadn't anticipated. Give yourself time to adapt, and be open to the possibility that you may need to use some of your talents and abilities that have just be sitting on a shelf. For circumstances which seem beyond your control, search out a response to them which feels liberating. In your relationships, trust of yourself is the key issue, and you may be surprised to discover that you've actually given up your own needs in favor of another. It's easy to rebelliously throw everything out the window, but first, be sure you really don't need it! There may definitely be a need to change things, but you want to become more real instead of more unrecognizable. You're holding your own personal revolution—a time of setting yourself free.

**If you were born from October 19–23, you're feeling a need to reach into the deeper recesses of your consciousness.** Pluto is semisextile your Sun, stimulating a sense of inner power and a need to know what lies beneath the surface. You may become more "research" oriented, personally and professionally. Superficiality can actually become uncomfortable, and you may find yourself taking a closer look at your value systems. You're experiencing a period of intensity which can help you amplify your talents and underscore your achievements. A time of healing and rejuvenation, this cycle prompts you to see the underlying truth in yourself and your world.

## Tools to Make a Difference

Make the most of your opportunities by incorporating them into a period of honest self-improvement. Take a careful look at yourself in the mirror. Give yourself time to look beyond your image into the essence of what lies behind your eyes. Concentrate more on increasing your inner beauty. See the part of yourself that is pure love.

Even though you may feel that much of your time is spent concentrating on yourself, you can also participate in outreach and community activities. Find a special interest and give it some of your energy. Your yearning to feel connected can lead you to find others who share your interests and can support your growth. You might also be drawn to a more socially conscious or environmentally active lifestyle, and can become highly effective in helping bring about social changes.

Surround yourself with items which feel personally empowering, instead of just superficially lovely. Consider building a shield, using your power stones and colors to amplify your strengths and provide a sense of spiritual and emotional support. Work with visualizations by doing more than just affirmations. Find ways to incorporate a sense of meaningful ritual into your life.

During your meditations and visualizations, concentrate on feeling the essence of the energy of attraction. This magnetic quality is part of your strength, and may need to be refined so that you can attract the experiences and circumstances into your life which allow you to express more of yourself. Learn to embrace yourself, and to become aware of that part of you which resists embrace. By loving yourself totally, you will become a more radiant expression of your true beauty.

### Affirmation for the Year
"I am my own Perfect Partner."

# ACTION TABLES FOR LIBRA

These dates reflect the best (but not the only) times for success and ease in these activities according to your Sun Sign.

| | |
|---|---|
| **Change Residence** | Jan. 1–13; Dec. 19–31 |
| **Request a Raise** | Oct. 5–6 |
| **Begin a Course of Study** | June 9; Dec. 2 |
| **Visit a Doctor** | Feb 1–20; Mar. 18–Apr. 8; Aug. 18–Sep. 3 |
| **Start a Diet** | Jan. 15–16; Feb. 11–12; Mar. 10–11; Apr. 7–8; May 4–5, 31; June 1, 28–29; July 25–26; Aug. 21–22; Sep. 18–19; Oct. 15–16; Nov. 11–12; Dec. 8–10 |
| **Begin a Romance** | Feb. 10–11 |
| **Join a Club** | Aug. 7–8 |
| **Seek Employment** | Feb. 1–20; Mar. 18–Apr. 8; May 29–July 2; July 10–Aug. 2 |
| **Take a Vacation** | Jan. 22–23; Feb. 19–20; Mar. 18–19; Apr. 14–15; May 11–12; June 8– 9; July 5–6; Aug. 1–2, 29–30; Sep. 25–26; Oct. 22–23; Nov. 18–19; Dec. 16–17 |
| **Change Your Wardrobe** | Jan. 14–31; Feb. 22–Mar. 17 |
| **End a Relationship** | Oct. 19 |
| **Seek Professional Advice** | Jan. 17–18; Feb. 13–14; Mar. 13–14; Apr. 9–10; May 6–7; June 2–4, 30; July 1, 27–28; Aug. 24–25; Sep. 20–21; Oct. 17–18; Nov. 13–14; Dec. 11–12 |
| **Have a Makeover** | Oct. 5–6 |
| **Obtain a Loan** | Jan. 20–21; Feb. 16–17; Mar. 15–16; Apr. 11–13; May 9–10; June 5–6; July 2–3, 30–31; Aug. 26–27; Sep. 22–23; Oct. 20–21; Nov. 16–17; Dec. 13–14 |

## PRIMARY FOCUS

Unrest within your family or home situation can lead to a breakthrough in understanding. Eliminate attitudes which leave you vulnerable to manipulation.

## HEALTH AND FITNESS

Calm excessive nervous energy by allowing time for adequate physical activity and thorough relaxation. Know your limits, and be cautious in high-risk situations and driving from the 14th–20th.

## ROMANCE AND RELATIONSHIPS

Family relationships can be the source of external or internal turmoil, but regardless of the outward appearances, it's important that you come to grips with your honest feelings. After the New Moon on the 11th, a fresh break from dependencies that are no longer necessary to your nurturance and growth can help you establish stronger security. Your attention turns to the playful and romantic after the 19th, when allowing time for creative and loving activities improves a relationship and confirms your deeper feelings. Share your love during the Full Moon on the 27th.

## FINANCE AND CAREER

Changes in the hierarchy can leave you feeling insecure about career prospects, but may actually lead to a better opportunity. Your flexibility widens your options from the 9th–22nd, although you may not reach an understanding until you confer on the 22nd–23rd. Financial prospects improve after the 22nd, but may not stabilize until next month.

## OPPORTUNITY OF THE MONTH

By keeping an open mind and adapting to changes, you can be in a position for personal advancement on the 22nd, 23rd, 27th, and 31st.

**Rewarding Days:** 4, 5, 8, 12, 13, 22, 23, 27, 28, 31
**Challenging Days:** 1, 6, 7, 10, 11, 17, 18, 19, 24, 25

## AFFIRMATION FOR THE MONTH
"I am safe and secure."

### PRIMARY FOCUS

Taking the initiative in creative endeavors brings excellent results, but there may be extra work involved which you hadn't anticipated. Budgeting your time can be frustrating.

### HEALTH AND FITNESS

Your mental attitude has a highly powerful effect on your health this month, when worry and negative thinking can be costly to your basic vitality.

### ROMANCE AND RELATIONSHIPS

Love relationships are more enjoyable through the 12th, and you may feel ready to take the lead in romance during the New Moon on the 10th. If you have concerns which are not being addressed, clarify the source of your feelings. Past traumas in love can haunt your dreams mid-month, giving you insight into any unfinished emotional issues. Misunderstandings are most easily clarified after the 21st. Allow extra time for personal contemplation during the Full Moon on the 25th.

### FINANCE AND CAREER

Stress emerges in situations which require you to work closely with others, and may be the result of time constraints. Before you agree to deadlines, be sure you're aware of possible delays or blocks, and allow for those in your estimations. Mercury's retrograde from Feb. 11 to Mar. 5 is complicated by static energy and power plays, so don't expect immediate results! Research, negotiate and review, when facts emerge that may lead you to change your mind.

### OPPORTUNITY OF THE MONTH

Meetings, presentations or conferences are most productive on the 1st, 4th, 27th, or 28th.

**Rewarding Days:** 1, 4, 5, 9, 19, 20, 27, 28
**Challenging Days:** 3, 6, 7, 8, 13, 14, 21, 22

### AFFIRMATION FOR THE MONTH
"I know and respect my boundaries
and the boundaries of others. "

### PRIMARY FOCUS

Demands from others may seem unreasonable or over-whelming, but communication is necessary to remedy the situation. Passivity works to your disadvantage.

### HEALTH AND FITNESS

Extra effort to keep fit is worth it, since you need the break in your routine to stay mentally alert and feel emotionally balanced. Watch a tendency to push yourself too intensely.

### ROMANCE AND RELATIONSHIPS

Partnerships, and your role as a partner, are more the focus of your energy after the 8th, but unrealistic expectations can create turmoil by the 24th. Control issues surface from the 13th–19th, when clarifying misunderstandings can stop a landslide of emotions. To divert the tendency toward disagreeable circumstances, take an honest look at the messages you've been sending! The Full Moon in Libra on the 27th can amplify unfulfilled hopes, and can mark a period of reaching true equanimity if you apply yourself.

### FINANCE AND CAREER

You may feel buffeted about by the hidden agendas of others at work, and just ignoring the situation will make it worse. Take the lead with your peers to reach consensus instead of breaking up into argumentative factions after the New Moon on the 12th. Budgetary or financial concerns may halt progress through the 18th, but will offer guidelines for the future. Adherence to agreed upon budgetary restraints works to your benefit.

### OPPORTUNITY OF THE MONTH

Honest self-awareness helps you avoid a temptation to project your discontent onto others, leading to progress in relationships.

**Rewarding Days:** 1, 4, 8, 18, 19, 23, 27, 28, 31
**Challenging Days:** 2, 6, 7, 11, 12, 13, 14, 20, 21

### AFFIRMATION FOR THE MONTH
"I am whole, healthy and strong."

### PRIMARY FOCUS

Social activities can be enjoyable, and may offer a chance to improve your career options. However, competitive circumstances can lead to feelings of jealousy if you're not careful!

### HEALTH AND FITNESS

Consider changing your fitness routine mid-month, with clear goals to help you measure your progress. It's a good time to work with a personal trainer or teacher.

### ROMANCE AND RELATIONSHIPS

Solidifying a relationship through a commitment or agreement during the New Moon on the 10th offers hope for the future. And if you're involved in a situation that needs to end, break away from those circumstances between the 14th and 24th. Your sexual energy is more intense from the 1st–25th, but unless you're communicating your needs you may feel unduly frustrated from the 19th–24th. Get away to a special place with your sweetie the 24th, 27th, or 28th, when you can create memorable moments.

### FINANCE AND CAREER

Support from others is finally forthcoming, and if you need to solicit investors or interested parties, you should see good results. Extra time spent with superiors or co-workers outside the workplace can lead to improvements in work situations. Be sure to double-check communications, contracts, or written agreements the week of the 17th. If you're persistent this month, you're likely to see financial rewards by the 28th.

### OPPORTUNITY OF THE MONTH

Interactions with others are the key to much of your success this month, and are especially promising on the 14th and 27th.

**Rewarding Days:** 1, 4, 5, 14, 15, 19, 23, 24, 27, 28
**Challenging Days:** 2, 3, 7, 9, 10, 17, 18, 29, 30

### AFFIRMATION FOR THE MONTH
"I am sensitive to my inner needs."

### PRIMARY FOCUS

Your diplomatic gestures work wonders and can give you the edge in important negotiations. Beneficial results arise from travel and educational pursuits, but keep your eye on your budget!

### HEALTH AND FITNESS

Your competitive urges need a healthy outlet, but choose your activities wisely from the 13th–21st when surprising changes can throw you off balance.

### ROMANCE AND RELATIONSHIPS

Time out to explore philosophical pursuits or travel to an inspiring locale adds exciting dimension to your personal life and can lead to romantic possibilities. Your magnetic energy builds to a level of peak intensity from the 10th–25th, and you may be willing to surrender to an intriguing diversion. If you're feeling flirtatious, be sure it won't upset the applecart, since your intentions may be taken seriously! Delightful interchange can spark romance during the Moon's Eclipse on the 24th.

### FINANCE AND CAREER

Make yourself more aware of your financial picture near the time of the Solar Eclipse on the 10th, when adding to your liabilities may not be in your best interests. Career opportunities can arise from workshops, conferences or presentations, and your ability to motivate and inspire others shines from the 11th–22nd. However, interruptions can make it difficult to stay on track. You can make these work to your benefit if you use your imagination!

### OPPORTUNITY OF THE MONTH

Get important projects moving from the 11th–22nd, when the momentum generated propels you toward long-term success.

**Rewarding Days:** 2, 3, 11, 12, 17, 21, 22, 25, 26, 29, 30
**Challenging Days:** 4, 6, 7, 10, 14, 15, 27, 28

### AFFIRMATION FOR THE MONTH
"I am guided by wisdom and inspired by truth."

### PRIMARY FOCUS

Career growth and financial considerations take first priority, and friendlier relationships through your work can soften on-the-job tension mid-month.

### HEALTH AND FITNESS

Immediately address any physical distress, since now it's easier to get to the core of any problems. Give yourself a little tender loving care after the 25th.

### ROMANCE AND RELATIONSHIPS

Keeping peace in the family may be impossible, so why give up your needs just to satisfy others?! But if someone's jumping to conclusions before seeking out the evidence from the 9th–14th, you may have some luck reviewing the situation and setting it straight on the 17th or 18th. Let the inspiration you feel after the New Moon on the 9th stimulate a clearer direction in relationships, and allow time to explore your natural spiritual path. You're likely to need the inner peace by the Full Moon on the 23rd.

### FINANCE AND CAREER

Dealings with authorities or superiors from the 1st–10th can lead to improvements in your work situation. But problems with details can arise during Mercury's retrograde from June 12–July 5. Seek out expert advice after the 16th to keep things in the proper perspective. Compromise may be in order. Disagreements over jointly held property or tax disputes can get out of hand after the 19th, so get your paperwork in order and don't get too rattled by the other guy.

### OPPORTUNITY OF THE MONTH

By keeping a clear awareness of your own boundaries you can more effectively answer the needs of those you love.

**Rewarding Days:** 8, 9, 17, 18, 21, 22, 25, 26
**Challenging Days:** 1, 3, 4, 6, 10, 11, 23, 24, 30

### AFFIRMATION FOR THE MONTH
"I am honest with myself and others."

### PRIMARY FOCUS

Achieving recognition for your efforts becomes more important, and may aid you in defining future goals. Put some energy into expanding your horizons.

### HEALTH AND FITNESS

Improvement in your vim and vigor comes more easily if you're involved in activities you really enjoy. Enroll in a class with a friend or join in a team sport. You're eager to see results.

### ROMANCE AND RELATIONSHIPS

You may feel like getting away and enjoy traveling with your partner or a group through the 10th. But traveling alone can be just as satisfying from the 11th–23rd. Improve your attitudes through incorporating spiritual needs into your personal relationship. In fact, finding new love through sharing an experience of spiritual renewal is highly promising the 13th–19th. Your fantasies can overwhelm your sense of reality from the 21st–30th, so set some personal boundaries. Keep family issues in perspective during the Full Moon on the 22nd.

### FINANCE AND CAREER

From the 3rd–9th, get back in touch with individuals or groups whose enthusiasm for your work or ideas supports your plans. Then, set a plan in motion which offers you a chance to improve your position. Conferences or presentations fare well on the 15th, 19th, 20th and 23rd. Take a more conservative stance from the 19th–25th, and move into more experimental possibilities on the 27th. Tighten up those purse strings this month, since spending can get out of hand.

### OPPORTUNITY OF THE MONTH

Follow-through from the 5th–10th strengthens your reputation for excellence and improves self-confidence.

**Rewarding Days:** 5, 6, 10, 11, 14, 15, 19, 23, 24
**Challenging Days:** 1, 7, 8, 9, 21, 22, 27, 28

### AFFIRMATION FOR THE MONTH
"I finish what I begin."

### PRIMARY FOCUS

With Venus moving into Libra on the 7th, you're set for a period of improvement in your self-image. Romantic or business travel can result in surprising alterations in your plans.

### HEALTH AND FITNESS

Advance your fitness levels by getting involved in pleasurable activities that appeal to your social needs. Consider working out with a friend or enrolling in a class.

### ROMANCE AND RELATIONSHIPS

Develop or enhance a friendship by sharing time or getting back in touch. Allow yourself to openly explore a refreshing turn in a friendship near the New Moon on the 7th, when you're more comfortable with changes. Romance is definitely a probability through improvements in an existing situation or the development of a new one. Leave time for special delights from the 19th to the Full Moon on the 21st. But be wary of distractions after the 26th when straying from a commitment can lead to a mess of trouble.

### FINANCE AND CAREER

Broaden your horizons, expand your base of operations or increase your field of influence from the 2nd–17th. Conferences or meetings offer you the right climate to advance and gain support from the 7th–21st. Special attention to budgetary expenses from the 17th–27th will help you avoid a shortfall. You can be disappointed if you expect someone else to cover your losses—you may, instead, have to cover their mistakes!

### OPPORTUNITY OF THE MONTH

Your confidence level is highest from the 3rd–21st, with the best time to move into new territory from the 10th–16th.

**Rewarding Days:** 1, 2, 6, 7, 10, 11, 15, 16, 19, 20, 29
**Challenging Days:** 4, 5, 14, 17, 18, 23, 24, 25, 31

### AFFIRMATION FOR THE MONTH
"My heart is filled with joy and love."

# ♎ LIBRA/SEPTEMBER ♎

## PRIMARY FOCUS

Feeling more strongly driven toward success, this can be a period of great accomplishment, but you can run into resistance if others feel threatened.

## HEALTH AND FITNESS

Overcome the tendency to ignore your physical needs, since allowing time for fitness helps you deal more effectively with stress. Review health needs during the Full Moon on the 19th.

## ROMANCE AND RELATIONSHIPS

You may still be dealing with fallout from last month's adventure, and can use this to your advantage through the 8th. But your feeling of restlessness grows to even larger proportions by the 18th, so it's a good idea to talk about the positive changes which need to be incorporated into your relationship. If you're ending a relationship, be sure you're leaving for the right reasons. The fires of passion can burn hot after the 19th, but may be ignited by dangerous elements. Know your emotional boundaries!

## FINANCE AND CAREER

Examine your work situation for circumstances which need improvement. Instigating changes after the New Moon on the 5th can bring support, but can also lead to alienation if you've been self-serving. Sudden changes made after the 16th can place you in a precarious position if you're unprepared, but you can take advantage of a surprising turn of events aligning necessary support and anticipating required information.

## OPPORTUNITY OF THE MONTH

Affirm your position by becoming positively supportive of others in the midst of changes.

**Rewarding Days:** 3, 7, 8, 11, 12, 15, 16, 25, 26, 30
**Challenging Days:** 1, 7, 8, 13, 14, 18, 20, 21, 27, 28

## AFFIRMATION FOR THE MONTH
"I am sensitive to the needs of others."

### PRIMARY FOCUS

Keep a close watch over finances—poor judgment during Mercury's retrograde from the 9th–30th can lead to long-term hassles. Review records, consider advice.

### HEALTH AND FITNESS

Build your stamina and endurance, taking advantage of your increased vitality to get back on track with your fitness. Team sports or group fitness classes can be supportive and inspiring.

### ROMANCE AND RELATIONSHIPS

With the New Moon in Libra on the 4th, you're likely to feel more aware of your needs and more comfortable talking about them with your partner. It's easy to go overboard with expectations (especially of yourself!) all month, but use that energy to positively enhance your self-esteem. Before making final decisions about personal needs, ask yourself if your actions will lead to positive growth. If not, reconsider. Partnerships take first priority near the Full Moon on the 19th, and you can mend misunderstandings after the 22nd.

### FINANCE AND CAREER

Keep credit cards under lock and key, since blowing your budget on impulse can leave you feeling low! Your income may be increasing, but it's not a good idea to deplete your resources. Find ways to make your money work for you, but think twice before you jump into new investments after the 9th. Good planning now can put you in an even stronger position for future growth.

### OPPORTUNITY OF THE MONTH

Launch into new projects from the 4th–6th, when a solid beginning helps you stabilize.

**Rewarding Days:** 1, 4, 5, 8, 9, 13, 22, 23, 27
**Challenging Days:** 2, 7, 10, 11, 17, 18, 19, 25, 26

### AFFIRMATION FOR THE MONTH
"My thoughts and actions are guided
by Divine Wisdom."

## PRIMARY FOCUS

Clear energy directed toward your goals brings you closer to realizing success. Take a closer look at your values, since you may be heading toward something you no longer want or need!

## HEALTH AND FITNESS

By putting increased effort into your fitness activities now you'll see faster progress and feel more vital. Fine-tuning your health regimen can make it less work and bring fruitful rewards.

## ROMANCE AND RELATIONSHIPS

Misdirected energy can drastically affect the substance of your relationships, and you need to be especially careful to communicate intended thoughts and feelings through the 10th. Ignoring trouble signals can create greater damage, it may be easier to stop and nip it in the bud! You're taking positive steps toward healing old emotional trauma, so be kind to yourself. After the 20th, be clear about motivations before you act on advice from another. You may have allowed yourself to be manipulated by their needs, not your own!

## FINANCE AND CAREER

The Solar Eclipse on the 3rd and Lunar Eclipse on the 18th bring a powerful emphasis to the material side of your life. You can see excellent financial growth, but you may also be more aware of the cost of your success! By setting priorities which support your personal growth, your professional life can become more rewarding. Otherwise, you may feel you've missed the mark.

## OPPORTUNITY OF THE MONTH

Rid yourself of situations which have proven themselves to be outworn or too costly on the 18th.

**Rewarding Days:** 1, 5, 9, 10, 19, 20, 24, 28, 29
**Challenging Days:** 3, 7, 8, 13, 14, 15, 18, 21, 22

## AFFIRMATION FOR THE MONTH
"I gladly release what I no longer need."

### PRIMARY FOCUS

Emphasis on communication, travel and sharing ideas builds your network of support, personally and professionally. You can be both teacher and student.

### HEALTH AND FITNESS

After putting forth such strong effort, you may need more time for relaxation. Continue to stay active, but be sure to take time out to rejuvenate after the 12th.

### ROMANCE AND RELATIONSHIPS

The powerful energy during the New Moon and Jupiter's conjunction to Pluto on the 2nd can be a real boost to the realization of your hopes. But you can go overboard if you're not careful. Be sure you're talking to a receptive listener, and giving to someone who truly appreciates your efforts. The love you've been seeking is likely to be right next door, so open your eyes and take a closer look. Take steps to initiate romance from the 11th–16th, and by the Full Moon on the 17th you may (gladly!) have your hands full!

### FINANCE AND CAREER

Your eagerness to take part in sharing knowledge and expertise from the 1st–18th can result in professional growth and the positive recognition of influential individuals. Careful attention to restoring or repairing valuables can be profitable and may also offer a previously unseen creative opportunity. The temptation to act with flamboyance after the 11th can alienate a more conservative supporter. Respect your own limitations.

### OPPORTUNITY OF THE MONTH

Using your creative ingenuity lays the groundwork for success, especially when coupled with your sense of grace and refinement.

**Rewarding Days:** 2, 3, 6, 7, 8, 16, 17, 21, 22, 25, 26, 30
**Challenging Days:** 4, 5, 11, 12, 18, 19, 20

### AFFIRMATION FOR THE MONTH
"My life is filled with abundance enough to share."

# ♏ SCORPIO ♏
## The Scorpion

### October 23 to November 23

**Element:** Water

**Quality:** Fixed

**Polarity:** Feminine/Yin

**Planetary Ruler:** Pluto

**Meditation:** "Mastery through Transformation"

**Gemstone:** Topaz

**Power Stones:** Obsidian, citrine, garnet

**Glyph:** Scorpion's tail

**Key Phrase:** "I desire"

**Anatomy:** Reproductive organs, genitals, rectum

**Colors:** Burgundy, black

**Animal:** Reptiles, scorpions, birds of prey

**Myths/Legends:** Hades and Persephone, Shiva, Ereshkigal

**House Association:** 8th

**Opposite Sign:** Taurus

**Flower:** Chrysanthemum

**Key Word:** Intensity

**Positive Expression:**

Passionate
Healing
Erotic
Penetrating
Regenerating
Investigative
Sensual
Incisive
Transforming

**Misuse of Energy:**

Extreme
Destructive
Violent
Overbearing
Lascivious
Jealous
Vengeful
Obsessive

# ♏ SCORPIO ♏

## Your Ego's Strengths and Weaknesses

With keen perception and an eye for intrigue, you possess a charisma which both fascinates and mystifies others. You're interested in probing beneath the surface to discover what lies at the core, and can be highly creative when sharing your discoveries. You enjoy the feeling of knowing what others have not yet discovered.

Your piercing insight into human nature and awareness of inner conflict is the result of your own internal experience. Because your natural sensibilities alert you to hidden agendas, those who have something to hide are often uncomfortable in your presence. And your tendency to keep the volcano of emotion under control beneath the surface may lead others to feel wary or mistrustful of you. They know something's going on, but you may be unwilling to expose the details!

Ruled by Pluto, the energy of regeneration and transformation, you are walking the path of the healer, and can experience the heights of joy and the depths of despair. Through directing this energy toward higher principles, you can rise to heroic action. But if you've been deeply wounded, you can become compulsively vengeful. By developing an awareness of your inner self, you can learn to forgive yourself and others, releasing pent-up emotions of guilt and shame, and experiencing true spiritual rebirth.

## Your Career Development

A career which allows you to be involved in bringing about changes will be most fulfilling. Work which involves research, scientific probing, or renovation can be gratifying. Healing arts, including counseling, can be gratifying and offer an opportunity to help others change their lives. Creative expressions such as painting, writing, or music may be strong outlets, and can also be transforming to others.

You're well-suited to influential positions and have a knack for making the most of the resources of others. In the entertainment field, these talents can be expressed in directing, producing, or performing. And in business, financial counseling, career management, insurance, and investment banking are excellent options. History and archaeology may be appealing as a career or hobby. Whatever your choices, you can transform what appears to be useless into something of value. Ultimately, you might even turn a tidy profit!

## Your Approach to Romance

When you're ready for love, you can weave an enticing and mesmerizing romantic web. You may long for the person who will share the depths of your soul, and then be unwilling to unlock the doors once you've sent out the invitation! Until trust has been established, you're likely to keep your feelings hidden. Once hurt, you can close the door to love forever, which protects your vulnerability, but also leaves you longing for tenderness.

With you, the art of lovemaking can be a continually intriguing experience, unlocking the gates to ecstasy. You search for a partner who accepts and shares your desires, and may need some patience before you find the right one. You may feel most comfortable with the water signs—Cancer, Scorpio, and Pisces. While another Scorpio may feel like your soul-mate, the relationship can go from extreme passion to volatility. Cancer may share your higher values and you'll enjoy the nurturance. And Pisces stimulates your romantic, creative side while providing plenty of imaginative sensitivity.

Aries can be interesting, but their teasing can lead to trouble. Your opposite, Taurus, demonstrates a sensuality and steadfastness which can be highly attractive. But disagreements can be highly frustrating, since neither of you will want to budge an inch. Gemini's entertaining wit can become distracting when you seek continuity and support. And although Leo's magnetism shivers your timbers, you may find them to be too self-absorbed.

Virgo's friendship and support can grow toward lasting passion. With Libra, you enjoy the feeling that they know what you want, but their indecisiveness can drive you nuts. The lusty, adventurous Sagittarian is inviting, but you may have difficulty accepting their carefree nature. Capricorn understands you and supports your growth and success. And although Aquarius may intrigue you, there's likely to be too much distance to achieve the far reaches of passion you desire.

## Your Use of Power

Scorpios certainly understand power. Even as a child you may have been drawn to powerful people or heroes of omnipotent power. Through your innate understanding of the natural transformational rhythms of life, the process of life and death, you know that changes are merely a part of existing. Yet your desire to hold onto life's richest experiences may be driven by a feeling that you want to control these natural processes in some way.

Instead of reaching deep within your own soul for your true needs, you may have built a massive shield against life's most sumptuous experiences. Once you've reached into that inner realm, you'll find a powerful warrior spirit residing at the core of your being, which constantly guards you from harm. This power does not have to emerge as threatening or negative once you've honestly allowed yourself to feel that you deserve to have your inner needs fulfilled. Through developing compassion for yourself you can reach out toward the world and bring about the changes which impart growth and hope for the future.

## Famous Scorpios

Roseanne Arnold, Edward Asner, John Candy, Indira Gandhi, Dwight Gooden, Larry Holmes, Mahalia Jackson, Bruce Jenner, Larry King, Joni Mitchell, Tatum O'Neal, Jane Pauley, Pablo Picasso, Pat Sajak, Martin Scorsese, Marlo Thomas

# THE YEAR AHEAD FOR SCORPIO

Now that you've worked to lay the groundwork, the cycles this year indicate a strong period of growth and fortification of your creative direction. You have ample opportunities to gain greater personal awareness without such intensive testing of your ego, although you're still in the process of changing many of your priorities. If you've been waiting for the right time to move forward, the balance of energy this year can help you develop the right blend of confidence and practicality that can help guarantee success. Your task is to put forth the necessary effort!

Jupiter's cycle has returned to Scorpio, a cycle which last occurred during 1982. You may feel you're ready to reach out beyond your current circumstances, but you have to stay aware of your reasonable limitations. This can be a period of positive growth, but it's just as easy to let things go too far. (Remember the lessons you learned during 1984–85 about the cost of reaching past your limits!) Used at its highest level, this energy can be the launching of your deepest wishes. You can manifest many of your hopes more effectively, and more quickly. Fortunately, throughout much of the year you have support from Saturn helping to balance a tendency to move too quickly. Your timing can be excellent, and you're in a great position to let your creative talents shine forth. Allow each moment to bring you a satisfying level of personal confirmation, and use that feeling to move forward into the future you desire.

The Solar Eclipses this year in the Taurus-Scorpio polarity are especially significant for you. By encouraging yourself to become more mindful and more aware of the energy within and around you, these cycles can help you become more attuned to your personal needs. You may question certain elements of your relationships, particularly partnerships, more from the standpoint of what is missing than what is there. Now you have the power to begin to fulfill those unanswered needs. First, you must become conscious of any blocks you've created, and determine if you can afford to let down those barriers. If you're ready, this period can be much like being reborn. But this time, you will have better recall!

Uranus and Neptune are separating from their conjunction, but are still traveling closely together and continue to have an impact on universal changes. For you, many of these changes may be connected to the way you think and the way you share your ideas with others. You're in a great position to learn or to try new approaches to existing situations. Rather than resisting new ideas, allow that aspect of yourself which accepts the positive process of change to help you make the most of new circumstances.

**If you were born from October 23–November 6 you're feeling the focused support of Saturn transiting in trine aspect to your Sun.** You can experience this period as one of positive self-affirmation. You're especially capable of consolidating your energy, and can accomplish more through positive discipline. If you're working toward achieving mastery in some area of your life, the concentration present during this year will aid you immensely. Projects or tasks which need disciplined effort are more easily accomplished, but you may have some difficulty if you're trying to diversify. This is a time to consolidate and complete. It's easier to structure your time, and you'll probably work better if you're functioning on a reasonably predictable schedule now. You may decide to seek out a teacher or mentor, or you may have the opportunity to teach others. Think of this as a period of creating a basic structure which leaves room for alteration and future growth.

**For Scorpios born from November 1–4, Neptune is transiting in quintile aspect to your Sun.** By incorporating imaginative ideas into your plans, you'll feel much more like you're heading in the right direction. You're likely to feel an enhancement of your sensibilities and special talents, but may have a bit of difficulty keeping your emotional boundaries intact. Allow yourself to be more aware of the impact of your environment and relationships on your emotions. Take some time each day to center and balance your energy so you'll recognize these outside influences more easily. As a positive attribute of this cycle, the spiritual element adds a special quality to your personal expression.

If you were born from November 2–7, you're feeling some erratic impulses while Uranus transits in quintile to your Sun. It's time to allow your creative insights room for expression. You're in a stable position to incorporate these changes without losing ground, and trying to ignore them will only cost you time. Stepping outside the bounds of your "usual" style of expression can add just the right touch to help you gain the effect you've been hoping to achieve.

Chiron's transit is sextile your Sun if you were born from October 26–November 16. Although this cycle is a subtle one, working consciously with this energy can help you realize your hopes more effectively. Make yourself more aware of the things you're doing each day, increasing your mindfulness. Life can become your meditation, and your ability to understand the experiences you face will increase. Develop a sense of direction, set some goals— even if you've never been a "goal person." Little by little, this period allows you to be more aware of your part in creating your life and manifesting your destiny.

If your birth occurred from November 12–16, you're experiencing an opening of consciousness while Neptune transits in sextile to your Sun. Creative activities can flow more easily, and you may feel a stronger sense of inspiration and love during your participation in them. This is a period of visionary insight and increasing psychic sensitivity, when dreams can be both symbolic and prophetic. Instead of just allowing life to float along while you drift in the stream, consciously move into this natural flow. By working with this energy, you can unleash levels of awareness which had previously eluded understanding. Enhancements in a relationship can occur. But perhaps most important is the experience of stronger unity with your spiritual essence, and more intimate communion with God/Goddess.

Uranus' transit sextile your Sun brings a period of awakening if you were born from November 14–18. Such excitement for life can add electricity to everything you do. Your special talents and unique self-expression are more easily expressed—you're more at home with yourself. Risks you might have avoided before seem less costly; you may simply be better prepared. But you're also experiencing more significant opportunities to do things in your own inimitable manner. Give yourself the chance to be more frank about your needs in personal relationships. Direct your natural ingenuity toward the areas that feel most enticing. This is your time to indulge in life's more rapturous experiences.

If you were born from November 17–23, you're feeling an increasing intensity in almost everything, since Pluto is transiting in conjunction to your Sun. Although you've had some sensation of this cycle for several years, the impact is at its fullest level. Talk about regenerative changes—this one is unsurpassed! Not everyone will experience such a cycle in their lifetime, and for you it has special significance. There's no need to panic, even if you do look into the mirror and wonder about the identity of the person changing before your very eyes. All the barriers to your inner self are falling away so you can find out who resides at the core of your being. Once discovered, that aspect of yourself empowers you to become more effectively and fully *YOU*. Old circumstances and attitudes which have been blocking your progress are now fading into the distance. Explore your motivations, since you may discover that you have been psychologically driven by messages you received from others when you were younger. You can now replace those with your own clear desires and needs. Through this level of healing, you're also assimilating life at its highest capacity. You're experiencing the restoration of your power. It just takes a period of adjustment to get used to it!

## Tools to Make a Difference

Focusing extra energy on creative expression during 1994 can provide significant self-affirmation. It's not necessary for artistry to be a source of income, but if you do use your artistry professionally, you'll likely desire an even higher level of mastery than you've previously achieved. Greater discipline in this area can be achieved through both teaching and learning, and teaching can be even more rewarding now than it has been in the past.

Develop your intuitive and psychic sensitivity through allowing some time each day to clear your mind, relax your body and listen to the messages from your internal sensors. By consciously working with the energies this year to open your awareness you'll feel even more positively in touch with life's natural rhythm. You might also enjoy learning martial arts such as karate or aikido, or other eastern body movements such as Tai Chi or hatha yoga.

Stay in touch with the natural cycles by maintaining an awareness of the Moon's phases and cycles. If you're so inclined, adding this awareness to your ritual practices or meditations can bring you into a closer affinity with the cosmic flow. Native American ritual, vision quest, and wiccan ritual offer significant opportunities to aid you in releasing and clearing your energy. Make it a point to create a special activity or environment during the eclipses this year, and consciously use these periods to evaluate your life situation and hopes for the future. Use these times to consciously release fear, pain and guilt.

Focus on the colors of your power stones—topaz, obsidian and garnet—during meditations. See them in your mind's eye and feel the impact of mentally placing yourself in a circle of light permeated by the colors of the stones. Use the power of your mind in harmony with your tremendous emotional power to create changes. See yourself standing in a desert under the light of the Full Moon. Feel the life around you, the results of changes throughout the ages. Own this vitality. Envision the silent rising of the morning Sun, the colors streaming forth over your face, filling you with life. Choose to walk the path of the warrior, knowing you carry with you wisdom and love which flow from the Source directly through you into the world.

## Affirmation for the Year

"I am filled with strength, love, and understanding."

# ACTION TABLES FOR SCORPIO

These dates reflect the best (but not the only) times for success and ease in these activities according to your Sun Sign.

| | |
|---|---|
| **Change Residence** | Jan. 14–Feb. 1; 22; Mar. 17 |
| **Request a Raise** | Nov. 3 |
| **Begin a Course of Study** | Jan. 11; July 8–9 |
| **Visit a Doctor** | Apr. 10–25; Sep. 4–27; Oct. 19–Nov. 9 |
| **Start a Diet** | Jan. 17–18; Feb. 13–15; Mar. 13–14; Apr. 9–10; May 6, 7; June 2–4, 30; July 1, 27–28; Aug. 24–25; Sep. 20–21; Oct. 17–18; Nov. 13–14; Dec. 11–12 |
| **Begin a Romance** | March 12 |
| **Join a Club** | Sep. 5–6 |
| **Seek Employment** | Apr. 10–25; Aug. 3–17 |
| **Take a Vacation** | Jan. 25–26; Feb. 21–22; Mar. 20–21; Apr. 17–18; May 14–15; June 10–11; July 7–8; Aug. 4–5, 31; Sep. 1, 27–29; Oct. 25–26; Nov. 21–22; Dec. 18–19 |
| **Change Your Wardrobe** | Feb. 1–20; Mar. 18–Apr. 8 |
| **End a Relationship** | Nov. 17–18 |
| **Seek Professional Advice** | Jan. 20–21; Feb. 16–17; Mar. 15–16; Apr. 11–13; May 9–10; June 5–6; July 2–4, 30–31; Aug. 26–27; Sep. 22–23; Oct. 20–21; Nov. 16–17; Dec. 13–14 |
| **Have a Makeover** | Nov. 3–4 |
| **Obtain a Loan** | Jan. 22–23; Feb. 18–20; Mar. 18–19; Apr. 14–15; May 11–12; June 8–9; July 5–6; Aug. 1–3, 29–30; Sep. 25–26; Oct. 22–24; Nov. 18–19; Dec. 16–17 |

## PRIMARY FOCUS

Take an active approach to getting your message across, and be sure to make contact with individuals who support your efforts. Find ways to take advantage of the changes around you.

## HEALTH AND FITNESS

Add more spirit to your life by gradually upgrading your physical activity level. Take time to get outside, since a natural environment can be positively stimulating.

## ROMANCE AND RELATIONSHIPS

All your relationships benefit from improved communication from the 1st–14th, but the New Moon on the 11th is especially significant for intentional expression of your feelings and needs. Try a different approach in order to improve your effectiveness. Contact with a sibling opens the door to better relations. Romance fares best on the 7th, 15th, and 16th. But be careful after the 25th, when you may give the wrong impression or become distracted at an inconvenient time! Deal with family issues before the Full Moon on the 27th to keep them from escalating out of control.

## FINANCE AND CAREER

Schedule important presentations or meetings between the 1st–13th when your most innovative ideas are well received. Initiate new programs from the 11th–18th for best results. Reach an understanding of expectations with superiors or authorities to avoid getting caught in the crunch from the 19th–27th. Your investments should be producing results now, and diversification from the 9th–17th can bring quick and lucrative results.

## OPPORTUNITY OF THE MONTH

Get exceptional results from efforts initiated on the 11th–12th.

**Rewarding Days:** 2, 3, 6, 7, 10, 11, 15, 16, 25, 29, 30
**Challenging Days:** 1, 12, 13, 14, 20, 21, 27, 28

## AFFIRMATION FOR THE MONTH
"I listen to my intuitive voice."

### PRIMARY FOCUS

Personal relationships may require more of your time, but can also provide greater satisfaction. Increasing activity at home can result in your feeling a bit strung-out, so pace yourself!

### HEALTH AND FITNESS

It's easy to push beyond your limits, especially if you're trying to satisfy everyone on your list. Go ahead and take time for that massage. You can use the break in your routine!

### ROMANCE AND RELATIONSHIPS

Familial pressures escalate unless you take a positive stand and create some structure out of the chaos. Effectively organizing a new approach to your routine looks promising from the 1st–8th, but you may have to deal with a difference of opinion over details on the 9th and 10th. Your willingness to move into a different direction after the New Moon on the 10th may bring surprising results. Your love life stabilizes after the 12th, when a commitment brings you closer. Plan a delectable diversion for the Full Moon on the 25th!

### FINANCE AND CAREER

Significant progress on your designs or projects results from focused efforts from the 1st–19th. You can even take advantage of Mercury's retrograde from Feb. 11–Mar. 5 by reviewing your material or product and making improvements. Disappointing financial news may have you worrying, but there's hope for a remedy from the 20th–27th. Use changes to your advantage by seeking out innovative approaches and redefining your aims.

### OPPORTUNITY OF THE MONTH

Information surfacing on the 21st and 22nd offers you a chance to get to the core of a problem.

**Rewarding Days:** 2, 3, 7, 8, 11, 12, 21, 22, 25, 26
**Challenging Days:** 4, 9, 10, 16, 17, 18, 23, 24

### AFFIRMATION FOR THE MONTH
"My life is filled with love and joy."

### PRIMARY FOCUS

Take direct action when crises occur, since you may actually be able to use these developments to further your position. Aiming for mere ego gratification can be costly, so watch your motivations!

### HEALTH AND FITNESS

Stress levels are highest early in the month. Get involved in an enjoyable recreational or fitness activity after the 7th, when emotional satisfaction is just as important as physical results.

### ROMANCE AND RELATIONSHIPS

Power struggles can disrupt the peace at home through the 7th, when you may feel that someone else has become too overbearing. Examine your own needs for control, and take a more open approach to sharing your feelings following the New Moon on the 12th. Children can play an active role, and may provide the impetus for many activities. But you can also bring romance back into your life, improve an existing relationship or open the way for someone new after the 20th. Intimate encounters fare best on the 21st, 25th, 29th, and 30th.

### FINANCE AND CAREER

Clarify budgetary problems from the 1st–9th, and deal with legal or contractual disputes by getting all the facts. The point of contention may not exist once the information is clearly presented. Improvements in work relationships benefit from innovative change after the 27th. But be aware of jealousy or undermining near the time of the Full Moon on the 27th, since it can be costly.

### OPPORTUNITY OF THE MONTH

Extra energy applied to personal expression or creative endeavors proves rewarding, but the gratification may be delayed.

**Rewarding Days:** 1, 2, 6, 10, 11, 20, 21, 25, 26, 29, 30
**Challenging Days:** 8, 9, 15, 16, 17, 23, 24

### AFFIRMATION FOR THE MONTH
"I am willing to share my love."

## PRIMARY FOCUS

Intimate relationships, especially partnerships, move into a prominent priority and can provide fundamental support for your self-esteem. Your influence can help another gain recognition.

## HEALTH AND FITNESS

Staying active continues to strengthen your vitality, but you may be tempted to try something for which you're not adequately prepared after the 17th. Get details before you jump in (or off!).

## ROMANCE AND RELATIONSHIPS

If you've been waiting for the right time to let that special someone know how you feel, it's here! Demonstrate your affection by sharing memorable experiences from the 1st–12th. You might even try something different (like talking about your feelings instead of just probing theirs) and discover that you can trust your feelings after all. Achieving a balance in an intimate relationship becomes increasingly important near the Full Moon on the 25th, with some old issues surfacing after the 18th, provoking you to reevaluate.

## FINANCE AND CAREER

Joint ventures provide successful results and bring positive recognition from the 1st–9th and again after the 16th. Be sure to clarify duties and responsibilities on the work front following the New Moon on the 10th. Sign contracts or finalize negotiations, making final adjustments and moving forward from the 10th–24th. Seek support or investment from others after the 20th, when you're in an excellent position to profit, in all respects.

## OPPORTUNITY OF THE MONTH

Flexible maneuverability is easier from the 1st–13th, but your position is stronger on the 21st, 26th, and 29th.

**Rewarding Days:** 2, 3, 7, 8, 17, 18, 21, 22, 25, 26, 29
**Challenging Days:** 1, 4, 5, 11, 12, 13, 19, 20

## AFFIRMATION FOR THE MONTH
"I easily express my gratitude."

### PRIMARY FOCUS

Others may demand more of your attention. Keep your priorities in order by sharing activities and responsibilities as much as possible. Search for solutions instead of provoking confrontation.

### HEALTH AND FITNESS

Pace yourself, since rushing about results in frustrating little accidents that cost time and energy. Your mental attitude goes a long way toward keeping you healthy.

### ROMANCE AND RELATIONSHIPS

Enrich an intimate relationship by exploring your sexual relationship more openly. Frank discussions from the 4th–15th may lead to discoveries that help you move closer to experiencing the ecstasy you desire. The Solar Eclipse on the 10th may prompt you to look more carefully at your relationship, but you're also needing time to explore your life direction. Seek guidance from a reliable individual if you're having difficulty reaching a solution to emotional issues following the Lunar Eclipse on the 24th.

### FINANCE AND CAREER

Working in concert with others can continue to be surprisingly resourceful, and you're in an excellent position to benefit financially from shared efforts. New information surfacing from the 15th–20th is likely to prove distracting, but does not have to sufficiently alter your direction. Take a conservative approach after the 16th, incorporating new ideas into the existing framework instead of laying costly new groundwork.

### OPPORTUNITY OF THE MONTH

Decide what you want from the commitments and situations in your life, and make reasonable adjustments on the 23rd and 24th.

**Rewarding Days:** 4, 5, 14, 15, 19, 23, 24, 27, 31
**Challenging Days:** 1, 2, 9, 10, 16, 17, 25, 29, 30

### AFFIRMATION FOR THE MONTH
"I am patient with myself."

### PRIMARY FOCUS

Business or personal travel is promising and offers inspiring insights into your life direction. You can also benefit from educational opportunities.

### HEALTH AND FITNESS

With the pace slowing, it's easier to find time to take care of yourself; but it's tempting to just forget about it and give yourself a break. Do both: stay active but take time to relax.

### ROMANCE AND RELATIONSHIPS

To bring life back into your relationship, get away from your routine, travel or spend time in more natural settings, getting back in touch with basics. You're ready for something different, and may be enticed by a unique individual from the 6th–12th. Although everything may not be as it appears, you can still enjoy the change of pace and may discover something especially wonderful. This energy can also bring fresh changes to an existing situation, and challenges you to break out of your shell. Laughter, intrigue, and excitement continue through the Full Moon on the 23rd.

### FINANCE AND CAREER

Momentum is building, and you're in a great position to take the lead. Apply your special talents to the challenge at hand from the 5th–12th, when you may actually see miraculous results if you're putting forth your best efforts. Cultural events, travel, or conferences provide you with additional opportunities. Use Mercury's retrograde from June 12–July 6 to complete negotiations or get back in touch with previously supportive individuals.

### OPPORTUNITY OF THE MONTH

Expand your horizons by moving into innovative directions from the 10th–17th, but don't burn all the bridges!

**Rewarding Days:** 1, 10, 11, 15, 16, 19, 20, 23, 24, 28
**Challenging Days:** 3, 5, 6, 12, 13, 25, 26

### AFFIRMATION FOR THE MONTH
"I am inspired by Divine Truth."

### PRIMARY FOCUS

Your efforts toward broadening your scope lead to valuable rewards, but you may have to deal with demands from others who want to be included in your moment of glory.

### HEALTH AND FITNESS

Taking assertive action when dealing with physical distress helps you quickly reach the core of the problem. Fine-tune your health regimen and evaluate your nutritional needs after the 11th.

### ROMANCE AND RELATIONSHIPS

Concentration on the circumstances at hand brings fresh energy into your emotional life. There's great promise in your love life after the New Moon on the 8th, when a different attitude toward your roles gives each of you more freedom. Even family relationships benefit from travel through the 22nd, and it's a great time to share an inspiring experience with loved ones. Emphasize communication through the Full Moon on the 22nd.

### FINANCE AND CAREER

Clear-up contractual issues from the 1st–9th, and be sure to clarify expectations involved in business agreements. Disputes over jointly-held property can escalate through the 17th, when you may reach a stalemate. Detailed investigation may reveal a simple solution, but there can be problems with insurance or taxes. Incorporate the necessary changes and move forward on the 21st–22nd. Business travel, conferences or presentations bring excellent results from the 11th–31st.

### OPPORTUNITY OF THE MONTH

Bring together those who are allied with your ideas on the 12th and 13th. Their support and feedback is extremely valuable.

**Rewarding Days:** 7, 8, 12, 13, 16, 17, 21, 25, 26
**Challenging Days:** 2, 3, 10, 11, 19, 23, 24, 30, 31

### AFFIRMATION FOR THE MONTH
"My life direction feels clear and supports my needs."

### PRIMARY FOCUS

Your career benefits from careful research and documentation. If you've been looking for the answers to pressing questions or dilemmas, this is the time to get to the heart of the matter.

### HEALTH AND FITNESS

Stress on the job can quickly drain your vitality, and although it seems impossible, take time to relax and include personal needs in your priorities. Boost B-vitamins for your nervous system.

### ROMANCE AND RELATIONSHIPS

Tension with superiors or parents can upset the peace, and may even add stress to your love life. Making adjustments which will help keep you out of the line of fire is easier after the New Moon on the 7th, although there can be a power struggle on the 15th–16th and 20th. Enjoying time with your loved ones is much easier from the 21st–31st, when you can put the pressures behind you and become more thoroughly involved in your favorite forms of distraction! Pay special attention to your partner on the 28th.

### FINANCE AND CAREER

Increased involvement with public activities improves your career status from the 1st–15th, but differences in philosophical or political issues can complicate the picture from the 15th–20th. Taking a stubborn position can be costly, so be sure you have the facts before you take your platform! A cautious approach is best with loans or investments. Jumping into a new financial arrangement from the 26th–31st can leave you vulnerable.

### OPPORTUNITY OF THE MONTH

Tension may be high near the Full Moon on the 21st, but it's still a good time to bring things to the surface.

**Rewarding Days:** 4, 8, 9, 13, 14, 17, 18, 21, 22, 31
**Challenging Days:** 2, 6, 7, 19, 20, 26, 27, 28

### AFFIRMATION FOR THE MONTH
"I am protected by a divine power."

### PRIMARY FOCUS

There are fewer ruts on your road to progress, and you can now concentrate on broadening the scope of your influence. It's a good time to improve your status and upgrade your image.

### HEALTH AND FITNESS

Consider a lengthy vacation, or at the least find ways to give your mind a rest from the grind. Soften your attitude and lighten your load!

### ROMANCE AND RELATIONSHIPS

Whether alone or in the company of your partner, travelling or participating in an inspiring retreat can instill peace and harmony. Your needs in an intimate relationship are more easily defined, and your self-esteem improves. Incorporating a greater sense of free expression during the New Moon on the 5th can lead to more satisfying romance by the Full Moon on the 19th. This period emphasizes your need to balance giving and receiving love, instead of just experiencing one side or the other.

### FINANCE AND CAREER

If you're pleased with your work, be sure to let others know. Consider the value of your services or products after the 7th, and find ways to improve that value throughout the long transit of Venus in Scorpio from the 7th through the end of the year. Clarify any misunderstandings occurring from the 18th–23rd, to avoid protracted disagreements. And be sure you possess accurate and clear information before proceeding with new ventures.

### OPPORTUNITY OF THE MONTH

Take bold steps on the 1st and follow-through on those efforts on the 18th to assure long-term success.

**Rewarding Days:** 1, 5, 6, 9, 10, 13, 14, 18, 19, 28
**Challenging Days:** 2, 3, 4, 15, 16, 22, 23, 24, 30

### AFFIRMATION FOR THE MONTH
"My thoughts and words and inspired by truth."

## PRIMARY FOCUS

Matters of the heart have a high priority, and you can also see beneficial results in your career. However, overindulgence in those things you love most can be extremely expensive!

## HEALTH AND FITNESS

It's tempting to be more spectator than participant, but staying active now will help you stay on track and keep your energy stronger.

## ROMANCE AND RELATIONSHIPS

You have some important choices to make, because the energy of Venus and Jupiter transiting together in Scorpio can add a high level of charisma to your personality. Your signals can definitely be seen, and you may have more than one fish on the hook. Look within yourself during the New Moon on the 4th to clarify your motivations. If you really feel good about yourself, then the situation you need will be clear. Take a second look at yourself and your choices after the 13th. You may change your mind!

## FINANCE AND CAREER

Positive results from investments of time and resources can change your financial picture from the 1st–19th. But you're in the best position to make decisions from the 1st–8th. Use the period after the 13th to get rid of things that have just been taking up space. Double-check all communications, documents, and arrangements after the 24th, when delays and surprising changes can be absolutely frustrating and may be costly.

## OPPORTUNITY OF THE MONTH

You're protected when reaching out or taking risks from the 1st–12th, but be sure to acknowledge your limitations!

**Rewarding Days:** 2, 3, 6, 7, 10, 11, 15, 16, 25, 30
**Challenging Days:** 1, 5, 12, 13, 14, 20, 21, 27, 28

## AFFIRMATION FOR THE MONTH

"My life is filled with love and abundance in all things!"

## PRIMARY FOCUS

You're still making progress, but may find competition when moving toward the recognition you hope to achieve. It's easy to be too abrasive, so be aware of the responses of others.

## HEALTH AND FITNESS

Extra attention to your physical needs keeps you in the pink, but ignoring problems now can lead to long-term hassles.

## ROMANCE AND RELATIONSHIPS

With the Solar Eclipse in Scorpio on the 3rd, you're likely to be experiencing everything as larger-than-life. This amplified emphasis gives you a chance to deal with reality instead of assumptions or hopes. You can sense the spiritual implications of your relationships more clearly, but may also be ready for a different approach. By the time of the Lunar Eclipse on the 18th you will have taken several looks at your partner, and might decide you're ready for a change. Changing partners is not the only answer; you could change your attitudes!

## FINANCE AND CAREER

Your drive to succeed can blind you to the circumstances or needs of others. It's easy to step on the wrong toes, particularly after the 20th. Before that time, improve your status and listen to the concerns of your co-workers, employees, and clients. Alterations in your approach and environmental changes can give you a more appropriate image. Expert advice is helpful from the 11th–16th. Investments look promising on the 21st, 22nd, and 27th.

## OPPORTUNITY OF THE MONTH

Give yourself time to take a personal inventory during the eclipses on the 3rd and 18th.

**Rewarding Days:** 3, 4, 7, 8, 11, 12, 21, 22, 26, 27, 30
**Challenging Days:** 1, 5, 9, 10, 16, 17, 18, 23, 24

## AFFIRMATION FOR THE MONTH
"I am aware of my true self."

### PRIMARY FOCUS

The impressions you make now are likely to stay with you for quite a while, so be sure you're projecting the image you want others to remember!

### HEALTH AND FITNESS

The intensity of stress decreases after the 11th. To maintain the balance you need, shift gears gradually. Watch your nutrition!

### ROMANCE AND RELATIONSHIPS

Now that Venus is moving in direct motion, your reservations or questions about your love life may be less bothersome. You're still needing to fine-tune your commitments. If you're ending an involvement, be sure you're actually reaching closure. But if you're at the beginning or stabilizing an existing situation, it's crucial to continue with honesty. Your reaction to family pressures from the 1st–12th may create a breech in your relationship, but this can be mended through discerning communication after the 22nd. Keep money out of the conversation.

### FINANCE AND CAREER

Be careful not to get caught in power struggles at work which have nothing to do with you from the 1st–13th. Stepping in where you don't belong is costly. Spend some time from the New Moon on the 2nd through the Full Moon on the 17th examining your financial picture. Errors discovered now can be remedied. If left untended, they are likely to cause long-term hassles. Consult with a friendly business associate the week of the 11th.

### OPPORTUNITY OF THE MONTH

Clear out those things which are no longer useful, since supporting excessive clutter now is emotionally claustrophobic.

**Rewarding Days:** 1, 4, 5, 8, 9, 18, 19, 23, 24, 28
**Challenging Days:** 6, 7, 13, 14, 15, 21, 22

### AFFIRMATION FOR THE MONTH
"I respect my limitations."

# ⚹ SAGITTARIUS ⚹
## The Archer

### November 23 to December 22

**Element:** Fire

**Quality:** Mutable

**Polarity:** Masculine/Yang

**Planetary Ruler:** Jupiter

**Meditation:** "All things in harmony with Higher Law are possible"

**Gemstone:** Turquoise

**Power Stones:** Lapis lazuli, sodalite, azurite

**Glyph:** Archer's arrow

**Key Phrase:** "I understand"

**Anatomy:** Hips, thighs, sciatic nerve

**Colors:** Royal blue and purple

**Animal:** Fleet-footed animals

**Myths/Legends:** Athena, Chiron

**House Association:** 9th

**Opposite Sign:** Gemini

**Flower:** Narcissus

**Key Word:** Expansion

**Positive Expression:**
Philanthropic
Optimistic
Adventurous
Athletic
Understanding
Wise
Generous
Jovial
Tolerant
Philosophical

**Misuse of Energy:**
Extravagant
Overzealous
Foolish
Gluttonous
Opinionated
Self-righteous
Condescending
Bigoted
Blunt

# ♐ SAGITTARIUS ♐

## Your Ego's Strengths and Weaknesses

Your exploration of life can lead you through many frontiers as you strive to reach an understanding of life's basic truth. As the philosopher of the zodiac, you're constantly questioning and eager to expand your base of knowledge. Your enthusiastic optimism often provides buoyant inspiration for others, and your honest, straightforward approach refreshes stale situations.

Through the energy of Jupiter, your planetary ruler, you're stimulated to constantly reach beyond your current limitations in order to experience as much of life as you possibly can. Your fascination with other cultures may lead to a desire to master at least one foreign language, and can be your stimulus to travel. Your discontent with the status of being "merely human" stimulates you to search for a higher level of consciousness.

Since you're always looking forward, you can easily grow impatient when the pace of life fails to keep up with your ideals. As you reach out for broader frontiers, those who yearn to be with you may be left behind. Your generous spirit instills an atmosphere of trust and understanding. However, you tend to expect more from others than they can deliver and can also undermine your own growth through feeling that you should be more than you are.

Although your zeal can blaze a path to wisdom it can just as easily lead you toward self-righteousness and judgmental fanaticism. The greater truth may be that you don't really know everything, and, more importantly, that you don't have to! You carry the torch of hope and can light a path which illuminates higher spiritual law.

## Your Career Development

Your career needs to give you plenty of room for independent action and should offer you a sense of unlimited potential. With an ability to relate to people from varied circumstances, you're a natural in sales situations and can be quite adept in public relations, advertising or as an agent or representative for others. Foreign service or diplomatic duties may also pique your interest.

With your abilities to sway others through your speech, you may be drawn to law, politics, or the ministry. Writing, journalism, or publishing may offer excellent opportunities to express your ideas. Speculative investments can be lucrative for you, whether in stock, sports, racing, or in other markets. Your constant desire to learn and teach may stimulate you to seek a profession in education where you can stimulate incentive in your students to reach high levels of personal mastery. No matter what your career choice, you think big!

## Your Approach to Romance

For you, love can be the most grand adventure of all, and the game of romance an absolute delight. You like to call the shots, and prefer not to become tangled in the lair until you're ready. Although you like to know another person's way of thinking before you get physical, you can be most intrigued by someone whose background is distinctively different from your own.

While you're experimenting with different relationship models, you may leave your former lovers behind in a cloud of dust. But once you're ready to make a commitment, you can be a steadfast and sensual partner. Along with the other fire signs—Aries, Leo, and other Sagittarians—you prefer a relationship filled with passionate interchange. And you're most comfortable when your easygoing nature is not too ruffled. With Aries, an invigorating excitement can keep your love strong. Leo's dramatic intensity warms your heart, and another Sagittarian is likely to share your favorite pastimes of reading and travel.

Taurus' slow pace may feel cumbersome to you. Your attraction to Gemini, your zodiac opposite can lead to exceptional discussions and may spark an exciting partnership. Cancer's need to take care of you can feel claustrophobic. And although you may appreciate Virgo's ideas, your broader view can spark disagreements. Libra's refined grace is fascinating and you may enjoy a lasting relationship. But you'll have to stay on your toes to avoid falling victim to the allure of Scorpio.

While Capricorn offers steadfast security, you may not feel completely open. Companionable Aquarius shows independence which supports your needs to grow. However, you may feel you cannot trust a relationship with Pisces, whose imagination is enticing but frequently hard to follow.

## Your Use of Power

Your sense of power arises when you have plenty of room to exercise your own ideas and actualize your potential. A power which confines is stultifying. Wisdom and understanding represent high levels of power to you, but the time it takes to develop them is a bit frustrating. You're willing to put forth the effort to get through all the foolish double-talk in order to achieve true enlightenment.

You realize that the truth does, indeed, set you free. And although you may seek truth, you have to be careful to avoid shutting your mind and looking for truth only as you see it. To have the abundant life, you may first be required to harmonize your actions with your Higher Needs. Otherwise, you can fall into a trap of hedonistic desire or fanatical beliefs which become, in themselves, your own prison.

The power of wisdom may come in many forms. Through travel, study, writing, teaching, or inspiring others you may recognize that your real power is connected to sharing the future through improving understanding among all humankind. Use your gifts and energy to unlock the minds of humanity to higher truth.

### Famous Sagittarians
Shirley Chisholm, Emily Dickinson, Joe DiMaggio, Amy Grant, Jimmy Hendrix, Sam Kinison, Don King, Howie Mandell, Monica Seles, Lee Trevino, Dick Van Dyke, Patricia Wettig

# THE YEAR AHEAD FOR SAGITTARIUS

Progress may come a bit more slowly than you like during 1994, but you can take deliberate steps to assure that you will continue to move forward. Your greatest freedom originates within your mind, and this is certainly a time of opening your consciousness and expanding your inner awareness. It's in translating your inner experience to external reality that you run into blockades! You're challenged to keep your awareness in the present while not losing your ability to see the vision of hope for the future.

Your planetary ruler, Jupiter, transits in Scorpio until December 9th, when it moves into Sagittarius. Throughout this cycle, you may feel you're on the brink of new opportunity, and that it's just beyond your grasp. In reality, while Jupiter travels through your Solar 12th House, you are reaching further than you may recognize. It's just that the reach is within the deeper realms of consciousness instead of just the outer realms of physical manifestation. This is a time of blessing and you may sense that you're more closely in touch with that quality some define as a guardian angel. Give yourself time to enjoy periods of inner contemplation, allowing your thoughts to become unified with a greater wisdom. Surrender your vision to the magnificent vantage point of a higher plane, and ask for guidance from that part of you which connects to The Source.

The Lunar Eclipse in Sagittarius occurs on May 25th, and marks a period when you may feel a need to get back in touch with your primary needs. Take stock of your inner self, and watch for the areas in which you feel vulnerable or extra-sensitive. The effects of this eclipse may last several months. By approaching this period with greater sensitivity to your own needs, you can use this time to naturally move away from the elements of your past which limit you, and move toward those things which encourage you to continue on a more satisfying path.

The Solar Eclipses in Taurus and Scorpio bring forth an emphasis of your needs to become involved in the drama of life on different terms. This year marks a time when you can reach out to others and make a difference in the quality of their lives and your own. But you cannot rescue by simply exercising your will over that of others. You're required to participate in experiences of service through developing true compassion. As you learn to see the part of you which is connected to the collective consciousness of humanity, you realize that by rescuing yourself from defeatist attitudes, you're aiding human evolution. This is your time to forge a path toward self-improvement and personal development which will actually change the focus of your life. Lip-service is no longer enough. This is the time to act!

**If you were born from November 23 to December 5, you're feeling a sense of restriction while Saturn transits in square aspect to your Sun.** Although this is not an entirely pleasant experience, it can give you a sense of direction and focus which helps you refine your path and redefine your identity. Now's the time to take stock of your life, measuring both your achievements and losses. It's easy to find all the things that went wrong, to discover everything that's not working, or to curse the elements of yourself you least enjoy. But that experience accomplished without self-love can be defeating. Your true challenge is to uncover the purest aspects of yourself and give them space to grow. Look carefully. You're likely to find a grain of wisdom which whispers into your ear the truth of yourself. Listen to that inner voice, feel the strength of the core of your being. Eliminate those things from your life which have been holding you back. Get rid of the attitudes, circumstances and relationships which no longer fit. Use this time to reach closure, to end the chapters that have been dragging on without completion. Let go of the pain of your past, which only serves to keep you in misery. Open to the element of yourself that is the wise teacher. Find ways to exercise this knowledge. Take time to teach what you know. Allow yourself to learn what you've desired to understand. Now you are becoming responsible in ways that will make sense. By taking control of your life again, you can feel good about the choices to be responsible. Physical health can be undermined during this cycle if you ignore symptoms or if you fail to handle stress in positive ways. Your body is your responsibility, and all the ways you've taken care of yourself in the past really pay off during this time. But if you need to change old habits or formulate a new health care regime, then this is one of your best periods to accomplish such goals.

You're experiencing some tension from Uranus and Neptune transiting semisquare to your Sun if you were born from November 27 to December 3. However, these energies spark a level of imagination and intuition which help you move more easily into a different life direction. Even though you may feel some restraints from Saturn's travels (above), you also sense that letting go doesn't have to be quite as painful as you might have imagined. Create a steady foundation, investigate the facts, and then take the risk of giving your creative individuality more room for expression.

Chiron is squaring your Sun if you were born from November 25 to December 16, and you're likely to feel a strong internal pressure to uncover a sense of life purpose. You make this discovery on your own, and with your sense of judgment and understanding. The pain which you feel may be coming from a sense that someone else's idea of your life path does not fit your own! In searching to find justification for your actions you may really be looking for an affirmation of your existence. From whom? Why? Stop; listen once again to your inner voice. You are becoming whole, and this process of healing brings remarkable needs for self-acceptance. In cherishing yourself, your traumas begin to fade away and your life direction is much more easily defined.

You're taking steps to incorporate a greater level of sensitivity into your life if you were born from December 12–15. By becoming more mindful in each of your daily activities, you can allow room for the energy of Neptune's transit semisextile to your Sun to help you enhance your sensibilities. The intangible realms of reality are more closely felt during this transit, and you may be driven by a need to feel more unified with the Source of All Life. This cycle can help you relinquish the barriers which have kept you from feeling compassion and love. Additionally, your creative activities are likely to flow more easily and may take on a more spiritual quality. If you've been struggling to emotionally release an old relationship or to find it in your heart to forgive another, this energy stimulates a deeper sense of true grace. It's a good idea to look deeply into yourself for the origins of old guilt, and to use this cycle to help you relinquish those negative feelings through self-forgiveness. Take the time to do something for others who reach out for help. With a sense of enhanced awareness and deep compassion, you really can make a difference.

**If you were born from December 13–17** you're stepping into new directions while Uranus travels in semisextile to your Sun. These are not drastic changes, but can stimulate a more exciting dimension of life experience. Listen carefully to the intuitive insights accompanying this cycle, since the mechanisms you incorporate now can help guide you for years to come. Find ways to allow individuality to emerge; reach out a bit more. This is the time to enjoy the freedom of being yourself and to share the unique elements of your personality with others. New relationships, especially friendships emerging now, can be more supportive of your special talents and abilities. At the core of this cycle is a feeling of discovery: discovery of your Self.

**For Sagittarians born from December 16–21,** Pluto is transiting semisextile to your Sun. This marks a period of self-realization and can signal a time to move beyond one circumstance into a different direction. The changes you're experiencing may feel like a gradual metamorphosis, and offer you the chance to drop some of your old defenses. Think of this as a cycle of removing layers, bringing you closer to your essential being. Scientific study or research undertaken now reveal remarkable results. Research into your own background will give you the liberty of knowing more about yourself. It's a good time to take some of your unused talents off the shelf and give them room to grow. Personal awareness intensifies, but just as readily, your perception of the world around you can shift. Incorporate your enhanced self-knowledge to make changes which will restore your power to fulfill your destiny.

## Tools to Make a Difference

Since many of the changes facing you during 1994 involve a shift in awareness, taking time to develop your consciousness can be highly beneficial. In addition to a period of meditation, begin to observe yourself throughout the day. Become more conscious during those times when habits take the driver's seat. If you want to change things, it's good to know what's already operating on "automatic pilot!" Listen to the messages you give yourself, and set out to replace negative thoughts with affirmations of support and hope.

You're more effective when you're in motion, and this is a great time to direct your actions in harmony with your changing awareness. As your consciousness grows, become more connected to the things that are happening in your body. If you're feeling tension or stress, use your periods of exercise and play to help relieve the tension and allow your energy to flow more smoothly. Use this time of increasing self-discipline to learn a sport or develop an exercise program. You're well-suited for martial arts, hatha yoga, or Tai Chi, but you also need to give yourself plenty of time to get outside and commune with natural life forms.

If you're feeling scattered, use your power stones (turquoise and lapis lazuli) to help you focus. Clear your mind and ask for divine protection and guidance. Then move forward with confidence. During your periods of meditation, see yourself standing under an azure sky. Breathe in the energy of this color. Listen for the sounds of peace; feel the presence of angelic beings who watch over your journeys and guide your way. Offer your gratitude and thanks for this guidance. Enjoy the knowledge that they are always with you (but drive your own car; angels are not good drivers!).

## Affirmation for the Year

"I am attentive, awake and aware!"

# ACTION TABLES FOR SAGITTARIUS

These dates reflect the best (but not the only) times for success and ease in these activities according to your Sun Sign.

| | |
|---|---|
| **Change Residence** | Feb. 1–20; Mar. 18–Apr. 8 |
| **Request a Raise** | Dec. 2–3 |
| **Begin a Course of Study** | Feb. 10; Aug. 7 |
| **Visit a Doctor** | Apr. 26–May 9; Sep. 27–Oct. 18; Nov. 10–29 |
| **Start a Diet** | Jan. 20–21; Feb. 16–17; Mar. 15–16; Apr. 11–13; May 9–10; June 5–6; July 2–4, 30–31; Aug. 26–27; Sep. 22–23; Oct. 20–21; Nov. 16–17; Dec. 13–14 |
| **Begin a Romance** | April 11 |
| **Join a Club** | Oct. 5 |
| **Seek Employment** | Apr. 26–May 9; Aug. 18–Sep. 3 |
| **Take a Vacation** | Jan. 27–28; Feb. 23–24; Mar. 23–24; Apr. 19–20; May 16–17; June 12–14; July 10–11; Aug. 6–7; Sep. 2–4, 30; Oct. 1, 27–28; Nov. 23–25; Dec. 21–22 |
| **Change Your Wardrobe** | Apr. 9–24 |
| **End a Relationship** | Dec. 18 |
| **Seek Professional Advice** | Jan. 22–23; Feb. 18–19; Mar. 18–19; Apr. 14–15; May 11–13; June 8–9; July 5–6; Aug. 1–3, 29–30; Sep. 25–26; Oct. 22–23; Nov. 18–19; Dec. 16–17 |
| **Have a Makeover** | Dec. 2–3 |
| **Obtain a Loan** | Jan. 25–26; Feb. 21–22; Mar. 20–22; Apr. 17–18; May 14–15; June 10–11; July 7–8; Aug. 4–5, 31; Sep. 1, 27–28, 29; Oct. 25–26; Nov. 21–22; Dec. 18–20 |

### PRIMARY FOCUS

Put your resources to work for you by making the most of existing circumstances. Concentrate on making contacts, attending meetings, and getting caught up on communications.

### HEALTH AND FITNESS

Incorporate exercises which build strength and endurance into your fitness routines this month. Stay alert from the 16th–22nd, when surprises can throw you off balance and lead to accidents.

### ROMANCE AND RELATIONSHIPS

Doubts or insecurity about your self-worth can have a detrimental effect on relationships from the 9th–20th, and you may find yourself on the defensive for no apparent reason. Watch a tendency to project your own insecurities onto others, resulting in mistrust or uncertainty. Get in touch with your deeper feelings, and talk about them with an intimate friend or partner. Contact with a sibling is positive from the 13th–15th. Communication improves after the 14th, and open sharing works wonders during the Full Moon on the 27th.

### FINANCE AND CAREER

Failure to pay adequate attention to the details of your financial picture can result in budgetary nightmares from the 1st–21st. Be sure to look at the current and the projected financial figures following the New Moon on the 11th, when reasonable planning can give you some breathing room. Following your intuitive sense about a deal from the 7th–17th can save you time and money! Network with influential resources after the 21st.

### OPPORTUNITY OF THE MONTH

Business travel, meetings or conferences offer potential longterm gain on the 23rd, 27th, 28th, and 31st.

**Rewarding Days:** 4, 5, 8, 9, 12, 13, 17, 27, 28, 31
**Challenging Days:** 2, 3, 7, 15, 16, 20, 22, 23, 29, 30

### AFFIRMATION FOR THE MONTH
"My life is filled with abundant love."

## PRIMARY FOCUS

Eager to get out and about, you can make progress in negotiations, benefit from travel, and enjoy sharing exciting ideas. But be sure to take care of responsibilities at home first.

## HEALTH AND FITNESS

It's easy to give in to a tendency to worry over family matters, and pressure in these areas can undermine your effectiveness. Reshaping attitudes and staying active helps improve your health.

## ROMANCE AND RELATIONSHIPS

Although family relationships draw much of your attention, a lack of agreement with them concerning your goals or plans can be uncomfortable near the time of the New Moon on the 10th. Share your ideas with those who can support them, or, better yet, keep them to yourself until you're certain! Solidify an intimate relationship by sharing time at home after the 12th. Time for contemplation and creative expression helps calm your mind from the 20th–26th.

## FINANCE AND CAREER

Take an assertive approach to business deals early this month, but be sure to respect boundaries and avoid sensitive areas from the 8th–11th. Mercury's retrograde from 2/11 to 3/04 can bring a chance to get back into a situation you thought to be hopeless, although you'll have to do some repair work before you're happy with it. A stalemate from the 16th–21st can be frustrating, but old allies come through after the 23rd.

## OPPORTUNITY OF THE MONTH

A hopeful, progressive attitude boosts you into a position of influence from the 1st–5th. Find practical ways to make changes.

**Rewarding Days:** 1, 4, 5, 9, 14, 15, 23, 24, 27, 28
**Challenging Days:** 3, 11, 12, 17, 18, 19, 20, 26

## AFFIRMATION FOR THE MONTH
"My words are inspired by truth."

## PRIMARY FOCUS

Expressing creative ideas and using your talents to their fullest brings positive attention and recognition. Share your celebrations with those who really care about you.

## HEALTH AND FITNESS

Emotional stress can undermine your sense of well-being. Extra attention to projects at home can actually help alleviate some of the tension. But time for recreation is crucial after the 8th!

## ROMANCE AND RELATIONSHIPS

Spending some extra time with a sibling goes a long way toward mending fences from the 1st–16th. But be sure your motivations are honest! Family interactions run a bit more smoothly, but you're ready for some romance and enjoyment after the 8th, and may prefer the company of an intimate partner. Find time to share your favorite forms of entertainment after the 13th. Your playful side emerges in droll circumstances, and you can find a superb outlet among friends or children near the Full Moon on the 27th.

## FINANCE AND CAREER

Dig into the details of financial or business negotiations from the 1st–17th in order to make a more satisfactory decision. Contracts signed from the 22nd–26th may have the best chance of success. You may be disappointed by evaluations of your performance made from the 24th–26th; show your best efforts and be prepared if your work is under scrutiny during this time. Money matters can become confusing after the 26th.

## OPPORTUNITY OF THE MONTH

A break in routine from the 13th–15th gives you time to enjoy loving energy, and can leave you with a fresh perspective.

**Rewarding Days:** 3, 4, 8, 9, 13, 14, 23, 24, 27, 28, 31
**Challenging Days:** 1, 7, 10, 11, 18, 19, 25, 26

## AFFIRMATION FOR THE MONTH
"I share my feelings of love with others. "

## PRIMARY FOCUS

Enjoyment is the rule, and if it isn't fun, you're probably not interested right now! It's easy to underemphasize responsibilities, which can lead to problems if you appear to be non-productive.

## HEALTH AND FITNESS

Activities around the house can fill your free time. Get involved in recreational sports after the 14th, when your play can keep you physically vital.

## ROMANCE AND RELATIONSHIPS

Family squabbles or harsh words can easily injure your feelings from the 1st–13th, but you can also be the instigator of problems if you fail to think before you speak or act! In your eagerness to get things done or to express your desires, it's easy to forget the feelings of others. Your passion gains momentum during the New Moon on the 10th, enlivening a love relationship and stimulating your creativity. Time spent alone or in a quiet setting with your lover during the Full Moon on the 25th helps to stabilize your feelings.

## FINANCE AND CAREER

You're ready to get a lot done, but may seem too abrupt through the 12th. If you're wondering why others are always challenging you, observe your own behavior. You may appear competitive when you're really just eager! It's easy to get carried away with spending after the 16th, so try to stay within your budget instead of yielding to impulse. Allow room for unforeseen expenses in creative projects from the 18th–24th. Try not to panic.

## OPPORTUNITY OF THE MONTH

Launch important enterprises after the 10th for best results. But be sure you're on a firm foundation or you may have to start over.

**Rewarding Days:** 4, 5, 9, 10, 19, 20, 23, 24, 27, 28
**Challenging Days:** 2, 6, 7, 8, 14, 15, 16, 21, 22

## AFFIRMATION FOR THE MONTH
"I feel safe when I share my feelings."

## PRIMARY FOCUS

By maintaining an equitable balance in personal and working relationships you'll see better cooperation from others. Sharing resources is much better than competing for them.

## HEALTH AND FITNESS

Enjoyable forms of activities continue to provide your impetus to stay fit. Stay alert to surprising environmental or circumstantial changes from the 14th–20th, when awareness is your best protection.

## ROMANCE AND RELATIONSHIPS

Partnerships are tested from the 1st–7th, and you may discover that you've been too easily swayed by influences from your past or family pressures. Examine what you need from your relationship instead of what others expect. Watch a tendency to rebel for the wrong reasons after the Solar Eclipse on the 10th! Confrontations with unresolved past emotional issues helps pinpoint your feelings of vulnerability. Focus on now and feel the difference during the Lunar Eclipse in Sagittarius on the 24th.

## FINANCE AND CAREER

Speculative ventures bring successful results, but there may be some delay in seeing profits. The temptation to jump into a new opportunity is powerful from the 13th–21st, but it can be costly to act without thorough investigation. Seek the advice of someone you trust before you make presentations or put yourself on the spot. Taking a risk can work, but if you're not prepared to handle the responsibilities, it works against you.

## OPPORTUNITY OF THE MONTH

Become more self-aware on the 24th and 25th, when you may discover or uncover aspects of your needs that you've ignored far too long.

**Rewarding Days:** 2, 6, 7, 16, 17, 21, 25, 26, 29
**Challenging Days:** 4, 5, 10, 11, 12, 13, 19, 23, 31

## AFFIRMATION FOR THE MONTH
"I am aware of myself and my environment."

## PRIMARY FOCUS

Frustrations with work can undermine your confidence and vitality unless you take time to balance stress, concentrate on the job, and avoid becoming distracted.

## HEALTH AND FITNESS

Staying active can increase your vitality, but a tendency to push beyond your limitations can lead to problems. Consult with a health professional to determine the root cause of any health problems.

## ROMANCE AND RELATIONSHIPS

Relationships may not seem to be worth the effort you have to put into them, but improvements result from honest communication (including listening to your partner!). Examine your own attitudes toward your role as a partner near the New Moon on the 9th. Misunderstandings over money issues may camouflage an underlying sexual frustration. Clarify the real source of conflict mid-month to avoid adding fuel to the fire. Share your spiritual yearnings, or spend time in natural surroundings to help balance your energies after the 15th.

## FINANCE AND CAREER

If piles of paperwork cover your enthusiasm for your job, tackle the problems and make room for new projects. Careful attention to financial details from the 5th–18th ultimately saves time, and may even safeguard your reputation. But complications during Mercury's retrograde period from June 12–July 6 call for a second look before you finally decide or agree to contracts. Listen to your intuition! You may not really need to take the risk.

## OPPORTUNITY OF THE MONTH

Schedule follow-up consultations or meetings from the 17th–19th or on the 21st, when you may feel more confident about your ideas.

**Rewarding Days:** 3, 13, 14, 17, 18, 21, 22, 25, 30
**Challenging Days:** 1, 6, 8, 9, 15, 16, 20, 27, 28, 29

## AFFIRMATION FOR THE MONTH
"I trust my inner feelings."

## PRIMARY FOCUS

Your competitive drive to reach your goals facilitates progress, but be sure you're aware of the effect of your actions upon others. Ignoring their needs or demands can cause tremendous set-backs.

## HEALTH AND FITNESS

Heightened activity levels after the 3rd increase vitality, but you can also be tempted to burn the candle at both ends. Eliminate those things you really don't have to do.

## ROMANCE AND RELATIONSHIPS

In an eagerness to have things your way, you can alienate the ones you're trying hardest to impress. You gain only temporary relief by riding off into the sunset. Try to find a common ground from the 1st–10th, and then deliberately slow down and take a look at the opportunities for growth from the 16th–24th. You may decide that your impulse to throw it all away is entirely too costly. Spend time examining your fears near the Full Moon on the 22nd, when you gain insights into the real nature of control and power.

## FINANCE AND CAREER

Taking action without adequate preparation can result in unexpected expenditures or delays near the time of the New Moon on the 8th. However, if you're willing to make adjustments, this can be a good time to reach agreements. You might prefer to take things at face value, but others may have hidden motives. Consult with a trusted advisor to guide you through the rough spots after the 22nd. Until then, watch out for sharks!

## OPPORTUNITY OF THE MONTH

Careful investigation on the 10th–11th proves worth the effort, and may expose facts which lead you to change your position.

**Rewarding Days:** 1, 10, 11, 14, 18, 19, 23, 24, 27, 28
**Challenging Days:** 2, 3, 4, 5, 6, 12, 13, 25, 26

## AFFIRMATION FOR THE MONTH
"My actions are guided by Divine Wisdom."

## PRIMARY FOCUS

Rewards for your valiant efforts are finally forthcoming, but you're still not out of the woods. Use your new resources wisely, and develop strong bonds with loyal allies.

## HEALTH AND FITNESS

Find a positive outlet for your competitive drive, and keep your goals within reasonable limits. Now's the time to trim away excess and fortify strength.

## ROMANCE AND RELATIONSHIPS

Inspirational experiences or travel can instill positive change in your love life. Develop trust by sharing your ideas and offering mutual support. The New Moon on the 7th opens the way for hopeful progress, and you may feel like you're on the brink of valuable self-discovery. Watch a tendency to withhold your true feelings from the 12th–16th. Honesty with yourself is most important, and a good friend can also provide strength. Explore your dreams and share fantasies with your partner during the Full Moon on the 21st.

## FINANCE AND CAREER

Opportunities for recognition can lead to advancement or strengthening of your position at work from the 3rd–22nd. Take the initiative on the 15th and 16th, but be sure you're thoroughly prepared. Mistakes in your accounting or simple absentmindedness can be expensive from the 13th–18th. Finances are improving, and others are more supportive. But there is a price for their support, and you need to understand it from the outset!

## OPPORTUNITY OF THE MONTH

You're poised to move forward from the 14th–20th, and gain real progress by staying aware of the larger picture.

**Rewarding Days:** 6, 7, 10, 11, 15, 16, 19, 20, 24, 25
**Challenging Days:** 1, 2, 8, 9, 18, 21, 22, 26, 28, 29

## AFFIRMATION FOR THE MONTH
"I am aware of my goals for the future."

## PRIMARY FOCUS

Friends and others who share your ideals and interests provide your best avenue for auspicious change. Offering support may also lead to unexpected rewards.

## HEALTH AND FITNESS

Now's the time to take direct action to get to the core of any physical discomforts or problems. Consider joining both alternative and traditional therapies to be your best avenue of treatment.

## ROMANCE AND RELATIONSHIPS

Reaching an understanding with your partner about your sexual needs can be uncomfortable unless you're both willing to take a more playful approach toward enjoying one another. An inability to achieve intimacy in either a new or an existing relationship may be an indicator that you're still stuck in the pain of an old trauma. Look at all your relationships as friendships, and consider ending those which show dishonesty or a lack of mutual understanding and respect. Be honest about your feelings toward parents near the time of the Full Moon on the 19th.

## FINANCE AND CAREER

You may be thrust into the spotlight, and will enjoy sharing your victory with friends and colleagues. But demands from your superiors are intense, and you'll progress faster by understanding their expectations. Review your own progress on the 5th, and take steps to strengthen your assets from the 7th–12th. Your flexibility during unexpected changes gives you an edge from the 19th–21st.

## OPPORTUNITY OF THE MONTH

Integration of more traditional values into your plans widens your support from the 25th–30th.

**Rewarding Days:** 3, 4, 7, 8, 11, 12, 15, 16, 20, 21, 30
**Challenging Days:** 5, 6, 10, 14, 18, 19, 25, 26

## AFFIRMATION FOR THE MONTH
"My mind is focused on the present moment."

## PRIMARY FOCUS

Spiritual inspiration and inner strength provide new direction for your creativity. Broaden your horizons through travel, study, teaching or writing.

## HEALTH AND FITNESS

Improve your vitality and resilience by getting involved in physical activities which discipline both your body and your mind. Concentrate greater effort on "inner" fitness exercises, too.

## ROMANCE AND RELATIONSHIPS

Time in private, intimate surroundings provides a greater incentive for developing your relationship. Add intrigue and excitement to enliven a love that's grown stale following the New Moon on the 4th; or, if you're single, risk an introduction. A new relationship may seem more dream than reality, but can take shape with surprising speed. In either case, you can create problems if you project too many expectations upon your partner! Romance can be intensely promising during the Full Moon on the 19th. After the 23rd, be careful of flirtations, since they may lead to trouble!

## FINANCE AND CAREER

Work to launch community projects early this month. Concentrate more energy on long-term developments from the 1st–19th, since much of what is begun now will require time and planning. Mercury's retrograde from the 9th–30th offers an incentive to familiarize yourself with what needs to be done behind the scenes. And watch your spending after the 22nd, since it's easy to be intrigued to something which is not what it seems to be.

## OPPORTUNITY OF THE MONTH

Be aware of your motivations before you decide to act. Selfish greed leads to high-priced lessons.

**Rewarding Days:** 1, 4, 5, 8, 9, 17, 18, 27, 28
**Challenging Days:** 2, 3, 7, 15, 16, 22, 23, 24

## AFFIRMATION FOR THE MONTH
"I am filled with love and joy!"

### PRIMARY FOCUS

Reach out to explore new ideas, share information and incorporate changes into your plans. Prepare your consciousness to allow room for growth, while still honoring your responsibilities.

### HEALTH AND FITNESS

Keep track of your progress and continue to move toward increasing endurance while enhancing resilience. You may need to adjust your routine after the 20th.

### ROMANCE AND RELATIONSHIPS

Misunderstandings can arise if you jump to conclusions or fail to confirm your plans from the 1st–8th. Reconsideration of an existing relationship exposes questions about your spiritual compatibility. Whether in romantic or family relationships, different spiritual pathways do not necessarily indicate a loss of love! The important question is for you to determine the best path for yourself. Take time for inner contemplation or meditation during the New Moon on the 3rd and the Full Moon on the 18th. Get your bearing, then act.

### FINANCE AND CAREER

Conferences, meetings, or business travel offer a chance for you to share ideas or products, but can be stressful if you're feeling overwhelmed by the competition. Do some research before you step into the spotlight. You're in a good position to work effectively with others, but may feel more comfortable in new surroundings after the 22nd. Background work can be rewarding, and gives you an edge in financial plans after the 20th.

### OPPORTUNITY OF THE MONTH

Your enthusiasm sparkles on the 24th, 25th and 28th. Sharing your energy with others leads to gain for all concerned.

**Rewarding Days:** 1, 5, 6, 9, 10, 14, 15, 24, 25, 28, 29
**Challenging Days:** 3, 8, 11, 12, 18, 19, 20, 26, 27

### AFFIRMATION FOR THE MONTH

"My mind is connected to the Source of All Wisdom."

### PRIMARY FOCUS
The freedom you're feeling gives a strong boost to your confidence, and may propel you into new circumstances. Keep your priorities intact to avoid feeling stretched too far.

### HEALTH AND FITNESS
Your drive can push you beyond your limits unless you allow yourself to release the stress you're feeling. Take time for a massage after all that power-brokering!

### ROMANCE AND RELATIONSHIPS
Romance is fine, but only if you feel it doesn't get in the way of your progress. Clarify your priorities during the New Moon on the 2nd, and let your family know about your needs. Otherwise, you may give the impression that everything is okay, even if you are in the midst of turmoil or change. Whether traveling or exploring your ideals together, concentrate on the spiritual side of your relationship from the 1st–18th. Be candid with your partner about any inner conflict near the time of the Full Moon on the 17th.

### FINANCE AND CAREER
Writing, lecturing, or attending conferences may offer an opportunity to boost your career. Use changes in the structure or bureaucracy from the 1st–10th to give you room to employ your best ideas. Business travel can be lucrative all month, but progress slows a bit from the 14th–22nd. Investments fare best from the 2nd–16th. Avoid impulsive spending the week of the 25th. Take time to go over finances and design long-range plans.

### OPPORTUNITY OF THE MONTH
In your eagerness to make progress, you may leave behind some important supporters. Be sure to invite them along.

**Rewarding Days:** 2, 3, 6, 7, 11, 12, 21, 22, 25, 26, 29, 30
**Challenging Days:** 1, 5, 8, 9, 10, 16, 17, 23, 24

### AFFIRMATION FOR THE MONTH
"My words and actions are inspired by love."

# ♑ CAPRICORN ♑
## The Goat

### December 22 to January 21

**Element:** Earth

**Quality:** Cardinal

**Polarity:** Feminine/Yin

**Planetary Ruler:** Saturn

**Meditation:** "Mastering the Challenge of the Physical Plane"

**Power Stones:** Diamond, quartz, onyx, black obsidian

**Glyph:** Head of goat, knees

**Key Phrase:** "I use"

**Gemstone:** Garnet

**Anatomy:** Knees, skin, skeleton

**Colors:** Black

**Animal:** Goats, thick-shelled animals

**Myths/Legends:** Cronus, Pan, Vesta

**House Association:** 10th

**Opposite Sign:** Cancer

**Flower:** Carnation

**Key Word:** Structure

**Positive Expression:**

Ambitious
Frugal
Conscientious
Cautious
Disciplined
Sensible
Patient
Responsible
Prudent

**Misuse of Energy:**

Controlling
Miserly
Rigid
Fearful
Repressed
Melancholy
Machiavellian
Inhibited

# ♑ CAPRICORN ♑

## Your Ego's Strengths and Weaknesses

Your persistence and determination go a long way in helping you accomplish the success you desire. You aim for victory, and know how to make the most of the materials at hand. When you're the one in charge, you can show responsible action, and can apply your sense of structure to keep things operating smoothly. Your aspiration to achieve your ambitions sets you apart from the crowd.

When faced with challenges and deadlines, you rise to the occasion, and may perform best when there's a bit of pressure to beat the clock. Even if everything around you has come to a grinding halt, your ambition to reach the ultimate can keep you moving forward. Through the energy of Saturn, your planetary ruler, you learn that manifesting your dreams requires building a strong foundation. But you can allow your fears or inhibitions to block your path. Getting back to basics can always help you get back on track.

Others may complain that you're taking advantage of them, when your motivation is to maintain control. Even though you may complain about the rules, you're more than happy to provide them (and change them as it suits your needs!). Your ability to create structure works best when based upon realistic needs. By balancing your sense of reality while maintaining a vision of your goals, you can stay motivated and continue to move ahead. You're challenged to achieve mastery over the physical plane without losing your connection with your Higher Self. By incorporating your connection to the spiritual realm with the tangible physical plane you can create a pattern for success which serves you well and which may be eagerly followed by others.

## Your Career Development

Your astute business judgement and sense of responsibility are strong assets in any career. Positions of management and authority are your preference, since you're at your best when you're in charge, and you're adept at delegating responsibilities to others. You might prefer to be self-employed, although your administrative and executive abilities can shine when working for others (or for the government).

Your ambition may lead you into positions as diverse as politics or the ministry. Or you may be drawn into the practice or teaching of geology, physics, life sciences, or medicine. Education or administration are also good choices for your instructional abilities. As a natural metaphysician, you may also be drawn into healing work such as chiropractic medicine, herbology or naturopathy. In the construction industry you might enjoy contracting, design or development. Managing a ranch or farm can answer your needs to stay in touch with nature. Whatever your choices, you're determined to make them successful.

## Your Approach to Romance

Because your self-worth may be tied up with your success in the outside world, you may feel restrained in matters of the heart until you've established a foundation in your career. You can cover your sensitivity with your trademark dry wit, although those who know you well probably suspect that there's sensitivity beneath that restrained veneer. Once you open up and allow yourself to share love, you may discover that the sensual pleasures can be your forte. Beneath the mask of control, you can be a highly sensitive lover.

With stability as an important factor in relationships, you're most comfortable in a loving relationships which gradually takes shape and grows over time. The Earth signs—Taurus, Virgo, and Capricorn—may be more patient with your "long-term" approach. Even though you may feel dedication and support with another Capricorn, you may both feel that the relationship becomes too stuffy unless you allow time to play. Taurus' earthiness gets your motor running and can be a perfect long-time lover and partner. With Virgo's companionship, your future feels assured.

The playful teasing of Aries is compelling, but may sometimes get on your nerves. Gemini's fickle nature can be frustrating. But Cancer, your Zodiac opposite, can become a consummate and patient partner. Before you decide if it can last with Leo, try to define who's in charge and get your territories established before it's too late.

Libra's refined tastes and gentility are attractive, but you may feel put off by their detachment. Yet Scorpio's enticing sensuality appeals to your understanding of the alchemy of love. Sagittarius' search for the best life has to offer inspires you, but you have to give them plenty of freedom. Aquarius offers life-long friendship and teaches you to let go of expectations, and Pisces' charismatic imagination provides a wondrous escape from the ordinary.

## Your Use of Power

Your quest for power may be tied to gaining greater control, although you may have to learn that control does not equal inflexibility. The struggle to keep the structure you've established in tact can lead to conflict if someone else suggests changes. By incorporating periodic review and evaluation, you can assess and initiate revisions on your own. You can easily undermine your own power by holding rigidly to patterns or traditions which have outlived their usefulness.

Since others are likely to look up to you, you can be of great influence and may become a mentor. Once you've established the position of respect you desire, others are quite likely to seek your counsel and guidance. But you may also find those control issues lurking behind the mask of "guidance." Remind yourself that you cannot be in charge of anyone's life other than your own. Only through support and direction which does not just serve your ego can you have the power to help them positively shape their destiny.

## Famous Capricorns

Debbie Allen, Kirstie Alley, Lew Ayers, Nicholas Cage, William Colby, Katie Couric, Federico Fellini, George Foreman, Mel Gibson, Germaine Greer, Annie Lennox, Barbara Mandrell, Hal Roach, Joseph Stalin, Betty White, Jon Voight

# THE YEAR AHEAD FOR CAPRICORN

Even though you've had to keep your nose to the grindstone for the past few years, you've always known that your focus and determination would lead to something. This is the year to see rewards for your efforts, and to develop a stronger base for future growth. By concentrating upon developing positive associations within your community and incorporating innovative ideas into your life, you can move in a more fulfilling direction. The cycles during 1994 bring positive support and inspiring challenge to continue personal development.

Relationships with friends and family play an especially important role this year, your best source of support when you're met with challenges from the outside world. Additionally, they can benefit from your steadfast determination. Jupiter transits in the sign of Scorpio through December 9, emphasizing the need to expand your contact with others of like mind. You might decide that you're ready to become more politically active, and may even be thrust into a role of leadership affiliated with those whose ideas are in harmony with your own. You're thinking more about the future, and can use this time to formulate a master plan. This is the time to manifest what may once have been only a dream. One of the keys to success now is in learning and truly expressing gratitude for the bounty you enjoy (even if it's not exactly *everything* you want!). If you greedily withhold what you could share, the opportunities during this cycle will be more limited. (This includes not only things, but information, time, and energy.)

The planets Uranus and Neptune are no longer exactly conjunct in the heavens as they were during 1993, but they are still traveling in tandem this year. You may be reeling from the changes you've been experiencing, and may yet have more to come. However, the foundations in your life are considerably more stable, giving you room to experience a less threatening element of change. If you've been resisting the urge to allow yourself to be as freely expressive as you need to be, there's still time to open to that intuitive voice whispering deep within your consciousness.

The Solar Eclipses this year emphasize the challenge to experience the process of giving and receiving love. Where you've failed to allow yourself to feel the flow of love into your life, you may finally be in a position to open your heart and be filled. Even though this doesn't sound like much of a challenge, if you've been resisting, it takes quite a bit of energy to allow those protective walls to fall! It's like a dam bursting—at first the force can overwhelm you, but it eventually levels out and just flows right through. This is *the* time to give your creativity a chance. Whatever you've dreamt of doing, effort applied now can lead you into a path that will support your best talents and abilities. But you must be willing to put forth the effort to express these gifts, to seek the guidance you require and to find the most harmonious circumstances for this expression. Otherwise, it's easy to waste those precious gifts or squander your resources in inappropriate directions.

**For Capricorns born from December 22–January 4,** Saturn's transit in sextile to your Sun brings an energy of discipline and crystallization. By applying this energy to your personal growth, you can use this time to become more positively aware of your real needs. This is a period of assessment which provides a supportive level of objectivity, and marks a period during which you may feel more synchronized with the rhythm of life. New beginnings are more viable, and if you've wanted to strengthen your position, your resources can support that change. Take advantage of educational opportunities which arise, since you may be more capable of the mental discipline. You may also have a chance to teach, write or travel—all of which can provide learning experiences of their own.

**If you were born from January 1–5,** you're feeling an inner urge to release the past while Pluto transits in semisquare aspect to your Sun. Many of these feelings will emerge from a very deep level, and may manifest as an unexplained compulsion to take a particular course of action. It's important to become aware of your motivations and to understand the needs associated with them. Taking time to become more acutely in touch with your feelings each day will help you experience a greater sense of control during this period of transformational change.

**For those born from December 23–January 15,** Chiron's transit trine to your Sun may offer you a sense that you're finally moving toward a more purposeful direction. Through consciously building a link to the Source of Divine Knowledge, you may become more confident that your ego is guided by your Higher Self. This inner partnership brings a more profound awareness of the spiritual dimension in all aspects of your life.

**You're feeling heightened sensitivity this year if you were born from January 10–15.** Neptune is transiting in conjunction to your Sun, a cycle which will not occur again in your lifetime. Your view of yourself is changing, and you may not feel quite sure of your identity. Surrendering to this energy, you'll discover many illusions you've held about yourself, but you may also fall victim to new illusions if you're not careful. To avoid getting caught in the deceptive side of this cycle, it's crucial to create a method of centering and grounding your energy. Sometimes, a creative expression—such as music, writing and art—or physical expressions—such as dance, Tai Chi, or Karate—can help you direct this energy. If you've been waiting for the time to allow creativity to take form in your life, this is an excellent period. Becoming more involved in the spiritual dimension of your life is also part of this transit, but you need to incorporate the spiritual into your daily routine, rather than using this time to evade your responsibilities. Escapist forms of behavior during this cycle will only exacerbate your confusion and can lead to a type of self-destruction. Do remember that you have a physical body, since it's all too easy to ignore those physical needs while experiencing this changing awareness. In fact, your body may be more sensitive now, and could require even more attention than you had planned!

**Uranus is transiting in conjunction to your Sun if you were born from January 11–16.** You're experiencing an awakening of energy, and may feel aspects emerging which have long been held in check. It's time to set yourself free, eliminate those things holding you back and move forward into the bright light of a new day. This cycle can occur only once in a lifetime, and does not happen to everyone (do you wonder if you really want to be that special?!). But you've been feeling these changes rumbling deep within for a long time, and may just now be willing, and ready, to take the chance to be yourself. This doesn't mean you have to alienate those you love, or that you have to leave behind the things you really need, but you will feel an urge to clear the way for a more honest form of personal expression, and your relationships are likely to undergo significant changes. You may feel that you need to take a new direction, or that your creativity is adapting to a different dimension. Rebellion alone is destructive now; you're needing to incorporate change within the dimension of true responsibility and to allow freedom for yourself and for others.

**If you were born from January 15–21 you're feeling the energy of Pluto transiting in sextile to your Sun.** During this period of restoration and rejuvenation, you're experiencing healing in many aspects of your life. Self-examination now can provide positive support, and you may finally be able to put some of your resources to work that have been lying dormant. Getting involved in political changes or taking an active part in working with a special interest group, you can easily move into a position of influence and power. The choice of how you direct this energy is up to you, although you may find that you're drawn into situations which need to be revitalized or repaired in some way. Instead of working alone, you may be much more effective by soliciting the assistance and support of others. You're in the perfect position to make changes which take you beyond your current life situation into a more complete realization of yourself.

## Tools to Make a Difference

To make the most of the energies providing the stimuli for growth in your life, spend some time examining your attitudes. There may be areas in which you've closed your mind, and that could be limiting your progress. Honest self-examination can be accomplished in many ways, but one of the best comes from journal-keeping. These "notes to yourself," can provide inspiration, but they can also give you a chance to work out solutions to problems, outline hopes and plans, or petition your inner self for greater support.

You can always profit by spending more time surrounded by the beauty of nature, and might want to schedule some time to regularly get outside and commune with this natural power. Since several cycles this year point to a need to expand, you might enjoy exploring areas you've never seen. Additionally, look for ways to add more natural beauty to your personal environment. You might benefit from gardening, even if you just grow a few herbs on your windowsill.

In your business endeavors, look for ways to incorporate your needs to become more supportive of our environment. Perhaps you'd feel better about investing in stocks or companies which are more environmentally aware! In your own business practices, be conscientious about recycling, and get behind your community's efforts to encourage recycle/reuse plans. You're perfectly suited to not only participate in such endeavors, but to turn them into personally profitable plans!

Continue to stay physically aware, since your connection to your body is more sensitive now. Martial arts, hatha yoga, Tai Chi or dance can be perfect ways to stay active and fit. But you'll also enjoy the challenge of improving your agility and strength. Work with your power stones—garnet, obsidian, quartz, or onyx—to keep yourself centered. During your meditations, contemplate a world of harmonious interaction. Envision yourself standing in the midst of a forest, surrounded by trees and animals and infused with light. Feel the peaceful connection between yourself and all life forms. Take this peace into your everyday life, and know that your actions are stimulated by a desire to enhance, create, and share love.

### Affirmation for the Year
"My life is filled with abundance in all things!"

# ACTION TABLES FOR CAPRICORN

These dates reflect the best (but not the only) times for success and ease in these activities according to your Sun Sign.

| | |
|---|---|
| **Change Residence** | April 9–24 |
| **Request a Raise** | Jan. 11 |
| **Begin a Course of Study** | Mar. 12; Sep. 5 |
| **Visit a Doctor** | May 10–27; Dec. 1–18 |
| **Start a Diet** | Jan. 22–23; Feb. 18–20; Mar. 18–19; Apr. 14–15; May 11–13; June 8–9; July 5–6; Aug. 1–2, 29–30; Sep. 25–26; Oct. 22–23; Nov. 18–19; Dec. 16–17 |
| **Begin a Romance** | May 10 |
| **Join a Club** | Nov. 3–4 |
| **Seek Employment** | May 10–27; July 3–9; Sep. 4–26 |
| **Take a Vacation** | Jan. 2–3, 29–30; Feb. 25–26; Mar. 25–26; Apr. 21–22; May 18–20; June 15–16; July 12–13; Aug. 8–9; Sep. 5–7; Oct. 2–3, 29–30; Nov. 26–27; Dec. 23–24 |
| **Change Your Wardrobe** | Apr. 26–May 9 |
| **End a Relationship** | Dec. 31 |
| **Seek Professional Advice** | Jan. 24–25; Feb. 21–22; Mar. 20–21; Apr. 17–18; May 14–15; June 10–11; July 7–8; Aug. 4–5, 31; Sep. 1, 27–28; Oct. 25–26; Nov. 21–22; Dec. 18–19 |
| **Have a Makeover** | Jan. 11 |
| **Obtain a Loan** | Jan. 27–28; Feb. 23–24; Mar. 23–24; Apr. 19–20; May 16–17; June 12–14; July 10–11; Aug. 6–7; Sep. 2–3, 30; Oct. 27–28; Nov. 23–25; Dec. 21–22 |

## PRIMARY FOCUS

Clear, definitive steps to put your plans into motion help you achieve remarkable progress in the face of surprising chances.

## HEALTH AND FITNESS

It's easy to push yourself beyond your limits, burning the candle at both ends. Safeguard your energy by setting a reasonable pace, and add extra nutritional support for your nervous system.

## ROMANCE AND RELATIONSHIPS

If you're stuck in stale patterns, this is the time to stir things up and put a little romance back into your life. Emotional conflicts can arise after the New Moon on the 11th due to miscommunication or deception. To honestly improve your love life you may simply need to alter your attitudes! Flirtations from the 9th–22nd can lead you to dangerously inaccurate conclusions, or may even create difficulties with your current situation. Maintain an awareness of your emotional boundaries before you leap blindly into unknown territory. Honor your needs.

## FINANCE AND CAREER

A shake-up in the hierarchy can leave an opening for you to step in and make a significant move. This time can be disastrous or miraculous, depending upon your level of preparedness for change. Risk only those resources you can afford to lose, since betting the farm can be costly. But do take the chance to move into a new direction after the 10th, making your most dramatic proposals before the Full Moon on the 27th.

## OPPORTUNITY OF THE MONTH

Get the facts straight and be ready to take reasonable risks from the 9th–16th. Strengthen your position to weather the storm.

**Rewarding Days:** 2, 3, 6, 10, 11, 15, 16, 20, 29, 30
**Challenging Days:** 1, 4, 5, 14, 17, 18, 19, 25, 26, 31

## AFFIRMATION FOR THE MONTH
"Change is safe."

## ♑ CAPRICORN/FEBRUARY ♑

### PRIMARY FOCUS

Avoid wasting your resources, and stay on top of all your communications. Avoid stretching beyond your limits; take a cautious approach to new situations.

### HEALTH AND FITNESS

Concentrate on building stamina and endurance, and remember to spend some time each day working on greater flexibility. Body and mind both benefit from developing resilience.

### ROMANCE AND RELATIONSHIPS

Everyday relationships require extra effort and attention, but can also bring positive rewards. Become more aware of the way you communicate, since your intention may be masked by an aloof or gruff attitude. Get back in touch with a sibling mid-month, and watch your expectations of your friends unless you really want an argument! Break up the routine from the 21st to the Full Moon on the 25th by planning a get-away with your sweetheart. You both could use a change of scenery.

### FINANCE AND CAREER

Details, details. Close scrutiny of all paperwork is absolutely necessary to avoid red tape. With Mercury's retrograde from Feb. 11 to Mar. 5 you may feel that things have come to a grinding halt. Actually, it's just a slower pace after the whirlwind. Use this time to research, double-check budgets and follow through on communications. Be wary of joint ventures until next month. And try not to force a situation that won't move.

### OPPORTUNITY OF THE MONTH

Instead of becoming frustrated with circumstances you cannot control, use the slow-down from the 10th–19th to catch your breath.

**Rewarding Days:** 2, 3, 6, 7, 11, 16, 25, 26
**Challenging Days:** 1, 4, 9, 13, 14, 15, 21, 22, 27, 28

### AFFIRMATION FOR THE MONTH
"My thoughts and actions are in harmony
with Divine Law."

## PRIMARY FOCUS

Extra efforts to clarify contracts and communication provide beneficial information and positive results. Patience, persistence and integrity are necessary if you want to achieve your goals now.

## HEALTH AND FITNESS

Deliberately take breaks in your routine after the 7th, when a change of pace freshens your outlook and stabilizes your vitality.

## ROMANCE AND RELATIONSHIPS

You may give the impression that you're not placing your love life at a high priority. Unless you want to create distance, take some time to be more attentive near the New Moon on the 12th, when you may find that you actually enjoy the closer contact. From the 8th–17th it's easy to disagree with a friend, especially if your priorities are in conflict. Family issues become demanding near the Full Moon on the 27th, but can be offset by prior communication with siblings. Flirtations from the 25th–31st can stir up trouble.

## FINANCE AND CAREER

Power plays and legal hassles seem to block progress from the 1st–16th, but can be in your favor if you've supported your position with factual evidence. Careful presentation wins support from the 12th–26th, and may even open the door for advancement or recognition. Business or personal travel are profitable after the 18th. Exploring the facts behind financial inconsistencies may uncover resources you had forgotten. Still, take time to double-check investments presented the 27th–31st.

## OPPORTUNITY OF THE MONTH

You can be highly influential in the midst of a challenge from the 10th–16th. Rely on your creativity.

**Rewarding Days:** 1, 6, 7, 10, 11, 15, 16, 25, 26, 29
**Challenging Days:** 2, 9, 13, 14, 20, 21, 22, 27, 28

## AFFIRMATION FOR THE MONTH
"I use my resources wisely."

### PRIMARY FOCUS

Travel and increased communication play a strong part early in the month, but business moves closer to home after the 15th. Take care of family issues immediately to avoid protracted difficulty.

### HEALTH AND FITNESS

Stress levels are more bearable from the 1st–14th, but you may feel torn in several directions and need extra time for relaxation after mid-month. Keep your well-being at a high priority.

### ROMANCE AND RELATIONSHIPS

Your love life gains momentum from the 1st–25th, but you still need to take an active role in creating the best opportunities to share special times. Children can be especially enjoyable now (or you may decide that you'd like to be a bit more foot-loose yourself!). The New Moon on the 10th may initiate family squabbles, and it's tempting to argue, especially since others may become rather obnoxious when making their point. Excessive turmoil is not necessary. Romance blossoms with the Full Moon on the 25th.

### FINANCE AND CAREER

Continue the momentum in business negotiations from the 1st–13th, and make a special effort to get involved in networking with influential individuals. Share ideas, and draw together the talent to get the job done on the 11th and 12th, targeting the 21st–26th to bring in your hottest products or concepts. Speculative investments fare better from the 17th–25th, but only if they do not involve a conflict of interests.

### OPPORTUNITY OF THE MONTH

Apply your creative abilities to the task at hand and you'll see remarkable results from the 10th–28th.

**Rewarding Days:** 2, 3, 8, 12, 13, 21, 22, 25, 29, 30
**Challenging Days:** 1, 5, 9, 10, 17, 18, 19, 23, 24

### AFFIRMATION FOR THE MONTH
"I am confident in my assertiveness."

## PRIMARY FOCUS

Bring improvements to your work environment, and take time to incorporate the requests of those under your supervision. Reaching the top can be highly competitive, and you need good support.

## HEALTH AND FITNESS

Pressures at work and at home can squeeze your vitality, and one of the best releases can be increasing your activity level. Just be sure you stay within your limits from the 8th–20th.

## ROMANCE AND RELATIONSHIPS

Turmoil at home can occasionally escalate to a high pitch, but becomes more marked from the 13th–21st. Take some extra time near the Solar Eclipse on the 10th to bring assurances to your intimate relationships, especially partner and children. And consider consulting with a friend to objectify the situation on the 23rd. You may need to break away from some old traditions and start a few of your own. Allow time for contemplative reverie during the Lunar Eclipse on the 24th and 25th. Greater clarity emerges on the 27th.

## FINANCE AND CAREER

Careful scrutiny of your professional image may expose some rough edges; polishing that image may bring just the right changes. Why not give yourself the advantage? Your tendency to be more brusque than usual can alienate those you're trying hardest to impress mid-month. However, it's important to be acutely aware of those who are jealous of your position or would undermine your progress. Be sure you're not undermining yourself!

## OPPORTUNITY OF THE MONTH

Confer with colleagues on the 4th, 5th, 9th, and 10th to create the best options for successful ventures.

**Rewarding Days:** 4, 5, 9, 10, 18, 19, 23, 24, 27, 28, 31
**Challenging Days:** 2, 3, 6, 7, 8, 14, 15, 21, 22

## AFFIRMATION FOR THE MONTH
"I am honest with myself and with others."

## PRIMARY FOCUS

Personal relationships need some extra care and attention, and you'll prosper by allowing more time to enjoy the beauty and love around you. Review your priorities and maintain your balance.

## HEALTH AND FITNESS

Try a fresh approach to staying healthy, and get a new program moving after the New Moon on the 9th. Create a routine that's actually enjoyable for a change.

## ROMANCE AND RELATIONSHIPS

Achieving the qualities you desire within a committed relationship is possible, but you have to take the risk of being honest with your partner about your needs. Otherwise, you may find that the relationship has become rather one-sided, and that your feelings have been pushed out of the picture. Love needs room to grow, and you're the one who provides the space for it. Look at your old attitudes, and allow fear to subside in exchange for the pleasure and joy of being yourself. Seek balance during the Full Moon on the 23rd.

## FINANCE AND CAREER

Your investments show successful results, and you may be tempted to jump back into the fire with another new plan. Before you sign contracts or agree to participate, make sure you're aware of all the details. Mercury's retrograde from June 12 to July 5 encourages a second look before you leap. Some changes in your business plans can bring success, and you're somewhat vulnerable to deception from the 6th–2th. Your shrewdness pays off on the 23rd.

## OPPORTUNITY OF THE MONTH

Enjoy the support of others, but be sure to extend your gratitude if you expect to see more of it.

**Rewarding Days:** 1, 5, 6, 15, 16, 19, 20, 23, 24, 28
**Challenging Days:** 2, 3, 10, 11, 12, 17, 18, 30

## AFFIRMATION FOR THE MONTH
"My life is filled with love."

### PRIMARY FOCUS

Demands from others can escalate now, but may also provide you with the best sources for advancement or good fortune. Educational pursuits bring rewards.

### HEALTH AND FITNESS

Honor your physical limitations instead of pushing your body beyond its limits. You may suffer some aches and pains from exposing yourself to environmental extremes or over-exertion.

### ROMANCE AND RELATIONSHIPS

If you get into some touchy territory in your love life early this month, try to find the best way to deal with your discomforts or fears instead of just shutting down emotionally. Patterns which are unhealthy are exposed during this cycle, giving you a chance to find better ways to meet your needs. Sharing inspirational experiences or travelling can provide a stronger foundation for intimacy from the 11th–31st. Integrate a more spiritual element into your everyday life and reshape your attitudes toward yourself.

### FINANCE AND CAREER

Disputes over jointly-held property or finances can escalate from the 1st–9th, when you may prefer to listen to the argument, then present the solid facts later, from the 16th–22nd. Negotiations and contracts signed on the 21st or before the Full Moon on the 22nd can be stable and profitable. Resistance from others whose attitudes lean toward excessive conservatism can clue you in to the more expedient direction for current pursuits.

### OPPORTUNITY OF THE MONTH

On the 16th and 17th, share insights and provide support to a friend or colleague whose advice has served you well in the past.

**Rewarding Days:** 2, 3, 12, 13, 16, 17, 20, 21, 22, 25, 30
**Challenging Days:** 1, 5, 7, 8, 9, 14, 15, 27, 28

### AFFIRMATION FOR THE MONTH
"I am one with my Higher Self."

### PRIMARY FOCUS

Concentrate on improving your work relationships, and strive to be more gracious when another person takes the lead some of the time. You might actually enjoy the break, if you let yourself!

### HEALTH AND FITNESS

Any chronic or troublesome physical complaints need to be examined for their root cause. Dealing with the deeper issues allows for more comprehensive healing.

### ROMANCE AND RELATIONSHIPS

Even your closest relationships may seem competitive now, so it might be a good idea to look at yourself and determine if you're pushing a bit too hard. The New Moon on the 7th emphasizes a period of greater awareness about your emotional attachments, and marks a good time to have a frank discussion with your lover. Issues over money within your family or your partnership are likely to be a smoke-screen for unresolved emotional trauma. Talk about it after the Full Moon on the 21st, when you're feeling less vulnerable.

### FINANCE AND CAREER

If you're falling short of your competitors at work, perhaps you've been lax in your responsibilities. Remedy the situation by careful research, then launch into a different direction or take a new approach from the 17th–27th. But don't be surprised if your superiors have a few questions; just be sure you have answers! Business travel can be profitable after the 24th, although staying close to home appears to provide better results.

### OPPORTUNITY OF THE MONTH

Setting reasonable goals provides a healthy target for your ambition. Otherwise you may just stir up defensive behavior.

**Rewarding Days:** 8, 9, 13, 14, 17, 18, 21, 22, 26
**Challenging Days:** 1, 4, 5, 6, 11, 23, 24, 29

### AFFIRMATION FOR THE MONTH
"I am aware of my motivations."

## PRIMARY FOCUS

Concentration on attainable goals helps expedite success and offers more options than you may have imagined. This is the time to manifest what you've envisioned.

## HEALTH AND FITNESS

A fairly hectic pace makes it difficult to relax and savor the moment. Even though you may feel that you're in a rush, slowing down will ultimately save you the time lost scattering your energy.

## ROMANCE AND RELATIONSHIPS

Before jumping to conclusions about a relationship, be sure to get the facts. A committed relationship matures through opening the gates and allowing more room for individual growth. But if you're beginning a love relationship after the 14th, you may be more inclined toward infatuation than drawn to a viable circumstance. Give yourselves time to explore all the possibilities. Travel can positively enhance any relationship from the New Moon on the 5th through the Full Moon on the 19th. Leave room for spontaneity.

## FINANCE AND CAREER

Opportunities to teach or share your knowledge offer you a chance to accelerate your career growth. You may be thrown into situations which feel foreign, but you can acclimate quickly through mid-month. After the 17th, there's a tendency to rush headlong into decisions before having all the facts. Even if expediency is important, moving too quickly can be costly. Use the best technological resources available to help you advance.

## OPPORTUNITY OF THE MONTH

An introduction to a mind-boggling idea offers a tremendous possibility for financial success; investigate it carefully first.

**Rewarding Days:** 5, 6, 9, 10, 13, 14, 18, 22, 23, 24
**Challenging Days:** 1, 7, 8, 11, 20, 21, 27, 28, 29

## AFFIRMATION FOR THE MONTH
"My intuition is open to clear truth."

## PRIMARY FOCUS

You're still driven to achieve the goals you've set; and if you haven't developed any plans, then get busy! Your confidence is at a powerful high and needs direction.

## HEALTH AND FITNESS

Everything you do may drive you to get beneath the surface. Work on developing muscular strength and flexibility, and devote some time to clearing your system of old toxic wastes.

## ROMANCE AND RELATIONSHIPS

Friendships play a powerful role and may be the source of a new love relationship. Supporting and sharing your dreams and victories with others of like mind boosts your confidence and provides mutual benefit. Review your motivations and needs in current relationships after the 13th, reflecting upon the conditioning you experienced from your parents during the Full Moon on the 19th. Breakthroughs in your creativity and ability to accept and share love improves all your relationships from the 16th–31st.

## FINANCE AND CAREER

Keep the momentum going, adding a boost during the New Moon on the 4th. Once Mercury enters its retrograde cycle (from the 9th–30th) you'll need to reorganize your plans. Difficulties with travel or mechanical breakdowns can stall your plans from the 23rd–1st, but doesn't have to create a permanent set-back. Have a contingency plan available, and be sure to double-check all your figures before making financial decisions.

## OPPORTUNITY OF THE MONTH

Create your Master Plan. Set long-term goals and also implement possibilities for shorter, interim goals from the 1st–8th.

**Rewarding Days:** 2, 3, 6, 7, 10, 11, 15, 20, 29, 30
**Challenging Days:** 1, 4, 5, 8, 17, 18, 25, 26, 31

## AFFIRMATION FOR THE MONTH
"I am flexible in the midst of change."

## PRIMARY FOCUS

Confusion early in the month may lead you to believe that things are hopeless. Have faith. Those changes are helping you to eliminate elements which stifle long-term success.

## HEALTH AND FITNESS

To avoid adding to your stress level, stay out of other people's arguments. Maintain a reasonable activity level; take advantage of professional medical advice.

## ROMANCE AND RELATIONSHIPS

Misunderstandings can create a collapse in communication with your family from the 1st–6th, but reasonable judgment begins to return on the 7th. Talk over concerns with a friend during the Solar Eclipse on the 3rd; treasure their insights. Part of the problem in your intimate relationships is related to expectations. You may even be expecting things of yourself that are unrealistic. Take time out for romance during the Lunar Eclipse on the 18th, when you can solidify a situation that needs some extra support.

## FINANCE AND CAREER

Pull back the reins a little early in the month and examine your progress. Scrutinize the viability of your business endeavors and eliminate those products, services, or options that are not producing or have become obsolete. Implement new growth from the 16th–18th, and nourish things that have proven their worth through the end of the month. Carefully consider the validity of partnerships or joint ventures. You may do better alone.

## OPPORTUNITY OF THE MONTH

Take a careful look at the cycles of investment and return, in financial and emotional circumstances. Are you doing your part?

**Rewarding Days:** 3, 7, 8, 11, 12, 16, 26, 27, 30
**Challenging Days:** 1, 2, 9, 10, 13, 14, 15, 21, 22, 28, 29

## AFFIRMATION FOR THE MONTH
"I am open to receiving love."

## PRIMARY FOCUS

Your affiliations may have a lot to do with your success this month. Be sure you're associated with groups, ideas or projects which are in harmony with your higher needs.

## HEALTH AND FITNESS

Those stress levels remain high through the 11th, and a relaxing massage might help take the edge off the tension on the 4th or 9th. Consider taking a vacation after the 13th.

## ROMANCE AND RELATIONSHIPS

Time spent with friends boosts your mood. Even though you may enjoy quiet times alone or with your sweetheart, getting out and enjoying the festivities after the 3rd and through the Full Moon on the 17th might actually be enjoyable! Family and friends become more the focus after the 18th, although you may choose to get away from it all and travel. Do plan something unique from the 26th–31st, when you're eager to break with a few traditions and explore the more imaginative side of life.

## FINANCE AND CAREER

After some major wheeling and dealing from the 1st–10th, you might appreciate a break in the action. Look into the ethical considerations of the projects you're planning for next year, and use the energy from the 12th–26th to break away from situations which don't really fit your particular philosophical approach. This is a good time to liquidate and seek out different sources for the investment of your energy and capital.

## OPPORTUNITY OF THE MONTH

Redirect your resources by getting some work done behind the scenes from the 4th–14th in preparation for the future.

**Rewarding Days:** 1, 4, 5, 8, 9, 13, 23, 24, 28, 31
**Challenging Days:** 2, 11, 12, 18, 19, 25, 26

## AFFIRMATION FOR THE MONTH

"I am willing to release the burdens from my past."

# ≈ AQUARIUS ≈
## The Water Bearer

### January 21 to February 19

**Element:** Air

**Quality:** Fixed

**Polarity:** Masculine/Yang

**Planetary Ruler:** Uranus

**Meditation:** "Creating new paths by focusing the mind"

**Power Stones:** Aquamarine, chrysocolla, black pearl

**Anatomy:** Ankles, circulatory system

**Key Phrase:** "I know"

**Gemstone:** Amethyst

**Glyph:** Waves of energy

**Color:** Violet

**Animal:** Birds

**Myths/Legends:** Deucalion, Ninkhursag, John the Baptist

**House Association:** 11th

**Opposite Sign:** Leo

**Flower:** Orchid

**Key Word:** Unconventional

**Positive Expression:**
  Altruistic
  Friendly
  Liberal
  Autonomous
  Unselfish
  Progressive
  Humane
  Unconditional
  Ingenious
  Futuristic

**Misuse of Energy:**
  Detached
  Thoughtless
  Intransigent
  Fanatical
  Anarchistic
  Aloof
  Rebellious
  Deviant
  Undirected

# ≋ AQUARIUS ≋

## Your Ego's Strengths and Weaknesses

As the individualist of the zodiac, you can become a pioneer for the unusual. Your inventive mind and grasp of the extraordinary give you the ability to see things from a universal perspective. Uniqueness is your trademark, and you can be full of surprises! You strive to be a genuine friend, and appreciate the power of boundless and unconditional love.

Freedom is among your highest values, and you may be inspired to champion the cause of individual rights and human liberty. Your tastes lean toward the unconventional, and you appreciate rare and abstract forms of musical and artistic expression. Even though some of your own ideas or creative efforts may seem nonconformist now, you may set a precedent for what later becomes classical style. Since you're frequently willing to risk stepping outside the boundaries of the mainstream, you may be viewed by others as rebellious. In your attempts to be different, you can become negligent when focused only on your selfish interests. Through connecting with the untamable energy of your planetary ruler, Uranus, you may feel alienated from many of the traditions which have been used by others as an excuse for a lack of progress. Trust your intuitive guidance to help you determine whether you are part of a gradual evolution or if you are called to carry the torch of revolutionary change.

Even when your intention may be to maintain objectivity, others may feel alienated by your aloofness. By developing at attitude of unconditionality and creating a connection to Universal Love, you can illuminate the path toward understanding and self-acceptance for all humanity.

## Your Career Development

In choosing a career path, you need to feel mentally challenged, with room to exercise your originality and express your ideas. Scientific fields may fascinate and reward you well; areas such as computer science, electronics, theoretical mathematics, astrology, meteorology, aviation, or the space industry may be appealing. Your talents may reside in working with people through advertising, public relations, broadcasting, news media, and you may have a special talent in writing.

An interest in politics may lead you to work in public service, especially in the areas of civil rights. In fine arts, your talents may range from original music, using the ultimate in technology, to visionary art. Owning your own business offers an opportunity to market your own or other uncommon creations. Whatever your career choice, your unique energy is unlikely to be overlooked.

## Your Approach to Romance

Your independent attitude and general friendliness draw a wide variety of people into your life. Even though you enjoy time to yourself, you may yearn for a companion who can be both your best friend and lover. You can be a steadfast and loyal partner, but only when the right person comes along. Your intuition tells you if it's love. But beware: your mind may try to talk you out of getting involved!

You may be most magnetically drawn to your opposite sign, Leo, whose fiery nature and playful warmth can be completely engaging, although occasionally challenging. You also love contact with the other fire signs—Aries and Sagittarius. Aries keeps you on your toes and provides stimulating, passionate exchange of energy. Sagittarius' adventurous attitude and good humor entice you, and you can both enjoy free self-expression.

As an Air sign, communication is important to you. Another Aquarian may be difficult to reach at an intimate level, but when you do connect, you can create a remarkable life together. Taurus' need to hold onto everything (including you), may feel too heavy. The allure of Gemini's wit and intelligence is hard to resist. Cancer's need for contact is not entirely compatible with your independence. And although Virgo may inspire you to search your soul, you may not always connect.

You're encouraged to explore the depth of your

heart with Libra, whose charm and quiet refinement inspire your love. With Scorpio, you may reach an uncomfortable feeling that you're submerged at a level which stifles your self-expression. Friendship with Capricorn may be easier than romance, since control issues can get in the way. Pisces' watery depths and high ideals entice you, although you can easily get lost in the vapors of a different reality with one another.

## Your Use of Power

You understand the power of the human mind and spirit, and may be drawn to merging your consciousness with a higher source to experience pure power. Misuse of power is distressing to you, therefore you may resist moving into a position of power and influence until you feel you're ready. A situation which allows you to represent a common cause or universal ideal may be more comfortable for you than seeking power for the sake of personal recognition.

Your outstanding abilities may bring recognition from others who boost you into a position of influence. Through winning trust, you can generate clear new directions for a group, company or nation. Your altruistic spirit may stimulate you to champion causes for those who are repressed. However, you may also find yourself in positions of notoriety which can damage your efforts if your personal actions have offended the sensibilities of society.

Because you possess the power of vision, you sometimes feel very lonely when stepping into directions that are foreign or uncomfortable for others. The future is quite real for you, and you can create ways to make that future brighter for the generations that follow.

## Famous Aquarians

Red Barber, Judy Blume, Lloyd Bentsen, Garth Brooks, Bobby Brown, Geena Davis, Wayne Gretzky, Arsenio Hall, Gregory Hines, Michael Jordan, Ted Koppel, David Lynch, Dinah Manoff, Joe Pesci, George Stephanopolous, Oprah Winfrey

# THE YEAR AHEAD FOR AQUARIUS

Nineteen ninety-four is the year to expand upon the stable base you've been struggling to create for the last two years. You may feel more willing to take a few more risks, within limits. It's time to make the most of your resources, and to eliminate false values which have kept you locked behind a facade which may have become woefully inadequate. Your real values emerge as a true test of your self-worth, and reflect qualities which are comfortable and supportive of your personal identity.

You may be ready to expand both the opportunities and challenges afforded by your career path, and may find that maintaining a balance between your personal and professional life is a bit of a struggle. Jupiter's transit in Scorpio this year energizes your Solar Tenth House, opening the doors to greater recognition, but also to increased ambition. As you gain greater influence during this time, remain aware of the manner in which you're responding to others in your environment. Used well, this time can become a period of increased influence, but you can also allow your ego to become too involved and may alienate those you've left on the lower rung of the ladder. To make the best use of this cycle, stay in touch with your real limitations, since there will be times you may feel that you don't have any! Certainly it's important to reach beyond your current circumstance, but only so far as your grasp will allow without toppling your stability.

Uranus and Neptune are separating from their exact conjunction which played such an important role during 1993. But these two planets are still travelling near the same degree of the zodiac. Since Uranus is your planetary ruler, this cycle has had a particularly influential role in your life, and you can still tap into that sense of feeling more closely in touch with the collective consciousness. The time you spend doing "inner" work is especially important this year, since the doorways to enhanced levels of awareness are still beckoning. On a practical level, you can still utilize this energy to help you release old emotional attachments and move into more freely expressive life experiences.

The Solar Eclipses during 1994 accentuate your need to adjust the balance between your personal needs and your professional growth. You're also breaking away from many of the old traditions which formed the basis of your stability, and may be creating pathways which are unique to your life experience. Sometimes, such a cycle will help to illuminate your need to get back in touch with those roots that you've so rebelliously shunned in order to become more fully aware of your sense of wholeness. You may not need to go back to the past and stay there, but instead may need to simply acknowledge where you've been.

**If you were born from January 21–February 2, you're feeling the urge to take the steps which will solidify your position.** Saturn is transiting in semisextile to your Sun, drawing your attention to the way you've handled your responsibilities. If you've built a good foundation by clearing away the unnecessary and focusing upon your real needs, then the steps you're taking now will seem to lead toward greater progress. However, if, during the last three years you've ignored those signals to change, then you may feel that you're not quite ready to move ahead, and that you're stuck with a lot of unfinished business. Now's a good time to focus on the practical side of life, to create building blocks for change by dealing with those necessities which are directly in front of you. It's also important to return some of those responsibilities you've been carrying for others to their rightful place. The key factor involved in your growth is related to adjusting your load. Are you trudging up those steps to progress with shoulders bent from too great a burden or gingerly stepping forward carrying only what's necessary?

**Chiron is travelling in quincunx to your Sun this year if you were born from January 23–February 13.** Extra attention to your physical needs now may bring greater awareness of the best solutions to some of those distressing symptoms or chronic problems. Your insights into the body/mind connection can become quite profound now, and you'll find that much of the healing which occurs in your life is the result of your willingness to change your attitudes and release some old attachments. Uncovering emotional scars which have been pushed into the deeper recesses of your consciousness also provides a sense of relief and can add a feeling of increased vitality.

**If you were born from January 31–February 9, you're feeling a special impact from the Solar Eclipses this year.** Issues surrounding home and family may loom larger now, and you're in an excellent position to put things in their proper perspective. Focusing only on the external factors in your life and simply responding to everything around you will seem too shallow now. You're needing to feel more closely associated with your inner self, and may feel driven to use that insight to help you achieve a sense of fulfilling your destiny.

**For Aquarians born from February 8–12,** your creative, imaginative processes are receiving a boost of energy while Neptune transits semisextile to your Sun. Your intuitive faculties may also be enhanced now, improving your sensitivity to the more subtle vibrations and helping you attune more readily to the inner plane of consciousness. If you're involved in artistic or creative pursuits, this energy can draw you into a feeling of expressing a greater sense of universality. By using the power of these increased sensibilities, you may find that you're creating just the right thing at the right time. If you feel a need for increased personal space or time alone, you can accomplish this in your life without alienating those you love. But there's a temptation to drift into a dimension where you're more unreachable than usual. Spend some time balancing your energy on a daily basis in order to keep a more powerful sense of wholeness, instead of feeling a strong need to disassociate from those things (and people) you truly need.

**You may finally be willing to break out of your self-imposed limitations and more into free self-expression if you were born from February 9–15.** Uranus is transiting in semisextile to your Sun, stimulating a need for greater freedom and independence. Personal relationships may need to undergo a few changes; and if you've been holding the lid on some feelings or needs for a long time, it's just about to fly off! You may plagued by inconsistency, since there are likely to be some times you're satisfied with your current situation and other times when you feel you have to make changes—immediately! Become aware of an increasing tendency to take action before you're really prepared for the consequences. This cycle can be like the exhilarating experience of navigating through the rapids—you have to be willing to get a little wet, stay alert to the unexpected, and realize that you really do need that life vest! It's time to try a new approach, to get out of your ruts and enjoy the surprises life has to offer.

If you were born from February 13–19, you're feeling an increasing intensity while Pluto transits in square aspect to your Sun. Circumstances or relationships counterproductive to growth can become intolerable, and you may feel you have no choice but to make changes. Even though you may be more than ready for some of these changes, you may still feel a great sense of loss as you incorporate these transformative experiences into your life. Self-destructive habits or attitudes can also be released now, and the resultant healing can be phenomenal. Feelings which range from rapture to grief often accompany these changes, and it's important to acknowledge any grief you're feeling, since that process in itself brings healing. Many times, this cycle marks a period which contrasts greatly with your previous life experiences, and you may not achieve a clear perspective on all the changes until several months after this transit is over. Listen carefully to your inner voice when you're faced with situations you had not anticipated in order to make better choices which resonate more clearly with your true self. Allow yourself to feel the essence of your real power, and be willing to acknowledge the power in others without reacting defensively. By taking a posture of strength and maintaining a willingness to stay connected to Divine Power, this period can mark a truly exceptional process of restoration. But fighting against the revisions which need to be made in your life can set you on a path toward self-destruction instead of the path of realization and renewal.

## Tools to Make a Difference

Since many of the internal shifts you're feeling can lead you to question your life choices, staying in touch with your inner self through contemplative or meditational exercises may be your best method of self-audit. If you're willing to take time each day to meditate, even for a few minutes, and quiet your mind, you're likely to discover a level of peace which allows you to transcend many of the everyday hassles. If you don't have much success sitting quietly, take a more active approach. Keep a journal or diary, and take time to write notes to yourself. Balance body, mind and spirit. Tai Chi, Qi Gong, or hatha yoga may offer a positive alternative which allows you to stay in touch with your inner self through connecting more effectively with your body.

Music can be an effective transformational agent in your life, and can help you alter your mood, increase your physical vitality, and enhance your awareness. You might also enjoy the experiences of resonate sounds from specially-tuned chimes, bells, or bowls. Work with aromas of essential oils to help you clear and balance your physical/emotional energy.

Make connections in your community and get involved with others. You don't have to make front-page news; in fact, working behind the scenes may feel better. But you are likely to feel a need to be part of the solution instead of creating the problems!

During your periods of visualization, create a place of beauty and serenity. Stand in the center of your special place, and become aware of the colors and sounds. See yourself walking toward two pillars which mark the first steps to a temple. Walk between the pillars, which electrify your consciousness. Once you enter the temple, look around for any special symbols or messages which speak to you. Feel yourself becoming charged with pure light and power, and allow your subconscious mind to register the messages you receive in this special place.

## Affirmation for the Year

"I am growing, changing and opening my mind
to pure truth and understanding."

## ACTION TABLES FOR AQUARIUS

These dates reflect the best (but not the only) times for success and ease in these activities according to your Sun Sign.

| | |
|---|---|
| **Change Residence** | Apr. 25–May 9 |
| **Request a Raise** | Feb. 10 |
| **Begin a Course of Study** | Apr. 11; Oct. 5–6 |
| **Visit a Doctor** | Jan. 1–13; May 29–July 2; July 10–Aug. 2; Dec 19–31 |
| **Start a Diet** | Jan. 25–26; Feb. 21–22; Mar. 20–22; Apr. 17–18; May 14–15; June 10–11; July 7–9; Aug. 4–5, 31; Sep. 1, 27–29; Oct. 25–26; Nov. 21–22; Dec. 18–19 |
| **Begin a Romance** | June 9–10 |
| **Join a Club** | Dec. 2–3 |
| **Seek Employment** | May 28–July 2; July 10–Aug. 2; Sep. 27–Oct. 19; Nov. 10–29 |
| **Take a Vacation** | Jan. 4–5, 31–Feb. 1, 27–28; Mar. 27–28; Apr. 23–24; May 21–22; June 17–18; July 14–15; Aug. 10–11; Sep. 7–8; Oct. 4–5, 31; Nov. 1, 28–29; Dec. 25–26 |
| **Change Your Wardrobe** | May 10–27 |
| **End a Relationship** | Jan. 27–28 |
| **Seek Professional Advice** | Jan. 27–28; Feb. 23–24; Mar. 23–24; Apr. 19–20; May 16–17; June 12–14; July 10–11; Aug. 6–7; Sep. 2–3, 30; Oct. 1, 27–28; Nov. 23–25; Dec. 21–22 |
| **Have a Makeover** | Feb. 10 |
| **Obtain a Loan** | Jan. 29–30; Feb. 25–26; Mar. 25–26; Apr. 21–22; May 18–20; June 15–16; July 12–13; Aug. 8–9; Sep. 5–6; Oct. 2–3, 29–30; Nov. 26–27; Dec. 23–24 |

### PRIMARY FOCUS

Although you may have some great ideas, you may be reluctant to put them forth until you test the water. Experiment with the 19th.

### HEALTH AND FITNESS

Allow extra time to rest and step away from stressful situations. A unique approach offers a path to wholeness the week of the 16th.

### ROMANCE AND RELATIONSHIPS

Fascination with someone who is unattainable can be a grand inspiration for a book or screenplay, but may be torturous in real life! Any new relationship begun between the New Moon on the 11th and the 18th may be built primarily upon speculation, rather than real needs. If you're involved in an intimate relationship, share your fantasies with your lover and find ways to break out of routine. Loving energy flows easier after the 19th. Use the Full Moon cycle on the 27th to make closer contact with your real needs.

### FINANCE AND CAREER

Changes in fundamental structures or shifts in hierarchy can alter your plans, and may afford you an unexpected chance to move forward in your career if you've proven yourself. But there are factors working behind the scenes that could undermine your success if you ignore them. Be alert to hidden agendas, and aware of signs of undermining or deception from the 7th–19th. Bring in allies and make your move on the 22nd, 23rd, or 31st.

### OPPORTUNITY OF THE MONTH

Research facts and be prepared for surprising changes. The more flexible your attitude, the greater your success.

**Rewarding Days:** 4, 8, 9, 12, 13, 14, 17, 22, 23, 31
**Challenging Days:** 1, 2, 16, 18, 25, 27, 28, 29

### AFFIRMATION FOR THE MONTH
"My intuitive mind is linked
to Divine Truth and Wisdom."

### PRIMARY FOCUS

Keep expectations in line with realistic possibilities to avoid getting in over your head from the 1st–16th. This is a time to actively expand, if you have a firm foundation.

### HEALTH AND FITNESS

With Mars transiting in Aquarius, you may feel that you're capable of burning the candle at both ends. It's more likely that you'll burn-out before you anticipated! Pace yourself.

### ROMANCE AND RELATIONSHIPS

Even though you may know what you're wanting out of a relationship, taking a posture which is too forceful could leave you shut out of the picture altogether. Be more aware of the impression you create during the New Moon on the 10th, when you make greater progress if your actions are in harmony with the needs of your sweetheart. Barriers can drop on the 9th, but you may also have a new aim in mind. Digging into your past after the 20th can stir up an old dragon, when honesty becomes absolutely necessary.

### FINANCE AND CAREER

Careful attention to your finances may expose an area of weakness. Early attention saves time and money. Mercury's retrograde from Feb. 11 to Mar. 5 emphasizes looking back into specifics of financial dealings through the 21st. After that, the tendency of management (or the government) to change the rules can create new problems. Avoid final agreements or binding contracts until later next month.

### OPPORTUNITY OF THE MONTH

Use your inventive, intuitive approach to balancing your needs to grow while consolidating your resources from the 10th–21st.

**Rewarding Days:** 1, 4, 5, 9, 10, 14, 19, 20, 27, 28
**Challenging Days:** 2, 3, 7, 16, 17, 23, 24, 25

### AFFIRMATION FOR THE MONTH
"I use my resources wisely."

### PRIMARY FOCUS

Before you jump to conclusions, be sure you actually know the facts instead of just assuming that you understand them! Then you can apply the best of your resources to the most logical solutions.

### HEALTH AND FITNESS

Concentrate on building stamina and endurance. Devoting some extra time to relaxation and release of tension can also help to extend your physical energy level to a higher capacity.

### ROMANCE AND RELATIONSHIPS

You may come on a bit too strong early in the month, when considering what you're about to say can save you from the embarrassment of putting your foot in your mouth! Initiating a fresh approach to personal relationships flows more easily once Venus moves into your Solar 3rd House on the 8th. If you're feeling guarded about exposing your more vulnerable side, take time to acclimate before you dive into intimacy. Travel or cultural experiences may offer pleasure from the 25th–31st.

### FINANCE AND CAREER

Take a conservative approach when projecting budgetary needs for business. Review productivity levels after the New Moon on the 12th to determine which areas need to be redesigned, emphasized, or eliminated. Presentations or conferences from the 17th–28th offer unique opportunities to share your ideas. Negotiations near the Full Moon on the 27th may offer a chance to incorporate new technology or innovative ideas.

### OPPORTUNITY OF THE MONTH

Power plays from the 1st–10th may leave you in a vulnerable position if you're unwilling to change. Loosen up and move forward!

**Rewarding Days:** 4, 8, 9, 13, 18, 19, 27, 28. 31
**Challenging Days:** 1, 2, 7, 15, 16, 17, 23, 24, 29, 30

### AFFIRMATION FOR THE MONTH
"My mind is open to new ideas."

### PRIMARY FOCUS
Your satisfaction with your job now is strongly dependent upon the rewards and opportunities for growth. If you're feeling stuck, now's the time to evaluate your position and make alterations.

### HEALTH AND FITNESS
Enjoy recreation or sports activities which take you outside or offer a chance to get back in touch with nature. Some fresh air may even stimulate a few fresh ideas!

### ROMANCE AND RELATIONSHIPS
Home and family ties gain emphasis now, and you may feel more inclined to expend your creative energy in home-oriented activities. Interaction with a sibling can bring mixed results, since you may not agree and can feel alienated if either of you express divergent opinions. Invite new experiences into your love life by taking a short trip or break in your routine from the 16th–24th. Take family considerations into account during the Full Moon on the 25th, when you may finally be ready to resolve old issues.

### FINANCE AND CAREER
Review your financial records and clarify problems before the 9th. You're ready to take action after the New Moon on the 10th, and will feel more confident if budgetary details are in place. A feeling that hidden activities or deceptive maneuvers could be undermining your progress may plague you from the 12th–19th. To avoid being thrown off balance by surprises from the 16th–24th, pay attention to your intuitive insights. Limit speculation.

### OPPORTUNITY OF THE MONTH
Get outside your everyday environment and allow room for spontaneous action from the 14th–24th.

**Rewarding Days:** 1, 4, 5, 9, 10, 14, 15, 23, 24, 28
**Challenging Days:** 3, 12, 13, 19, 20, 21, 25, 26

### AFFIRMATION FOR THE MONTH
"I am an excellent communicator."

### PRIMARY FOCUS

Invigorate your career by emphasizing programs or ideas which incorporate your individuality. Your need to share love extends not only into your personal life, but can positively alter your work.

### HEALTH AND FITNESS

Improve physical health and mental attitude by increasing your activity level. Avoid high risk activity from the 13th–20th; watch out for the other guy when driving.

### ROMANCE AND RELATIONSHIPS

Allow time for reflection upon your past near the Solar Eclipse on the 10th, when you may find that old psychological messages are still behind many of your motivations and needs. Children can play a special role, and, by sharing their experiences and reflecting upon your own childhood dreams, you may gain creative illumination. An existing love relationship can take a surprising turn from the 15th–20th, or you may discover a new love during this time. You're awakening to an important aspect of your inner self, and need room to express it during the Lunar Eclipse on the 24th.

### FINANCE AND CAREER

Networking and reaffirming important career connections assures your future development. You cannot afford to remain stuck in a circumstance which does not allow room for your unique input, and may feel restless if you're too confined. Presentations are well received from the 10th–30th.

### OPPORTUNITY OF THE MONTH

Using your talents opens the pathway to recognition. Career challenges and growth enhance your development after the 10th.

**Rewarding Days:** 1, 2, 3, 6, 7, 11, 12, 13, 21, 22, 25, 29, 30
**Challenging Days:** 4, 9, 10, 16, 17, 18, 23, 24, 25

### AFFIRMATION FOR THE MONTH
"I use my talents wisely and in harmony
with my highest needs."

## PRIMARY FOCUS

By concentrating on self-improvement, you may find it easier to meet demands from others while also experiencing greater satisfaction from yourself.

## HEALTH AND FITNESS

Evaluate your daily routine, dietary needs and personal habits for their effectiveness in providing the support you need to stay healthy. Boost supplements which benefit your nervous system now.

## ROMANCE AND RELATIONSHIPS

Friction at home can lead you to escape into a routine of overwork, but avoiding issues will only increase the tension. Conflict can help you identify areas which need improvement or expose problems at their core. Loving relationships show promise near the New Moon on the 9th, when sharing memorable entertainment or recreation can smooth ruffled feathers. Show appreciation to your partner after the 15th, when their support helps you deal with pressures from authority figures.

## FINANCE AND CAREER

Caught in the grip of strong expectations from your superiors while dealing with the undercurrents of competitors, your work can be bittersweet. Co-workers may be more cooperative through the 8th, but sudden changes can throw this situation out of balance by the 12th. Mercury's retrograde from June 12 until July 6 emphasizes a need to pay special attention to daily routine, and your attitude can turn the tide by the time of the Full Moon on the 23rd.

## OPPORTUNITY OF THE MONTH

Improvement in collaborate efforts from the 1st–4th and 21st–28th streamlines efficiency and stimulates fruitful results.

**Rewarding Days:** 3, 4, 8, 9, 17, 18, 21, 22, 25, 26, 30
**Challenging Days:** 1, 5, 6, 12, 13, 14, 19, 20

## AFFIRMATION FOR THE MONTH
"I gladly express my gratitude toward others. "

### PRIMARY FOCUS

Put fire into your love life by pursuing the object of your affection. Allow your talents and creativity to lead to personal satisfaction and professional success.

### HEALTH AND FITNESS

To hold your interest, fitness needs to be enjoyable. Invigorate yourself by getting involved in a class or sport you like. Take time to learn more about your body's needs after the 11th.

### ROMANCE AND RELATIONSHIPS

Partnership can be more rewarding, but you may need to take direct action in rekindling the flames of love. An old relationship may surface from the 2nd–10th, and you may still have unresolved feelings. Take an honest look at your needs, and allow your emotional spontaneity some room. If you've avoided real intimacy, you're in an excellent cycle to address your fears and open to the healing energy of love. Stay in touch with your inner self, especially during the Full Moon on the 22nd.

### FINANCE AND CAREER

Unfinished business projects linger on through mid-month, offering you a chance to revise or improve a situation. Bring greater cooperation into interactions with coworkers after the New Moon on the 8th. New options are launched more successfully from the 15th–24th, although you may meet some resistance from conservative factions. By incorporating reasonable restraint in spending with speculation in new ideas you'll see more success. Joint ventures show promise after the 27th.

### OPPORTUNITY OF THE MONTH

Instead of trying to outrun the past, deal with incomplete or unfinished business directly, opening a pathway for the unexplored.

**Rewarding Days:** 1, 5, 6, 14, 15, 19, 20, 23, 24, 27, 28
**Challenging Days:** 2, 3, 10, 11, 16, 17, 21, 30, 31

### AFFIRMATION FOR THE MONTH
"My heart is filled with love and joy!"

## PRIMARY FOCUS

Effective communication, educational pursuits, travel, or conferences provide your best sources for outreach and professional success. Diversify and increase your social contacts.

## HEALTH AND FITNESS

Avoid scattering your energy, and be sure to allow time for your physical needs. Work time can crowd your schedule after the 21st, when adequate attention to health keeps your mental energy sharp.

## ROMANCE AND RELATIONSHIPS

After a few adjustments early in the month, your love life shows improvements. An existing relationship needs room for airing differences near the New Moon on the 7th. Your need to feel more spiritually connected can lead to an air of projected detachment and may confuse your partner. It's easy to get caught in the trap of pursuing your "dream" relationship instead of working with the real situation before your eyes. Honestly evaluate yourself during the Full Moon on the 21st. Have you made yourself unreachable?

## FINANCE AND CAREE

Speculative interests and investments fare well through the 12th. Consultation with a financial advisor offers illuminating insights from the 18th–26th. Avoid the temptation to jump into a new situation after the 27th unless you're clear about all the details. Safeguard your belongings if you're traveling after the 24th. Creative pursuits appear successful throughout August.

## OPPORTUNITY OF THE MONTH

Outreach from the 10th–20th open the way to broadening your horizons and may lead to recognition or advancement in career.

**Rewarding Days:** 1, 2, 10, 11, 15, 16, 19, 20, 24, 29, 30
**Challenging Days:** 4, 5, 6, 7, 13, 22, 26, 27

## AFFIRMATION FOR THE MONTH
"I listen to my intuitive voice."

## PRIMARY FOCUS
Educational pursuits, fine-tuning your skills and business travel may increase your professional connections and add viability to your position. Creative artistry figures prominently in career.

## HEALTH AND FITNESS
Increasing demands from your work can add to your physical and emotional stress. Increase your nutritional support, and take time out for relaxation or a short vacation from the 19th–24th.

## ROMANCE AND RELATIONSHIPS
Explore the intimate side of love now that you feel encouraged by easier communication with your partner. Travel can boost the love quotient, especially if you're looking for a new relationship. Watch for sudden infatuation from the 16th–23rd, when you may be enticed by what you think you see rather than real substance. Changes would be welcome now, but try to keep them within your emotional safety zone! Think carefully before becoming intimately involved with someone at work.

## FINANCE AND CAREER
Broaden business contacts now. The New Moon on the 5th highlights joint finances, and review of jointly-held resources helps you determine if you're seeing benefits. New contracts or agreements show promise from the 7th–16th. Caution in pursuing unknown ventures is best after the 18th, when you may not have all the facts. Stick with your budget, since you may be tempted to buy things you don't need (and may not want!).

## OPPORTUNITY OF THE MONTH
Attend meetings, conferences, or travel to open your professional horizons. You're well-received on the 7th, 12th, 16th, 17th, and 25th.

**Rewarding Days:** 7, 8, 11, 12, 15, 16, 20, 25, 26
**Challenging Days:** 2, 3, 4, 9, 10, 18, 22, 23, 24, 30

## AFFIRMATION FOR THE MONTH
"My words and actions are guided by Divine Truth."

## PRIMARY FOCUS

Competitive urges may seem to be the results of a drive to achieve greater rewards from your career. Honestly consider your personal values and the true motivation behind your efforts.

## HEALTH AND FITNESS

Set reasonable goals for your fitness and strive to achieve them without overexerting your physical limitations. It's tempting to burn the candle at both ends.

## ROMANCE AND RELATIONSHIPS

Open conflicts can arise in personal relationships, including interactions with parents. Deal with anger directly, using it to help you explore the deeper nature of your discontent. Questioning a relationship may lead you to disclose a more pure sense of the real love you need in your life. By incorporating the spiritual and physical elements of your intimate relationship you'll find that love flows much more easily. A new approach offers hope in transforming the nature of your commitment after the 19th.

## FINANCE AND CAREER

To achieve progress in your career you may first have to decide if you're on the right path! Confer with a trusted advisor to help you determine your options. The complexities of reaching agreements can be highly frustrating during Mercury's retrograde from the 9th to 30th, but you may find answers by reviewing the situation from a different perspective. Clear out things which are no longer producing the results you desire to achieve.

## OPPORTUNITY OF THE MONTH

Even though you may feel like you're fighting a war, you'll at least have an idea of where your competitors stand.

**Rewarding Days:** 4, 5, 8, 9, 12, 13, 17, 22, 23, 31
**Challenging Days:** 1, 2, 6, 7, 11, 20, 21, 25, 27, 28

## AFFIRMATION FOR THE MONTH
"I am honest with myself about my feelings."

## PRIMARY FOCUS

Necessity may dictate that you stay in a situation which does not meet all your desired specifications, but you can make tremendous progress by maintaining your focus and completing the task at hand.

## HEALTH AND FITNESS

Increasing stress undermines your physical vitality unless you take some time to consciously release the tension. Schedule a massage or spa treatment on the 11th, 12th, 19th or 21st.

## ROMANCE AND RELATIONSHIPS

Work may leave you little time for personal pleasures, although travel or time spent sharing inspirational experiences from the 1st–9th can take the edge off any conflict. The Solar Eclipse on the 3rd and Lunar Eclipse on the 18th emphasize family ties. Your response to pressures from family may determine the difference between an honest, open relationship and a situation which increases your internal conflict. Make peace within yourself before asking for concessions from others.

## FINANCE AND CAREER

Be a keen observer in business meetings or presentations from the 1st–4th, when deception behind-the-scenes can create difficulties. Your ideas for change may be well-received on the 5th, 6th, and 9th. Power-struggles may result in a restructuring of the hierarchy from the 13th–22nd, and you can meet increasing expectations after the 21st. You can make progress in the face of change, but only if you're willing to be more adaptable.

## OPPORTUNITY OF THE MONTH

Meeting the challenges before you leads to accomplishment by the 29th, but you need to pace yourself. Consider this a marathon.

**Rewarding Days:** 1, 5, 9, 10, 13, 14, 19, 28, 29
**Challenging Days:** 3, 4, 8,, 16, 17, 23, 24, 25, 30

## AFFIRMATION FOR THE MONTH
"My values are in harmony with my highest needs."

### PRIMARY FOCUS

Setting long-range goals becomes imperative during this time of achievement and personal advancement. A tendency to become too egocentered can alienate those you desire to bring closer.

### HEALTH AND FITNESS

Stress continues to run high, although many of the pressures are greatly reduced. Continue to boost your nutritional support and gradually redirect your energy toward more relaxation by the 21st.

### ROMANCE AND RELATIONSHIPS

Your real friends have definitely emerged from the tests of the last few months. Enjoy their company from the 1st–17th, and take measures to bring greater equanimity into your friendships and your love relationships. Plan a special gathering or pleasurable experience for the Full Moon on the 17th, when sharing time with those you love can be highly gratifying. A new or an existing relationship is enriched through creating a unique expression of yourself and your individuality becomes highly appealing.

### FINANCE AND CAREER

Although some power issues may remain in your professional life throughout the month, the intensity level subsides considerably after the 10th. Greater success is achieved by beginning a project just after the New Moon on the 2nd, with momentum continuing through the 17th. But business contacts also fare nicely after the 26th, especially if you're planning for the future. Finances show improvement throughout the month.

### OPPORTUNITY OF THE MONTH

Your enthusiasm can be contagious, bringing substantial support from others on the 6th, 7th, 11th, and 16th.

**Rewarding Days:** 2, 3, 6, 7, 11, 12, 16, 17, 25, 26, 30 **Challenging Days:** 1, 5, 13, 14, 21, 22, 27, 28, 29

### AFFIRMATION FOR THE MONTH
"I have abundance enough to share."

# ♓ PISCES ♓
## The Fish

### February 19 to March 21

**Element:** Water

**Quality:** Mutable

**Polarity:** Feminine/Yin

**Planetary Ruler:** Neptune

**Meditation:** "Surrender to the heart of Divine Compassion"

**Gemstone:** Aquamarine

**Power Stones:** Amethyst, bloodstone, tourmaline, sugilite

**Anatomy:** Feet, lymphatic system

**Key Phrase:** "I believe"

**Glyph:** Two fish joined, swimming in opposite directions

**Colors:** Violet, sea green

**Animal:** Dolphin, whale, fish

**Myths/Legends:** Aphrodite, Buddha, Jesus of Nazareth

**House Association:** 12th

**Opposite Sign:** Virgo

**Flower:** Water lily

**Key Word:** Transcendence

**Positive Expression:**

Empathetic
Compassionate
Poetic
Imaginative
Visionary
Impressionable
Tenderhearted
Idealistic
Quiet

**Misuse of Energy:**

Confused
Addictive
Co-dependent
Escapist
Susceptible
Unconscious
Self-deceptive
Victimized

# ♓ PISCES ♓

## Your Ego's Strengths and Weaknesses

Through your heightened sensibilities, you experience life at the level of sensual, imaginative, and visionary possibilities. You're likely to express a mystical and magical personality, although you can be rather like a chameleon, constantly adapting to the energy around you. The plane of vibration is real for you, and your enjoyment of music and the arts is an extension of this awareness. Your perceptive abilities may be expressed through your visionary ideas and creative talents. The magic of sunrise, the light in the eyes of a child, and the tender touch of love inspire your trust in the continuity of life.

When others are trapped in their own despondency your faith in your beliefs is strong, and often carries you through. Your compassion for life includes an awareness of suffering and despair, and you may be drawn to reach out to those less fortunate. Despite occasional feelings of vulnerability, you can always imagine different possibilities. However, the fine line between the different levels of reality can be unclear, and you can become victimized by illusion or deception. It's important that you safeguard against unscrupulous individuals who would misuse your sympathetic understanding. Your unassuming nature may lead you to choose a quiet life; but if you are strongly involved with the public, you still need plenty of time and room for personal reflection or seclusion.

Because you are aware of the more subtle planes, you may feel drawn to escape from the heaviness of the physical plane through creative expression or meditation. But you can also fall prey to addiction, whether in the form of substances, situations, or relationships. Finding ways to stay in touch with your own inner self helps you maintain those boundaries which balance your relationship with life. You have the capacity to become a vehicle for divine compassion and transcendent inspiration, and can easily connect with the haven within yourself which radiates true compassion for yourself and for others.

## Your Career Development

You may use your career as a vehicle for expressing your vision of life, and need plenty of room to exercise your talents and imagination. Although ambition may not be your incentive, your desire to reach beyond the mundane may drive you to achieve strong success. A desire to beautify life may inspire you to work in the floral industry, landscape design, interior design, make-up artistry, fashion design, or hairdressing. You may also be a talented actor, musician, artist, dancer, or photographer.

Your ability to stay in touch with the collective consciousness can aid your success in the businesses of advertising media or movie-making. Counseling, social work, medicine, or the ministry can be outlets for your desire to uplift the human spirit. Or you may have a taste for the restaurant business. A special sensitivity to animals may draw you to a career focusing on their needs. Whatever your choice, your happiness is assured when you're in the flow.

## Your Approach to Romance

Romance can be your forte, since life without love would seem meaningless to you. Your search for your soulmate may lead you into many opportunities, but your trust may not always be met by another who understands your depth. You seek the enchantment of love, and can create a magical space into which you and your true love retreat from the harshness of the outside world.

You have the capacity to relate to almost anyone, but may feel most comfortable with the Water signs—Cancer, Scorpio, and another Pisces. Sharing special joys and creative moments is easy with Cancer, who offers caring and nurturance. Scorpio's magnetic sensuality carries you into another dimension. Another Piscean understands your special dreams and desires.

With Aries, you can enjoy spontaneous pleasures but may sometimes feel left behind. Taurus' taste for the good things blends well with your imaginative ideas. Gemini's changeability can throw you off balance, but you may enjoy the feeling—temporarily. Love with Leo can be too much work, since their demands can take much of your energy. Your Zodiac opposite, Virgo, can be highly attractive and may offer a direction for your hopes and dreams.

Libra's elegance and charm are interesting, but you may feel you're not quite perfect enough. You're inspired by Sagittarius' spiritual yearnings, but you'll have to stay alert to keep up with them. And even though Capricorn's stability feels safe, you need to carefully maintain your boundaries. Aquarius may be a better friend than lover, since they can be difficult to reach, even when you use your imagination!

## Your Use of Power

You're drawn to power from the ultimate Source of All Life, and desire to surrender to that energy as it pulses through your soul. Your life can become the instrument for the expression of divine love, which conceives and nourishes life itself. Staying in the flow of the currents of creativity keeps you charged with vitality, helping you become a radiant vision of faith and hope.

You may choose to follow a spiritual path or practices which require great devotion as part of your link with Divine Love. Even when you lose yourself or your direction in this release, you're hungry to stay connected. By focusing your energy and mind you can find the true illumination you seek and locate the true spiritual teacher residing deep within yourself. By touching the Source, you can become empowered to return that energy to the physical plane through your creative and imaginative endeavors. You can become the true healer, glowing with the light of love, returning a true sense of joy and hope to those you touch.

## Famous Pisceans

Edward Albee, Justine Bateman, Glenn Close, Billy Crystal, Sam Donaldson, Hubert Givenchy, Alan Greenspan, Jerry Lewis, Rue McClanahan, Liza Minnelli, Kate Nelligan, Linus Pauling, Philip Roth, Willard Scott, John Updike

# THE YEAR AHEAD FOR PISCES

By maintaining your focus and concentration upon your path, this can be a tremendously rewarding year. The opportunities presented during 1994 can bring a re-affirmation of your faith, beliefs, and ideals. This is a period of learning, and may also offer you an opportunity to teach others. Your relationship with the community and with your friends can become highly significant, extending your feeling of becoming more connected to all of humanity. Even though you may feel that you're leaving behind some old pathways, the new directions before you offer hope and can inspire you to become a more positive expression of yourself.

Jupiter's transit in Scorpio in trine aspect to your Sun can add a sense of ease and flow, and inspires increased optimism and self-confidence. Education, travel and the exploration of cultural and religious teachings can extend your understanding of the world around you, and may also bring situations which lead to your career advancement. It's tempting to just let things work out, rather than taking control of the reins and directing your life, but you may find greater reward in combining your options. By using your willpower to keep your life on track, and taking advantage of this period of expansion, you can move further and faster toward your goals. If you choose to slacken your self-control, you may instead lose some of the opportunities which await you. Self-indulgence during this cycle can be dangerous, since it's sometimes difficult to know your limits until you've gone too far. Find reasonable outlets for your increased feelings of generosity.

The Solar Eclipses during 1994 emphasize your connection to the world through travel, communication and interaction with others. If you're inclined to write, this is an excellent period to discipline your efforts or seek out publication of your ideas. At the least, maintaining a journal can be an illuminating experience, and may help you sort through some of the larger questions which challenge you. Many of those questions may be answered through your own inner processing, but you may also feel drawn to seek a teacher or guide whose influence can help you fine-tune your path. Find ways to share ideas with others—discussion groups, correspondence or other forms of networking. Most importantly, this cycle marks a time of broadening your horizons and connecting more fully to the source of wisdom and understanding.

**If you were born from February 19–March 3, you're feeling the focus and restraint of Saturn transiting in conjunction to your Sun.** This cycle of testing can be more enjoyable if you create some of the tests for yourself instead of just meeting them from the outside world. By using this energy to help you scrutinize your life choices, you can develop a greater sense of direction and control. Responsibilities can weigh heavily, and become more tolerable if you eliminate those things from your life which you no longer need. By lightening your load, you can then balance and carry those responsibilities which truly belong to you in a much more tolerable manner. Not only are you faced with the reality of your life situation, but you may discover that you've been carrying a load which actually belongs to someone else. Additionally, if you've been shirking your own responsibilities, they come to roost now, and you're staring them squarely in the eye. Rather than feeling overcome by the sight, take a good look at yourself and recognize that you're faced with situations which can stabilize your life and confirm your true identity. Allow yourself to surrender the responsibility for those things which really belong to someone else. Frequently, relationships with parents or authorities play a more significant role during this period. If you feel that you've been carrying some of the emotional pain for those you love (especially hold-overs from childhood), this is an excellent time to walk away from that burden and move into the experience of your true personal needs. You're challenged to assert your real identity, and may choose to leave dependent forms of behavior behind while you stand firmly on your own two feet. Your physical health may need closer scrutiny, and can also be improved now, when it's crucial to eliminate behaviors or attitudes which compromise your vitality.

**For those born from February 24–28,** maintaining a balance between opportunities for expansion while keeping your life on track can bring significant rewards. By taking advantage of Saturn conjunct your Sun while Jupiter trines your Sun, you may see this as one of the most powerful period of progress you've experienced in many years.

**If you were born from February 22–March 15, you're feeling some internal pressure from questions about your life purpose.** Chiron is opposing your Sun, and you may be faced with a sense of frustration, wondering if you'll ever grasp the meaning of it all. Bring your focus into the moment, concentrating on your feelings and senses about where you are now. Identify those things which are working and determine for yourself which situations are undermining your sense of feeling connected to your inner self. Recognize that no force or person outside yourself can point out your purpose— you must locate it for yourself through your connection to each breath, thought, word and deed.

**Neptune, your planetary ruler, is transiting in sextile to your Sun if you were born from March 10–14.** The emphasis now is that of connection to your hopes, dreams, and desires to share the love which resides deep within yourself. That love involves not only giving, but opening and receiving! Not only can relationships improve during this period, but you're in an excellent position to enhance your creative and artistic talents and abilities. An enhancement of sensitivity allows you to fine-tune creativity, bringing a more transcendent quality to your endeavors. If you do not feel artistically inclined, use this time to become more aware of the depths of color, the vibration of sound and music, and the essence of beauty around you. This expansion of consciousness not only elevates your sensitivity, but heightens your awareness. You may also feel more strongly inclined to offer energy and services to your community or to others who need help. When seeking out direction for these expressions, allow yourself to flow toward something that feels comfortable and to individuals who truly appreciate your assistance.

If you were born from March 12–16, you're experiencing the electrifying energy of Uranus transiting in sextile aspect to your Sun. This energy provides a sense of inner freedom and may stimulate you to move into untried territory. By exploring those ideas or experiences which intrigue and enliven your interest you can bring a fresh perspective to your life circumstances. Seek out groups or friends who share your interests, and become involved with change in your community. Surprising or unexpected situations can arise which offer unique opportunity to move into the forefront. You can also be part of creating a revolution, beginning within your own life. Use this energy to break away from attitudes, circumstances or relationships which inhibit your self-expression. Allow yourself the freedom to overcome your personal inhibitions and enjoy the realization of your dreams.

For Pisceans born from March 15–20, Pluto's transit in trine to your Sun brings a period of restoration and healing. Your need to incorporate a deepening awareness can be applied to every situation in your life, but you may find the most positive elements of change within your intimate relationships. It's time to heal the past. Where you've felt scattered, this energy helps you integrate. Where you've experienced loss, you're learning to feel wholeness. If given the opportunity to influence change, you can take your place of power with grace and ease. Primarily, this is your time to bring together the totality of your life experience, eliminate those elements which no longer work effectively and manifest a reality which suits your needs.

## Tools to Make a Difference

Even though many cycles this year positively support your ego self, you may also feel a sense of heaviness and sense that everything seems to drag on a bit too long. Seek out programs or experiences which enhance your own need to bring peace and comfort into your world. Utilize the transits of Uranus and Neptune through your Solar 11th House by connecting to a group who share your interests. Community programs which reach out to those less fortunate can provide an especially significant form of expression. Your personal involvement becomes an instrument for change. You might also benefit from a support group whose focus helps you deal with some of your own life issues, such as any types of addictive or co-dependent behaviors.

Learn more about the plants, herbs, and naturally occurring elements in your immediate environment. These substances can have a profound influence upon your health. During the times when the world seems to crowd in around you, use your element, water, to help you release some of the intensity. Soak in a bath sprinkled with fragrant herbs which rejuvenate your spirit and relax your mind. Take a walk by the seaside, lake, or stream. Consciously participate more closely in the everyday processes of life, and develop a sense of mindfulness in all that you do.

Music has an especially significant influence for you, and can become one of your primary tools to balance, invigorate, rejuvenate, or enhance your life. If you play an instrument, sing or dance, spend more time in these activities. Clear your energy each day through transcendent musical experiences. Allow time to be in touch with your body through movement, dance, or exercise with music as the background.

During your period of meditation, bring your energy into focus by first centering and balancing. Envision a large crystal before you, and see the bright light of the Sun shining through the stone. As the rainbow of colors reflects around you, draw in all the colors with each breath. Allow your higher self to direct these colors into the different parts of your body. Bring your focus to the top of your head and draw energy into your head, directing it throughout your body and connecting you to the grounding energy of the earth. Follow this practice with a period of deep reflection and quiet. When you return to your conscious state, feel refreshed and know that you can draw on this powerful energy which resides within you at any time.

### Affirmation for the Year

"My mind is focused, my heart is open
and my life is filled with joy!"

# ACTION TABLES FOR PISCES

These dates reflect the best (but not the only) times for success and ease in these activities according to your Sun Sign.

| | |
|---|---|
| Change Residence | May 10–27, July 3–9 |
| Request a Raise | March 12 |
| Begin a Course of Study | May 10–11; Nov. 3–4 |
| Visit a Doctor | Jan. 14–31; Feb. 21–Mar. 18; Aug. 3–17 |
| Start a Diet | Jan. 27–28; Feb. 23–24; Mar. 23–24; Apr. 19–20; May 16–17; June 12–14; July 10–11; Aug. 6–7; Sep. 2–4, 30; Oct. 1, 27–28; Nov. 24–25; Dec. 21–22 |
| Begin a Romance | July 8–9 |
| Join a Club | Jan. 11–12 |
| Seek Employment | Aug. 3–17; Nov. 30–Dec. 18 |
| Take a Vacation | Jan. 6–7; Feb. 2–3; Mar. 1–2, 29–30; Apr. 25–26; May 23–24; June 15–16; July 16–17; Aug. 12–13; Sep. 9–10; Oct. 6–7; Nov. 3–4, 30–Dec. 1, 27–28 |
| Change Your Wardrobe | May 28–July 2; July 10–Aug. 2 |
| End a Relationship | Feb. 26–27 |
| Seek Professional Advice | Jan. 2–3, 29–30; Feb. 25–26; Mar. 25–26; Apr–21–22; May 18–19; June 15–16; July 12–13; Aug. 8–9; Sep. 5–6; Oct. 2–3, 29–30; Nov. 26–27; Dec. 23–24 |
| Have a Makeover | Mar. 12 |
| Obtain a Loan | Jan. 4–5, 31–Feb. 1, 27–28; Mar. 27–28; Apr. 23–24; May 21–22; June 15–16; July 14–15; Aug. 10–11; Sep. 7–8; Oct. 4–5, 31; Nov. 1, 28–29; Dec. 25–26 |

### PRIMARY FOCUS
Begin the year by setting goals which broaden your options for success and allow you to interact with those who share your ideals and interests. Complete tasks, making room for new options.

### HEALTH AND FITNESS
Team sports or group fitness activities can offer your best resource for staying physically active. Excellence and progress are marked in competitive activities from the 11th–20th.

### ROMANCE AND RELATIONSHIPS
Your friends provide increasing support and also offer you the chance to show encouragement of their efforts. Open broader gates in your intimate relationship, allowing greater personal expression and independence. After the New Moon on the 11th, you may be drawn to a unique individual or into an unusual situation which piques your imagination. Try to maintain a realistic perspective, since it's easy to allow infatuation to influence better judgment. But do enjoy the romantic intrigue!

### FINANCE AND CAREER
Recognition and advancement in career can alter your plans for the future. Presentations, conferences, or meetings with your peers provide opportunities to share talents. Be alert to the undercurrents in the workplace after the 17th, when another's jealousy can undermine or weaken your position. It's important to maintain ethical standards, but that doesn't mean it's okay for someone to walk over you. Ask your allies for support.

### OPPORTUNITY OF THE MONTH
Find ways to share your visionary ideas and talents from the 10th–16th, when you can garner the support of powerful individuals.

**Rewarding Days:** 6, 7, 10, 11, 15, 16, 20, 25, 26
**Challenging Days:** 2, 3, 8, 9, 22, 23, 29, 30

### AFFIRMATION FOR THE MONTH
"I am confident and optimistic."

## PRIMARY FOCUS

To make progress in your personal and professional development you may need to take a serious look at your life situation. It's time to begin eliminating those things which you no longer need.

## HEALTH AND FITNESS

Your attitudes have a tremendous impact on your sense of well-being. Gain greater physical resilience through caring for your needs instead of ignoring them.

## ROMANCE AND RELATIONSHIPS

By opening yourself to love and acceptance, you pave the way for greater fulfillment in your relationships. Meditative reflection during the New Moon on the 10th can aid you in releasing old emotional pain, opening the way for greater happiness. Even if you choose to be alone, Venus transiting in Pisces after the 12th marks a positive period for expression of your feelings and needs, stimulating a greater capacity for love. Follow your intuitive feelings—you may still need time before you're ready to bare all.

## FINANCE AND CAREER

Paperwork, regulations or incomplete agreements stifle forward progress. Instead of pushing to finalize all details, use this time to investigate resistance and thoroughly research the questions. Mercury's retrograde from 2/11 until 3/04 can signal a time to concentrate on existing business instead of diving into new options. Finances improve considerably through financial planning from 20th–28th. Settle legal disputes after the 25th.

## OPPORTUNITY OF THE MONTH

Thoroughly investigate details of contracts, research, or long-range plans, but postpone final decisions until next month.

**Rewarding Days:** 2, 3, 7, 11, 12, 16, 21, 22
**Challenging Days:** 1, 4, 5, 10, 18, 19, 20, 25, 26

## AFFIRMATION FOR THE MONTH
"I trust my creative instincts."

## PRIMARY FOCUS

You're eager to move forward but may feel caught in the mire of unfinished details. Pace yourself, set priorities and eventually you'll reach the goals you desire.

## HEALTH AND FITNESS

Mars transits in Pisces after the 7th, and you may feel more strongly driven to increase activity levels. However, it's easy to overextend unless you consciously balance your priorities.

## ROMANCE AND RELATIONSHIPS

Taking short breaks in your routine from the 1st–7th to enjoy special moments with your sweetheart helps bring some sanity into what can be a stressful time. By the New Moon in Pisces on the 12th you're ready for more meaningful interaction with those you love and may feel that it's time to make commitments which you've previously avoided. These promises which you make to yourself can actually lead to a new level of freedom. That "antsy" feeling from the 20th–28th is just a test of your honesty!

## FINANCE AND CAREER

Legal disputes may lead to the emergence of information which finally settles a case. You may also be involved in contractual negotiations which had previously reached an impasse. The waiting appears to be over by the 17th, although all the details may not be in writing until after the 21st. Follow your budgetary spending guidelines after the 24th to avoid wasting resources on impulse. A careful review on the 27th (Full Moon) reveals your next move.

## OPPORTUNITY OF THE MONTH

Clarify misunderstandings from the 1st–5th, and prepare to make significant forward progress on the 12th.

**Rewarding Days:** 1, 2, 6, 7, 10, 11, 12, 16, 20, 21, 29
**Challenging Days:** 3, 4, 14, 18, 19, 25, 26, 31

## AFFIRMATION FOR THE MONTH
"I take responsibility for my actions and words."

## PRIMARY FOCUS

Concentrate on improving communication. By allowing your ideas to be known and becoming personally involved, you can facilitate the types of reforms which allow you to reach an important goal.

## HEALTH AND FITNESS

Allowing plenty of time to stay active and also to relax helps maintain stamina. Watch a tendency to overindulge in sweets from the 10th–14th. Use caution during travel from the 22nd–26th.

## ROMANCE AND RELATIONSHIPS

An existing relationship gains momentum through the 9th, but you may have to take some direct action to express your needs and desires before you see much progress. After the New Moon on the 10th thru the 15th, take time to get away from pressure. Your needs to feel spiritually and emotionally connected to your partner can be achieved, even with different philosophical approaches. Travel, inspirational experiences and animated discussion about ideals enliven your relationship near the Full Moon on the 25th.

## FINANCE AND CAREER

Instead of just watching the parade, get involved and make the contacts necessary to get yourself back into the picture. The connections you make now can open doors for long-range growth. Put your resources to work by investing time and energy in a new technology or system from the 16th–25th. Find ways to use your uniqueness within the existing framework.

## OPPORTUNITY OF THE MONTH

Surprising changes can open the way for you to take advantage of unusual situations from the 17th–29th.

**Rewarding Days:** 2, 3, 7, 8, 11, 12, 17, 18, 25, 26, 29
**Challenging Days:** 1, 5, 14, 15, 21, 22, 23, 27, 28

## AFFIRMATION FOR THE MONTH
"My mind is filled with creative concepts
and imagination possibilities."

### PRIMARY FOCUS

By making the right connections now, you have access to greater resources. However, you may feel that your timing is off a bit. Evaluate carefully before you jump into new circumstances.

### HEALTH AND FITNESS

Your motivation to stay active can be at a low ebb. Some attention toward building endurance can actually stimulate your overall energy level. Time out-of-doors is invigorating mid-month.

### ROMANCE AND RELATIONSHIPS

Strive to achieve greater harmony with those who spend time with you on an everyday basis, especially in your home. To achieve the comfort you desire, you can benefit from redecorating or rearranging your personal surroundings. Sibling relationships may be highlighted during the Solar Eclipse on the 10th. All your personal interactions may require you to evaluate the effectiveness of the communication of your feelings and needs. Jumping to the wrong conclusion can damage an intimate contact from the 13th–20th.

### FINANCE AND CAREER

Business travel, conferences, or meetings from the 1st–8th may provide contacts for broadening your professional horizons. By avoiding impetuous reactions to changing circumstances mid-month you're in a better position to strengthen your situation. Changes in the hierarchy or involvement with different superiors near the Lunar Eclipse on the 24th can be beneficial.

### OPPORTUNITY OF THE MONTH

Managing your resources in a responsible manner leads to an excellent situation for speculation or experimentation later on.

**Rewarding Days:** 4, 5, 9, 14, 15, 23, 27, 28, 31
**Challenging Days:** 2, 7, 11, 12, 18, 19, 20, 25, 26

### AFFIRMATION FOR THE MONTH
"I use my energy and resources wisely."

### PRIMARY FOCUS

Love's in bloom, and you may wax poetic. At the least, your creative and imaginative insights can draw positive support and attention from those you most desire to attract or influence.

### HEALTH AND FITNESS

A more consistent level of energy inspires you to improve your fitness routine. Recreation, play, or sports may be your best options for staying active this month.

### ROMANCE AND RELATIONSHIPS

An intimate love affair grows (or may begin) from the 1st–14th, although you may experience some inconsistencies which cause you to question your desires. Honest reflection may expose your own fears of losing your freedom, or perhaps you're looking for an unhealthy escape through your passion. It's time to break those negative patterns in achieving intimacy and experience greater fulfillment. By the Full Moon on the 23rd, you're ready to declare your feelings. Just be sure you know what they are!

### FINANCE AND CAREER

If your work involves the use of your artistic or creative talents, you're likely to have the chance to show them now. Mercury's retrograde from the 12th can lead to a second venture or a repeat of your earlier opportunity. If you're trying something different, you may have better luck on the 10th and 11th, although you'll need to have alternate plans in case it doesn't work out! Power struggles over joint resources loom from the 24th–29th.

### OPPORTUNITY OF THE MONTH

Put forth your best efforts during your Rewarding Days to assure that others can adequately evaluate your strengths and abilities.

**Rewarding Days:** 1, 5, 6, 10, 11, 19, 20, 23, 24, 27, 28, 29
**Challenging Days:** 3, 8, 9, 15, 16, 21, 22, 26

### AFFIRMATION FOR THE MONTH
"I have confidence in my creative abilities."

## PRIMARY FOCUS

Expression of your talents continues to open new vistas, but you may feel an undercurrent of competition. The strongest competitor could be within yourself; look honestly before placing blame.

## HEALTH AND FITNESS

Emotional turmoil can drain your physical vitality unless you acknowledge your feelings and deal with them directly. Staying active is important now to help alleviate stress.

## ROMANCE AND RELATIONSHIPS

Strengthening of your most cherished love relationships arises from your willingness to share. You may have to deal with jealousy from family members or criticism from parents (or their beliefs). Your priorities and ability to keep your emotional boundaries intact help you remain committed to your needs. Room to express your love is necessary during the New Moon on the 8th, when children can play a strong role. Receiving affection is important during the Full Moon on the 22nd.

## FINANCE AND CAREER

Details in contractual agreements need review from the 1st–10th, when you may discover all your requirements have not been met. A partnership provides positive support after the 11th, but you may feel that there are some conflicts which weaken its effectiveness. Competitive actions from others can inspire you to work harder, but you can undermine your own efficiency if you concentrate too much on the other guy.

## OPPORTUNITY OF THE MONTH

During the challenging period from the 17th–23rd you can rise to the top by maintaining your focus and self-discipline.

**Rewarding Days:** 3, 8, 9, 16, 17, 21, 25, 26, 30
**Challenging Days:** 1, 5, 6, 12, 13, 18, 19, 20

## AFFIRMATION FOR THE MONTH

"I am open to giving and receiving the love I need."

## PRIMARY FOCUS

Self-improvement efforts lead to more successful relationships and greater personal satisfaction from your work this month. However, it's tempting to concentrate your energy on the needs of others.

## HEALTH AND FITNESS

A class or informative source provides good information on the best ways to improve your health. Make an effort to put the things you learn into use.

## ROMANCE AND RELATIONSHIPS

Some of the romance may have disappeared from your relationship, and now you're dealing with the more realistic demands of intimacy. If you're feeling dissatisfied, look at your own expectations and attitudes. Decide first the type of partner you want to become. Address your needs to remove many of your own barriers toward intimacy, and seek escape from your self-imposed martyrdom. Rise above those limitations, spending time in personal reflection during the Full Moon on the 21st. Open to the love within.

## FINANCE AND CAREER

Bring improvements into your working conditions from the 3rd–17th. Listen to the needs and requirements of others, but recognize your own essentials. Launch new projects at work following the New Moon on the 7th, and provide room for flexible options. Review your finances from the 7th–26th, and be careful of newly-conceived speculative ideas after the 27th. You can achieve significant rewards on the 28th, if you're prepared.

## OPPORTUNITY OF THE MONTH

Your efforts can coalesce into a period of significant increase from the 18th–31st, but you must be realistic and responsible.

**Rewarding Days:** 4, 5, 13, 17, 18, 21, 22, 26, 27, 31
**Challenging Days:** 1, 2, 8, 9, 10, 15, 16, 29

## AFFIRMATION FOR THE MONTH
"I am open to change."

### PRIMARY FOCUS

Your spirited efforts to move beyond your current circumstances can bring you into contact with new people, ideas and situations which challenge your flexibility and imagination.

### HEALTH AND FITNESS

Seek out activities you enjoy, and incorporate some fun into your fitness routine. Dancing, swimming, classes, or other recreation offer a chance to meet new friends.

### ROMANCE AND RELATIONSHIPS

An existing partnership can be revitalized by experimenting with new ideas or options which enliven your sex life. Since you're likely to feel more open, you can encourage your partner to share fantasies and desires which perhaps felt inappropriate earlier. If you're seeking a new love, it's a good idea to recognize your vulnerability to easy infatuation, especially near the time of the Full Moon on the 19th. Channel your energy into activities which inspire your imagination after the 20th.

### FINANCE AND CAREER

Cooperative ventures provide ample opportunities to increase your financial worth, but you may also encounter some deceptive actions or practices which undermine your stability. Before agreeing to contracts or situations which increase your liability, be sure you know the nature of your responsibilities. Loaning money to friends or lovers can prove costly. Investigate claims and avoid making assumptions based on the "word" of someone else from the 18th–25th.

### OPPORTUNITY OF THE MONTH

Taking a new approach to an existing situation from the 14th until the Pisces Full Moon on the 19th paves the way to success.

**Rewarding Days:** 1, 9, 10, 13, 14, 18, 19, 23, 28
**Challenging Days:** 3, 5, 6, 11, 12, 25, 26, 30

### AFFIRMATION FOR THE MONTH
"My vision is clear and focused."

## PRIMARY FOCUS

Travel, educational opportunities or exposure to cultural activities provide an excellent situation for reaching beyond your limitations into broader horizons.

## HEALTH AND FITNESS

Be cautious in new activities in order to avoid excessive muscle soreness or injury, especially after the 20th. Take adequate precautions if you're in high-risk circumstances.

## ROMANCE AND RELATIONSHIPS

Your love life takes a dramatic turn as the result of travel or involvement in activities leading to greater enlightenment. You search for a soulmate may lead you to question the validity of your current relationship or can result in hesitation in a new situation. By making an effort to surrender to your higher needs, you may be ready to experience the true ecstasy of love. Rather than trying to duplicate a previous experience, allow yourself to open to fresh possibilities and exciting self-discovery.

## FINANCE AND CAREER

Presentations, conferences or meetings offer you a chance to influence the opinions of others. You can also gain in knowledge and insight by following the guidance of a masterful teacher until you feel confident. Mercury's retrograde from the 9th–30th emphasizes agreements, contracts or joint ventures—all of which require special consideration before you proceed. New options presented after the 24th are likely to be flawed in some way.

## OPPORTUNITY OF THE MONTH

Taking the time to reevaluate your commitments and choices allows you the option of making needed change.

**Rewarding Days:** 6, 7, 10, 11, 15, 16, 20, 25, 26
**Challenging Days:** 2, 3, 8, 9, 14, 22, 23, 29, 30

## AFFIRMATION FOR THE MONTH
"My thoughts are guided by Divine Truth."

### PRIMARY FOCUS

You can make significant progress in your career, but only if you remain aware of your strengths, limitations, and personal ethics. Incorporate a multi-cultural influence whenever possible.

### HEALTH AND FITNESS

Alternative therapies may offer relief from physical ailments from the 1st–8th, but you must also participate by shifting your attitude to one of wholeness. This can be a time of true healing.

### ROMANCE AND RELATIONSHIPS

Exceptional changes can occur in your romantic relationship. If you're in a situation which is open to growth, you can reach a level of commitment and bonding which confirms your love. However, if it's time to end a relationship, you're in an excellent position to walk away; each of you moving toward your higher needs. The Solar Eclipse on the 3rd emphasizes a need to communicate your needs and feelings, leading to greater understanding. During the Lunar Eclipse on the 18th, you're ready to move beyond your current limitations.

### FINANCE AND CAREER

Professional growth occurs as the result of taking advantage of business travel, educational opportunities (whether teaching or learning), or reaching into a newly opened territory. Power struggles brew after the 20th, and are likely to be the result of misplaced expectations. Avoid other's disagreements, since you may not even be involved! Make investments after the 24th.

### OPPORTUNITY OF THE MONTH

Your expertise may be sought to solve a problem from the 11th–13th, when you can easily impress others with your abilities.

**Rewarding Days:** 3, 4, 7, 11, 12, 16, 17, 21, 22, 30
**Challenging Days:** 1, 4, 5, 6, 18, 19, 20, 26, 27

### AFFIRMATION FOR THE MONTH
"I am comfortable in new situations."

## PRIMARY FOCUS

Career aims take top priority, and you can definitely make progress. Be certain you're aware of the responsibilities before you jump into advancement, since you could get in over your head.

## HEALTH AND FITNESS

Ignoring physical discomfort can lead to a break in your activity from the 1st–8th. Work may demand much of your time, but you still need to take care of your body.

## ROMANCE AND RELATIONSHIPS

Demands from others may seem unreasonable unless you discuss their concerns and understand their needs. It's also important to clearly illustrate your position, since you could offer misleading signals from the New Moon on the 2nd until the 7th. Take some time away from your routine on the 8th or 9th to enjoy your sweetie or indulge in your favorite entertainment. Family concerns can quickly grow out of proportion near the Full Moon on the 17th unless you address them directly.

## FINANCE AND CAREER

Even though you may experience recognition or advancement in your career, you may not trust the permanency of the position. A trial period from the 10th–31st can give you a better sense of the situation, but you may not have that luxury. Avoid the temptation to expect the same support from others that you would give to them. Be clear, direct, and forthright with your expectations to avoid disappointments. Financially, plan and budget your expenditures.

## OPPORTUNITY OF THE MONTH

In your eagerness to impress the right people, you may overlook the little guy. Remember your humanity from the 15th–24th.

**Rewarding Days:** 1, 4, 5, 8, 9, 10, 13, 18, 19, 28
**Challenging Days:** 2, 3, 15, 16, 17, 23, 24, 29, 30

## AFFIRMATION FOR THE MONTH
"I am humble, confident, and capable."

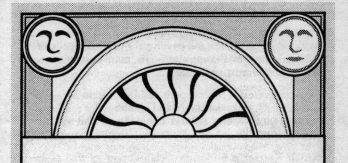

# SUN SIGN
# FEATURES

Ninah Kessler
Jude C. Williams
Vince Ploscik
Ralph Pestka
Tom Bridges
Jeraldine Saunders
Barbara Everett
Noel Tyl

# About our Features Writers

**Tom Bridges,** an astrologer in Big Rapids, Michigan, works at Matrix Software, developer of astrological software for personal computers. His main interests are horary and Uranian astrology.

**Barbara Everett,** a Minneapolis resident, teaches at spiritual retreats, does astrology and numerology readings, and enjoys traveling around the globe to visit various sacred sites.

**Ninah Kessler** is a Florida social worker as well as an astrologer. A regular contributor to the *Llewellyn Sun Sign Books*, and *Astrological Calendar*, she also writes about astrology for local publications, and does consultations.

**Ralph Pestka** is a professional astrologer, doing consultations, writing, and lecturing on astrology. With Priscilla Schwei, he co-authored *The Complete Book of Astrological Geomancy* (Llewellyn Publications, 1990).

**Vince Ploscik,** a full-time astrologer in northeastern Ohio, studied under Sophie Mason, He teaches classes, lectures, and does consultations, and has written eclipse articles for the *Sun Sign Book* for a number of years.

**Jeraldine Saunders** is the author of 11 books, including the best-selling *The Love Boats,* and *Signs of Love* (Llewellyn Publications, 1991), and creator of "The Love Boat" television series. She lectures and writes about astrology, numerology, graphology, and palmistry, and frequently appears on radio and television talk shows.

**Noel Tyl** lectures extensively throughout the U.S. and Europe. His most recent book is *Prediction in Astrology* (Llewellyn Publications), and he also edits Llewellyn's New Worlds Astrology anthology series.

**Jude C. Williams** is a master herbalist, with 25 years of study and practice behind her. She is the author of *Jude's Herbal Home Remedies* , and co-author of *Healing Herbs & Health Foods of the Zodiac* (Llewellyn Publications); also publishes *Back to Basics—A Newsletter on Natural Living.*

# Saturn in Pisces:
# Let Your Fear be the
# Gateway to Your Dreams

### Ninah Kessler

I once had a friend from Mississippi. She charmed me with her colloquialisms, like "we had a good harvest of beans. We froze most of 'em and just saved some for table use." When she had a gathering of women at her farm one March 17, we celebrated the snakes that St. Patrick drove out of Ireland, and cut apples into circles, making mandalas for the goddess. She told us that our fear was the gateway to our power. With Saturn in Pisces there is a corollary; let your fear be the gateway to your dreams.

If you want to see the fear in an astrological chart, just look at where Saturn is placed. Initially, this fear will block and frustrate us. Liz Greene states, "It is possible that each delay, disappointment, or fear may be utilized as a means for greater insight into the mysterious mechanisms of the psyche, and that through these experiences we may gradually learn to perceive the meaning of our own lives."

Our fears are even stronger when Saturn is in Pisces, the sign associated with the 12th House—what we repress. They take on the power of the shadow, and we will do anything to avoid them, so in 1994 we will be dealing with fear, both on a global and on a personal level. Unresolved issues from childhood and from past lives are apt to come up in ways that will be extremely difficult to ignore. We will be tempted by all kinds of escapes and addictions, but none will do the job. The only real answer is to confront what scares us and find out what it has to teach us. Then the flip side of this planetary configuration will emerge, and we will find that if we can dream it, we can do it. Pisces provides the imagination and Saturn gives the know-how.

There are many ways of looking at Saturn in Pisces, but maybe the best place to start is to look at the planet, since Saturn rules the Earth, our physical home in the universe. Pisces corresponds to the oceans, so this placement impacts our marine environment.

Globally, few would disagree that the Earth is at a crossroads. There are only so many toxins, ruled by both Saturn, Neptune, and Pluto, which can be released into our environment before the planet becomes unlivable. Just as we can only put so much into a landfill before it leaches into the water supply, we can only dump so many waste products into the ocean before it becomes a sea of sewage.

This year, 1994, is a good time for some ecological riddles. How many PCBs does it take to kill off all the marine life? How much nutrient runoff and algae bloom will be irreversible and totally kill the oceans? How many species of fish will we allow to become extinct before we do something about it? When will whales and dolphins stop beaching themselves, dying from mysterious illnesses? How do you feel about eating oysters when you know that they were raised in sewage?

While you're pondering the answers to these questions, remember that Pisces also rules chemicals, and check the headlines for accounts of oil spills which will dwarf anything that occurred with the tanker Valdez. Even routine drilling operations disturb the marine habitat, and each additional offshore drilling rig increases the chances of an oceanographic disaster.

Saturn is associated with the coral reef, since it is composed of the skeletons of sea creatures, and Saturn has dominion over the bony parts of the body. The reef is already in trouble, both from decay within and from careless boaters and divers. Will all the reefs in the world become extinct when Saturn enters Pisces? What will happen to all the sea life that is sustained in this rich marine habitat? One of the first people to draw our attention to this pollution was Rachel Carson, author of *The Silent Spring*, who has Saturn in Pisces in her birth chart.

It seems unbelievable that we are in the process of destroying our oceans, and you may be wondering how this could happen. One explanation is provided by Barbara Hand Clow, who notes that we have crystals in our bodies which are "programmed so that it is possible for people on Earth to destroy our planet with radiation and chemicals and not feel their actions." However, we will not be able to do this forever, for she also adds, "In the very center lies the Goddess who says, 'The poison you pour into my body is the poisoning of your body, and soon you will hear the screams of the protozoa in the seas.'"

The destruction of the oceans is particularly scary, since they are the source of all life, and the human body is primarily composed of a saline solution very similar to sea water. Neptune has been in Capricorn for ten years, and much of the population has been aware of the destruction of the oceans for about that length of time. The most excellent difference in 1994 is that Saturn in Pisces is in Mutual Reception to Neptune in Capricorn. This means that Saturn, which rules Capricorn, is in Pisces, while Neptune, which rules Pisces, is in Capricorn. Mutual Reception suggests that both planets can manifest their positive qualities, and makes it possible for us to make a difference.

Instead of functioning as a watery graveyard, the oceans could be a source of nourishment, recreation, and inspiration. Underwater farms, producing both seafood and sea vegetables, could feed a prosperous and thriving planet. First we need to face the horrible condition of our oceans, then we need to believe (Pisces) that our efforts (Saturn) will make a difference, and work (Saturn) to transform our dreams (Pisces) into a new reality (Saturn) And what usually stops us from doing this is our fears (Saturn), which need to be dissolved (Pisces).

Luckily there are a number of organizations that are already working to save the oceans. Greenpeace, Reef Relief, and the Nature Conservancy are the ones that come to mind, and I know that there are others. They need your support. Donate money and time. Stop eating dolphin with your tuna. Use baking soda instead of chlorine bleach, creating fewer toxins when you clean. Laugh when the plastics industry tells you that styrofoam is a gift to humanity, and write to your senators and to your television station, letting them know you don't like the ads. Saturn in Pisces suggests that if you like the coast you need to stop coasting.

Since Saturn in Pisces has traditionally been associated with financial troubles, you may wonder how this will affect our perennial recession. Saturn was last in Pisces between 1964 and 1967, and in 1966 the Dow Jones Industrials hit a significant bear market low. In Saturn's previous transit of Pisces, 1935–1937, we were experiencing the depths of the depression. Soon after this Roosevelt said that we had nothing to fear but fear itself. Much of the problem with Saturn in Pisces is that our fears (Saturn) are magnified by our imaginations (Pisces), and the more that we focus energy on scarcity and lack, the more we create this as our reality.

This certainly seems to be the case with our current economic difficulties, which have coincided with Neptune in Capricorn. We don't spend money because we are afraid things will get worse, there is a crisis in consumer confidence, and since consumer spending makes up two-thirds of the gross national product, the economy does not improve.

The most effective way to deal with this is to connect with our divine birthright and remember that we can manifest whatever we really need. Access your right livelihood, practice your prosperity affirmations, and review *The Dynamic Laws of Prosperity* by Catherine Ponder.

Another reason why Saturn in Pisces is not associated with boom times is that it is not really interested in making more money just to be able to have one more BMW. The "beamer" mentality is associated with Saturn in Capricorn, the era of yuppie consciousness. With Saturn in Pisces, even those who are young and upwardly mobile realize that earthly (Saturn) possessions are not very secure. The hurricanes, earthquakes, and layoffs of Saturn in Aquarius have shown us the folly of putting our faith in things that can rust, decay, collapse, get fired, or be blown away.

When Saturn transits through Pisces, we focus on more universal concepts like sharing the wealth. Saturn was last in Pisces from 1964 to 1967, and the hippies symbolized flower power, peace, free love, and communal living. In the thirties, when Saturn made its previous Piscean sojourn, Franklin Delano Roosevelt inspired us with New Deal National Socialism. Karl Marx, who has Saturn in Pisces natally (1818) published his book, *The Communist Manifesto,* in 1848, during his Saturn Return.

It is not so much that nobody makes money when Saturn is in this sign, but that money is made in Piscean ways. Aristotle Onaissis (1906) had Saturn here, and he made his fortune in ocean shipping. Bugsy Siegel (1906) made his through crime and the development of Las Vegas. Las Vegas was incorporated in 1905, and guess where Saturn was then.

Since Saturn rules authority figures, Saturn in Pisces dissolves the rigid hierarchy, facilitating more equitable forms of social interactions. Hence, in 1994 we are apt to see the transformation of the family. Since Neptune entered Capricorn the nuclear family has been changing to single-parent families and extended families. Additionally, with Saturn in Aquarius, there is less attention to biological relationships, and our families can be composed of friends. With Saturn in Pisces, expect to see more blended families and communal forms of living.

Interest in feminism also peaks during Saturn in Pisces, partially because it dissolves the hierarchy of the patriarchy. Consciousness raising was heightened in the 60s and Susan B. Anthony (1820) has Saturn in Pisces in her natal chart. Some famous female writers also share this placement—Emily Bronte (1818) and George Eliot (1819). Perhaps they expressed themselves this way because it was one of the few avenues open to women at the time.

Some of what mattered to us when Saturn was in Pisces were forms of entertainment that titillated our imaginations. In the thirties it was the glamour (Pisces) of the movies and Hollywood. Many stars were born when Saturn transited Pisces between 1935 and 1937, including Jane Fonda, Mary Tyler Moore, Alan Alda, Robert Redford, Burt Reynolds, Warren Beatty, Vanessa Redgrave, Albert Finney, and Julie Andrews. The previous transit gave us Katherine Hepburn (1907), Josephine Baker (1906), and playwrights Clifford Odets (1906) and Lillian Hellman (1905).

In the sixties our fascination was psychedelic music. While I do not yet have the chart data to back it up, I would hypothesize that many of the rock musicians now turning thirtysomething were spawned during Saturn's transit there from 1964 to 1967.

For those of us who need more of an escape than the movies or music, with Saturn in Pisces there are always drugs. Interestingly the glyph of Pisces is two fish swimming in opposite directions, and we use the expression, "he drinks like a fish" to describe someone who's into alcohol. The 30s marked the end of prohibition. Nicotine became stylish, and it's hard to find a movie from that period without someone seductively lighting up. In the 60s the motto was "turn on, tune in, drop out," and the drug culture was born. With all this abuse of chemicals, it's no wonder that Saturn in Pisces is associated with liver problems.

While crack is likely to remain popular in 1994, the biggest growth is likely to be in prescription medications developed by the big pharmaceutical firms.

But with the combination of Neptune in Capricorn and Saturn in Pisces, we'll be able to do other things than to escape into fantasy land. We could discipline (Saturn) our imaginations (Neptune) to accomplish what has only been dreamed of before. This could happen from our connection with our higher selves, the accessing of the akashic records, or the development of astral travel. Robots, computers, and virtual reality could enhance the scope of our visions and enable us to translate our conceptualizations into finished products.

Since Pisces rules institutions like psychiatric hospitals, we're likely to see changes here, particularly in the use of psychopharmacology. During Saturn's transit of Pisces in the thirties, lobotomies and Electroconvulsive Shock Therapy (ECT) were first used. In the 1960s psychotropic drugs enabled millions to be released from institutions.

The psychotropic pharmacopoeia continues to expand, and often produces results that are truly miraculous. Yet how many will just take Prozac rather than exploring what their depression has to teach them. It is easier to pop a pill than to face our fears, but sometimes the more challenging path is where the real growth is.

Perhaps in 1994 we'll be able to create sanctuaries for souls needing help on their journeys. These could be havens where one could stay as long as needed, with spiritual, psychological, and pharmacological help available.

There's apt to be an increase in the variety and use of medications at the general hospitals, as well as an increase in socialized medicine. Perhaps with Saturn in Pisces we'll see the development of drugs from more natural substances, like those found in the rain forest. During previous episodes of this transit, antihistamines, amino acids, sulfa drugs, and vitamins were synthesized, the term "allergy" was coined, new techniques were invented for growing cells outside of the body, the whooping cough bacillus was identified, Wasserman introduced the serum reaction test for syphilis, artificial insemination was used on animals, birth control pills were declared to be safe, and Christiaan Barnard performed the first open heart surgery. This time we're likely to develop drugs (Pisces) that retard aging, (Saturn),

© 1979 VOLK

especially as the baby boomers start getting wrinkles. Saturn in Pisces has traditionally been associated with cosmetics, as they are a product (Saturn) that gives us a more glamorous (Pisces) appearance. Interestingly, cosmetics giant Elizabeth Arden was born with Saturn in Pisces in her 12th House.

There are moral implications to the development of these preparations, and our species has misused chemicals before poison gas, DDT, biological warfare. Some say we misused technology in Atlantis. With the ecosystem in the critical care unit now, what we do is likely to impact the future growth of our species.

On a psychological level, Saturn in a water sign suggests that we are learning about healing our emotional or astral body. According to Liz Greene, with Saturn in Cancer we build an emotional foundation, with Saturn in Scorpio we blend our emotional bodies, and with Saturn in Pisces we merge with life itself.

Saturn is not really happy in Pisces, as form is dissolved. But we must let go, for it is only in yielding that our energy can be rebirthed in Aries. At this point in our evolution, many of us are attached to our emotions, and, as they say in Zen, "attachment is the cause of all suffering." If we let our fear of emotional pain dominate us, we are likely to become sick or crazy. But we can let our fear become the gateway to our dreams.

How can we do this? Saturn in Pisces, especially with the mutual reception to Neptune in Capricorn, enables us to imagine other options and work at building foundations on the earth for our castles in the air. The lesson here is that if you can dream it, you can do it.

Now most of us are not enlightened beings, able to instantaneously transform the material plane with our thoughts like Jesus, who had Saturn in Pisces natally. I believe that the miracles he performed were to show us that it could be done, and that during this transit of Saturn in Pisces, more and more of us may be able to do it. And this is likely to be what it takes to heal the planet.

As we evolve, we need to allow our visions to guide us as we work to preserve the planet. Jan Spiller notes in *Spiritual Astrology*, "By acknowledging yourself as creator of your private visions and dreams, you can gain confidence in your ability to bring about a true manifestation of that which has already been created in your imagination."

With this combination of the tangible and the spiritual, we can learn to communicate telepathically with other people, with animals, with plants, with rocks, with extraterrestrials, and with other planetary bodies. We started this process with Neptune in Capricorn, as we began to unlock the wisdom stored in crystals, and to communicate with the dolphins. Some will have access to the akashic records, and can use them to get information about other times and other lives. The rest of us can open to a higher power and get in touch with the spiritual purpose for this incarnation.

The spiritual component is very important with Saturn in Pisces. Neptune, the planet that rules spirituality, was discovered in 1848 when Saturn was in Pisces. Important religious leaders have it natally in their charts, like the Dalai Lama XVI (1935) and Pope Pius XII (1876).

Fear is associated with spiritual evolution. Pisces dissolves Saturnian boundaries, and we are summoned to interact with the cosmos. Here mystical rules apply, with karmic consequences. We must fortify our spiritual strength, cleanse the planet, clean up our acts, and facilitate the birth of a new awareness when Saturn enters Aries.

## Opportunities and Challenges

Each sign will have special opportunities and challenges with Saturn in Pisces. They are:

♈ *ARIES:* Time to stop being so rambunctious, Aries, so chill a little. For the past decade you were out there focusing on worldly concerns and on interacting with others, but all that is about to change. To get ready for the new cycle when Saturn enters Aries, you need to pay up old debts and even the score. While you're apt to be well rewarded for the positive work that you've done, since nobody's perfect (except for enlightened beings), you'll feel intensely what went wrong. While personal growth is not necessarily a picnic, if you do face your fears and learn from your mistakes, you'll be way ahead on the karmic scale. You may want to allocate a good bit of time for yourself, as you're like a caterpillar going into the cocoon. They don't call the 12th the House of Seclusion for nothing. Evaluate where you stand and plant seeds for the next 29 years. You may want to study hatha yoga, the martial arts, or take an aerobics class—something that centers you so you can open yourself to the intuitive insights that the universe is waiting to bestow. If you get discouraged, remember that in a few years you'll be making your debut as a butterfly.

♉ *TAURUS:* Some Bulls are likely to be happier than others this year. For those on the path of right livelihood, business interests are paying off, friends are supportive, and you're making the most of networking opportunities. Additionally, there's the satisfaction that comes from following your heart's desire. If you have just been working to pay the bills, you're finding out that no amount of money can compensate for selling your soul. Those acquaintances you've been cultivating because they're good for business are so superficial, and your material goodies are just not that satisfying. As always with Saturn, that cruel taskmaster, probably the best advice is to accept the situation, continue to act responsibly, and know that this too will pass. Don't miss opportunities to cut your losses and get in touch with what really turns you on. Humanitarian causes and focalization groups can be just what the doctor ordered. You'll feel better about yourself if you do something positive for the planet.

Ⅱ **GEMINI:** Congratulations, Twins, it's harvest time. You're reaping the fruits of your labor. Those seeds that you planted 21 years ago finally came through. Enjoy the recognition that comes your way, you've worked hard for it. You're likely to be very busy enjoying your business success; however the responsibilities that come with it may crimp your style. Remember that to whom much is given, much is expected, and the higher you rise, the steeper the fall. You're not likely to have too much of a problem if your professional self is a reflection of your spiritual self. If you're one of those Twins that has been confused about what you want, you may not be receiving those corporate kudos, but it is an opportunity to decide what you want to be known for in the next thirty-year cycle.

♋ **CANCER:** On your mark, get set, go. You're on the brink, so make the final adjustments before lift-off. Enrolling in a university or professional institute can assist your career. You may find yourself in some far-away places, but not just to have a good time—it's travel for work. Saturn in your Solar 9th House can mean some problems with the courts, and the judge will only see it your way if your case is karmically correct. These lawsuits could be about business finances, or you could be renegotiating your alimony. Another drawback is that it's kind of scary out there in the world; you're usually more comfortable at home. But the opportunities are too good to miss, so pack your security blanket in your flight bag and prepare for takeoff.

♌ **LEO:** If you've been relying on someone else for financial assistance, Saturn could be showing you the error of your ways. You'll be in a better position if you're self-supporting and the balances on the credit cards are low. Financial setbacks may plague a partner, or some insurance money that you were counting on could elude you. If you're divorcing, there could be some difficulties dividing the assets. But when it comes to relationships, it's not just the money that's bothering you. Maybe you thought you understood your spouse more than you really did. The 8th House is related to merging with a significant other, and you may have an inability to connect. Once you accept responsibility for keeping yourself separate, you increase the chances for contact. You may experience the death of someone close, or it just could be a sense of being apart. You may have a tendency to want to use drugs to escape from the pain, but that will only compound the problem. Instead, use these dark thoughts to help you appreciate just how wonderful and precious life really is, and share your Leonine warmth with your special someone.

**♍ VIRGO:** No man is an island, and you are likely to be involved with a partnership that means more to you than you may want to admit. A mutually supportive and loving relationship will only be strengthened by the challenges that can come up at this time, but a weak one could be stressed to the breaking point. Asking for help seems wimpy to most Virgos; instead, they attract people they can take care of, like a good codependent. This solution works fine until they really do need help and find that their partner is out in the ethers. The opposite scenario is that the spouse gets it together, doesn't need a relationship to survive, and starts to evaluate whether the partnership is viable. In either case, with Saturn in Pisces, relationships aren't likely to be easy. The best thing to do is to let go of your perfectionist standards for others, assess whether your current relationship has enough going for it to stand the test of time, and either cut your losses or work to create the divine union that you are seeking. If you are not in a significant relationship at this time, you may realize that keeping people out of your life can get lonely, so start doing your affirmations and taking responsibility for creating your reality. You could also be offered a business partnership at this time. Evaluate it very carefully; if it looks good, it could be the beginning of a "beautiful friendship."

**LIBRA:** Have you been a good Libra for the past 12 years? Have you been working on yourself, getting to know who you are, and building a strong foundation? Then just put on the finishing touches, for your debut is coming. Take that computer course if you need to be electronically literate, join a gym if your body needs work, or make a commitment to be of service to the planet. However, if you are still in the middle of an identity crisis, don't panic and try to get your act together all at once. It's likely to throw you off balance, and you know that you get sick when that happens. This is really not the best time for your health anyway, so don't make things worse. Instead of giving yourself a hard time, use your organizational skills and prioritize what needs to be done. Make some changes so that the picture you present to the world reflects who you really are. Watch your diet, drink plenty of liquids, and find an exercise program you can live with. You need to be in good shape for the climb to the top of the heap in the years ahead.

**SCORPIO:** Remember all those books you wanted to write, those pictures you wanted to paint, that instrument you've promised yourself you would learn. Use Saturn's transit of your 5th House to combine the perspiration with the inspiration and get down to work. While this is not likely to be the time that you win the lottery, and speculation is not encouraged, you may surprise yourself with what you can accomplish if you're willing to work at it. Your children need your attention now, so don't take on so many other commitments that you can't be there for them. While this could seem like work at times, you'll be repaid in spades. If you have any illusions about romantic liasons, the rose-colored glasses could come off about now. While this may be more than you care to deal with, it's an opportunity for a stronger, more lasting commitment a few years down the road.

**SAGITTARIUS:** When did you last have your house checked for termites? Improve things at home, starting with the foundation and working your way up to the attic. This is an opportunity for symbolic house-cleaning as well. Get your life in order, beginning with the recesses of your psyche. If you rent, this might be a time to consider purchasing real estate. You won't make a killing from it, but you'll have a place to live. You may think that a base is unnecessary, as home is where your heart is, but sometimes even Sagittarians need some territory that they can call their own. It's time to get to know who you really are and to deepen relationships with the people who really care about you, and you have to do this somewhere. If a home seems confining, it's probable you have some unfinished feelings about mom and dad. You're the one who chose to incarnate with them as parents, so you might as well find out what it is that they have to teach you.

♑ **CAPRICORN:** Are you experiencing one of your periodic depressions? Seeing the glass as half empty instead of half full? Maybe you're being too sensitive to the neighbors. Remember Fritz Perls—you're not here to live up to other people's expectations, and they're not here to live up to yours. Your true friends will accept you for who you are, and it's a good way to weed out those hangers on. Besides, you may not really be depressed, just quieter because you prefer to talk about what really matters, and you're looking for someone who's interested. You might find it helpful to take a canoe trip down the river, read some inspirational books, or listen to some soothing and rejuvenating music.

♒ **AQUARIUS:** Although you may want to be known for your humanitarian generosity, this isn't the time to buy a boat for Greenpeace; that is, unless you have a trust that will pay for it. Organize a recycling co-op in your neighborhood instead. While the universe will provide you with all that you really need, it wouldn't hurt to keep your desires to a minimum. But these financial restrictions aren't likely to bother you too much, as your money has an elusive quality about it anyway. You need to pay attention to what you value, and you may find that some things that you thought you believed in no longer matter to you. If you realize that you do care about what happens to the planet, there is no better time to do something about it. Rather than striving to accumulate possessions, remember that it is who you are and not what you have that is most important.

♓ **PISCES:** Have you enjoyed that sweet ride to the top of the charts, or are you nursing your wounds because things didn't go as well as you wanted them to. In either case, it's time to say good-bye to the past and get ready to begin a new cycle. Stop facing backward and look at who you are and what you want to create. Remember that this is a special opportunity for you to align your heart's desire with what needs to get done, and to be practical about what you want to be doing with your life. Begin with an assesment of who you really are, and throw away those masks you've been hiding behind. It's pretty lonely when your persona wins all those popularity contests, and the real you slinks around incognito. It's not likely to be a particularly high energy time, so you may want to cut back on your commitments and focus on getting to know the one person who's always there for you. Invest in what's really important— what you really want to create for yourself and for the planet.

## Summary

If we look at the planetary configurations over the past five years, a pattern emerges. In 1989, Saturn conjuncted Neptune in Capricorn. Now, Saturn is in Pisces in Mutual Reception to Neptune in Capricorn. The cosmic forces are facilitating the blending of the spiritual and the material worlds. Saturn, the planet of limitations, is opening up, and in the spaces that are created we get to confront and to transcend our fears. As we do this, the boundaries between the physical and the etheric worlds are dissolving.

In the words of Barbara Hand Clow in *Heart of the Christos*, "Saturn teaches that we must experience all levels of life on Earth. Saturn is the planet that reveals that we are not separate from matter, that density is an illusion, that vibration is what really forms reality . . . We are mere thoughts in the mind of God."

Since Saturn is associated with world governments, this could be the dawning of the new world order.

Whether this will be a totalitarian police state or a golden age of peace, prosperity, and harmony is up to us. Any belief system can be used or abused. It depends on what is happening in the heart.

## Bibliography

Clow, Barbara Hand. *Heart of the Christos: Starseeding from the Pleiades*. Santa Fe: Bear & Company, 1989.

Greene, Liz. *Saturn: A New Look at an Old Devil*. York Beach, ME: Samuel Weiser, Inc., 1976.

Jansky, Robert Carl. *Astrology and the Feminist Movement*. Van Nuys: Astro-Analytics Publications, 1977.

Spiller, Jan and McCoy, Karen. *Spiritual Astrology*. New York: Simon & Shuster, Inc., 1988.

*The Timetable of Technology*. New York: Hearst Books, 1982.

# Astrological Healing With Herbs

## Jude C. Williams

Astrology means "star wisdom." Ancients believed that events in the heavens reflected and affected the destinies of each and every person on earth. Early practitioners found that the heavens foretold the changing seasons, weather, and other important events. This information was used to plant and harvest crops under particular conditions according to the zodiac; still a popular practice today. An Egyptian named Hermes is believed to be the first authority on botany, mathematics, and medicine—and how the planets and stars influenced all these sciences. While it is not clear whether Hermes was an actual person, or one of Egypt's great gods, he is credited with many books on the subject. *The Book Of Hermes On The Plants Of The Seven Planets* and *Medical Mathematics* are attributed to his authorship and have been handed down from generation to generation.

In the first century a man named Manilius wrote several books on astrology. He wrote of two theories that are still a part of that science today. He determined that there are "houses" that have a particular influence over events in daily lives. The second idea was that each of the twelve signs matches a part of the physical body. He pictured the figure of a man bent in a curve around the zodiac. Zodiac is a Greek word that means "circle of figures" or "circle of life."

Today, the practice of using astrology to treat particular illnesses is becoming common. Tests have been done on the effect of the moon on certain mental illnesses. The results show that the new and full moon cause changes of mood and behavior, just as the ancient astrologers claimed. The medical field has found that even the time it takes for blood to clot is affected by the moon. The full moon has been found to stimulate births—midwives have long known this to be true. Scientists have found that even the sex of children can be determined by the position of the moon. If conception occurs during the time the moon is in a positive sign of the zodiac, there is a 96 percent chance of the child being male. If the moon is in a negative sign during conception, the child will be female.

Hospital staffs have learned to watch liver patients closely between the hours of 11:00 P.M. and 1:00 A.M. because that is the time that the liver is most active, and problems are most apt to occur then. Our body temperature also changes on a regular pattern during a twenty-four-hour period.

Early practitioners of medicine were accomplished astrologers. This was the first way to diagnose and treat patients. Diet was also attended to in order to correct physical illness. The whole system was treated as one. They knew that the physical was only a part of the whole. Herbs were a part of the natural world and thus came under the influence of the heavens. This was a new science that the healers had to become proficient in, in order to be of help to first the royalty, then the common masses.

The early shamans practiced medicine using the herbs and plants that surrounded them. Medicine as we know it today began with the use of herbs for healing. Our scientist today are testing these herbs and finding that early knowledge was correct. Most of our modern-day miracle drugs are plant-based, and we are now finding that herbs have a lot of value medicinally. We literally spend billions on research of the information given by shamans worldwide. They long ago learned, through trial and error, the properties of the herbs. Modern science now wants validation of that knowledge and they are getting it through research.

The early shamans had to be proficient in the art of astrology in order to diagnose and treat illnesses. We know by trial and error the right time to plant and harvest using the moon signs—why would this not hold true to harvesting and using herbs to treat the body ills that mankind is afflicted with. I have long held the theory that the herbs that grow in a given area are best used to treat the people that live in that particular area, because the mineral content in the herbs is common to that area; and that the individual body has adjusted to it, through the water in the area as well as the eating of vegetables grown there. Our scientists and physicians have found that our health is dependent upon certain mineral salts found in the plants. Astrology has long maintained that these salts are associated with certain Sun signs. We now know that many foods can lower cholesterol and blood pressure as well as alleviate other life-threatening diseases. All other illnesses that afflict mankind are caused by, or are affected by, our diet.

Native Americans have always believed that our health is dependent upon what we eat. This relates to the way we treat our soil. We will get only from the soil what we put back into the soil. I trust my instincts when it comes to my health, and my experience has been that most of the old beliefs ring true. I grow more interested in the correlation between astrological signs affecting certain herbs and plants and thus affecting the foods I grow and ingest, which in turn affects my physical health and well being.

We must realize that the wisdom of the past is of value to us and learn more about the natural world of astrology, natural healing, and we need to make our walk on the earth more compatible with nature. All of life is a circle and we must learn this if we are to survive. All is connected, whether we like it or not. Manilius wrote of the zodiac as a circle with the human figure bent in a curve around the circle. Each of the twelve signs relate to a part of the human body.

I am including a small list of herbs that are pertinent to each sun sign. I do want to caution you that herbs alone won't heal. They are not miracle workers. Your physician alone does not heal you. He is not a miracle worker. Pure and simple, your body heals itself. All you are doing by using herbs is to strengthen your immune system so that it has a better chance to heal itself. By keeping as much of the chemicals away from our systems as we can and using as many natural products as we can, we are helping our system to respond faster by using natural medicines.

We all need to take a look at some of the chemicals that are in commercial products. We put substances on our skin that we would never dream of ingesting orally, yet our skin absorbs what is placed on it, and the chemicals that are in that hand lotion end up being stored in our liver. We can and should learn to produce the products that our families use daily. We should and can learn to grow and store as much of our food supply as we are capable of. We can and should learn enough about the natural methods of treating simple illnesses by using the knowledge passed down to us by those early astrologers and shamans.

The following list shows what part of the body is affected by the sign ruling our birth dates. Then we will go into the remedies for each sign.

## Signs in Relationship to the Body

| | |
|---|---|
| ARIES | Head, face, and brain |
| TAURUS | Throat and neck area |
| GEMINI | Hands, arms, nervous system, and lungs |
| CANCER | Breast and stomach |
| LEO | Heart, spine, and generative organs |
| VIRGO | Bowels, solar plexus, and alimentary canal |
| LIBRA | Back, kidney, and bladder |
| SCORPIO | Uterine and generative organs |
| SAGITTARIUS | Thighs and nervous digestion |
| CAPRICORN | Knee area and disorders of the skin |
| AQUARIUS | Calf and ankle area |
| PISCES | Foot and toe |

# Herbs in the Sun Signs

The herbs listed in this section are especially important to each Sun sign. Following each listing are herbal remedies that show different ways to use some of the plants. *

## ARIES

Skullcap *(Scutellaria laterifolia)*
Honeysuckle *(Diervilla lonicera )*
Hops *(Humulus lupulus)*
Lettuce *(Lactuca sativa)*
Valerian *(Polemonium caeruleum)*
Violet *(Viola odorata)*
Passion flower *(Passiflora incarnata)*

**Valerian**

Blue flowers are the signature of certain herbs, indicating that they have sedative value. Aries has a tendency to get nervous headaches and a sedative herb works very well for her or him. This tea has three herbs that have the signature and is a pleasant way to treat a headache caused by mental strain. Add 1 tablespoon each of passion flower, violet leaves or flowers, and skullcap. Mix well and add 1 teaspoon of the mixture to 1 cup of boiling water. Cover and steep 10 minutes. Strain and sweeten with honey.

A tincture made from valerian is an excellent way to treat any nervous disorder. Place the powder or root of valerian in a pint jar and fill the jar with vodka. Place in a warm area and allow to steep for at least two weeks, shaking daily. Strain and place in a sterile container. Dosage is 5–15 drops in tea or other liquid. Guaranteed to stop headaches. Valerian has similar properties as Valium, without the side effects.

---

* This work is no substitute for proper medical care. It is not intended to be a medical guide, but to discuss alternative, traditional remedies that have been found effective. Herbs can be very potent and must be used responsibly. Some of them can be poisonous, or stimulate allergic reactions. The publisher assumes no responsibility for the efficacy of any of these recipes, nor do we promise any cures. Use caution and common sense with the recipes found in this article.

## TAURUS

Horehound *(Marrubium vulgare)*
Irish moss *(Chondrus crispus, Gigartina mamillosa)*
Slippery Elm *(Ulmus fulvus)*
Coltsfoot *(Tussilago farfara)*
Thyme *(Thymus vulgaris)*
Sage *(Salvia officinalis)*
Balm of Gilead *(Populus candicans)*

**Sage**

Taurus seems to have trouble with sore throats. Thyme is a good antiseptic to use when treating disorders of the bronchial system. Place 1 teaspoon of the herb in 1 cup of boiling water. Cover and steep until cool. Strain and use as a gargle to relieve sore throat.

Balm of Gilead gargle; Balm of Gilead has pain-relieving properties, as well as being an expectorant and antiseptic. Place 1 tablespoon of the balm of Gilead in 2 cups of boiling water. Cover and steep 20 minutes. Strain and use as a gargle. It has a numbing effect on the throat and relieves pain immediately.

## GEMINI

Parsley *(Petroselinum crispum)*
Boneset *(Eupatorium perfoliatum)*
Carrots *(Daucus carota)*
Comfrey *(Symphytum officinale)*
Yarrow *(Achillea millefolium)*
Calendula *(Calendula officinalis)*
Fennel *(Foeniculum vulgare)*
Sage *(Salvia officinalis)*

**Yarrow**

Boneset has two good reasons for being the herb of preference for Gemini. It serves to eliminate mucous from the bronchial system and is also a wonderful muscle relaxant. When combined with comfrey and yarrow it will also serve as an expectorant and yarrow has pain-relieving properties for aches and pains associated with colds and flu, and acts as an astringent. Combine 1 tablespoon each of yarrow, comfrey, and boneset. Place 1 teaspoon of the mixture in 1 cup of boiling water. Cover and steep 15 minutes. Strain and sweeten with honey. Drink at the first sign of chest congestion as Gemini has a tendency to suffer from pleurisy.

Pleurisy treatment; Mix 1 tablespoon each of boneset, yarrow, ginger, sage, Irish moss, elder flowers, milkweed root, and elecampane root. Add two tablespoons of the mixture to 1 quart of water. Boil down to half the liquid. Strain well and add 1 teaspoon oil of peppermint and 8 ounces of honey. Dosage is 1 tablespoon every 2 hours.

# CANCER

Chickweed *(Anagallis arvensis)*
Hyssop *(Hyssopus officinalis)*
Peppermint *(Mentha piperita)*
Red clover *(Trifolium pratense)*
St. John's Wort *(Hypericum
  perforatum)*
Dock *(Rumex spp.)*

**Red Clover**

Cancer seems to suffer most from indigestion and stomach upsets. Peppermint is an excellent treatment for heartburn and helps ease digestive upsets. Add 1 teaspoon of the dried herb to 1 cup of boiling water. Cover and steep 10 minutes. Strain and sweeten with honey. Drink to relieve heartburn.

Red clover tea helps to relieve the pain of ulcers as well as treat all stomach disorders. Red clover relieves excess acidity in the system. It is also great to strengthen the blood as it has many minerals. Add 2 teaspoons of dried or fresh red clover to 1 cup of boiling water. Cover and steep 10 minutes. Strain and add honey to sweeten. Drink 1 cup before meals and before bedtime as a treatment.

## LEO

Sweet woodruff *(Galium odoratum)*
Ginger *(Zingiber officinale)*
Roses *(Rosa spp.)*
Borage *(Borago officinalis)*
Cranberries *(Vaccinium macrocarpon)*
Hawthorn berries *(Crataegus oxyacantha)*

Ginger is frequently used as a blood thinner, and can be used as a flavoring in any tea. It also helps to keep the platelets in the blood healthy and

**Ginger**

slippery. Hawthorn berries have long been used to prevent or treat heart problems. Pour 2 cups of boiling water over 3 tablespoons of the berries. Cover and steep overnight. Next morning strain, being sure to squeeze the berries to extract all the juice. Drink 1 cup twice daily as a tonic for the heart.

Rose Hip tea to strengthen the heart. Place 2 teaspoons of crushed rose hips in 1 cup of water. Boil gently for about 3 minutes. Strain and sweeten with honey. Drink as often as desired. Rose hips contain vitamin P which heals ruptures of small blood vessels as well as vitamin C. Vitamin C is another great help to prevent heart disorders. A lack of vitamin C causes a roughness to the interior of the arteries and leads to susceptibility of small breaks in the arteries. This causes the rush of clotting agents in the blood to cement the breaks. This can lead to blockages in the arteries.

## VIRGO

Licorice *(Glycyrrhiza glabra)*
Caraway *(Carum carvi)*
Dandelion *(Taraxacum officinale)*
Watercress *(Nasturtium officinale)*
Aloe Vera *(Aloe spp.)*
Costmary *(Chrysanthemum balsamita)*

Virgo has problems with the bowels and alimentary system, and tonics

**Dandelion**

will help to strengthen the whole alimentary system as well as to regulate the bowels. Plenty of fresh fruits and vegetables seems to help this Sun sign very well as the digestion of these serve as regulators. Aloe vera tonic; Place the juice from aloe vera in water and refrigerate. Drink daily as a tonic and regulator.

Watercress has been used as a blood purifier for centuries and also acts to clean the kidneys. The minerals in watercress are of great help to Virgo. Add 2 teaspoons of chopped watercress to 1 cup of boiling water. Cover and steep 10-15 minutes. Strain and sweeten if desired. Drink several cups daily as a tonic.

## LIBRA

Feverfew (*Chrysanthemum parthenium*)
Chamomile (*Matricaria chamomila, Anthemis nobilis*)
Pansy (*Viola tricolor*)
Thyme (*Thymus vulgaris*)
Burdock (*Articum lappa*)
Apple (*Pyrus malus*)
Skullcap (*Skutellaria laterifolia*)
Hops (*Humulus lupulus*)

**Apple**

The back, kidney, and bladder of this Sun sign will benefit from tonics used to cleanse and strengthen the kidneys. There is no better treatment to rid the body of toxins than apple pectin. Apple tea is simple to make and is great to treat the whole system. Add several slices of dried apple to 1 cup of boiling water. Cover and steep 10-15 minutes. Drink as often as desired. Great way to rid the kidneys of all toxins.

Many times when we are bothered with back pain a good relaxant herb works to release tight muscles and reduce the pain. Mix together 1 tablespoon each of hops, chamomile, and skullcap. Add 1 teaspoon of the mixture to 1 cup of boiling water. Cover and steep 10 minutes. Strain and drink warm. Honey may be added if desired. Great to relax tight muscles.

## SCORPIO

Horehound *(Marrubium vulgare)*
Ginseng *(Panax quinquefolius)*
Mullein *(Verbascum thapus)*
Marsh Mallow *(Althaea officinalis)*
Willow *(Salix spp.)*
Strawberry *(Wild, Fragaria virginiana, Garden, Fragaria vesca)*
Hyssop *(Hyssopus officinalis)*

**Horehound**

Scorpio has problems with the uterine and generative organs. There are many tonics to help with the strengthening of these organs. For men the best well-known herb is ginseng. It has been used for centuries to treat these disorders. Add 1 teaspoon of ginseng to 1 cup of boiling water. Cover and steep 10 minutes. Strain, sweeten with honey and drink several times daily.

Women have long used the strawberry as a female treatment for uterine problems such as menstrual cramps. Add willow as a pain reliever and you not only have a tonic but a pain reliever. Mix together 1 table-spoon each of strawberry leaves, willow, and hyssop. Mix well and add 1 teaspoon of the mixture to 1 cup of boiling water. Cover and steep 10–15 minutes. Strain and add honey to sweeten. Drink several times daily as need-ed. Both male and female of this sign would do well to increase their intake of honey. This not only thins the blood but adds many needed minerals to the diet.

## SAGITTARIUS

Solomon's Seal *(Polygonatum officinale)*
Chicory *(Cichorium intybus)*
Oak *(Quercus varieties)*
Sassafras *(Sassafras albidum)*
Nettle *(Urtica dioica)*
Primrose *(Primula)*
Dandelion *(Taraxacum officinale)*

Sagittarius is affected in the nervous system and needs to insure that they pay close attention to their emotional and spiritual

**Nettle**

needs as well as the physical. We are becoming more aware of the treatment of the person as a whole and do not need to concentrate solely on the physical to heal. A good balance in our life of work and play goes a long way to ensure good health. We need to slow down long enough to appreciate the spiritual side of our nature. The tonics are so important to keep the body healthy and toxins flushed from the system. The herbs listed with each sign have the minerals and cell salts needed in particular for each sign. Dandelion tea is an excellent way to get the needed minerals from this herb. Place 2 teaspoons of the leaf or root of the dandelion in 1 cup of boiling water. Cover and steep 10–15 minutes. Strain and drink several times daily.

Many in this sign seem to have high blood pressure. Primrose is an excellent way to lower the pressure naturally. Add about 1/4 cup of chopped primrose leaves and flowers to 1 cup of boiling water. Cover and steep 10 minutes. Strain and sweeten with honey. Drink with meals.

## CAPRICORN

Shepherd's purse (*Capsella bursa-pastoris*)
Skullcap (*Scutellaria laterifloria*)
Fennel (*Foeniculum vulgare*)
Sage (*Salvia officinalis*)
Cinquefoil (*Popentilla reptans*)
Sheep Sorrel (*Rumex acetosella*)

Shepherd's Purse

Capricorn suffers from skin disorders. Because most skin disorders are caused by internal factors there are many tonics to use that would remove the harmful toxins from the system. One of the best to use is the sheep sorrel, as this herb is a great way to remove toxins from the blood. Add 1 tablespoon of the herb to 1 cup of boiling water. Cover and steep 10–15 minutes. Strain and drink several times daily. Burdock root can be added as it too is a great internal cleanser. If burdock is added to the tea psoriasis can be treated by applying the tea to the affected area. Apply externally to the area several times daily and drink the tea several times daily as an internal help also.

For treatment of acne, thyme is an excellent astringent. Make a tea using 1 teaspoon of thyme to 1 cup of boiling water. Cover and steep 10 minutes. Strain and apply to face as a compress. The tea can be refrigerated and used as a final rinse daily to treat acne.

## AQUARIUS

Valerian *(Polemonium caeruleum)*
Violet *(Viola odorata)*
Honeysuckle *(Diervilla lonicera)*
Plantain *(Plantago major)*
Nasturtium *(Tropaeolum majus)*
Dock *(Rumex spp.)*
Ginger *(Zingiber officinale)*

Plantain

Because the ankles are often affected in this sign it would be good to add several of the diuretic herbs to your diet. Plantain is a great diuretic and can help to reduce swelling of the ankles. Place 1–2 tablespoons of dried plantain in 1 cup of boiling water. Cover and steep 15 minutes. Strain and sweeten with honey. Drink several times daily for 1 week if used as a treatment.

Ginger removes viscid matter from the kidneys and helps to clear the system of toxins. Place 1 teaspoon of fresh ginger in 1 cup of boiling water. Cover and steep 15 minutes. Strain and sweeten with honey. Drink several times daily.

## PISCES

Kelp *(Fucus vesiculosis)*
Cherry *(Prunus)*
Goldenseal *(Hydrastis canadensis)*
Parsley *(Petroselinum crispum)*
Heartsease *(Viola tricolor)*
Irish Moss *(Chondrus crispus, Gigartina mamillosa)*
Calendula *(Calendula officinalis)*

Pisces suffer in the foot and toe area. There are many problems with the feet and I suppose gout is about the most painful of any of the ailments. The most common remedy used is cherries as a treatment for gout. Place 1 cup of cherries, with the stems on, in 1 pint of water. Simmer for 30 minutes. Strain and add 1 pint of honey. Refrigerate and take 2 tablespoons daily to prevent gout attacks. Again I want to emphasize the use of tonics that are important to each sign.

**Parsley**

Goldenseal has long been considered a heal-all and all-around tonic. Adding parsley helps the diuretic action of the tea. Add 1 teaspoon each of goldenseal and parsley to 1 cup of boiling water. Cover and steep for 15 minutes. Strain and sweeten with honey if desired. Drink 2 times daily for 1 week as a treatment.

Because we may have a tendency to develop problems in certain areas due to our Sun sign does not mean that we will indeed have problems. It simply means that we may want to take extra precautions in these areas. I firmly believe that our health is affected by attitude and we may want to become more familiar with the Sun sign relationships so that we will know what area of our life we may want to work with. A physical illness is simply a symptom. We can try to treat the symptom, but when the spirit and soul are left out of the treatment, we cannot get a healing that will be lasting. Modern physicians sometimes forget that we are more than just physical; those who take a second look at these old remedies sometimes reach startling conclusions. One who comes to mind immediately is Dr. Bernie S. Siegal, who has written many books on the subject.

Herbalism, along with astrology, is making a comeback in popularity—and the opportunities to learn about both were never better. Both have been in practice since the beginning of time and have been proven through trial and error. Doesn't it make sense to use these arts for the betterment of ourselves and our families?

# Are You Two Compatible?

If you and your partner's Suns are located in the relative positions shown in this chart, your relationship may be either Harmonious (bold type) or Difficult (italic).

| Sun in | Relationship |
| --- | --- |
| Same Sign ♉ / ♉ | **Close rapport and understanding from beginning, mutual admiration.** *Boredom; weakness, bad habits annoy the other.* |
| Adjacent Signs ♉ / ♊ | **Pronounced Life Style and personality differences are fascinating; one compliments the other.** *Nothing in common, complete disinterest.* |
| Alternate/Sextile Signs ♊ / ♌ | **Comfortable, amiable relationship; just enough variety to maintain stimulation.** *Disagreements are mild; long-term commitment lacking.* |
| Signs in Square (same quality): Cardinal, Fixed or Mutable ♋ / ♎ | **Differences spark strong attraction; close, warm friendships are likely.** *Fundamental differences in attitude bring about disagreements.* |
| Signs in Trine (same element): Fire, Air, Earth, Water ♍ / ♑ | **The most compatible combination for close relationships or friendships.** *Weaknesses on the part of both partners interfere with relationship.* |
| Signs in Quincunx ♏ / ♈ | **Similar to adjacent signs relationships.** *Similar to adjacent signs relationships.* |
| Opposite Signs ♊ / ♐ | **Opposites experience intense attraction. Each balances the other, providing what the other lacks.** *In close relationships, differences can be irritating, leading to disagreements.* |

# The 1994 Eclipses

## Vince Ploscik

As the Moon orbits the Earth, it deviates up to five degrees from the plane of the ecliptic (the apparent path of the Sun in the heavens). Eclipses occur when a New Moon or a Full Moon takes place when the Moon is right on the plane of the ecliptic, and it's this straight line alignment of the Earth, Sun, and Moon that makes eclipses such potent astrological events. Eclipses are also generally cyclical in nature, often repeating in the same sign and degree every nineteen years. Hence, astrologers look to eclipses to help time events suggested by our birth charts or by the transiting planets, as well as to better understand how history repeats itself against a backdrop of circumstances that continuously change over time.

There are four eclipses in 1994, and they will have the greatest impact upon individuals whose birthdays coincide with or fall within a day or two of their occurrence. The birthdays associated with each particular eclipse date will be discussed in both "favorable" and "unfavorable" terms, and it will remain up to the individual to determine if their affected Sun degree is free of affliction (if favorably aspected by an eclipse) or receives mitigating positive aspects (if unfavorably aspected by an eclipse). (Note: Llewellyn offers a complete line of professional chart readings if help is needed here).

Solar Eclipses are said to last for a year, and Lunar Eclipses are said to last for six months, but any eclipse is capable of generating events or changes that may last long beyond these time frames. Since eclipses receive an

opening square aspect after about three months and an
opening trine aspect after about four months, their energies are certain to be active during the five months that
follow their occurrence. Hence, this article will furnish
possible "trigger dates" for each eclipse through a six-
month period. These trigger dates all feature a lunation
or a transiting planet in aspect to the eclipse along with
the transiting Moon as a possible catalyst, so they may
all have the *potential* to generate hard events, whether
positive or negative.

## The Solar Eclipse of May 10, 1994

The first eclipse in 1994 is a Solar Eclipse at 19°
Taurus 49' on May 10. This Solar Eclipse may be the
most problematic for anyone born around Feb. 8, May
10, Aug. 12 or Nov. 12 (any year). This eclipse may also
generate some degree of mental or emotional stress or
spark potentially difficult adjustments and adaptations
for anyone born around Mar. 25, June 26, Sept. 28, Oct.
13, Dec. 11 or 26 (any year).

The May 10 Solar Eclipse occurs in a Virgo decanate (every ten degrees of a sign [decanate] has a ruler)
and in the eighth duad of Taurus, which is ruled by
Sagittarius (every two and one-half degrees of a Sign
[duad] also has a ruler). This suggests that individuals
born around the unfavorable birthdates cited above
may experience stressful changes, restrictions, or frustrations related to joint finances, insurances, taxes,
alimony and child support or material security, and
there may also be possible work or career instability.
Much emotional intensity and willfulness or stubbornness may be generated by this eclipse, all of which may
translate into intense arguments and confrontations or
power struggles and tests of will over the control of
finances, unless there is a willingness to compromise
and cooperate with others. The idea here is to show
emotional flexibility and to adapt to these changes or
concerns rather than stubbornly resisting them or
indulging in emotional over-reactions or extremes.

The May 10 Solar Eclipse degree has received
repeated stress aspects from transiting Pluto; and then
from transiting Saturn in May 1992 through January

1993, as well as a sesquiquadrate aspect from transiting Jupiter in November 1992 and in May and June of 1993. Consequently, the financial or work concerns outlined above may constitute yet another round of

**Solar Eclipse**
from Johannes de Sacrobusco's *Opus Sphaericum*, printed by Erhard Ratdolt, Venice, 1482

problems in conflicts and stresses that have been going on for years. Transiting Jupiter will oppose the eclipse degree in October 1994 (along with transiting Venus), and this may increase the potential for possible legal stress, relationship problems, or additional financial frustrations, unless there is a willingness to put aside long-standing resentments and try to find grounds for compromise. With this eclipse in a Virgo decanate, it's possible that permanent changes in diet or lifestyle or in the work environment may be mandated, again as the result of stresses that may be traced back to the early 90s.

With all the above in mind, individuals born around the unfavorable birthdates cited above should guard against the negative potential of this May 10 Solar Eclipse around May 23, June 20 or 26, July 1 or 17, Aug. 12 or 23, Sept. 6 or 27, Oct. 10, 13, or 24; Nov. 10 or 13, and Dec. 26, 1994. Around these dates, use extreme care in the handling of finances, avoid confrontations with others, and try to find constructive means of venting anger or frustration.

The May 10 Solar Eclipse will make favorable aspects for anyone born around Jan. 10, Mar. 10, May 10, July 12, or Sept. 12 (any year). Individuals born around these favorable birthdates may enjoy financial increases or positive resolutions for any longstanding financial legal or emotional disputes. This eclipse trines the much-celebrated conjunction of Uranus and Neptune that occurred back in February, August, and October, 1993, so individuals born around these favorable birthdates may experience continued work and career opportunities or reap the benefits of investments and financial decisions that were made in 1993. Watch for the positive potential of this eclipse to be possibly triggered around June 6, July 8, 13 or 26, Aug. 27, Sept. 10, 14, and Oct. 11, 1994.

## The Lunar Eclipse of May 25, 1994

The second eclipse in 1994 is a Lunar Eclipse at 3° Sagittarius 37' on May 25. This Lunar Eclipse may be the most problematic for anyone born around Feb. 22, May 25, Aug. 27, or Nov. 26 (any year). This eclipse may also generate some degree of mental/emotional stress or spark potentially difficult adjustments and adaptations for anyone born around Jan. 9, Apr. 8 or 24, June 25, July 11, or Oct. 12 (any year).

The May 25th Lunar Eclipse occurs in a Sagittarius decanate and in the second duad of Sagittarius, which is ruled by Capricorn. This suggests that individuals born around the unfavorable birthdates cited above may experience work or financial instabilities that may be accompanied by enormous mental emotional and physical stress. These work or financial concerns may be exacerbated by nervous tension and restlessness, communication problems, erroneous assumptions, confusion, indecision, and impatience or intolerance, all of which suggests a possible need to slow down, to double-check facts and figures and to avoid rash or reckless reactionary responses. Sagittarius is a dualistic sign, so there is likely to be more than one source of stress and concern, and this suggests a possible need to eat right, get proper rest, and avoid physical (and financial) over-extension as a means of mitigating this eclipse's possible nervous tension.

Much of the instability associated with this eclipse may be rooted in concerns stemming from February, August, and October, 1993, when the Uranus-Neptune conjunction semisquared the eclipse degree from Capricorn, as well as from concerns stemming from September 1993, when transiting Jupiter and Mars semisquared the eclipse degree from Libra. All of these possible work/career and financial stresses may crop up again in February and March, 1994, when transiting

Saturn and Mars squares the eclipse degree from Pisces, generating possible increased difficulties in balancing work or career stresses with domestic or familial concerns. With this eclipse in Sagittarius, there is at least the possibility that irreconcilable differences may result in legal action, and relocation or matters at a distance may also factor heavily into this stressful equation.

With all of the above in mind, guard against the negative potential of the May 25 Lunar Eclipse around June 5, July 8, 12, 15, or 28, Aug. 19 or 26, Sept. 14 or 17, and Oct. 11, 1994. Around these dates, try to avoid arguments by exercising tact and diplomacy, and avoid attempts at imposing religious or philosophical convictions upon others. Stress management may also be important around these dates, as individuals born around the unfavorable birthdates may experience great anxiety and nervousness that may be capable of "torpedoing" their better judgment.

The May 25th Lunar Eclipse will make favorable aspects for anyone born around Jan. 23, Mar. 24, July 26, Sept. 26, or Nov. 26 (any year). Individuals born near these favorable birthdates may experience work or career opportunities that may involve possible retraining or relocation, or possible financially rewarding legal settlements; travel and educational opportunities may also accompany this eclipse. The key point to remember here is that a Lunar Eclipse is a Full Moon, so a major decision may be required or someone may need to be appeased in order to realize the positive potential of this eclipse. Watch for the potential opportunities associated with this eclipse around June 17, July 22 or 27, Aug. 10, Sept. 6 or 25 and Oct. 8, 1994.

## The Solar Eclipse of November 3, 1994

The third eclipse in 1994 is a Solar Eclipse at 10° Scorpio 54' on November 3. This Solar Eclipse may be the most problematic for anyone born around Jan. 31, May 1, Aug. 3, or Nov. 3 (any year). This eclipse may also generate some degree of mental/emotional stress or spark potentially difficult adjustments and adaptations for anyone born around Mar. 16, Mar. 31, June 1 or 17, Sept. 19, or Dec. 18 (any year).

The Nov. 3 Solar Eclipse conjuncts transiting Venus in a Pisces decanate and in the fifth duad of Scorpio, which is ruled by Pisces. This suggests that individuals born around the unfavorable birth dates cited above may experience relationship conflicts or financial stresses involving taxes, insurances, alimony and child support or joint finances. Extreme emotional sensitivity, emotional pride or obstinacy and/or emotional confusion and misunderstandings may accompany this eclipse, and its double-Pisces inference further suggests possible secrecy or deception. Sexual or romantic indiscretions and/or attempts at emotional or psychological manipulation should be avoided along with get-rich-quick schemes, and caution should be used in all financial dealings or decisions. Open and honest communications and emotional flexibility may go a long way toward mitigating these eclipse-related concerns and stress.

Transiting Jupiter conjuncts the eclipse degree in January, April, and September, 1994, and this may spark emotional excesses, financial extravagance or legal concerns that may culminate in possible relationship or financial instability when the negative potential of the Nov. 3 Solar Eclipse is possibly triggered around Nov. 16, Dec. 13, 17, or 21, 1994; Jan. 14 or 30, Feb. 2 or 27, Mar. 13 or 26, Apr. 19 and 22, 1995. Children, religious/philosophical convictions and/or relatives at a distance may also factor heavily into these eclipse-related concerns. Around these negative trigger dates, try to exercise emotional objectivity, and try to avoid emotional extremes or excesses.

The Nov. 3 Solar Eclipse will make favorable aspects for anyone born around Jan. 1, Mar. 1, July 3, Sept. 3, or Nov. 3 (any year). Individuals born around these favorable birthdates may enjoy very special energies for creative and spiritual transformation as well as heightened intuition and perception that may be successfully applied to research studies or self-expression. This eclipse may favor couples who are desirous of children and individuals who are seeking romance, and individuals born around these favorable birthdates may also enjoy possible financial gains (which may again stem partly from Jupiter's transit over the eclipse degree in January, April, and September, 1994). Watch for the positive potential of this eclipse to be possibly triggered around Jan. 1, 5, 24, or 28, Mar. 1 and Apr. 7, 1995.

## The Lunar Eclipse of November 18, 1994

The fourth and final eclipse in 1994 is a Lunar Eclipse at 25° Taurus 35' on November 18th. This Lunar Eclipse may be the most problematic for anyone born around Feb. 14, May 16, Aug. 18 or Nov. 18 (any year). This eclipse may also generate some degree of mental or emotional stress or spark potentially difficult adjustments or adaptations for anyone born around Jan. 1, Mar. 31, July 2, Oct. 3 or 19, or Dec. 17 (any year).

The Nov. 18 Lunar Eclipse occurs in a Capricorn decanate and in the eleventh duad of Taurus, which is ruled by Pisces. Hence, much like the individuals who receive stress aspects from the May 10 Solar Eclipse, individuals born around the unfavorable birthdates cited immediately above may encounter possible work or career frustrations and/or financial stresses or instabilities that may be accompanied by enormous emotional intensity and possible power struggles and tests of will with family members. Once again, stubbornness, obstinacy, or insecurities may result in unreasonable emotional demands and expectations, so it can't be stressed enough that emotional flexibility and a willingness to compromise and cooperate with others may be needed to mitigate these eclipse-related conflicts.

The possible work or relationship disputes outlined above may trace back to January–March 1993, November 1993 and June–September 1994 and transiting Pluto's opposition to the eclipse degree (along with transiting Saturn's square in December 1993), which suggests that this eclipse may be accompanied by a good deal of pent-up frustration and repressed anger or resentment. Transiting Jupiter opposes the November 18 Lunar Eclipse, and this may prompt these intense emotions to boil over into intense confrontations, possible legal problems or potentially extreme emotional overreactions, all of which may prompt relationships to encounter increased polarization. Again, these eclipse-related concerns are calling for adaptation and flexibility, and so resistance/defiance will only exacerbate matters.

Individuals born near the unfavorable birthdates cited above should guard against the negative potential of the Nov. 18 Lunar Eclipse around Nov. 25 or 28, Dec. 26, 1994; Jan. 1 or 4, Feb. 13, 15, or 18, Mar. 11, 24, or 30, Apr. 3 and 7, 1995. Around these dates, use extreme caution in financial dealings/decisions, and try to find constructive outlets for pent-up anger or frustrations. Once again, taxes, insurances, and joint finances, as well as children, may play prominent roles in these eclipse-related concerns.

The Nov. 18 Lunar Eclipse will make favorable aspects for anyone born around Jan. 15, Mar. 16, May 16, July 18 or Sept. 18 (any year). Individuals born around these favorable birthdates may enjoy work or career opportunities and possible financial gains, but here again, major decisions and compromises or possible relocation or retraining may be needed in order to realize the positive potential of this eclipse. Early in 1995, transiting Uranus and Neptune begin trining the eclipse degree, which suggests that many individuals born around these favorable birthdates may be beginning a two-year period of career growth, spiritual development or community involvement that may be richly (as well as financially) rewarding. Watch for the positive potential of the Nov. 18 Lunar Eclipse to be possibly triggered around Jan. 2 or 16, Feb. 26, Mar. 16 or 29, and Apr. 17, 1995. Again, this eclipse is a Full Moon, so major decisions or a willingness to compromise may be needed in order to realize its positive potential.

One final note: three of 1994's eclipses—the May 25 Lunar, the Nov. 3 Solar and the Nov. 18 Lunar—are repeats of eclipses that occurred nineteen years ago, in November 1975. Hence, individuals affected by 1994's eclipses may want to use 1975–76 as a point of reference and look for similar events/areas of concern in 1994–1995, even if the differing transiting planets behind these two series of eclipses alters the circumstances behind these events or concerns.

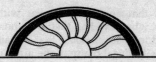

# Your Sun Sign Guide to Gambling

**Ralph Jordan Pestka**

Different people have different approaches to attempting to win money at games, contests, or other activities. The ways people speculate and gamble can be refined down to twelve basic attitudes and styles of approach that can then be correlated to the twelve basic building blocks of astrology—the twelve signs of the zodiac.

The Sun is the planetary ruler of the sign of Leo, and the 5th House of the horoscope in the natural zodiac of astrology. The Sun, the sign of Leo, and the 5th House rule over activities related to risk, speculation, games, and gambling. Your Sun sign shows your basic inclinations, talents, and abilities that you can build on to increase your chances of winning at gambling. Of course, risk is risk, and you can't win all the time. Your Sun sign also reveals the things of which you should be cautious, in order to minimize your losses in the things on which you do wager.

In this article we will look at the twelve Sun sign personalities and how each approaches wagering their money on the outcome of speculative events. Before reading the description of your personal Sun sign, I suggest you read the description for the sign of Leo. The sign of Leo reveals many of the general qualities inherent in human nature, and present in each of us to some degree, that incline us toward finding challenge, thrill, and enjoyment in risking our money in the hope of gain. (We all have the sign of Leo somewhere in our horoscope.)

Readers that are more familiar with astrological analysis, and who have had their own horoscope calculated, should look at the house that contains the sign of Leo as this will reveal many of the areas in which they are more interested in taking risks. Regardless of where the sign of Leo is placed in your horoscope, however, your basic attitudes and approaches to gambling are primarily influenced by your Sun sign and the 5th House from your Sun sign. These are the factors we will concentrate on in the following descriptions. (If you want to have your horoscope calculated, Llewellyn offers this service. For the more serious gambler, Llewellyn also offers a personal speculation reading that includes your more fortunate time periods for one year ahead. A description of this service and an order form can be found at the back of the *Sun Sign Book.*)

Learn more about your personal nature in regard to risk, speculation, and gambling. Find out what you should be doing more, and understand those things of which you should be cautious, in order to increase your overall chances of winning. Then go out and take a chance of *some kind.* As the saying goes among gamblers, "You can't win if you're not in." Good Luck!

## Aries—March 21 to April 20

As an Aries, you are eager, assertive, and fearless in your approach to gambling. Your attitude toward gambling is, "Hey, let's go for it; let's do it; let's get it on!"

You are ready for action, particularly when you can compete directly against others. With the Sun-ruled sign of Leo in the 5th House, you display many of the Leonine qualities in your personal approach to speculation, gambling, and competition for money. You enjoy the thrill of risk, the excitement and energy of high-powered gambling environments, and the adrenalin-stimulating rush in the battle to be a winner.

Your strengths lie in your willingness to take risks, in your understanding of the nature of competition, and in your direct approach to gambling. You won't be overcome by self-doubt or overburdened by too many details in figuring out what you want to bet on. You are more attracted to sporting events, prize fights, and competitive situations in which people are directly pitted against each other. You are better able to figure out who has the upper hand in competitive situations as you are more naturally attuned to what it takes to win in these. You can assess strengths and weaknesses and base your betting decisions on this analysis. You are also more likely to bet on yourself in direct competition with others.

You can profit from sports handicapping, card games in which you play against others in direct competition, and high action casino games such as craps.

You'll increase your chances of winning in direct proportion to the degree with which you control your impulsiveness and impatience. Your eagerness to get in the action can cause you to throw caution to the wind, forget the importance of strategy and tactics, and to bet too much too fast. You must learn to balance your eagerness and enthusiasm with a bit of cautious forethought and realistic appraisal. Be aware of the mathematical probabilities and the practical monetary realities of any gambling situation you enter. Recognize that there are times and situations where you should just pass on taking a chance. Don't be too willing to enter into any and every gambling proposition—no one wins every single time they play. For you, it is important to learn to recognize when not to bet. Your eagerness and enthusiasm to be in the action can blind you to situations that are just too unpredictable to give you a winning edge.

## Taurus—April 20 to May 21

As a Taurean, you are stable, steadfast, and practical in your approach to gambling. Your attitude toward gambling is, "I think I'll wait until the odds are in my favor." You are careful, conservative, and analytical when it comes to gambling. With the Mercury-ruled sign of Virgo on the 5th House, you are truly going to think before you put your money down. You are conscious of the value of money and the importance of probabilities and odds. You understand that to win in the long run you have to get the odds in your favor most of the time. As with the other earth signs, you tend to have less inclination to gamble in you than, say, the air or fire signs. When you do bet, you will be looking at it more as an investment than as fun and games.

Your strengths lie in your ability to evaluate situations and spot a good risk. You can pass up betting opportunities and wait until the odds are in your favor. You do not have to be in the action constantly, and thus save a great deal of money that others would lose on more risky propositions. For a Taurean, gambling may mean loaning a friend money or buying rental property—you can be *that* conservative. When you do gamble, you'll be attracted to betting small amounts in the hope of hitting it big—a single lottery ticket, a two dollar bet at the race track, the quarter slot or video poker machines, or a small investment at the bingo hall.

You can increase your chances to profit most by learning the odds and technicalities of what you bet on, taking the long view, and setting limits on your losses. Taurean steadfastness and determination can turn into stubbornness when losing. You can feel the money you have lost is still yours and pursue it until you go broke. The red ink of losses can become a red flag that gets your blood cooking and raises the internal pressure. In this case, you can become blinded to the practical realities of good money management. It is important for you to learn to bet more when things are going your way and to pull up and quit gambling when you have lost your limit for the day.

## Gemini—May 21 to June 22

As a Geminian, you are lively, intellectual, and adaptable in your approach to gambling. Your attitude toward gambling is, "I think I can find a way to beat this game." You are in motion, both in body and in mind, and are attracted to all the mental and physical activity surrounding the gambling environment. With the Venus-ruled sign of Libra on the 5th House, you are interested in the numbers, percentages, probabilities, and odds that go with whatever type of gambling you choose. Mentally active, you are greatly stimulated by the ever-changing possibilities involved in picking the winning numbers.

Your strengths lie in your rational, logical, and analytical approach to gambling. You can be attracted to any sort of gambling in which variable numbers and odds are important. This could include lotteries, keno and bingo, sport and race handicapping, and card games, particularly blackjack card counting. You like to have your hands in the action, literally, and any game that allows you the continual use of your hands is likely to interest you. You are also very talkative. Gambling environments that allow you to communicate with others are more stimulating to your basic nature.

You can profit best from gambles that require rapid and continual decision-making. You can then use your lightning-quick computer brain to greatest advantage. Gambles in which your decisions *really* matter, such as poker, blackjack, or sports handicapping, will allow you to make the best use of your talents.

Games of pure chance, such as lotteries, keno, bingo, roulette, and craps require few truly critical analytical decisions—you place your bet and see what happens. But the numbers, the combinations, and the fast-paced changes surrounding these types of gambles can stimulate your high-strung need for variety and change. This can be your undoing, as you can become more obsessed with the repetitious motion and action, and move further away from using your more critical, analytical faculties in the betting decisions you make. Do not become too enraptured of the motion and change surrounding your gambling. Take the time to step back and do a reality check occasionally. Remember the most basic factors for winning at gambling, such as the analysis of the true odds, good money management, and the ability to pull back or quit when things are not going your way, or to quit with a profit once you get ahead.

## Cancer—June 22 to July 22

As a Cancerian, you are cautious, shrewd, and resourceful in your approach to gambling. Your attitude toward gambling is, "If I lose this much, I'm out of here." Accumulative, protective, and security-minded by nature, you are somewhat less inclined than most others to truly gamble. With the Mars- and Pluto-ruled sign of Scorpio on the 5th House, you bring an intensely emotional desire to win into anything at which you gamble. When you do take a shot at a risky venture you become more emotionally involved than most. Changeable and moody, your emotions will fluctuate with the tides of fortune.

Your strengths lie in your shrewd, cautious, and thrifty approach to gambling. You will get the most gamble for your dollar. You will look for the best odds, the more favorable situations, and will keep tight control over your bankroll. As one of the cardinal signs, you will take the initiative in carrying out your own agenda. As a water sign, you are greatly affected by your environment and the people around you when you gamble. You will tend toward gambles that are more competitive and action-oriented, such as sports, races, direct competition with others, and casino games such as craps, rather than such sedate gambles as keno, bingo, or video poker. But any form of gambling can attract particular Cancerians as it is the promise of accumulation that attracts them in the beginning.

You can profit most by staying sensitive to your emotional and intuitive promptings. When you feel comfortable, secure, and internally in balance, your sensitive intuition can lead you to find the winning situations and the winning bets. With the fast-moving Moon as your planetary ruler, your moods can shift and change every few days. This can cause you to be up one day and down the next; to be right on the money one day and do everything wrong the next. Maintaining your emotional self-control is essential if you are to win at gambling.

The experience of losing can cause you to become too cautious, too hesitant, and therefore cause you to make poor betting decisions—decisions that are motivated by a desire to protect yourself rather than a true desire to win. Everyone definitely needs to remain a little cautious and protective when gambling. This is the equivalent of a good defensive position in warfare. But to win, to occupy the enemies' territory (gain their money), you must at some point take the offensive and strike out. For you, it is important to balance your emotionally defensive nature with the willingness to let go and take a chance.

## Leo—July 23 to August 23

As a Leo, you are courageous, dynamic, and self-confident in your approach to gambling. Your attitude toward gambling is, "Here I am, deal me in!" You understand, more than most, that nothing is certain, things can change, and that life itself is, to a great degree, one big gamble. Because of this, you are more willing than most to take risks; and if you should lose, you are more willing than most to pick yourself up and get back in the action. With the Jupiter-ruled sign of Sagittarius on the 5th House, you approach gambling and risk with an optimistic and adventurous spirit. You are not as concerned with odds and probabilities as much as you are concerned with opportunity and the chance to win. You respect winners, and want to be a winner. You understand you have to play the game, whatever game the others are playing, in order to win the gold and receive the admiration of the crowd that goes with being crowned the winner.

Your strengths lie in your optimism, self-confidence, and determination—all essential attitudes for attracting good fortune and winning at gambling. You intuitively understand that everyone has a bit of gambler in them, and are willing to take some kind of risk at something; if others can do well, you are confident that you can do even better. You are more attracted to action-oriented games, sports events, and risks in which people are directly pitted against each other. Winning, for you, is more than just monetary reward—it is the ego satisfaction of knowing you bested the rest; that you overcame the odds; that others lost *their* money to *you*. You will learn the games, develop your abilities, and directly compete with others and bet on yourself.

The sign of Leo rules casinos and playgrounds—places where people gather for fun and games. Your attraction to gaming is so strong you may organize gambling activities to be certain the game goes on. You may be the organizer of the sports pool at the office, solicit friends to take a junket to Vegas, or take up employment in a field involving gambling or direct contact with other gamblers.

You can profit from direct contact with other gamblers. You can learn the technicalities of a particular type of game or event from them and apply their techniques in your own betting. Your desire to climb to the top of the heap will motivate you to get closer to the winners, and to avoid the losers. Attitudes rub off, and the right attitudes are as important to winning as are a knowledge of odds, a sufficient bankroll to risk, and good timing.

The down side of your nature—the attitudes that can cause you to lose—are pride, willfulness, and extravagance. In short, your ego can drive your desire to win to such a degree that you just feel you deserve to win, and therefore *will* win. You should remember that a balance of many different things go into winning. Along with a positive, confident attitude, you *do* need to be knowledgeable about odds, the technicalities of the game, and be open and willing to learn from the best.

## Virgo—August 23 to September 23

As a Virgoan, you are analytical, meticulous, and practical in your approach to gambling. Your attitude toward gambling is, "Wait! Let me figure this out before

I bet." You are methodical and discriminating in anything you consider taking a chance on. With the Saturn-ruled sign of Capricorn on the 5th House, you are cautious and calculating when it comes to gambling. You will learn the odds, evaluate the detailed factors, and consider the pros and cons before you commit yourself to a course of action. You naturally tend to worry a little more than most gamblers. Your concern comes from a desire to make the perfect choice and, due to this, you can be somewhat reticent or inhibited in your approach to gambling.

Your strengths lie in your ability to assimilate varied data and make detailed analysis of the important factors involved in arriving at winning decisions. You are quite capable of understanding the racing form, recalling all the sports statistics, and remembering the exposed cards in a deck. Because you can recall many details and evaluate many factors, you are better able to find the lucrative bets in situations where analytical decision making counts the most.

You can profit by gambling at things in which a systematic approach is required. This would include sports and racing handicapping in which statistics and past results are so important to finding winners. In direct competition with others, you would do well at card games such as gin rummy, blackjack, or poker, in which you can use your ability to remember exposed cards. Since Virgo rules small animals, you may do well in handicapping dog races.

Your greatest weaknesses lie in getting so concerned with the many details that you lose sight of the larger picture. You may become so preoccupied with the statistics that you forget basic tactical and strategic principles. For example, you may make numerous small bets instead of placing several larger bets on your very best choices. You may become short-sighted, thinking only of the immediate betting situation and losing track of the long-term trend. You should periodically step back and review the total picture. Be certain that all the little pieces are fitting into a larger framework that leads to winning results.

# Libra—September 23 to October 23

As a Libran, you are socially oriented, logical, and often indecisive in your approach to gambling. Your attitude toward gambling is, "Oh, there are so many choices, I'm not sure what to bet on—what are *you* going to bet on?" In other words, you can see so many sides to any single decision you can have difficulty arriving at exactly what to do. As one of the air signs with the Saturn- and Uranus-ruled sign of Aquarius on the 5th House, your mind can logically take into account the many variables of any betting proposition. As the sign of balance and partnership, you will feel more certain if you gamble in partnership with another, or at least have someone around to bounce your ideas off and help you to make up your mind. At the very least, you will probably ask others what they gamble on, how they arrived at a particular betting decision, or may go into partnership with them and let them make the decisions. You would do well to seek out the insight and advice of the best gamblers you know in order to make more winning decisions yourself.

Your strength lies in your ability to consider the many important variables that enter into a betting decision. You can be more impartial and a bit more emotionally detached than most gamblers when considering what to bet. As the opposite polarity of Aries, the sign of combat and competition par excellence, you could be attracted to sports and competition. Your planetary ruler, Venus, relates to numbers and probabilities, so in anything you gamble at the odds and percentages will carry a great deal of weight in your final decision.

You can profit from gambling in partnership with others. An extension of this is to make knowledgeable people your partners, in that you follow their best advice; for example, reading up on past results and statistics in sports or racing and considering the opinions of different handicappers. The socializing aspect of gambling is important to you. You can use your gracious and refined social skills to rub elbows with the winners, get them to share their winning techniques or winning picks and help you to spot the winning combinations.

Recognize that your greatest strength can also be your greatest weakness. You can become lost in the multitude of factors available for consideration. This can cause indecision and paralysis. In the end, you may just bet the favorites or toss out all analysis and everyone else's opinion, and bet against conventional wisdom. The point is, you must learn to take into account the opinions of others, but then take the responsibility to make your own decisions.

## Scorpio—October 23 to November 23

As a Scorpian, you are purposeful, powerful, and determined in your approach to gambling. You attitude toward gambling is, "I *must* win." Your desire to win is so deep and pervasive that you will probe to the inner workings of anything you gamble at to determine how you can win. With the Jupiter- and Neptune-ruled sign of Pisces on the 5th House, you will explore the mysteries and seek out the necessary insights in order to increase your chances of winning. You see the money you risk as the seminal seed from which a monetary fortune can be born. You appreciate the fact that money *is* power. You are attracted to gambling for the sake of the power that winning will bring.

Your strength lies in the intense sense of purpose you bring to your gambling. Motivated by the passionate desire to win, you will leave no stone unturned, will seek out every advantage and will persist to the end in your battle with the odds. You can combine piercing perception, mental analysis, and intuitive promptings to arrive at winning bets. You are able to maintain more self-control as to when you bet, how you bet, and on what you bet than most other gamblers are capable of. You can be attracted to any number of forms of gambling as it is not necessarily what you gamble at that is as important as how much you can win. However, due to your deeper insight into gaining the advantage in any situation, you will take into account odds and probabilities, percentages and payoffs.

You can profit from the weaknesses and lapses of others. In handicapping sports or races you can spot the errors of the crowd, and determine when the long-shot actually has hidden strengths and advantages. Games of pure chance, such as lotteries, bingo, or roulette may not attract you that much, as you would rather have some degree of control or use your own decision making to gain a favorable advantage. If you are attracted to a game of pure chance such as craps, it will be because you appreciate the potential for a big score and understand that the casino has a very small percentage advantage.

Your undoing can be in the very strength you bring to your gambling—an intense desire to win. Desire springs from a deep emotional energy and this can cause you to become obsessed with winning. This obsession can lead you down dark alleys and dead-end streets, as your intense emotional desire can cause you to become blinded to the realities of the gambling situation at hand. You must learn to give it up, to go home a small loser when things are not going your way. Otherwise, you could find yourself losing way too much when it is simply not your day.

## Sagittarius—November 23 to December 22

As a Sagittarian, you are adventurous, optimistic, and adaptable in your approach to gambling. Your attitude toward gambling is, "This is boring, I'm going to the track (or casino, or bingo parlor, or card game, or . . .)." You require movement, exploration, and challenge in your life in general, and gambling can provide an outlet for all these needs. With the Mars-ruled sign of Aries on the 5th House, you are attracted to the excitement and competition of such gambles as sports contests and horse races. Whatever you gamble at, you will set your sights high and look for a big score. You rarely think small, but rather look for expansion and abundance.

Your strengths lie in your ability to see the larger picture, to become motivated to learn how to win by the pure challenge of it all, and to be adaptable, open-minded, and teachable. You are more attracted to the fast-paced action of sports and races, and to the excitement and comraderie of such games as craps. When you do opt for more sedate forms of gambling such as bingo or card games like poker, it will largely be due to the fellowship, jokes, and laughter that often accompany these. You are able to approach the challenge of winning from several different angles and to reassess your ideas. This makes you able to learn about and understand the mathematical and psychological principles that make winning possible. Once you are in the action you won't be a timid and worrying bettor. When the odds look good or you're on a roll you'll be willing to make the big bet.

You can profit from training and disciplining your mind to consider the many details that go into the larger framework of betting propositions. You can study the racing form or review the statistics, and then consider these in the context of the larger and more basic factors important to finding the winning bet. You should always look to stretch your goals and objectives beyond your more recent accomplishments. Your ability to understand problems and arrive at solutions is great. If you discover something you don't quite understand or are unfamiliar with, you should ask questions of experts or read and study until you understand it more completely. The foundations of all gambling rest in mathematics and probabilities. Be certain you understand the odds involved in any gamble you take.

Your weaknesses lie in a tendency to impatience, extravagance, and blind optimism. In your driving need of adventure and freedom you can forget that your funds are limited, that money management is important and that you cannot win every time you gamble. If you do not manage your money you won't have any to gamble with, or, worse yet, you could go into debt chasing a losing streak. You should learn to balance your optimism with careful consideration and self-control.

## Capricorn—December 22 to January 21

As a Capricorn, you are ambitious, prudent, and rational in your approach to gambling. Your attitude toward gambling is, "I never gamble, I take calculated risks." Your responsible and frugal attitude rarely lets you be comfortable in taking great risks like a Leo or Sagittarian would. With the Venus-ruled sign of Taurus on the 5th House, you will wait it out, evaluate the odds, and structure your betting so that you protect yourself from big losses. You are the money manager par excellence when it comes to gambling. When the stakes are high, when all your chips are in the center of the table, you will remain cool and calm, however, confident that the odds are in your favor; otherwise, you never would have risked so much to begin with.

Your strengths lie in your cautious approach, your ability to discipline yourself and in your determination to give yourself the greatest advantage by calculating the odds before you wager. You remain sensible and realistic in your approach to gambling. You'll like to bet small amounts with the chance of making a big score. If you do evolve into a high stakes bettor you will probably gravitate toward no-limit poker, baccarat, or the craps table—games in which you can win a great deal while also giving up very little advantage to your opponents or the casino.

You can profit from a systematic and structured approach to your gambling. You'll want to learn everything you can about the things you gamble at. You can keep records, track results through time, and use this information to structure your betting activities. You can recognize the importance of setting winning goals and loss limits before you begin to gamble.

Your greatest weaknesses lie in plodding along and being unwilling to step out and risk enough to make the effort worth your while. You can become too structured and controlled due to a fear of losing. You may want to protect your downside by betting very small amounts, but this can often mean your winnings are equally small. You can become pessimistic and miserly when losing. This attitude can prevent you from recouping your losses because, when your fortune turns back around, you are not betting enough to get the most value for your money.

## Aquarius—January 21 to February 20

As an Aquarian, you are detached, ingenious, and progressive in your approach to gambling. Your attitude toward gambling is, "Wait a minute, there has to be a system to this that will increase my chances of winning." You won't just jump into risky situations without first considering the best way to increase your chances of winning. With the Mercury-ruled sign of Gemini on the

5th House, you are going to want to apply your rational intellectual skills to analysis of your betting propositions. You may read books, study forms, analyze past results, and appreciate systems that have a rational basis. The combination of Saturn and Mercury point to careful consideration, observation, calculation, and planning. For you, gambling is an opportunity to show yourself and others that *you know how* to win, as much as it is an opportunity for financial gain.

Your strengths lie in your willingness to learn, your determination to find the best systems that are realistic and practical, and your ability to ingeniously and creatively experiment until you find the winning system that works for you. You won't be led astray by all the hype and temptation toward winning the lottery or busting Vegas. You won't be distracted by the bright lights, the pretty girls, or the free drinks when you gamble. Rather, you'll be more capable than most of staying focused on your goal of gambling and winning.

You can profit from being certain to take the whole picture into view and remaining adaptable to changing circumstances. Remain emotionally detached and analyze the odds in each betting situation. Be certain to remain flexible, adaptable and able to drop any system that is not working. Your undoing can be in your fixed sign determination to prove that you have developed *the* winning system. Do not become so enthralled in your efforts to test the system that you lose sight of the bottom line. Be cautioned against deviating radically from time-proven procedures that have shown themselves to increase a bettor's chances of winning. Recognize that there are basic principles of odds and probabilities that must be taken into account. Also recognize that no amount of knowledge, analysis, or creative effort can bring in winners every time you gamble. For you, it is important to understand that luck and fickle fate can intervene and upset the best system you devise. It is true that, to a great degree, we make our own luck by our preparation and effort. However, understand that you can make your best and most intelligent choices, but you cannot force, control, or command the inconsistent and fickle nature of fortune herself.

## Pisces—February 20 to March 21

As a Piscean, you are impressionable, adaptable, and intuitive in your approach to gambling. Your attitude toward gambling is, "I can't explain why, but I just feel I'm going to win this time." Your imaginative and impressionable mind is attracted to visions of great wealth available from hitting it big at gambling. With the Moon-ruled sign of Cancer on the 5th House, you will bet your feelings, follow your hunches and often seem to receive winning information from some higher realm. Since you operate with a great deal of faith, and are so impressionable and idealistic, you must make an effort to remain practical and realistic when you gamble—otherwise, you can be too easily led down the path of habitual losses as you pursue the pot of gold at the end of the rainbow.

Your strengths lie in your ability to gain a transcendant vision of the total picture in whatever gamble you involve yourself. You may not be able to exactly verbalize all your reasons for doing what you do that leads to winning results. You should always attempt to stay attuned to your inner promptings and intuitive feelings. Certainly learn the technicalities and odds of the game you play, but do not let these control your every decision. Rather, once you have taken these into account, relax, meditate, get in touch with your subconscious sensations—then bet your gut-level feelings.

The Piscean tendency can be to overlook or avoid the details of what you gamble at, but proper technique and an understanding of probabilities and odds are the foundations on which winning at gambling is built. Once you have this foundation, you can proceed to follow your transcendant intuitive mind.

Your weaknesses lie in a tendency to gamble for escape or to follow self-deceptive intuitions and hunches. Gambling environments can be brutally expensive for those that bet every impulse and hunch. You will have to develop a degree of sensitivity to know when your intuition is operating correctly. Be more cautious when your hunches are vague or you feel a great deal of indecision. When your intuition is on target you will have a better sense of direction, confidence, and decisiveness.

# Chart Comparison Techniques

© **Tom Bridges**

Chart comparison, or synastry, is a popular astrological pastime. It's just hard to resist comparing yourself to other people, finding out your likenesses and your differences, and astrology is quite a tool of comparison. Where are your two Moons in relation to each other, or one's Moon to the other's Sun? There are many possibilities and comparing two charts can be a fairly involved matter. Quite a bit has been written and is available on traditional chart comparison techniques (witness Llewellyn's recent two-volume account of the subject in its New Worlds Astrology series). Therefore I thought it would be interesting to cover some techniques that are accessible but perhaps lesser known, as well as some terms that crop up but seem strange because not much information is out on them—namely the vertex, the equatorial ascendant, parallels, and antiscia. We'll start with the better known midheaven and ascendant.

In this article I will be throwing a few terms around, ones with which you may not be familiar. The astronomy of what all these points are is beyond the scope of this article. If the interpretations intrigue you, you can seek out how these points end up in your chart. Meanwhile (and this is partly a result of the computer's revolution in astrology, that you're sometimes just handed a chart with "vertex" on it but no explanation) you can start working with these points in your own life. If you don't know where these points lie in your own horoscope,

Llewellyn's Personal Services can provide the information; make sure you request a horoscope including these points specifically.

## Angles

"Angles" is the generic name by which the mid-heaven and ascendant—and their opposite points, the lower midheaven and descendant—are known in astrology. We talk about significant "turning points" in our lives—aspects to angles show various turning points or signposts in our personality; and by transit or progression, planetary aspects to angles show shifts in direction or understanding. These points are called angles because they all demarcate a change in the celestial scheme from above to below, or approaching and leaving the highest and lowest points on the ecliptic. At one of these places in the horoscope, a planet "turns a corner" and enters a new realm of meaning. The vertex and equatorial ascendant are also angles in that they demarcate similar changes from different perspectives on the heavens.

## Planet-Angle Aspects

Aspects between the planets and the angles of the horoscope figure prominently in both natal astrology and chart comparison. What's special about the angles is that they are the most time-sensitive factors in the horoscope; more than anything else, they define the astrological character of the moment of your birth; and aspects between planets and angles are prime fodder for character description. Say your Jupiter is in close trine aspect to your midheaven—great for success in career. Or say your Saturn is in close conjunction with your ascendant (Saturn was rising when you were born)—you probably have a serious demeanor, are known for your hard work and diligence, but sometimes feel very challenged to accomplish things. Or say Venus is square your descendant—you may find yourself in many dynamic relationships.

## Relevance to Locality Astrology

Not only are the angles time-sensitive, but they are place-sensitive as well. Casting a birthchart as if you were born where you are now living (assuming you weren't in the first place) is the beginning of the great art of locality astrology. When you think of it, time and place bear much in common. Shifting time and place accomplish pretty much the same thing in terms of the Earth's orientation to the heavens. You can't alter your time of birth, but you can move, and the fact that different places have different effects on you is not just due to favorite restaurants or weather conditions—the fate of your response to surroundings and environment is more up to you than you may have thought possible, and aspects to the angles are the key astrological indicator of these influences. Since two of the angles in particular—the ascendant and descendant, cusps of the 1st and 7th Houses—have a lot to do with social and personal relationships, it makes sense to look at them in chart comparison.

## The Importance of an Accurate Birthtime

The angles move rapidly with the daily motion of the earth on its axis, covering the full 360 degrees of the zodiac in about 24 hours. Every two hours, a new sign is at the midheaven; thus, if your birthtime is in question, you may not be sure what the angles of your horoscope are, and so you cannot be sure how the other planets are aspecting them. If you are not certain of your time of birth within 15 minutes or so, it is best to ignore the angles in chart interpretation; there is still plenty to cover without the angles. (If you're not sure of your birthtime, Llewellyn's Personal Services offers a chart rectification service that gives you "working" angles based on past significant events in your life. By "working" is meant a chart that resonates reliably by transit and progression.)

## The Angles Give a Horoscope Its Distinction

To give you an idea how time-sensitive the angles are, the midheaven moves about one degree every four minutes; therefore, in the space of half an hour, it approaches and leaves a close aspect with another planet. Compare this to the Moon, which moves about 12 degrees per day and remains within orb of aspecting another planet for practically a full 24 hours. Jupiter, moving on average only one-twelfth of a degree per day, spends about two months approaching and leaving an aspect with another planet—more if the aspect occurs during a retrograde cycle. But the angles are fast and hits to planets are more distinctive. Let's say you were born on a day when the Moon trined Mars. This aspect would also show up in the charts of pretty much anyone who was born that day, anywhere in the world. But let's say that the Moon is smack at your ascendant, so Mars is trine your midheaven too. This is something much rarer; only those born within about half an hour of you *and* in the same location would have this configuration (on that day).

## The Midheaven

But while angle aspects move quickly across the heavens, they are nonetheless important, the midheaven and ascendant considered the most important of the four. You've probably heard more about the ascendant, but many astrologers consider the midheaven the most important point in the chart. It symbolizes many things, and perhaps you have heard about its role in vocation and your public role. But at a deeper level, the midheaven signifies the soul, the "very self," the spirit, as well as intellectual and social attitudes. An aspect to your midheaven goes right to the core of your being. The closer the aspect's orb, the stronger its influence.

## The Ascendant

The ascendant signifies your environment and surroundings, your acquaintances and (like the lunar nodes) connections, and, in short, the place where you are. It's the effect others are having on you. It's what they see in you and remember about you. It's likely their first impression of you. The ascendant is the first foot most people put forward. Aspects to the ascendant influence your style and "delivery"; they are the wake of the boat we call life.

Together, the ascendant and midheaven signify the rising, cresting, and setting of events and ideas in your life. The halfway point between the ascendant and midheaven is sometimes called the "karmic ascendant," signifying a unity of soul and surroundings, the presence of yourself just where you are, and hence is a point of accountability and awareness in the horoscope.

Now for some terms with which you may not be familiar—the vertex and equatorial ascendant. I'll spend a little more time on these points than I did for the midheaven and ascendant since less information is available.

## The Vertex

The vertex and equatorial ascendant are less used but important points, especially (I have found) in chart comparison. The vertex is seldom far from the descendant in your chart (the point opposite the ascendant) and twice each day it actually coincides to the descendant. When either 0° Aries or 0° Libra rises on the ecliptic; if you are one of those rare birds whose descendant and vertex are identical, you have a special connection to the Earth; "second nature" is first nature. The point opposite the vertex is called the anti-vertex. It likewise seldom strays far from the ascendant and is actually identical to the ascendant, twice each day, just as the vertex. When looking at aspects to the vertex, a square to one is a square to both, and a trine to one is a sextile to the other.

The vertex signifies fate and destiny. Because its daily cycle usually takes it through only the 5th, 6th, 7th, and 8th Houses, and because these houses define a find of "relationship quadrant" in a horoscope, the vertex is important in relationships. By fate or destiny is meant that sense of inevitability about the relationships you establish in this world. Some demand your attention more than others, and often in these cases the vertex is involved. The vertex is also associated with out-of-the-blue and unexpected social contacts. Because it is driven by the inscrutable engines of destiny, the vertex is an indicator of what seems to be your lot in life, your role, what is put into your hands, and what is left for you to undiscover, in the sense that what you have you didn't find, but somehow were born having. Some say our challenge is to understand not having what we have so easily. The vertex relates to that theme. Vertex contacts between charts can be heavy and burdensome, but they also contribute to self-knowledge.

In Charles Jayne's words:

> Planets which are strongly linked by aspect to the vertex are . . . very much bound up with the impersonally fated part of the life of the native. One cannot really change the things signified by that which is involved with the vertex, since it has to do with one's 'lot in life', actually determined by one's past and thus peculiarly karmic.

## The Equatorial Ascendant

The equatorial ascendant signifies connection with your environment or surroundings. Where the ascendant signifies the environment itself, the equatorial ascendant links you to it through a dynamic of comparison between you and other people. The equatorial ascendant generally appears in either the 1st or 12th House (of house systems where the ascendant marks the first cusp). Uranian astrologer Arlene Kramer has noted that the equatorial ascendant in the 1st House shows that you never feel the real you is coming across to others; there is a veil between what you say and what others hear. But when the equatorial ascendant is in the 12th House, this is not a problem, and there's no trouble getting yourself across to others. More on the equatorial ascendant shortly.

## The Lunar Nodes

The lunar nodes—there are a pair, always opposite each other in the horoscope—signify unions, connections, and communication. They also signify the limits of a situation, the walls you run into as well as the doors you walk through. Many astrologers draw a distinction between the north lunar node as where you're going and the south lunar node as where you're coming from; this is certainly valid, but together, and more broadly, the nodes signify the tissue that connects this before and after. The lunar nodes are your limits in this life, not in the sense of Saturn, which is restrictions, but in the evolutionary sense of what you're bumping into to prod your being onto greater awareness and understanding. When you have a real sense of connection, you may wonder what else is there, and the nodes serve this very karmic function in our lives. Aspects between planets and the lunar nodes describe your process of connecting and the types of limits you are likely to run into. In relationships, node contacts describe the rules or parameters of your getting along. And rules are made to be broken.

You have seen that the lunar nodes and the ascendant both signify connections. What is the difference? The nodes are a little more literal and a little less fluid than the ascendant. If the nodes are like a land border between countries, the ascendant is like a water border, a little harder to pin down and define. The lunar nodes also have more to do with communication than the ascendant. You may be thinking that communication is Mercury, but more fundamentally Mercury is thinking, sort of "preconnective," where the lunar nodes are definitely connective.

## All These Points Relate to "Connection"

The ascendant, midheaven, vertex, equatorial ascendant, and lunar nodes describe five "orbits" of consciousness. They define your "angle on" life, or what your view is. Are you looking at things flat, or more inclined; are you high up, or on the level— aspects to angles indicate our perspective on life. The common thread connecting these points is connection, different forms of togetherness, and hence their importance in relationships. All but the midheaven, which is the base or fundamental point in the chart, are types of nodes in their own right, in the astronomical sense of crossing orbits.

The ascendant is actually a node of the midheaven, in that it takes our "flat earth" perspective and directs it from whatever direction we may be viewing to the vicinity of the rising Sun; thus the ascendant has a lot to do with the cycle of birth, death, and rebirth.

The vertex is a second node of the midheaven, in that it is where the horizon—always connected to the point in the sky directly overhead—comes "down to earth," and meeting up with the Earth's orbit in the east. In the old maxim "as above, so below," the ascendant is the bridge.

The equatorial ascendant, as its name suggests, is the node of the celestial equator, emblematic of the earth's daily rotation, which accounts for the rising and setting of the sun. The equatorial ascendant is a fundamental point in the chart, yet frankly one with which astrologers are only in the childhood of understanding. The simplest way to think of the equatorial ascendant is that it is the ascendant in your chart had you been born at the equator. It is therefore your primary connection to the spinning earth and the daily cycles of light and darkness. Since into every life a little sleep or darkness must fall, and since the chasm between one end of the cycle of waking and the other end can be vast, the equatorial ascendant signifies a connection with ourselves—who we think we are, or remember we are, or are reminded we are. It is like suddenly being dropped, on a daily basis, into a country whose language you once knew fluently but now—at least at the dawning of your arrival— eke along in. But by the end of the day you have regained your former fluency. Have you ever felt like you have an important thread of understanding, that you're really onto something, but are afraid that after sleeping and in the morning things won't be what they seemed the night before? We all have. This is the equatorial ascendant functioning in your life, and it therefore signifies various forms of attachment, which of course has a lot to do with relationships. How much do we allow ourselves to get attached to others? That is the question posed by the equatorial ascendant. Answers can be discovered in the aspects of the planets to it.

The lunar nodes are exceptional in that their traverse of the zodiac is comparatively very slow, on the order of 19 years, where all the others move full revolutions in a single day. The nodes, as the crossing points of the orbits of the earth and the moon, have to do with our connections to other bodies on this earth. They are some kind of lifeline between the coming into and the leaving of this world. Hence the attribution of "karma" you read in reference to the nodes. The nodes are what's always matting down the path of life at least one step ahead of when we get there; and they are the grass slowly springing back up and rising into our consciousness where we have already walked.

## Astrology's Vertical Dimension

Most aspects or planet comparisons in astrology occur along the ecliptic. Parallels are an exception. They, along with antiscia, form part of what we might call astrology's vertical dimension, in which a planet's distance above or below the ecliptic or equator is the key factor. See the following diagram to help you visualize the vertical and horizontal dimensions of astrological space.

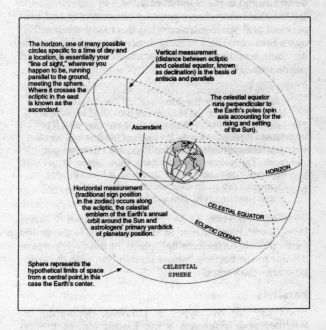

The horizon, one of many possible circles specific to a time of day and a location, is essentially your "line of sight," wherever you happen to be, running parallel to the ground, meeting the sphere. Where it crosses the ecliptic in the east is known as the ascendant.

Vertical measurement (distance between ecliptic and celestial equator, known as declination) is the basis of antiscia and parallels.

The celestial equator runs perpendicular to the Earth's poles (spin axis accounting for the rising and setting of the Sun).

Ascendant

HORIZON

CELESTIAL EQUATOR

ECLIPTIC (ZODIAC)

Horizontal measurement (traditional sign position in the zodiac) occurs along the ecliptic, the celestial emblem of the Earth's annual orbit around the Sun and astrologers' primary yardstick of planetary position.

Sphere represents the hypothetical limits of space from a central point, in this case the Earth's center.

CELESTIAL SPHERE

This may seem terribly basic, but one of the key issues in astrology is how to measure the planets. It's not as simple as it may seem. For one thing, the planets are "not just out there"—they don't conveniently reside upon some celestial ruler, like a number line in math class. We have to put them there. How we do that is the subject of a separate article, but the fact that we do brings the multi-dimensional reality of space into account; we don't just measure *along*, but *up and down* as well. (Not to neglect the third, *in and out*, dimension, known as distance value, but we probably have our hands full already.) The diagram shows the two main measurement styles in astrology—horizontal and vertical. There's more than one horizontal measurement, and more than one vertical, but for now let's cover the most common: horizontal, along the equator, and vertical, perpendicular (at a right angle) to the celestial equator.

Michael Erlewine, computer programmer and pioneer of Local Space astrology, has this to say about astrology's horizontal and vertical dimensions, which he calls by their traditional names, azimuth (horizontal) and prime vertical:

> Where the azimuth . . . has to do with action and outreach on our part, the prime vertical dimension has to do with reaction, the response of the world to us. In a word, the prime vertical tells us about that which is fated or destined for us, the areas of life that will happen automatically and don't require effort on our part. The prime vertical charts those areas of life where we can't help but be involved. It is our destiny. None can say no to us where the prime vertical (and vertex) are involved. It is fated.

The reference to vertex clearly echoes Charles Jayne's statement earlier in this article—it is the prime vertical circle on the celestial sphere, or the circle perpendicular to the horizon, whose intersection with the ecliptic marks the vertex.

## Parallels

There are two types of parallels, depending on whether your reference is the Earth's annual motion around the Sun, or its daily motion on its own poles. Planets are in "parallel by declination" when they are the same distance from the celestial equator, the circle representing the Earth's daily motion (see diagram). This distance is called declination and, as long as planets have the same declination—it doesn't matter if they're in a traditional sign aspect, such as trine or square—they are parallel. Because the ecliptic and celestial equator bear a fixed relationship to each other, a planet's position in the zodiac (by sign) does have bearing on its declination; but the planets' orbits undulate above and below the ecliptic, thus their actual distance from the celestial equator differs from the distance of their ecliptic degrees from the equator (unless the planets are exactly on the ecliptic).

What's interesting is that you might have two planets whose ecliptic degrees are not in traditional aspect, or wide of orb (too wide to be of much interest), yet their declinations might be identical—for example, Mars at 15° Leo and Jupiter at 23° Scorpio. Going by traditional ecliptic aspects, these planets are in wide square—too wide if you've got several other tighter aspects at your disposal. But let's say that both planets are 17.5° from the celestial equator, in exact parallel—this could happen. If so, you've got a dynamic planetary duo on your hands.

## Contraparallels – Splitting Hairs

Actually, in this example, Mars would be north of the equator and Jupiter south, and so in what is technically called a contraparallel relationship—the same distance from the equator but on opposite sides of the equator. But I think the parallel and contraparallel act the same way, or at least it seems like a niggling distinction when there are so many other and weightier factors to consider in interpreting a chart. It's analogous to comparing a conjunction and opposition, the difference being more a factor of what planets are involved than any intrinsic difference between the aspects.

## How Much Orb?

How close to having the same declination do planets have to be in order to be in a parallel or contraparallel aspect? Beyond 1° is getting a little loose—just a degree; it's a much tighter tolerance than you have with traditional aspects on the ecliptic, the reason being that you're dealing with less than a sixth as much possible range of distance. With more than 1° orb, there's too much overlap.

There are also parallels and contraparallels of latitude, which occur when planets are the same distance from the ecliptic rather than from the celestial equator. Usually astrologers pay less attention to parallels of latitude, but they shouldn't overlook them. After all, eclipses are a powerful phenomena whose determining factor is that the Sun and Moon are not only in the same (or opposite) place in the sky, but both are smack on the ecliptic. In case you're wondering why not every Full or New Moon is an eclipse, the reason is that while the Sun is always on the ecliptic (has zero latitude), the Moon undulates in a monthly cycle above and below it. In order to have an eclipse, not only need the Moon be conjunct or opposite the Sun, but it must have zero latitude—be right on the ecliptic with the Sun. If you use parallels of latitude, you should allow even less orb than you would for parallels of declination, since there's even a smaller range of possible separation.

### "Cut Me Some Slack"

Enough theory ... what do parallels mean? Basically that there is "no latitude"—no breathing room, no margin for error, or tight as tics, depending on what planets are involved. Often it's the case that in a dynamic between two people there's a certain margin for misunderstanding, an allowance of differences, a latitude of forgiveness—there are many ways of referring to it. But sometimes this is not so—the two·people see eye to eye on things, or, if not, they're easily at odds. In short, there's "no latitude"—no difference in the distance from the equator (or ecliptic).

### Cooperation

Parallels and contraparallels place high demand on cooperation. When Robert Bly says we should "follow our gold," the "gold" of two planets in parallel or contraparallel is **cooperation**—learning to get along. It can be glorious and tough simultaneously. If you find two planets in your own chart in parallel or contraparallel, it means that you are "put here" to learn to have them get along, to be their diplomat. And if you're lucky, you'll have diplomatic immunity, but when Mars or Saturn and, to a lesser extent (I think), the outer planets are involved, it can be like dealing with two opposing countries.

## Example – Gloria Steinem and Robert Bly

Now there's a pair!—*Ms. Magazine* meets Iron John. Gloria Steinem is a widely recognized voice of feminism, ironically known today for a somewhat uncompromising traditionalism vis-à-vis her originally more radical-sounding precepts. Robert Bly is the "cry, man, cry" voice of modern "masculinism," known for his poetry, translations, and redux of the old Iron John story.

You may wonder what an astrological comparison of Bly and Steinem would reveal, since these two are not (as far as I know) personal associates. But, as respective champions of male and female gender causes, they are certainly social or world associates. Comparing their charts, you'll find an interesting parallel (by declination): namely Bly's Mars at 14°48' declination, contraparallel Steinem's Saturn at -14°31' declination—only 17 minutes of arc, or about a quarter degree, separated from exact. If you compared Bly's Mars at 6° Taurus and Steinem's Saturn at 24° Aquarius, you will indeed see an aspect in the horizontal dimension, in fact an exact one, if you work with quintiles. Quintiles are fifth-portions of the zodiac circle, or 72°. Bly's Mars and Steinem's Saturn are less than 11 minutes of arc—about a tenth of a degree—from being in exact quintile. So what to do and which to choose? If you work with quintiles, you'll note the tremendous "action of separation" (Alfred Witte's phrase for the Mars/Saturn dynamic) these clarion criers of gender issues have mustered socially among their respective adherents, and all with the lights-out creativity that characterizes the quintile. But there's another way to look at this, especially if the quintile isn't in your astrological bag of tricks. This is the contraparallel. Here the interpretation, with Mars and Saturn involved, is that there's no margin for misunderstanding. The forces of cooperation are interrupted. Bly and Steinem, mavens of the masculine and feminine, epitomize the periodic (keyword for Mars/Saturn) gender separation known as the battle of the sexes.

## Antiscia (Solstice Points / Equinox Points)

Antiscia (also called solstice points) and parallels are related. The zodiac degrees of two planets are each other's antiscia when they are the same distance from the equator. It is important to say "the zodiac degrees of two planets" rather than "two planets" since the planets, with their orbits that seem to undulate with respect to the Earth's, may or may not be on the ecliptic.

I don't think it makes much difference whether the planets are above or below the equator. When the two planets are on the same side of the equator—both above or both below—you have a traditional solstice point or antiscia relationship, but when one planet is above and the other is below, you have what would naturally be called an equinox point relationship.

The explanation of this terminology is that when the zodiac degrees of two planets are the same distance from the equator and on the same side of the equator, they are also the same zodiacal distance from either of the two solstice points on the zodiac—0° Cancer, 0° Capricorn—so-called because they mark the two annual solstices, or the beginning of Summer and Winter. You can set up an analogous scenario with the equinox points, 0° Aries and 0° Libra, the markers of the two equinoxes and the beginning of Spring and Fall. This is in fact what you have when the zodiac degrees of two planets are the same distance from the celestial equator but on opposite sides of the equator. At least so far, I don't see any point in making an interpretive distinction between these phenomena; solstice points and equinox points work identically. The table on the next page will let you find antiscia in your charts. (Computer programs are available to do the work for you—see resources section at the end of this article).

Note that due to the quadrant symmetry of the zodiac circle—four equal 90° quarters—it is necessary to cover only the first 90 degrees of the zodiac; the other quadrants are mirror reflections—hence the alternative name for solstice points, mirror points.

# Antiscia Table

|  | VII | V | III | I |  |  |  |  |
|---|---|---|---|---|---|---|---|---|
|  | 270 | 180 | 90 | 00 | 90 | 180 | 270 | 360 |
| CARDINAL | 271 | 181 | 91 | 01 | 89 | 179 | 269 | 359 | MUTABLE |
|  | 272 | 182 | 92 | 02 | 88 | 178 | 268 | 358 |
|  | 273 | 183 | 93 | 03 | 87 | 177 | 267 | 357 |
|  | 274 | 184 | 94 | 04 | 86 | 176 | 266 | 356 |
|  | 275 | 185 | 95 | 05 | 85 | 175 | 265 | 355 |
|  | 276 | 186 | 96 | 06 | 84 | 174 | 264 | 354 |
|  | 277 | 187 | 97 | 07 | 83 | 173 | 263 | 353 |
|  | 278 | 188 | 98 | 08 | 82 | 172 | 262 | 352 |
|  | 279 | 189 | 99 | 09 | 81 | 171 | 261 | 351 |
|  | 280 | 190 | 100 | 10 | 80 | 170 | 260 | 350 |
|  | 281 | 191 | 101 | 11 | 79 | 169 | 259 | 349 |
|  | 282 | 192 | 102 | 12 | 78 | 168 | 258 | 348 |
|  | 283 | 193 | 103 | 13 | 77 | 167 | 257 | 347 |
|  | 284 | 194 | 104 | 14 | 76 | 166 | 256 | 346 |
|  | 285 | 195 | 105 | 15 | 75 | 165 | 255 | 345 |
|  | 286 | 196 | 106 | 16 | 74 | 164 | 254 | 344 |
|  | 287 | 197 | 107 | 17 | 73 | 163 | 253 | 343 |
|  | 288 | 198 | 108 | 18 | 72 | 162 | 252 | 342 |
|  | 289 | 199 | 109 | 19 | 71 | 161 | 251 | 341 |
|  | 290 | 200 | 110 | 20 | 70 | 160 | 250 | 340 |
|  | 291 | 201 | 111 | 21 | 69 | 159 | 249 | 339 |
|  | 292 | 202 | 112 | 22 | 68 | 158 | 248 | 338 |
|  | 293 | 203 | 113 | 23 | 67 | 157 | 247 | 337 |
|  | 294 | 204 | 114 | 24 | 66 | 156 | 246 | 336 |
|  | 295 | 205 | 115 | 25 | 65 | 155 | 245 | 335 |
|  | 296 | 206 | 116 | 26 | 64 | 154 | 244 | 334 |
|  | 297 | 207 | 117 | 27 | 63 | 153 | 243 | 333 |
|  | 298 | 208 | 118 | 28 | 62 | 152 | 242 | 332 |
|  | 299 | 209 | 119 | 29 | 61 | 151 | 241 | 331 |
| FIXED | 300 | 210 | 120 | 30 | 60 | 150 | 240 | 330 | MUTABLE |
|  | 301 | 211 | 121 | 31 | 59 | 149 | 239 | 329 |
|  | 302 | 212 | 122 | 32 | 58 | 148 | 238 | 328 |
|  | 303 | 213 | 123 | 33 | 57 | 147 | 237 | 327 |
|  | 304 | 214 | 124 | 34 | 56 | 146 | 236 | 326 |
|  | 305 | 215 | 125 | 35 | 55 | 145 | 235 | 325 |
|  | 306 | 216 | 126 | 36 | 54 | 144 | 234 | 324 |
|  | 307 | 217 | 127 | 37 | 53 | 143 | 233 | 323 |
|  | 308 | 218 | 128 | 38 | 52 | 142 | 232 | 322 |
|  | 309 | 219 | 129 | 39 | 51 | 141 | 231 | 321 |
|  | 310 | 220 | 130 | 40 | 50 | 140 | 230 | 320 |
|  | 311 | 221 | 131 | 41 | 49 | 139 | 229 | 319 |
|  | 312 | 222 | 132 | 42 | 48 | 138 | 228 | 318 |
|  | 313 | 223 | 133 | 43 | 47 | 137 | 227 | 317 |
|  | 314 | 224 | 134 | 44 | 46 | 136 | 226 | 316 |
|  | 315 | 225 | 135 | 45 | 45 | 135 | 225 | 315 |
|  |  | II |  | IV |  | VI |  | VIII |

## Working with Antiscia

You may want to get the feel of antiscia by working with your own chart. Write down a list of all the zodiac degrees of the planets in your chart. One by one, find each degree in the table, but first . . .

## A Simple Conversion

To use the table on the previous page, you may have to convert the position of a planet from its normal notation to what's called 360° notation. The easiest method is to determine what number the sign of the planet is in the standard zodiacal sequence:

| | |
|---|---|
| Aries | 1 |
| Taurus | 2 |
| Gemini | 3 |
| Cancer | 4 |
| Leo | 5 |
| Virgo | 6 |
| Libra | 7 |
| Scorpio | 8 |
| Sagittarius | 9 |
| Capricorn | 10 |
| Aquarius | 11 |
| Pisces | 12 |

Then subtract one from that number; for example, if the sign is Capricorn, your result would be 9. Now multiply that number by 30; if it's Capricorn, the answer would be 270 (9 x 30). Finally, add the number of degrees the planet has in the sign; if it's 15° Capricorn, the result is 285 (270, the previous result, plus 15). Now go to the table and look for 285. There's a trick to finding the numbers in the table, which may at first glance appear to be out of sequence. Use the roman numerals at the top and bottom of the columns to find you way. I starts the counting, down to 45°, then column II goes bottom-up to 90°, followed by column III from top to bottom, and so on. 285° is a third of the way down column VII (the first column listed).

The next step is the key one. Take all the numbers in the same row as 285°, so what you have is this:

**285 195 105 15 75 165 255 345**

These numbers represent all the antiscia points of 15° Capricorn (285° in 360° notation). This list includes both solstice points and equinox points. Now that you have your contact points for the original planetary position of 15° Capricorn, it's time to convert the positions back to regular sign notation (with enough practice, you'll start doing this in your head). It's easy: divide each of the numbers by 30 and *add* one to get the number of the sign. For example, from the list above, 30 goes into 195 six times, with 15 as a remainder. Seven is therefore the number of the sign, which is Libra. *The remainder becomes the number of degrees of Libra, so the result is 15° Libra* (note that when the number is less than 30, the sign is automatically Aries). The other points in this set of solstice and equinox points for, in sequence, are 15° Cancer, 15° Aries, 15° Gemini, 15° Virgo, 15° Sagittarius, and 15° Pisces.

## Learning Antiscia Degrees

Notice anything about this list besides the fact that all are 15° of some sign? All are Cardinal or Mutable signs—four of each. This is a good way to remember what points in the zodiac are sensitive to each other. If you go back to the table, you'll see you get similar patterns with the rest of the rows. For example, three rows down you have 18° of Cardinal signs and 12° of Mutable signs. The Cardinal signs are Aries, Cancer, Libra, and Capricorn; the Fixed signs are Taurus, Leo, Scorpio, and Aquarius; and the Mutable signs are Gemini, Virgo, Sagittarius, and Pisces.

## Interpretation – "We Are the World"

I think of antiscia as the "we are the world" aspect in astrology, especially in relationships. They represent a back door out of the "solitary confinement" that seems to characterize modern existential reality, but don't be depressed—antiscia are a connection to the world. They are world links. Like parallels, they have the flavor of fate or destiny, as any personal interface with the interpersonal world seems to have, but beyond that they kind of harpoon our hearts to each other—when the degree of a planet in my chart is the antiscion (singular form of antiscia) of a planet in yours. It may or may not be love, but it feels like you've got Moby Dick on the other end—a wild ride. How could it not be, when we suddenly find ourselves connected to the world?

Antiscia also represent a way through the miasma of self-doubt and the "I can't believe this is happening to me syndrome." With antiscia, there's more than just "me"—there's you too, and you probably have a different take on what I'm up to. Depending on your predisposition to change (stubbornness quotient) and the planets involved, antiscia aspects belong to the astrological college of hard knocks, or learning the hard way. But antiscia also leave an indelible impression.

## Example – Hugh Heffner and Jesse Helms

It'll be a cold day in hell when these two share a table, but let's look at one way this reveals itself in their charts. As with Gloria Steinem and Robert Bly, we have two world figures who represent diametrically opposed phenomena—"Heff," publisher of *Playboy* magazine and radical entrepreneur, and Helms, moralizing politician and our modern-day St. Augustine (without the sense of humor).

Helms' Mars is at 18° Virgo. The question is, does Hugh Heffner have anything at 12° of a Cardinal sign? He has Pluto at 12° Cancer (and some change). So Helms and Heffner are roped to the world via Mars and Pluto. That seems terribly fitting, the two rulers of Scorpio and, at the risk of oversimplification, the two great sex planets. Heffner is Pluto in this drama, the greater transformer, while Helms, with his Mars in Virgo, is something of a prude (no offense, all you Mars in Virgo people; Helms has other stuff going on in his chart, such as that Mars tightly square his ascendant, representing his environment and surroundings, and closely sextile Mercury in Scorpio, putting his brain in overdrive).

## Double the Fun

If you really want to see a connection, compare an antiscia pair in one chart with an antiscia pair in another chart. Not all charts, of course, have antiscia, but when the two people involved both do, there's going to be some bonding, one way or another. We have such a case with Heffner and Helms. Heffner has Mercury and Uranus as antiscia in his natal chart. This is revolutionary thought, which fits, considering the radical nature of his publication. Helms has Moon and Neptune as antiscia in his natal chart. Alfred Witte has the following to say about Moon/Neptune:

> To fall asleep. To dream. State of dreaming. Cerebral state of sleep. **Not quite clearly conscious.** Dazed. Receptive brains. Delicacy, tact. **To have a scent for something** [my emphasis].

The revolutionary thinker meets the hound dog of morality and tact. Is the quality of their mutual connection to the world any surprise?

(Comparing charts with pairs of antiscia is actually a refinement of the Uranian system of astrology. Two such pairs form what is called a "planetary picture." For a fuller description of the Uranian system, you are referred to an article by Arlene Kramer in Llewellyn's *Special Measurements* volume of the New Worlds Astrology series, edited by Noel Tyl. This volume contains a more detailed essay on antiscia, also by Tom Bridges.)


## Acknowledgements and Resources

The quote by Charles Jayne is from *Horoscope Interpretation Outlined*; that of Michael Erlewine from an essay on Local Space astrology printed with the documentation to Michael's computer program covering this technique. The ideas of Uranian astrologer Arlene Kramer are from personal communication. The interpretations of Alfred Witte, founder of the Uranian system of astrology, are from a book called *Rules for Planetary Pictures*. Readers may be interested in checking out the correspondence course in horary astrology offered by Gilbert Navarro, who uses parallels and antiscia extensively in his work; information on the course is available by writing to 112 Palmetto Drive, Edgewood, Maryland, 21040. I would like to thank all the astrologers I have mentioned for their inspiration and assistance, including Michael Erlewine for his work with Local Space and the nodes in astrology. The celestial sphere diagram in this article was produced by the author and is the copyright of Matrix Software. The table of antiscia degrees is an elaboration of a table, found in Ptolemy's *Almagest*, pairing degrees of the ecliptic with degrees of declination. The astrological charts for celebrity examples used in this article are from Richard Nolle.

If you wish to pursue the subject of locality astrology, Llewellyn has books on Astro★Carto★Graphy (Jim Lewis and Ariel Guttman) and Local Space (Steve Cozzi). For a detailed personal report comparing two horoscopes, including the angles, see the ad in the services section. Computer software can save you a lot of time by calculating the astrological factors mentioned in this article. The programs of Matrix Software for home computers—endorsed by Llewellyn for many years—are top notch. Besides chartwheels showing the exact position of the ascendant, midheaven, vertex, and equatorial ascendant in your chart, you can print tables and grids showing aspects between the planets and these points. It's a great time-saver, especially when you're looking at a lot of charts. For a catalog of Matrix programs, call 1/800/PLANETS, or write 315 Marion Avenue, Big Rapids, Michigan 49307.

> The contemplation of celestial things will make a man both think and speak more sublimely and magnificently when he descends to human affairs.
>
> —Cicero

# The Planets' Effects on Romance

## Jeraldine Saunders

> Sure; man was born to meditate on things
> and to contemplate the eternal springs of
> God and Nature; glory; bliss and pleasure
> that life and love might be his heavenly
> treasure.
>
> —Troherne

All of us are interested in love. Sigmund Freud said;
"People need at least two things in life; love and orbit."
Orbit meaning work. Astrology tells us so much about
how each sign relates to love and romance. Ralph Waldo
Emerson said; "Astrology is astronomy brought down to
earth and applied to the affairs of man." Astrology
shows that without the Sun there is no life. Starting with
Aries, the natural 1st House of the zodiac, look for its 5th
House of love which would be Leo. Leo is ruled by the
Sun; the giver of life. Each sign has its own solar 5th
House and 7th House which gives reasons why each are
attracted to certain types of lovers and mates.

As I wrote in *Signs of Love* (Llewellyn Publications;
1991) "And now we will strive for a mood of mystic
thoughtfulness using astrology for the quickened appreciation that causes us to be attentive to the significance of
living and loving. Right-mindedness is the directing of
attention to those matters that are first in importance. We
must not allow isolation and the false feeling of separate-

ness to keep us from being able to realize what the true significance of love is all about. The enemies of love are: 1. Low self-worth (low self-esteem) and 2. Fear. They are very prominent in our society, but the good news is that we can make them disappear if we face them. The past must be released and we must let go of everything that doesn't help promote a beautiful future."

# ♈ Aries ♈

Aries is ruled by Mars, the planet of action, personality, and attraction. In the animal kingdom the plumage of the male bird is brighter to attract the female. The purpose is union and ultimately offspring. Aries is the aggressor. It takes two to tango and so somebody has to start things. That is why Aries is called the pioneer; being the self-starter and willing to experiment and to take risks. Most persons are so vulnerable and so afraid of rejection where love is concerned. The fear of rejection ranks almost next to the inborn fear of falling. Aries teaches us that we have to take the risk. Philosophers, writers, and poets tell us never to be afraid of making a fool of ourselves over love.

If you are an impulsive Aries (March 21–April 20), or if your gentleman friend or lady friend is an Aries, here are some traits you'll need to know about. This is a "cardinal fire" sign. The other cardinal signs include Moonchild (Cancer), Libra, and Capricorn. These signs are presumed to be leaders.

Aries tend to be easily excited about anything or anyone new. One of the negative traits is that Aries often fail to stay with situations or persons long enough to capitalize on new career opportunities or personal relationships, in order to take full advantage of their good fortune.

They have a me-first attitude and a desire to be at the head of the line; often causing them to take chances in love and in traffic. They are prone to fall in love at first sight and get distracted by any potential new love interests. It is their nature, because their planetary ruler is the planet Mars, to be aggressive, ambitious, bold, lacking in patience, quite enterprising, original, and full of energy—properly directed, we hope. They know how to make money and are not always frugal about hanging on to it.

In romantic matters; they are spontaneous and appreciate persons who are equally spontaneous.

They are feisty and they enjoy a good scrap; quick to anger and just as quick to forgive and forget. Often home base or real estate-oriented, they love to create a comfortable and attractive ambience where they live. The bad news is that they are apt to move more often than some other signs. Their romantic sector is ruled by the sign of Leo and they are likely to be attracted to persons who are showy and regal.

Their 7th House, the house of marriage and partnerships, is Libra, ruled by romantic Venus, a sign not noted for making snap decisions. Both tend to try to see all sides of offers, the plusses and the minuses; often agonizing over decisions, while do-it-now Aries needs this stability.

Everything must be done immediately or the day before. If you know someone like this who is not an Aries the possibility is that the person may have Mars or some other planet in Aries.

Why do people change?

One of the reasons is that if the birth Sun, for instance, is in Aries, by astrological progressions, the Sun moves into the next sign for approximately 30 years. Then it moves into the next sign, each time picking up some of the characteristics of that sign, and dropping a few built-in traits of the original birth sign.

If we do not change, we have not grown—presuming that we have not changed for the better. Then there are those who change all right, but for the worse.

Life and love has been described by gamblers as a crap shoot. Some people always seem to win and others win less often. Those who have faced the challenges of dealing with occasional or continual defeats are supposed to develop more character.

Because of the Aries craving for excitement they often get a reputation of being promiscuous, when they are actually just surveying the field for a person who is sensually and romantically suitable for a long-term arrangement. If you can cope with the idea of spending time with a person with many irons in the fire and some of the other qualities mentioned above, you may be very stimulated by this often one-of-a-kind, action-oriented specimen.

If you are not an Aries; you have missed out on being in some pretty fast company. If you like the excitements offered you might consider a fling with someone of this sign. You will probably get the rush act and wind up with some interesting memories.

# ♉ Taurus ♉

"If music be the food of love, play on," (William Shakespeare from *Twelfth Night*). Shakespeare said, "Tis the stars above that govern us." This Taurus also said; "It is better to have loved and lost than never to have loved at all." So astrology now verifies what we instinctively know, that we don't really enjoy life without love. Shakespeare's sign, Taurus, is ruled by Venus, the planet that symbolically represents love. It is the second sign in the zodiac. Taurus represents our ability to be secure materially and emotionally, and the sensitivity of Venus. It rules the throat, the voice, the sound. Taureans help us to evaluate possessions. Our ability to earn income from our talents is a possession.

There are many astrological references to astrology in Shakespeare. The word jovial is from Jupiter. When we say Martian we mean Mars, sunny is the Sun, of course, Venus is Venusian, Mercury is mercurial, and on and on.

If you are a Taurus or if someone of this sign has touched your life or your heart, here are some of the facts you need to know about this fixed, Venus-ruled, Earth sign. The other fixed signs are Leo, Scorpio, and Aquarius. The fixed signs are the money signs.

Taurus is generous, gentle except when angered, charming, practical, interested in art, music, possessions, and making money. Of the fixed signs, Taurus is without a doubt the most intransigent, and least likely to compromise in stressful interpersonal relations. They exude a kind of sexual romantic vibration that is extremely attractive to the opposite sex. Many consider music and art their major interest—after money-making and loving.

Their key words are "I possess," inferring a certain acquisitiveness and a desire for material objects that they want to share with their loved one; including jewelry, property, an upscale model automobile, musical instruments, or the paraphernalia of the artist—depending upon the creative path that they've chosen.

The first thing you are apt to notice is the sexual quality of the speaking or singing voice. It is likely to be rich and resonant because the sign rules the throat, the thyroid gland, and the shoulders.

361

Like "Auntie Mame," Taurus feels they should be sitting at the head table of life and dress the part with good taste, plus flair. They have an aura of sensuality and appreciate the romantic aspects of life. Flowers and gifts in general are recommended, in case you are attempting to make points with this luxury-oriented sign.

With Aries natives, their personal rule is "Do it now." With Taurus the pace is slower and their approach is "take time to enjoy it." They are more patient, less impulsive, more cautious, and often quite intuitive. They need lots of affection. Some Taureans seem to associate affection with love more than they do sex, but must recognize the trinity: affection, sex, and love. They are somewhat of a connoisseur. This applies to sex as well as other areas.

They are often very good cooks; liking rich foods, along with a love of fresh vegetables and fruits. They need a spacious kitchen and a large home in a prestigious neighborhood. Entertaining guests is one of their strong suits. Children are apt to be pampered, but much is expected of them: good manners, good grades, and good vocational prospects when they reach the adult stage.

Taureans are potentially hard working, with a lot of financial smarts. The old-time astrologers felt that Tauruses should marry persons of their opposing sign, Scorpio, the intense, secretive, charismic, power-hungry and often over-sexed. The over-sexed tendency appeals to sex-pot Taureans. If the partner is guilty of flirtations or affairs, another side of Taurus comes into play. They can be jealous, possessive, and vindictive. Be warned!

This Venus-ruled sign is satisfied with only the best, in wares, servants, and, if a female, is definitely a luxury-item woman that some men could not afford as mistress or wife; in matters of sex they are romantic and insatiable. They opt for the lavish life style.

In courtship, the males are seen as big spenders; but in marriage there are moments when they seem a little conservative with money. They often consider themselves experts on wines, and most Taureans, male or female, are second-helping people, and are quite at home in the kitchen as well as the bedroom.

They are dress-for-success people. Taurus's 5th House of love is Virgo. This knowledge can be helpful to anyone aspiring to be loved by this financially capable Taurean, for where Virgo falls in the chart a person is very particular and discriminating. The loved ones apparel and grooming must be impeccable. Taurus's Venus, together with this Mercury significator of the solar 5th House, combine to indicate variety, excitement and analysis. A sense of humor will help them obtain the basic goals they seek, one of which is often an insatiable sex desire.

For Taurus the solar 7th House of partnerships and marriage would be Scorpio. After an argument it is important for this Taurus lover to keep communications open. Taurus would have to overcome the tendency to be sullen during this time. When Taurus learns to give up the desire to possess, and can be open to suggestions and verbalize, then this sexy, 7th House influence will bring them an exceptionally happy life with an emotionally intense and extremely sensual spouse who may have some of the Scorpio qualities.

## ♊ Gemini ♊

Gemini is associated with Mercury, the planet of the mind, communications, the written word, reports, dissemination of information, all related to love. Geminis are attracted first to the mind, and then follows the physical attraction. A clash of ideas is more exciting than the clash of guns. Virgo is also ruled by the planet Mercury. Gemini and Virgo are the writers and communicators. You might hear one of them say, "If it isn't on the page, it isn't on the stage." Gemini's solar 5th House of love is Libra, Venus ruled. So we have here a combination of Mercury and Venus which means mind and love and flowers and music. They are attracted through the excitement of ideas, and the sensual voice. Love birds whispering sweet nothings—tantalizing with their silver-tongued use of language.

If you or someone you care for was born under the sign of Gemini they are a fascinating, mutable air sign, ruled by the planet Mercury. Mercury is also the planet of ideas, writing, selling, words, short trips, paper, advertising, buying, debating or arguing, delivering mail and packages. Gemini longs for affection and understanding. If they control the urge to be critical and learn to take the bitter with the sweet, they will enjoy the blessings of their lucky Sagittarius-Jupiter ruled 7th House of marriage. They are attracted to the type of lover who won't make them feel imprisoned, someone who is as independent as they are.

They are born storytellers and may become writers; lecturers, teachers, or work in the media. They love words, puns, and may even be avid crossword puzzle fans. They often interrupt people and finish their sentences for them, if the speaker is a slow talker.

If you aspire to attract and hold on to a Gemini lover or mate, you had better be a full-time interesting person. Geminis have a very low boredom threshold. If you fail to be stimulating and interesting, you are going to wind up being a short-timer in their life.

Geminis, in general, are apt to be taller, have longer arms, and longer fingers. A few of them become amateur or professional magicians, their hands being quicker than the eye. A good magician also has a diverting line of patter that goes along with each trick.

In a lover, they are looking for a sounding board to bounce ideas off and may not hold on to the same point of view from day to day. If another person makes a statement that they believe should be carved in stone, the Gemini is apt to butt in and poke all sorts of verbal holes in the other person's opinions.

Versatile describes Gemini. They are often romantically involved with persons where they work or someone they met through a brother, sister, or neighbor.

Clothing-wise, they are often ahead of trends, and because of their slimness they present a sleek profile to the world. In the presence of the opposite sex or in a crowd they are apt to get off some quotable double entendre remarks. They can pass anything but a book store, library, or an intelligent-seeming member of the opposite sex. They often annoy dates by table-hopping at a banquet or in a restaurant. Their memory is somewhere between superficial and encyclopedic.

As dates, they look good because their interests are varied and enthusiastic; and they display a fascinating package of presentability. A single and admiring friend of yours may ask you if your date has an equally vivacious brother or sister.

If you marry a Gemini the good news is their living quarters are usually neat and their books, tapes, CDs, or other possessions are displayed in an orderly fashion. It was probably a person with strong Gemini in their chart who said; "A room without books is like a room with no windows."

Though Geminis are often pretty good in bed, their way of communication, boredom may set in. The rule for hanging on to this quicksilver sign is to be perpetually interesting and continually full of stimulating ideas, and a conversationalist *par excellance*.

You have to be well-read, amusing, and pretty presentable in public yourself. Ideally you should also be tall, have nice fingernails, and not be packing around too many pounds. You should also be able to do some of the cooking, because Geminis have been labeled, or libeled, as "the soup and stew sign."

## ♊ Cancer ♊

If your desire in lovers is an experimental, cheerful, and chatty person who often cannot sit still very long, you cannot go wrong with a flirtatious Gemini.

We know through empirical observation and written reports that there is more human and animal mating activity during a full moon. The moon relates to Cancer, the Crab, the natural fourth zodiacal sign. The 4th House is the home, security base, the family, negotiations for our own script, taking charge of our own destiny, our own fate. The moon relates to love making, physical expression of deep feelings, the offspring and family, loyalty, integrity, sustenance, food, and restaurants.

Cancer also represents the ability to enjoy the zest of living as well as the zest for the feel and taste of things, the taste buds. Of course, we need water and food to exist. Our bodies are made up of at least 70 percent water. Cancer—the water, the tides, moods, all relate to the moon. Professor Ralph N. Morris of the University of Illinois in Chicago has provided us with a very long list of things that can occur during a full moon, everything from convulsions and riots, to post-operative hemorrhaging, so if we are wise we will save the full moon nights for romance.

Cancer is ruled by the moon. What lovely songs have been sung about love and the moon. Everyone knows instinctively that the moon relates to love; "Wait till the full moon," they say. "Lets not waste the moonlit night." Vigor returns. The solar 5th House for Cancer is the powerful Scorpio ruled by Pluto. Where Cancer is concerned it is not only family orientation, procreation, but delving into the mystery; the hidden side of life itself, Pluto, the hydrogen bomb. When Cancer loves it's intense—yes, love can be explosive. If you or someone dear to you is a Moonchild you will notice that they are very changeable. That is because their ruler, the moon, spends two and a half days in each sign every 28 or 29 days.

This can be puzzling to their intimates because they take on the characteristics of the sign the moon is in during its transit though the twelve signs. One day they are scrimping and saving their money; and then they may be quite extravagant when the moon is in another sign.

With this lover you get the twelve-for-the-price-of one sign. They are apt to cry when they are sad *and* when they are happy. They tend to be collectors; sometimes of antiques, menus, souvenirs, and just about anything that has an emotional tie to it. They enjoy being embraced and touched. They are the huggers and touchers of the zodiac.

In matters of romance, it is their heart and their sentimentality that colors their impression of their intimate one. However, they do have some questions that nag at them. If the Moonchild is a female, she wonders if, after she has given her body and soul, will her lover propose marriage? On top of this question is the one, "Would he be a good provider?" The other one, "Would he welcome the idea of several children to sire and to love?"

If this Moonchild is male, his approach to a woman is sentimental and sensual, and may very well have something to do with his relationship with his mother as a boy and during his teens.

He would want a woman who was, to some extent, maternal in nature, with a generous brassiere size and equally at home in the kitchen as in the bedroom.

The natives of this sign tend to become very emotional at the approach of full moons. They can get cantankerous and/or amorous, or both.

Ask Cancer a question and they do not answer with "I think . . ." It is more likely that they will say, "I feel . . ." because they are sentimental and empathetic persons.

Making love is a way of expressing their deep feelings. The bad news is that if they are single and think of their intimate other as a potential soul mate, the moment will come when the scary subject of marriage comes to the fore. If it becomes very clear that the lover is just playing around and not in the mating mood, he or she will become history.

You may very well be looking for a lover or mate who is complex, changeable, who offers the multiple personalities of all 12 signs; depending on the position of their ruler, the moon, during its two-and-a-half-day transit of each sign—then you are seeking an emotional and sexy Moonchild. You will need patience, understanding, a sense of humor, and the ability to avoid making cutting remarks because of their sensitivity.

## ♌ Leo ♌

The solar 5th House, the house of love and romance for Leo, is Sagittarius ruled by Jupiter. This planet represents expansiveness, the higher mind, and spirituality. Despite what some may think, lovemaking goes hand in hand with spirituality. Passion and beliefs don't always find their way into the act of sex. It is being enthusiastic as opposed to ennui, as contrasted to indifference.

With love there is a dynamism. When creative juices we all have within us occur, the phenomenon can be transformed into life. The persons Leo may be attracted to could be foreigners or of a different religion, or persons who have traveled widely. This house, the solar fifth, also describes the kind of amusements that are likely to interest Leo and include horsemanship, trips to the track, and the great out-of-doors. Since there is an affinity between Sagittarius and the wide-open spaces, your Leo lover may like to make love on the top or side of a mountain, on the beach or the shore of a pond, stream, or the ocean where Nature is putting on her best shows, or in the hayloft of a barn, since that is where horses are kept. Leos are likely to be lucky in love while traveling away from their town, state, or country.

For fun, games, and friendship they may choose an Aries, Gemini, Libra, Sagittarius, or Aquarius. Leos like to have their commands followed, and although the Aquarians can be very obliging if asked civilly to do something, they definitely do not like to take orders.

If you need a loan, you will find your Leo lover to be quite generous. The bad news is that to maintain their regal life style they are more likely to be big spenders than savers. They need to avoid going into debt for things like impressive and expensive cars and other creature comforts.

A Leo's home is his or her castle and must be furnished with costly furniture and preferably be on a hillside or hilltop from where they can look down upon those they feel are beneath them in rank. Your Leo lover will like to wear clothing that shows them off to their best advantage when making grand entrances. To keep them happy remember their zodiacal animal symbol is the lion, and they do need and like to be stroked, to be flattered and to be applauded. We astrologers think of them as those who sing, dance, tell jokes, teach or administrate, and love to give orders. They crave an audience, and need willing listeners and watchers. To those who teach, the class is their audience. Titles and honors are bestowed on them; they are buoyant, sociable, regal, loyal, dignified, energetic, and a very affectionate lover.

When famous astrologer Sydney Omarr was asked; "What sign do you claim is the best lover?" he replied without blinking an eyelash, "Why Leo, of course." He is, as you might have guessed, a Leo.

They do not stay long in subordinate positions and their target job is in management. If they are into sports, they are often chosen to be captain of the team. Acting is natural to them, as is directing. Leo's 7th solar House of marriage is gregarious Aquarius, which might bring them a mate who would be extremely interesting and unusual, since this house is ruled by Venus. Remember these Leo lovers like strokes to make them purr. If you aspire to mate or date this lion or lioness you'll find them loving, protective, entertaining, and maybe sometimes a bit pompous, but almost always very loveable, because they are warm, generous, humorous, and loyal.

# ♍ Virgo ♍

Virgo, the natural sixth sign of the zodiac, has to do with the sign of service. Virgo, the Virgin; meaning purity on its positive side. Remember what Freud said; "Love and Orbit go together." Virgo teaches us to accept, to study, to learn, to share knowledge through teaching others, and helping with vocational guidance and providing knowledge so love can enter the door.

Virgo's planetary ruler is Mercury. They can be critical, discriminating but flexible, adaptable. Their adaptability allow Virgos to be able to get along with more signs than any of the other twelve signs. Their search is for perfection and what they often find is someone that needs shaping up and civilizing. Often they say, "You have to clean out your clothes closet and get some more suitable wearing apparel." They often go along with you to make sure you too can dress to impress.

If your living quarters are cluttered, in need of vacuuming, your kitchen is disorganized or not spotless, you are bound to hear some constructive criticism and a lecture on cleanliness and neatness.

If the lover is a diamond in the rough and capable of being, with the sandpaper of Virgo's criticism, made closer to their ideal of perfection, one of two things could happen. The first is that you will be cut loose on your own, after the treatment, and the Virgo may seek out another poor devil who is in worse shape than you were.

They never embarrass you in public by failing to dress appropriately and neatly. Every item of dress is wrinkle free and with simple good taste in style. Men of the sign are also very particular about clothing, shoes, nails, and hair style.

The bad news is that there are exceptions to the above. There must be some Virgo you know who is hopelessly untidy.

The ideal Virgo is well read, and has not neglected to read the sex manuals and knows more positions for the enjoyment of their earthy desires and yours. Remember that motto of theirs; "Do it right or do it over." In their search for impossible perfection in a mate, they are likely to have had a number of lovers or none at all.

If a Virgo is attracted to you maybe you should feel honored, because they felt, at the time, that you had some improvable possibilities. Because of their obsession with body cleanliness, you are expected to shower before and after lovemaking.

Virgo's solar house of romance, the 5th House, is Capricorn, so Virgos like signs of status, success, and dependability in their lover. This makes them sometimes attracted to the older or more mature lover who has many business responsibilities, exactly the sort of person who needs the humanizing benefits of love and fun, and association with a practical Virgo. They often feel responsible for the health, clothing, and morale of their lover. If you are attracted to a Virgo you are an elitist.

Their 7th solar house of marriage is Pisces. They need a protective, supportive, intelligent partner who is moderately frugal but with a dash of generosity and excitement. They need an orderly partner, preferably without a drinking problem. Their offspring are taught the virtues of brushing their teeth after each meal, good nutrition, washing behind their ears, etc. They are very selective but, assuming that you pass muster and like a hard worker, really adaptable and intelligent, personable lover or mate; you cannot go wrong if you go Virgo.

## ♎ Libra ♎

Libra is a cardinal air sign ruled by the luxury-loving planet Venus, which also rules money and love. Their symbol is the Scales; implying a person who is balanced, serene, just. This sign of partnership is apt to use words like "we" and "our," rather than "me" and "mine,"

Diplomacy is their forte. The darker side of their nature has been described as "the iron fist in the velvet glove." Reputed to be the sign of peace and harmony, it is also the sign of war. Ghengis Khan had 40 percent of his planets in Libra.

They are born with, no matter how humble their earlier years may have been, a feeling that they are of the better classes. They manage to find living quarters in the part of a city where the elite live, through their own creative efforts, and sometimes with marriage to an affluent and work ethic-oriented mate.

Careers in management, the law, art, music, acting, writing, medicine, and politics attracts them; in fact, any work that involves dealing with the public suits them.

In matters of decisions and alliances, they are slow to make up their minds because they try to see both sides of situations and people. Before the loving they must be entertained, and must be wined and dined in a place where the select of society meet and greet. The prospective lover must be well dressed, well mannered, well groomed, civil and attentive, with compliments and endearments.

Librans dislike vulgarity and scenes. Many of them have had a Sagittarian in their romantic life at some time. The air and fire signs are usually compatibles, but they often wind up married to hard-working Capricorns who are also status conscious and are of the executive class.

They are lovers of beauty and are often described by society columnist as the "beautiful people." Their Venusian nature makes them very romantic. Are you worthy of and able to keep up with this elegant paragon with expensive tastes?

Because Libra is ruled by Venus, this planet usually brings beauty. Libra feels like Aldous Huxley, the author and lyricist, when he or she says "Love and marriage go together." Libra is the natural seventh house, the house of partnership and marriage. If we look into St. Valentine's Day via astrology, we understand he was made a saint because of a dictatorial emperor who said, "When men are married they won't fight for me. They won't be great soldiers so I hereby outlaw marriage." A priest named Valentine refused to condemn marriage. He was given a chance to be saved from execution if he would only say; "I condemn marriage," which he would not and so died rather than condemn the beautiful sacrament of marriage. People who love life and the procreation of life made Valentine a saint.

He was, of course, an *avant-garde* Aquarian. Aquarius is Libra's 5th House of romance. He became a martyr to love and marriage. People who allow themselves to love are less apt to fall prey to ignorance and prejudice.

Libra's solar 7th House of marriage is ruled by Mars. Librans are attracted to mates who are more impulsive and make quick decisions. It may take them a little longer to find the perfect mate because there is a constant searching for the idealized version of what love, marriage, and physical relationships should be. Their personal standards are higher than average. When the ladder is higher, the climb is longer. When it does happen it could happen quickly—a love-at-first-sight kind of thing, because their solar 5th House of love is ruled by the unpredictable planet Uranus. Their Venus and this Uranus combination, to say the least, is unorthodox. They are giving and affectionate and fair, and don't like discord, all ingredients for a great marriage partner.

## ♏ Scorpio ♏

One way or another, a relationship with a Scorpio is usually an unforgettable experience. This is one of the most complex, unnecessarily secretive, magnetic, persistent, dynamic, intense, and smoldering, sensual of all signs of the zodiac. They are complex, the powers of others do not impress them. They can do what others don't have the fortitude to do.

Scorpios have, when it comes to romance, a certain hypnotic magnetism. To quote from my book, *Signs of Love*, "cat and mouse games are one of Scorpio's specialties; they carry a form of these to the arena of love. They touch, fondle, and caress every inch of you before the final business begins. So be prepared to be indulged—and to indulge—in foreplay. Let the partner of a Scorpio be prepared to accept the challenge of their potentially delicious wickedness, and be ready for a feast of the senses and a crash course in sexual education."

Scorpio's 5th House of love and romance is Pisces, the sign of dancers, mystics, those who act, model, take photographs, and indulge in other arts, including poetry. Scorpio's 5th House would keep them searching for more stimulating emotional experiences; so it is not surprising that Scorpios have a rather prolific track record in the romantic conquest and seduction department. If you are looking for a mate who is a good provider you may find that Scorpio's ability to make money with other people's money is phenomenal.

For Scorpio, the 7th House, the house of partnerships and marriage, would be ruled by Venus, so here is another need for a sensual connection. The blending of Scorpio's Pluto with Venus is pure delight; nothing remains the same.

If you are looking for a lover or a mate of this charismatic sign you must be a strong person who is willing to submit, on many occasions, to their leadership. Color them exciting.

## ♐ Sagittarius ♐

Sagittarius is a mutable or flexed fire sign with the planetary ruler, Jupiter, called the Greater Benefic. This is probably the luckiest, most optimistic of the signs and least tactful. Most of them have traveled more than any other sign and are often fluent in other languages.

If there were such a thing as the typical Sagittarian, the hair would be light with a hint of red; height, very tall; build athletic, with well-muscled thighs. They would be described as daring, adventurous, sportsmen or sportswomen, very comfortable in the saddle of a fine horse or motorcycle. They would have a collection of hunting rifles and possibly a bow, sheath of arrows, and golf clubs. They don't mind taking a risk, so you might meet them at the race track.

The pursuit of the opposite sex goes along with their hunting instinct, and their conquests are their trophies, to go along with their other trophies. Many have RV's, and many have horses. They love the wide-open spaces and the wild animals that are found there. Besides their regular living quarters, they are apt to have a mountain lodge. They love the flora and the fauna.

Conversationally, they have a great deal to say; tales to tell, jokes to share, and are no slouches when it comes to the gift of persuasion. Nothing pleases them more than an excuse to board a plane and head for the horizon. If they had a theme song, it would be "Don't Fence Me In" or "The Best Things Are Yet to Come."

The grass, for them, is greener someplace else.

No one is a stranger to them for long. In business, they are expansive and the world is their oyster. They dine in the most expensive places and are big tippers; their attitude toward money is that there is plenty more where that came from.

The professions are engineering, teaching in college, public speaking, often on motivational subjects, philosophy, or theology. Some of them get involved in the publishing industry, travel industry, the law, writing, and professional sports—to name a few fields. Potential lovers and mates need to be good sports about their frequent trips out in the wilds or out of the country. Both the females and the males have a strong streak of independence, a sense of humor, a generous and sensual nature. Obviously they do marry, reproduce, and enjoy the company of their lover with great enthusiasm.

The Sagittarian's solar 5th House would be Aries, the sign of the eager and impetuous, the sign of the hasty heart. Some Sagittarians may be considered a tease because they can unknowingly be very provocative. They shun the possessive type as they would a jail, or because they like to feel they are a free spirit. The heat of their passions are quickly ignited; sometimes by inappropriate persons. No matter, they are good sports and variety is the spice of their life. Affairs that flame high with this fire sign and eventually sputter out often become lasting friendships. Some of their affairs are short because they may be traveling so much they can't stay around long enough to build a relationship.

They do eventually make strong commitments when they get to really know someone special. They are straight shooters and can become somewhat conventional.

Sagittarius' solar 7th House of partnership and marriage is ruled by Mercury. This means they need companionship, interesting communication and lack of stodginess, intellectual stimulation and, of course, romance—but with a touch of idealism in their mate. What they don't need is a partner who is a tightwad or too rigid in his or her opinions or too set in his or her ways. They need a companion who is understanding, flexible but practical, aware, and not slow to compliment them when they need a morale boost.

They are good sports, generous and full of warmth and optimism. They entertain lavishly, dress extravagantly, and live with opulence and flair.

The problem is to get them down that aisle when running free is so much fun and the game is afoot.

# ♑ Capricorn ♑

Capricorn is quite serious about love in their youth, but become more playful as they mature. Their Saturn rulership and their being the natural 10th sign of the zodiac emphasizes their career, destiny, fate, ability to lead others, to guide. The leadership role is there. It is permanency, it's being loyal, not frivolus where love is concerned. The solar 5th House of love for Capricorn is ruled by Venus. The warmth of the Taurus Venus warms up the cold Saturn. We put Saturn and Venus together and we talk about true love. When Capricorn commits, takes an oath, a vow to be faithful, they remain true.

Many Capricorns remember having adult-type responsibilities thrust upon them at an early age and so they learn that method, order, system, ambition, and need to achieve is a built-in program, because climbing that mountain is slow and arduous; they learn to be patient and to persist doggedly, no matter the set-backs or frustrations along the way. To achieve high goals there is hard work to be done and long hours of planning, wheeling, dealing, choosing options and often waiting to act.

On the lighter side, persons who are attracted to Capricorns appreciate their earthiness and the feeling that they may be having a date with Destiny. Because marriage is a responsibility, the prospect of the trip down the aisle and resultant need to provide for the fate of offspring is bearable. The children are expected to be achievers, to do chores, and to behave. They will learn discipline, whether they like it or not.

The Capricorns are the sign least likely to say the word "Whoopie!" unless it is in a humorous situation. Astrologers accused them of being "Sayers of Nay." This is often because they believe the time is not yet right.

Timing is their forte. Ask anyone who has been made love to by the randy Goat. They tend to live longer than many of the other signs and are active even when forced to retire. The childhood pleasures they may have been denied they can now enjoy without guilt. What they have accomplished often lives on after them—an example being the number of people that still think Capricorn "Elvis Lives!" The Capricorn seeks a mate that will hang in there for them and won't wear out or poop out. Do you have the stamina and understanding to go the distance with a person who may love their work more than they seem to love you? Just for the record; the females of the species are as driven by ambition as the males.

Capricorn's solar 5th House of romance is Taurus. This house also represents hobbies and other recreation. Take away Capricorn's 5th House and their life would be work, work, work, duty, duty, duty. Their solar 5th House brings them an invitation to take up music lessons, study, dream, and dance, and, of course, love. The Capricorn becomes more playful in this department as they grow older. Because their 5th House is ruled by Venus, the planet of love, they are lusty in this area. How wrong those people are who consider them cold. That may be how they appear because of their outer demeanor, but they are inwardly warm, hopeful, and naive. Their lofty ideals can propel them to great heights.

Capricorn's solar 7th House, the house of marriage, is Cancer, associated with the Moon. The Moon, Saturn (their significator), and Venus (5th House ruler) paint a portrait of a person who craves warmth and security, constantly reaching out for love and permanency. The Capricorn lover is cautious about revealing his or her true feelings but when the armor is off, it is all the way or nothing. They are so passionate—that is why they are so cautious.

## ≈ Aquarius ≈

Aquarius is considered to be the friendliest and most humanitarian of the signs, but this description does not begin to describe them.

They are known by their differences to the norm. They are inventive, sometimes rebellious, independent, idealistic, well read, and attractive to the opposite sex, who find them to be startling. They are usually beautiful, both on the inside and on the outside. Many of the males have the high foreheads of the scientist. They are not given to bragging because they feel secure within themselves. They are self-sufficient and calm in temperament, except when an enthusiasm seizes them.

The fixed signs are called the "money signs" and the Aquarians know how to make it and how to hang onto it, though they have their moments of extravagance. Usually they will see a new must-have gadget, a book, or tool for one of their many hobbies. In fact, an avocational pursuit is often turned into a business or sideline source of money. Like the Moonchildren, they tend to hoard things and have to keep moving into larger and airier quarters to make room for their treasures.

Their bedrooms usually have an extra sound system to better entertain their lover and get them in the mood. Relationships usually begin as friendships and the party of the second part becomes a loving friend in the process.

Both the males and females are apt to have a dress code like no one else's. It can be a little bizarre or merely quite striking. A sweater would be an ideal gift for your Aquarian lover.

Aquarius is the natural eleventh zodiacal sign. The 11th House represents hopes, wishes, desires, and friendships. Aquarius' significator is Uranus. We must remember that Uranus is the only planet in the solar system that can roll over on its side. It can roll over and look down and have a big laugh at us.

So Aquarius is the sign of the unconventional, the element of timing and surprise. Aquarius in connection with romance and love teaches us yet another lesson; that we need not be structured, conventional, or planned. Uranus is spontaneity and releases us from the prison of feeling we must do things a certain way. Furthermore, a very important lesson Aquarius teaches us about love is that love and friendship go hand in hand. Aquarius in love can win friends and influence people from the low and the lonely to the high and the mighty. They are so lovable theycan win powerful friends, because all the world loves a lover. Aquarius finds love in helping those they respect to gain greater financial security. They are timeless, being the 2nd House from Capricorn. Gertrude Stein, an Aquarian, said; "A masterpiece has nothing to do with time." She was concerned with astrology. She understood that a masterpiece is timeless because as an Aquarian she created her own traditions.

The solar 5th sign for Aquarius is Gemini–Mercury, the mind, the mental. Let us not forget the yin and the yang—the opposites. Leo is the opposite sign; so look at this dramatic link between love and friendships and also between love and the mind; the mental attitude. The largest sexual provoker, of course, is the mind, and the Aquarius solar 5th House is Gemini. The mind, Mercury, is experimentation, developing ideas into valuable concepts. Astrology teaches us not only about love but about life; that love and life go together.

Aquarius is the sign of the mental aristocrat with an uncommon ability to fit in among both higher and lower echelons of society. They are the cosmic person with arms outstretched to embrace the world. This lover is friendly, loving and lovable, usually calm, confident, and poised. Of course there may be moments when they may be outrageous, shocking, and downright eccentric, but not temperamental. When love is involved they need mind-to-mind contact for real gratification and fulfillment. Be patient with this "Ahead of the Times" thinker. You may not understand what he or she is trying to do because nobody ever did it before. Maybe that is why there are more Aquarians in the Hall of Fame than any other sign.

A failing of theirs is to tell their lover or mate that something which had upset them is "no big deal." If sharing your life with an unconventional articulate person who is full of surprises and who loves a good rap and loves to party appeals to you, look no farther. Aquarians can make you laugh, irritate you off and on, but you have bagged yourself an original.

## ♓ Pisces ♓

Pisces, the natural 12th sign of the zodiac, is ruled by the planet Neptune. With Neptune, the mirage seems real, the pictures move—without Neptune we have no motion pictures, no psychic intuitive ability. When Pisces is in love it's "One Enchanted Evening." You look across a crowded room and there is your soul mate. That's Neptune, that's Pisces; sensitive, and without whose qualities life itself would lack spice, imagination, surprise, mystery, intrigue. Pisces persons are said to be ruled by the feet. That may be true, but a Pisces can raise an eyebrow and cause others to be weak-kneed. Think of the eyebrows of Elizabeth Taylor. Pisces exudes a subtle kind of sensuality and sex appeal which is vital to love. The solar 5th House from

Pisces, the house of love, is Cancer; ruled by the moon. Put Neptune and the moon together and I don't think you would ever want to be separated.

This sign is very intuitive, creative, thrives on the arts—acting, writing, poetry, photography, psychology, art, and politics. They are nearly always great dancers and may sweep the opposite sex off their feet with their emotional and romantic power. Because their motto is "I believe," it is no surprise that they are into religion, mysticism, and astrology. Scorpios, Moonchildren, and Virgos gravitate toward them. Their empathy with the underdog make them vulnerable to flawed relationships

Some of them are blessed with great physical beauty and bedroom eyes. Those who eat sweets in times of sensual deprivation or head for the bar tend to put on a great deal of weight between crash diets. Their life veers from being loners and creators of fantasy to the more public life and pursuit of vocational obligations.

Candlelight, wine, and stirring music are likely to be on tap when they are in a romantic mood. When married, they believe in large families and are apt to collect animals that have been abandoned.

They are too trusting and need a practical companion to steer them away from those who would deceive or impose on them. Those who are musically-minded gravitate toward stringed instruments and composing. Peter Ilich Tchaikovsky comes to mind, a composer of very sensual and emotional music.

Ideally their home should be near a stream, pond, or ocean, and provide them with a retreat and the privacy they crave. Their solar 7th House of marriage and partnerships is Virgo; their complimentary opposite. Both are adaptable and service oriented. Pisces isn't obsessive about having things in the right place but they are attracted to neat, orderly mates. For Pisces sex is home and family, a roof over their head, privacy, enough to eat, satisfaction and emotional stability, contentment, the opposite of sensationalism. They want change and excitement, yet desire security. For Pisces, sex is moonlight and roses and violin music, beauty and sensitivity. They can transform dreams into realities if they apply self-discipline.

Pisces exude a quiet sexuality. They are subtle and love intrigue. They have a special charm, a "Mystique." To keep their sexy figure they must stay away from refined sugar; especially if they were born on the 6th, 15th, or 24th. They then will have the energy and enthusiasm to carry out their beautiful dreams.

If you are looking for someone to inspire you, who has volatile emotions, who can be changeable, sometimes stubborn and romantic to a fault, then you may be looking for Pisces, the Dream Boat of the zodiac.

When we traverse the twelve signs of the zodiac it represents all of us, that's why there are twelve persons needed for a jury, the twelve disciples. We are all a bit of the twelve signs. We are all interrelated and only through astrology can we wisely choose our mates, intelligently choose our healers and the people we want to play important roles in our lives.

## Planets' Effects in Romance

Here is my condensed version of the planets' effects on the twelve signs in the matters of romance.

| | |
|---|---|
| ARIES | Do it immediately or forget it. |
| TAURUS | Take time and enjoy it. |
| GEMINI | Let's talk about it first. |
| CANCER | It's got to be an emotional experience. ' |
| LEO | Do it dramatically. |
| VIRGO | Is it a service or a treatment? |
| LIBRA | It is the social thing to do. |
| SCORPIO | Do it intensely. |
| SAGITTARIUS | Let's do it out of doors or in another state. |
| CAPRICORN | With the right person, it may be a useful move. |
| AQUARIUS | Do it differently. |
| PISCES | Do it because this is my fantasy. |

# Tracking World Trends

## Noel Tyl

The United States horoscope (July 4, 1776 at 2:13 A.M. in Philadelphia, PA) is under very interesting pressure for a change of national image. I think the outlines of this new national image will be defined around September 1993, go through critical growing pains in March and April 1994, and then again in November 1994.

In April–May of 1993, Bill Clinton surely had unexpected setbacks: he will have had to find better ways of doing things; his political honeymoon will have ended abruptly. But he will have recovered strongly in the last weeks of July through staff changes and political maneuvering. Hillary will have come to the rescue and probably received even more power and responsibility (Clinton's Solar Arc Moon conjunct his Midheaven and trine his Ascendant, with transiting Mars square his Uranus). At the same time, he will have reacted impulsively, pushing to use the country's force, in what is an ever-ongoing, caretaker relationship between the United States and the rest of the world.

The question will be, "Who are we now that Russia is no longer a threat, that we are the world's sole super power? Who are we with this weak president?" Clinton will continue struggling, and times will have been very difficult for him, in September especially. In October-November, the probability is extremely high that Clinton will have flexed our national foreign-affairs muscle and used force in intervention abroad. The effort will be successful. Clinton will appear to have great emotional conviction, but the U.S. will be confused over its role in the new world order.

1994 will begin with lots of international criticism of the United States for our intervention in Yugoslavia. Clinton will seize the spotlight with satisfaction, and Hillary will present her Health Program for approval.

In the spring of 1994, we will have to learn how to manage rather than deploy our power as the world's only supernation. I think we will be learning that we can not police the world with the deployment of armed force. Our national standard of living may suffer greatly. This is a major issue for the United States and for Bill Clinton, not just in the spring of 1994, but, as well, in September-November 1994 when *the United States surely will flex its muscles once more*, and the whole issue will arise again. There will be a very vocal public outcry dividing those who favor the "give 'em hell" posture from those who favor a "let them take care of themselves" position. As our new national image stabilizes, there will be an intense spring and an intense autumn, as force or no-force as our image will signify the United States' out-reach to the world.

President Bill Clinton's horoscope (August 19, 1946 at 8:51 A.M. in Hope, Arkansas) simply has no strength: he has loads of charisma, almost to the point of dandy-ism, and is fired with enormous self-confidence, loads of education, loads of communication skills. But, his inauguration address notwithstanding, he is unable to effect change; when others deputized to do the job make their recommendations, he will delay. Privately, although pompous about his personal views, he has great difficulty making decisions. Behind the rhetoric and gloss, there is little innovation and power. Bill Clinton is our president. I must predict that he will be a weak president.

It is absolutely no secret that Clinton's wife is his greatest asset; Hillary Clinton dominates Bill Clinton's horoscope. She is his claim to fame.

Clinton will be a changed (and perhaps beaten) man throughout all of this enormous responsibility. Bench-mark times for his maturation within the heady allure of power tactics are certainly April–June and September–November 1994.

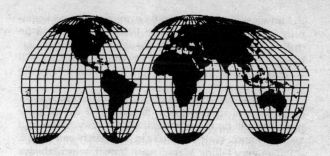

### Conjunction Signals Unrest

Transiting Mars and Saturn make a critical conjunction at 5 Pisces 19 on March 14, 1994 at 05:01 A.M. GMT. This powerful conjunction which occurs approximately every two years is then reinforced by the Full Moon Eclipse on May 25 at 3 Gemini-Sagittarius 43 at 3:39 A.M., GMT. Both these phenomena make a square aspect with the United States' Ascendant, signifying again a strong developmental tension toward a new national image (SA Sun conjunct the Moon at the Midheaven).

The Eclipse of the Sun on May 10 at 5:07 P.M. GMT occurs directly overhead at 77 West 03 and 12 South 03, bringing Lima, Peru into the news. There we can expect to see activity to change the government in power; the unrest is most focused during the periods June 18–20 and November 10–13, 1994 and is probably vitalized within the voice of labor.

The tensions in Peru can easily share news with unrest in Uruguay and Argentina (Montevideo and Buenos Aires, the capital cities, are very closely related to the occurrence of the Full Moon Eclipse, May 25.

Very interestingly, in Rome—where the May 25 Eclipse is precisely rising—there is the potential for similar civil unrest. The focus there could very well be finance, bank fraud, government collusion. The particularly apt time for this to come to light is within the first 10 days of July.

Germany will begin to make headlines in the spring, signalling a build-up to the federal elections at the end of 1994. Chancellor Helmut Kohl (April 3, 1930 at 6:30 A.M.

in Ludwigshafen) will be under extreme pressure, beginning in November–December 1993; his voice will be dulled, labeled ineffective by the aggressive bloc of German voters. Between June and December 1994 Kohl will wage a losing battle. Look for him to withdraw from the election process by October 20, 1994.

Populist uprisings in South Africa will continue, especially forceful in Capetown. Beyond civil rights, there probably will be the introduction of money, wage, and taxation issues. Watch carefully in late March–early April.

The very telling Mars-Saturn transit, which always traces the lines of unrest and upset in the world, has with its occurrence this March 14, 1994 a special quality: it is peregrine. This astrological term comes from the Latin word meaning "foreign." When a planet makes no conventional (Ptolemaic) aspect with any other planet in the horoscope and is not in a sign of essential dignity, it is said to be peregrine, and the observed effects are that the planet "runs away" with the horoscope. In the case of this conjunction, both Mars and Saturn are peregrine and the hot-and-cold nature of the conjunction, the aggressive-in-spite-of-controls thrust will dominate. Their symbolization is "foreign" to the horoscope at hand.

We see this phenomenon promised in all the cases outlined above. Additionally, we can anticipate governmental disruptions in New Zealand, continuing chaos in Yugoslavia, upsets in Czechoslovakia, and the beginnings of rebellion in Nigeria. The hot times in all these locations will be in May 1994. Interestingly, the cause of religion will somehow inflame and/or rationalize these upsets. In Japan, as well, there will be national business tension around foreign debt balance. The squeeze is on Japan as its mercantile power grows and living space diminishes.

## Israel on the Move

The predictions regarding Israel (May 14, 1994 at 4:00 P.M. EET in Tel Aviv) I made in 1991 came to pass: a new government was elected in 1992 and the land-for-peace negotiations with the Palestinians resumed in February 1993, and probably will have been completed successfully for both parties in September 1993. Behind the scenes, Israel is sorely hurting for money, with enormous debt pressures at home. Munitions, money, and mercy are all mixed up in the Israel outreach to the world. All the bluffing and hidden agendas should clear out by the end of 1993 and Israel will begin to make some deals in 1994.

Yet, 1994 steers Israel to a very important change: one of astrology's strongest and most reliable measurements, transiting Uranus conjunct the fourth cusp, i.e., opposed the Midheaven, takes place in Israel's national chart early in March, at the end of June, and late in December 1994. The three "hits" tell us that Israel will be working out a "new start" somehow, a revolutionary stance with regard to its world position. The probability of armed skirmishes is very strong in the spring, and at the end of 1994. This new stance will take all year to develop; it is motivated by the need for money; bargained for by the trade-off of land for peace and commerce, all designed to improve its international trade position. The new party in power will hear considerable static from the hard-liners now out of power, but after almost a year of haggling, Israel will mark its history with as much stabilization as it has ever had . . . after the next series of concessions, negotiations, and aggressive tactics . . . culminating in November-December 1994. A quiet period of integration with the rest of the world will then follow.

## Russia—Still a Nation in Transition

The predictions made so successfully for the USSR and its leader Gorbachev in 1991 were possible because of an extraordinarily reliable chart for the former Soviet Union, the chart for the Revolution, November 8, 1917 at 2:12 A.M. EET in Petrograd. The exact time had been frozen on a clock face, perhaps by a stray bullet, when Bolshevik Red Guards, under the direction of Lenin, had arrested the Provisional Government. The fall of the Soviet Union was keyed by the Solar Arc of Pluto square the Midheaven of that chart.

But that chart is not valid any more, what with the changes in that enormous nation. Until a regeneration chart becomes clear within the corroboration of historical events linked to timings that have been suggested and, indeed, may yet be coming, as politics still jostles national identity, the chart of the leader, Boris Yeltsin, must be used for the thrust of the many countries to become one country. Yeltsin's horoscope is apparently also well-timed: February 1, 1931, 3:32 A.M. R3T, (-4:00H) in Swerdlowsk, USSR. Yeltsin's political tensions with the old communist guard were predicted in last year's publication, with the promise that he would prevail in the Spring of 1993. Indeed he did: the tensions began with the powerful transit of Uranus opposed his natal Pluto in February (a tremendous clash between demand and power) and was resolved in a public Referendum, clearly in Yeltsin's favor, in late April 1993, with SA Node semi-square Mars and transiting Jupiter exactly conjunct his 4 Libra 10 Midheaven (and other measurements). This Jupiter was extremely powerful for Yeltsin, establishing a station upon the Midheaven just as the Referendum was completed.

When we look ahead with Yeltsin, we see more of the same: enormous energy and enormous good luck. The man's horoscope is filled with tension and drive—it is singularly remarkable. In his meeting with President Clinton, I can not help thinking that Yeltsin behaved properly and was grateful for the aid he solicited and received but, in private, scoffed at the unseasoned and not-so-deep American president.

Yeltsin lives on adrenalin, on Mars. Transiting Mars aspects make personal headlines for him whenever they occur. Yeltsin will have risen to secure popularity and a more peaceful country image at the end of 1993 (Progressed Moon trine Jupiter; SA Venus sesquiquadrate Jupiter, Venus ruling the Midheaven). Then transiting Jupiter takes over in square to Yeltsin's Sun in January; a propitious start for the year, indeed.

That Jupiter squares his Sun again in April 1994 and still again in September 1994. I think Russia will continue to grow in stability throughout 1993 and 1994. Only toward the end of 1994, in early November perhaps, will we see Yeltsin a bit confused in international negotiations that may well have to do with global or space communications and/or oil commerce. Overall, the picture through Yeltsin's horoscope appears very good. Though the growing pains are audible, a new Russia will be born from Yeltsin's efforts.

## Pluto's Transits Lead to New Order

On May 8, 1993, just as these predictions for 1994 were going to press, headlines everywhere read "U.S. Links Iraq to Plot to Assassinate Bush in Kuwait," bearing out the prediction I'd made fourteen months earlier that "the United States will be duped somehow, very dramatically . . . coming to light in early June 1993. The deception will be from Iraq." I could find no more appropriate words than "duped. . . . very dramatically" for Iraq's insidious use of force that I saw emerging out of secrecy.

Iraq is still a presence to be feared, especially as the planet Pluto—stark power, crucially defined perspective—weaves its way around the Sun and within the life maps of our leaders and their countries. From now to the end of 1995, transiting Pluto at the very end of Scorpio continues to symbolize a revolutionary spirit of change, the focus of force, and the screaming efforts for so much of the world to renew life perspective. The Uranus-Neptune conjunction has helped punctuate this grand Plutonic background (as we discussed last year) and our planet has witnessed extraordinary upheaval of the oppressed, wanting to change out-dated structures, confronting force with force, establishing perspectives for the new Millennium.

We have seen the change of government in Israel (as predicted) as Pluto opposed the national Sun. This is a critical change for Israel as it prepares for a dramatic new stance within world politics and trade (discussed earlier in this article). Transiting Pluto is now approaching opposition with the national Mars in the spring of 1994 and at the end of the year. These are key times for the Israel change, and there will be force, struggle, and extraordinary ruthlessness, probably cloaked by the accord of a Palestinian settlement. The force will be part of the martyrdom politics favored by Israel—i.e., we have made peace with the Palestinians, now help us financially in our impoverished state, and let us get away with murder in our other squabbles.

The problems in Serbia are obviously Plutonic as well: transiting Pluto will continue its onslaught to square with Serbia's Uranus all through 1994. At the same time, transiting Pluto will square its own natal position. This is about as rough as it gets, and 1994 will be worse for Yugoslavia.

We see the Plutonic influence in South Africa as well, with transiting Pluto square to the Ascendant of the Union of South Africa. These apparently unending struggles so far to the south will continue through 1995.

Gentle Norway is not exempt from the world tensions. King Harald V is a retiring individual (February 21, 1937 at 12:45 P.M. CET in Skaugum, Norway) with a powerful, high-presence wife. His seventh cusp—his presentation of self to the world, his wife—is being highly stressed throughout all of 1993 by the conjunction of transiting Uranus and Neptune. His country is having extreme financial problems and is facing the extraordinary financial drain of hosting the upcoming Winter Olympics.

Transiting Pluto opposes Norway's national Midheaven (the Norwegian Independence chart, June 7, 1905 at 11:00 A.M. CET in Oslo). I feel this portends far more than publicity for this small nation. I feel that a major change is in store for the royal family, precipitated by Harald's private life and by the country's economic woes, all brought to the surface by the exposure of the Olympics.

Gorbachev will be heard from again, in a sad way, a way of desperation out of frustration, especially in December 1993 and January 1994. The issues—impulsive, out-spoken rebellion against what he sees as wrong principles in his country's government—will bring him into the headlines repeatedly in May and October . . . if his efforts are not silenced.

Back to Iraq: With every predictive thrust into Iraq's future, we come closer and closer to confirming the reliability of the Iraq national horoscope (August 23, 1921 at precisely 6:00 A.M. in Baghdad) and the conjectural horoscope for Saddam Hussein (presented in my book, *Prediction in Astrology* as April 28, 1937 at 8:18 A.M. in Tikrit, Iraq). The transiting Mars-Saturn conjunction discussed earlier in this article occurs in conjunction with the seventh cusp of the Iraq chart. The chart for the moment of this powerful conjunction, viewed from Baghdad, has the Uranus-Neptune conjunction directly overhead. All this means more forceful aggression from Iraq, hidden, collusive, insidious.

The key times will be late in March 1994, with Saddam himself very much in the news, and at the end of May, triggered by the Lunar eclipse. This is the period that begins a grand arcing effort for Iraq to become a world power, controlling the Middle East. Transiting Pluto begins its application to square with the national Mercury and Sun, ruling the nation's Ascendant and Midheaven, and 12th House, respectively! This means the peacocks are coming home to roost during the summer of 1994 and continuing all through 1995.

The Plutonic power thread is tightening throughout the fabric of all these nations. It is also present within the personal horoscope of President Clinton, especially during the period June–September 1994. The pressure on Clinton is enormous. The structure that was missing at the beginning of his administration must somehow be created by those around him, including the Republicans, especially by the intercession of his wife. He stands for change, but he is unable to stand up and make it happen. In actuality, the astrology of our president suggests, all too strongly, only a band-aid maintenance of the status quo—not the establishment of the new image the country is calling out for so strongly.

Perhaps with our own national image in the re-making, the United States will look more to the homefront, as the economy improves, as Israel fights its way to stabilization, as the Middle East itself focuses almost entirely on Iraq, as we overlook the bubbles of anxiety in South America, let Germany straighten out its leadership problems, commiserate with a still-stalled Yugoslavia (in our embarrassment from intervening), as we buttress the new Russia with funding and know-how, and see the world resolutely working itself out of chaos into a new order.

## A Final Note

In late 1993 and throughout 1994, the force of Pluto focuses very, very strongly on the Vatican in Rome and on Pope John Paul II.

The chart for Vatican Independence as a City State (June 7, 1929 at 11:00 A.M. in Rome) is very reliable. The tests of astrological measurements for the demise and installation of five Popes since 1939 show remarkable congruence between measurements and occurrences, especially in 1978 when Pope Paul VI died on Aug. 6; Pope John Paul I took office on Aug. 26, and himself died 33 days later on Sept. 28; with the present Pope, John Paul II, taking office on Oct. 16, 1978.

The present pope (born May 18, 1920, probably near 1:00 P.M. in Wadowice, Poland) has his Sun and Moon almost exactly conjunct the Midheaven of the Vatican chart; and his Saturn is exactly conjunct the Vatican Ascendant. This is an extraordinary congruence.

Both the Vatican and Pope John Paul II are under extreme signals for change. The tension is for change of world status, public perspective and, indeed, leadership. They began in April 1993, December 1993, and will probably peak in March 1994. Should the changes be delayed by understandings beyond our astrology, another critical time will be in late October 1994.

Grand changes in the Vatican over the past 54 years include strong measurements involving Mars, the Ascendant, and/or the Midheaven in the Vatican chart. In three of the five major shifts in the papacy since 1939, solar arc measurements have involved the Midheaven, Saturn, and Pluto. Early in 1994 the basic astrological picture for change is suggested by transiting Saturn square and transiting Pluto opposed the Pope's Sun; transiting Pluto opposed the Vatican Midheaven, transiting Jupiter square the Vatican Mars, and, above all, solar arc Saturn square to the Vatican Midheaven.

Born in the Eastern bloc, the first non-Italian pope since Adrian VI of Utrecht was elected in 1522, Pope John Paul II's work to internationalize the papacy and support the voice of oppressed peoples everywhere focused strongly first in his native Poland. His inspiration reinforced the heroic "Solidarity" movement there and stimulated greatly the major changes still underway throughout the Near and Middle East. We could say that the Pontiff's work has been completed. New perspectives beckon.

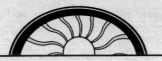

# Uranus and Neptune— a Healing Combination

## Barbara A. Everett

The wonder of the Uranus-Neptune conjunction is in its infrequency, once every 171 years. Its unusual power and influence should make us grateful that it does take that long to return again! Let us remember that the last conjunction of these two planets took place in 1822, longer ago than any one of us can personally remember, unless you consider a previous lifetime.

At that time Neptune had not been discovered, so its power was still veiled. Thus the 1993 conjunction, in many ways, was the first with its dual identities unveiled, and in full view of an interested public.

The energy of Uranus is always dramatic, extraordinary, a gigantic thunderbolt which can create havoc, panic, and even fear when first observed. Its great gift is change and freedom. Uranus is a planet of mental energy, giving itself to break-through, intuition, higher creativity, higher consciousness, and inventiveness. As we are in the doorway of the Aquarian Age, Uranus will ignite the minds of individuals to see and experience beyond the limitation of concrete mind. Its very nature can be enigmatic. Its message is not of the mundane, but of the magnificent.

Until Uranus was discovered in 1781 by Astronomer William Herschel, the sign of Aquarius was ruled by the serious planet Saturn. When Uranus was discovered, it was given the rulership of Aquarius. In retrospect, the period after its discovery and assignment to Aquarius can now be seen as the entrance to the Aquarian Age. However, as we understand the nature of Aquarius more, both Uranus and Saturn will have their own unique expressions within it. In 1993 we began to see the influence of Uranus become even stronger within the sign of Aquarius, as well as in the endeavors of the human mind and future possibilities.

Let us look at Neptune also. Until its discovery in 1846 by Astronomer Johann Galle, the sign of Pisces was ruled by Jupiter, the planet representing the doorway to the expansive universe. At Neptune's discovery, the new planet was accorded rulership of Pisces. So these two magnificent signs, Aquarius and Pisces, began to have two rulers each. Even now they continue to be co-ruled, giving added dimension to both the signs and planets so involved. Both Uranus and Neptune, then, could be said to be learning to co-work, one of the great emerging concepts for this time.

Neptune is known for its many exemplary qualities, among them mercy, devotion to an ideal, zealousness, and the ability to merge with the mystical and the divine, the creator of beauty. Neptune's energy is compassionate, empathetic, paranormal, spiritual. The nature of Neptune is to dissolve, and to absorb, in contrast to Uranus, which is to bring change, to sweep away outworn concepts. We can envision Uranus in the form of Shiva, the Hindu deity which destroys the old in order to create the new. We can envision Neptune as the cosmic concept of the Universal Christ, which through its divine essence brings renewed life and inspiration. Both planets are representative of change, but their methods are very different. The results, however, are a better and more liberated humanity, more intelligent (Uranus), and more compassionate (Neptune).

We can see Uranus as the higher octave of Mars, with the expanded power to create an environment for ideals, inventions, innovations, independence, freedom, and futuristic possibilities. We can see Neptune as the higher octave of Venus, with the expanded power to love with true caring, a love that is Universal, holding spiritual goals and ideals, forgiveness, dissolution of barriers, and the emergence of the transcendent. Both planets are transpersonal in their effect upon humanity, and in the course of human affairs.

As can be seen, these two planets are quite different in their influences. Joined in close relationship now, they make a most interesting cosmic marriage, each so unique, and each with its own message for this cusp period. As with all marriages, time will bring forth its flowering.

## Healing Opportunities

Let us consider the opportunities for healing during this unusual period which will extend over many years to come. Healing itself has always been an important component for the human race. As human consciousness has taken its leaps forward, new developments for healing naturally emerge. With this Uranus-Neptune conjunction, very unusual and creative approaches are evolving into what is being termed "New Therapies." Some of these have been developing over the last 100 years, probably since the previous conjunction in 1822. We build upon the former times, just as one building block is placed on top of, or next to, the original blocks to form a new structure. We could also term this the new wine being poured into old wineskins.

As more Uranian energy was recognized, the many inventions of time and space were brought to birth, also bringing with them great discoveries about the intricacies of the human mind, its shadow self, the darkness, and also the freedom of the mind to tap into inner dimensions. Into human consciousness sprang the therapies we would eventually call psychiatry and psychology, the in-depth probing of levels of consciousness, regression therapy, hypnosis, visualization, prayer therapy, and meditation.

Simultaneously, the illnesses and therapies of Neptune filtered through to human awareness. Even the development of hospitals, sanatariums, and asylums came into being through Neptune, in an endeavor to create places for those who were suffering mind and body trauma. The many abuses and injustices which have been part of this growth are the negative side of

Neptune, which often goes to extremes; too much, too little, too late.

The development of drug therapy has been guided by Neptune, as well as the growth of psychedelic drugs to expand and explore the levels of the mind, or escape the challenges of the personal world. Here, too, the more damaging excesses emerged, creating dependence, addiction, or madness—all Neptunian effects—often leaving the body, mind, emotions, and spirit hampered and damaged. Now we know that with care minds can heal, bodies can rebuild, and emotions can be restored.

Whenever a danger appears, destiny sends an antidote. As consciousness expanded, and various new illnesses emerged to be understood and experienced, so did the possible therapies to relieve and heal them.

We think of the aid that has come to suffering humanity through "miracle" drugs, drugs to help rest an injured mind, surgeries to repair the body, vaccines to stop and prevent disease, techniques of communication to probe the emotions. Spiritual paths for the illumination of the spiritual self continue to come forward as we must be aware of this vast territory beyond the ordinary limits of the mind.

## Spiritual Healing

We stand on the brink of new discoveries for the healing of all levels of self, physical, emotional, mental, and spiritual. We know now that these components influence the entire person; the untapped potentials at each level which can promote healing on other levels. Already greater emphasis is being given to the power of the mind to heal both itself and the body. We are beginning to tap the power of feelings, of emotions, to comprehend its effects on other levels. The self-rejuvenating abilities of the body vehicle to repair and restore itself, often with only minimal or gentle corrections, amazes us.

Ancient knowledge and wisdom is re-emerging, but in ways now suitable to the world of the 20th and 21st centuries. In the great civilizations of the past, especially in Persia, Egypt, and Greece, healing with sound and color had been perfected and applied to cure illnesses and promote total well-being, to rejuvenate the body, and extend the life span. Today these possibilities are returning, as the effects of sound and light are investigated from both the aspects of their detriment to the bodies as well as the beneficial use in recovering and repair. We know now that the repetition of affirmations and positive words help to forge new pathways into the brain/mind connection, leading to renewed self-esteem, development of will, and the ability to transform old forms into new and positive ones.

Music is used to increase healing, to soothe the chaos of emotional suffering, to encourage the birthing of babies, and to assist the dying. Exercise is now valued as an accepted means to overcome depression, to reduce life-damaging stress, and to alleviate the effects of serious illnesses.

Rhythmic breathing is used to restore emotional balance and to clear confusion from the mind, and to become aware of the inner process occurring. Meditation is known and accepted as a method of building a spiritual environment for mind, body, and emotions to expand, create, and to heal. Biorhythms show the high and low periods of energies, especially helpful when considering surgery and healing. Biofeedback machines have helped thousands control pain, and allow the natural healing process to happen.

Medical astrology is gathering its practitioners, who tabulate information and validate results from the awareness of illness already shown in a birth chart. Etheric healing is now a technique taught and being used to diagnose illness and problems in the etheric body before they even appear in the physical. Hands-on healing of many kinds is available, and it is being used in conjunction with traditional medical treatments in innovative environments. The ancient uses of herbs, plants, and flowers are easily ascertained, and are being studied with renewed interest. The esoteric understanding of the body energies, and their blockages, is no longer considered strange.

As expansion of consciousness continues, numbers of people will develop etheric vision (Neptune) and be able to view the energy systems in the body, seeing the potentials for disease in order to heal them before their appearance in the physical.

Water therapies will emerge as we understand more completely the healing properties of this element. Water has always been the domain of Neptune.

The use of electricity in therapies will develop at a rapid rate as the human mind creates new methods of diagnosis, therapy, and treatment to all the systems, mind, body, emotion, spirit. Here we see Uranus at its best.

Massage, in all its variations, and chakra balancing will aid in maintaining good health. Nutrition will be accepted as a science, to utilize the vitality of foods for body health and mental clarity.

Best of all, the mysterious power of Love (Lots of Vital Energy) will be tapped and understood, so that love will be accepted as a transformative energy, not limited to romantic love as we usually see and experience it.

The regenerative powers of all elements, earth, air, fire, and water will be seen as positive and practical ways to deal with fatigue, illness, depression, and all diseases and discomforts which plague humanity today.

The new era being initiated by the Uranus-Neptune conjunction will abound with old ideas transformed into regeneration. Every method now known will take huge steps forward, breaking through as human consciousness leaps and dances to the infiltration of ideas and concepts from within itself and from cosmic sources, including planetary energies.

## Doorway to Aquarian Age

During this incredible conjunction time, which will extend for many years to come, humanity stands gazing through the doorway of the Aquarian Age. We speculate and theorize, as Uranus demands of us. We dream of a more enlightened and compassionate humanity, as Neptune inspires us. We stretch to learn to forgive our own trespasses as we know we must now learn to forgive the trespasses of others, as Neptune insists.

We know in the very core and depth of our beings that we must create and intuit new forms, new technologies, new styles of learning, of healing, of government, of communication, in the arts, and through ritual and spiritual forms. We must be daring in our creativity (Uranus) and loving in our relationships (Neptune) if we are to move into the new era.

The planet Earth itself cries out for the family of humanity to bring healing and renewal to it. We experience its pain and panic as the earth convulses through storms, hurricanes, tornadoes, earthquakes, floods, winds, and the like. Those in humanity who are awakened seek to enlighten others to the dangers of pollution, and the damage to soil, water, and air. Many already seek the ingenuity to restore the beauty of the earth, and bring safety to the other kingdoms which share the earth with humanity. We know we must protect nature, the animals, the minerals, or we, too, will perish.

The power of the unconscious level of the mind will be unveiled through new methods, including new therapies and dreams. More and more will dreams be accepted as valid avenues to the inner world. The inner world itself will be understood as the link to an ever-expanding universe, within ourselves, and also the doorway to exploring outer space.

Knowledge and wisdom will be gleaned through the intuitive sciences of astrology, numerology, and intuition, joining the natural sciences of mathematics, astronomy, quantum physics. Even the little-understood power of nuclear energy will be harnessed for healing. People will be more intuitively in touch with what is correct and necessary for their spiritual, mental, and physical well-being. The dependence on doctors and healing professionals will be altered. Patients will assume greater responsibility for their own well-being. Doctors, therapists, and health professionals will be accepted as they are, not as the super-humans we have tried to make them become.

The conjunction definitely implies that the old order and ways must surrender to the new realities. Resistance to change often impedes the speed and efficiency of necessary changes. At this time, the need for available and affordable health care can no longer be denied. As we endeavor to become aware of the suffering of others, this crisis is unavoidable. Technology is often financially impossible, necessary care is often beyond the means of many. This crisis is not confined to the United States alone—this is a world-wide humanitarian need—and let us remember that Uranus and Neptune are "outer" planets whose influence is universal and dedicated to the uplifting of the entire human family.

## The Final Experience

One often-forgotten facet of healing is the death process. Usually we have viewed death as the end of all experiences. But such is no longer the view. Over 18 million people have had near-death experiences, the re-emergence of life after what is called clinical death. Books now abound about this subject, with inspiring personal experiences being used for articles, television specials, and films. Those who have had a near-death experience report of a tunnel of light, the meeting with a Light Being, the return to their body, resulting in the complete re-working of all their life patterns over a period of years. These reports often include amazing reports of physical and health situations which improve dramatically after the n.d.e.

Dying itself is a healing component. In past times death was seen as a friend, a natural aspect of living. Only in more recent centuries has death been termed the Grim Reaper, and viewed as an enemy to be avoided at all costs. We are struggling with these incredible issues: who can live, who can die. We are slowly beginning to build bridges of consciousness between these parts of life experience; that life exists always, sometimes with a body, sometimes without a body. The fear of death, as an unknown reality, will dissolve with the understanding and mercy of the coming era.

## The Future of Healing

The mental strength of Uranus demands that we understand more and more about everything. The compassion of Neptune demands that we learn forgiveness and compassion necessary to accomplish the mighty deeds which are emerging in the human mind. The great sanctuaries where Will, Love and Wisdom, and Intelligence reside beam their messages constantly. We are awakening, we are listening, we are responding.

Healing is a natural phenomenon, as is consciousness. As co-workers, these qualities seek to cooperate with each other to restore the great plan on earth. These visions for the future will take years to become easy and natural. In fact, probably the entire 171 years before the next conjunction of Uranus and Neptune will go by. All things have a time of growing and a time of reaping. We are planting seeds now, including new healing styles, methods, discoveries, and inventions. The use of light and lasers is seen in small applications now, but the needs of the future will expand their capabilities.

Healing will not be complete or inclusive enough until it includes the healing of male-female relationships, the injustices and intolerance within the human group mind, including the terrible memories of pain, neglect and abuse. With the belief in the ultimate good, and the maturity of the human spirit connected to a larger Universal concept of Love and Wisdom, all things are possible.

# Associated with the Sun

**Sun Dance:** Traditional religious ceremony performed by North American Plains Indians at the time of the summer solstice.

**Sun Disk:** Ancient Near-Eastern symbol representing the sun god (depicted above).

**Sun Drops:** A flowering plant related to the evening primrose (*oenothera*).

**Sunfish:** Freshwater fish of family Centrarchidae, name derived from its flat disk-shaped body covered with irridescent gold-shaded scales.

**Sunflower:** So-called because the flower turns on its stem, following the movement of the sun in the sky. Heliotrope (*helianthus*).

**Sunflower State:** Kansas.

**Sunglass:** Convex lens used to focus the sun's rays, producing heat or igniting fire; burning glass.

**Sun Gods/Goddesses:** Apollo, Hebe, Helios, Horus, Nergal, Ra, Shamash, and others.

**Sun King, the:** Louis XIV of France.

**Sun, Land of the Rising:** Japan, whose national flag displays that image, and whose rulers were said to be descended from the Sun goddess.

**Sun Pillar:** A halo phenomenon in which a streak of light appears above and below the sun.

**Sunstone: Aventurine,** a brilliant variety of oligoclose flecked with scales of hematite.

**Sun Wheel or Gear:** The central wheel around which the planet wheels or gears revolve.

# PRODUCTS

and

# SERVICES

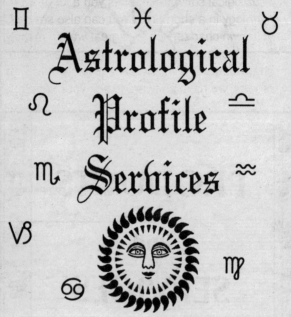

# *Get A New Start On Losing Weight*

## A Complete 30 Day Herb Tea Program For A Slimmer And Happier You!

## HERB TEA DIET and Cleansing Program

**Herb Tea Diet and Cleansing Program contains the six most important Herb Teas you need for a slimmer you!**

## Natural Herb Tea

Nature's Herbs have been used for over 4000 years in China for healing and balancing the body's energy. The use of herbs as body cleaners, rejuvenators, tonics and relaxers has been practiced by mankind all over the world, since the beginning of time. These natural remedies are still in use today.

## Safe & Gentle

Herbs work safely and gently so they do not have dangerous side-effects on your body as many drugs do. Join the millions of people who have discovered the health benefits of natural and delicious herb teas.

## One Cup A Day

Just one cup of fresh and delicious herb tea everyday will put you on the right track losing weight. Because the Herb Tea Diet and Cleansing Program is a 30 day program it makes sure you get all the valuable herbs your body needs to function at its peak and lose weight fast.

BEFORE | AFTER

**Feel Better & Look Better Takes Just 30 Days!**

## Results in 30 Days

Because herbs are so mild in action, enough time is needed for positive and lasting results. That's why Herb Tea Diet and Cleansing Program gives you a 30 day program. Isn't 30 days a small price to pay to feel and look your very best?

## Your Guarantee

Try Herb Tea Diet and Cleansing Program for 30 days. If you're not 100% satisfied that Herb Tea Diet and Cleansing Program has helped you lose weight, just return the unused portion for a full refund! That's how sure we are! Available in Tea or Tablets.

## FREE With Tea Order!

*Stainless Steel*

**$1.95 Value**

**Herb Tea Infuser**

Isn't it time you got a new start? Order Herb Tea Diet and Cleansing Program and get a FREE Herb Tea Infuser for brewing your delicious, healthful Herb Tea Diet and Cleansing Program.

## Herb Tea Diet & Cleansing Program Contains These Important Herbs

| Ginger | Cascara Sagrada |
|---|---|
| Ginger root has a warming, stimulating effect. Ginger is a carminative, soothing to the stomach. | **Cascara Sagrada** Tones large intestine and helps maintain regular elimination. |
| **Yellow Dock** | **Bearberry** |
| Yellow Dock is beneficial for the liver and large intestine. | Bearberry is a mild diuretic, cleansing to intestinal and urinary tracts. |
| **Prickly Ash Bark** | **Psyllium Seed** |
| Prickly Ash Bark acts as a blood purifier, cleansing the blood | The highest fiber available, bulking agent gives a full, satisfied feeling; speeds intestinal transit time and removes waste & toxins. |

## HOW TO ORDER [HT29]

Please specify Tea or Tablets
Send Check or Money Order for
$9.95 plus $2.00 for shipping to:
**Indiana Botanic Gardens**
P.O. Box 5 Dept. LAHI, Hammond, IN 46325
*"Keeping America Healthy Since*

# Classifieds

## Ancient Teachings

RECEIVE ANCIENT POWERFUL spell, for fulfilling your desire. Win with real magickal help. State desire, $1/ SASE. Wizeworld(LL), P.O. Box 1337, Huntington Beach CA 92647

## Announcements

WILL PAY UP to $100 for stories about psychic powers, extraterrestrial, afterlife, ESP and reincarnation experiences. Free information. MTCF, Box 720104, San Diego CA 92172

## Astrology

IN-DEPTH COMPATIBILITY REPORT (lowest price). Send $12.95 to: Lisa Burton, P.O. Box 2564, Riverside CA 92516-2564. Include two birthdates: month, day, year, birthplace, name and sex.

WOW! 45/60 PAGE ASTROLOGY reports. Depicts all characteristics. Send birth info. and $24.95 to: Carol Corsi, Box 221254, Hollywood FL 33022

## Books

FREE METAPHYSICAL BOOKLIST. Astrology, healing, earth changes, occult, etc.! Sunbooks, Box 5588 (SSB), Santa Fe NM 87502-5588

## Crystals

CRYSTALS, FREE GIFTS! $1 refundable for details and price list. Ariels' Crystals, Box 387L, Marcy NY 13403

## Instruction

WITCHCRAFT SPELLS. REVEALING ancient power secrets show how to cast spells to get whatever you want. P.O. Box 9133SS, Greensboro NC 27429

## Magick

FREE! ONE BLACK or white magic spell! Tell me what you need! Menor, 18533 Roscoe, Northridge CA 91324-2932

## Personal

HOW TO ATTRACT more money than you need. For true peace of mind write: Universal Ideas, Box 8465-S, Bartlett IL 60103

DATES "R" US. MEET that special one. Fast, Effective. Inexpensive. 33,000 members. 19 years experience. Call 1-800-723-2496 for free information.

## Products

ASTROLOGICAL STATIONARY. 25 pieces with sun sign, 25 plain, 25 envelopes. $12.95, indicate sign, to: Carol Corsi, Box 221254, Hollywood FL 33022

## Products

NEW AGE SOFTWARE. Astrology, numerology, tarot and much more! Great prices. Catalog $1. Amazons' Realm, Box 60591, Reno NV 89506

QUARTZ CRYSTAL NECKLACES on silk rope. Enhances psychic ability (Holy Ice). Send $8.95 to: Carol Corsi, Box 221254, Hollywood FL 33022

ASTROLOGY FLASH CARDS. Learn astrology's symbolisms (planets, signs, houses, aspects). Send $16.95 to: Carol Corsi, Box 221254, Hollywood FL 33022

## Publications

CIRCLE NETWORK NEWS – Quarterly newspaper/journal of Paganism, Wiccan Spirituality, Goddess Studies, Shamanism, Magic and Nature Spirituality. FREE sample copy. Box 219, Mt. Horeb WI 53572

EXCITING NEW NATIONWIDE photo magazine for singles. Send name, address, age. Send no money. Exchange, Box 2425, Loveland CO 80539

## Readings

CLAIRVOYANT, TAROT, NUMEROLOGY or astrological readings. Taped: $35. Free information! The Psychic Network<sub>sm</sub>, Box 499-M, Deerfield FL 33443

EXTRAORDINARY PSYCHIC COUNSELOR, Randal Clayton Bradford, will tell you the best possible future in any situation, and how to make it happen. "Cuts straight to the truth…accurate, detailed and specific." Established worldwide clientele by telephone. AMEX/MC/VISA, 310-823-8893 or 213-REALITY

LIVE 24 HOURS! One on one! Psychics, astrologers, tarot. 1-900-773-7374. The Psychic Network<sub>sm</sub>, Box 499-M, Deerfield FL 33443

PSYCHIC PHONE READINGS, incredibly accurate. Need answers on love, health, finances? JoAnna 516-753-0191, NY, $35

GIFTED PSYCHIC TAROTIST shares insight and wisdom on love, health finances. Phone consultations, $30. Call Jerel-Lynn 516-271-8540.

# Llewellyn's Computerized Astrological Services

Llewellyn has been a leading authority in astrological chart readings for over thirty years. Our professional experience and continued dedication assures complete satisfaction in all areas of our astrological services.

Llewellyn features a wide variety of readings with the intent to satisfy the needs of any astrological enthusiast. Our goal is to give you the best possible service so that you can achieve your goals and live your life successfully.

When requesting a computerized service be sure to give accurate and complete birth data including: exact time (a.m. or p.m.), date, year, city, county and country of birth. (Check your birth certificate for this information.) *Accuracy of birth data is very important.* Llewellyn will not be responsible for mistakes made by you. An order form follows for your convenience.

## Computerized Charts

### Simple Natal Chart
Before you do anything else, order the Simple Natal Chart! This chart print-out is programmed and designed by Matrix. Learn the locations of your midpoints and aspects, elements, and more. Discover your planets and house cusps, retrogrades and other valuable data necessary to make a complete interpretation.
APS03-119 . . . . . . . . . . . . . . . . . . . . . $5.00

### Personality Profile
This is our most popular reading! It makes the perfect gift! This ten-part reading gives you a complete look at your "natal imprint" and how the planets mark your destiny. Examine your emotional needs and inner feelings. Explore your imagination and read about your general characteristics and life patterns. Very reasonable price!
APS03-503 . . . . . . . . . . . . . . . . . . . . . $20.00

## Life Progression

Discover what the future has in store for you! This incredible reading covers a year's time and is designed to complement the Personality Profile Reading. Progressions are a special system with which astrologers map how the "natal you" develops through specified periods of your present and future life. We are all born into an already existing world and an already existing fabric of personal interaction, and with this report you can discover the "now you!"

APS03-507 . . . . . . . . . . . . . . . . . . . . . $20.00

## Transit Report

Know the trends of your life—in advance! Keep abreast of positive trends and challenging periods for a specified period of time in your life. Transits are the relationships between the planets today and their positions at the moment of your birth. They are an invaluable aid for timing your actions and making decisions. This report devotes a paragraph to each of your transit aspects and gives effective dates for those transits. The report will begin with the first day of the month. Be sure to specify present residence for all people getting this report!

APS03-500 – 3-month report . . . . . . . . . . . $12.00
APS03-501 – 6-month report . . . . . . . . . . . $20.00
APS03-502 – 1-year report . . . . . . . . . . . . $30.00

## Biorhythm Report

Ever have one of those days when you have unlimited energy and everything is going your way? Then the next day you are feeling sluggish and awkward? These cycles are called biorhythms. This individual report will accurately map your daily biorhythms. It can be your personal guide to the cycles of your daily life. Each important day is thoroughly discussed. With this valuable information, you can schedule important events with great success. This report is an invaluable source of information to help you plan your days to the fullest. Order today!

APS03-515 – 3-month report . . . . . . . . . . . $12.00
APS03-516 – 6-month report . . . . . . . . . . . $18.00
APS03-517 – 1-year report . . . . . . . . . . . . $25.00

## Compatibility Profile

Find out if you really are compatible with your lover, spouse, friend or business partner! This is a great way of getting an in-depth look at your relationship with another person. Find out each person's approach to the relationship. Do you have the same goals? How well do you deal with arguments? Do you have the same values? This service includes planetary placements for both individuals, so send birth data for both. Succeed in all of your relationships! Order today!

**APS03-504** . . . . . . . . . . . . . . . . . . . . . **$30.00**

## Personal Relationship Interpretation

If you've just called it quits on one relationship and know you need to understand more about yourself before you test the waters again, then this is the report for you! This reading will tell you how you approach relationships in general, what kind of people you look for and what kind of people might rub you the wrong way. Important for anyone!

**APS03-506** . . . . . . . . . . . . . . . . . . . . . **$20.00**

## Tarot Reading

Find out what the cards have in store for you! This reading features the graphics of the traditional Rider-Waite card deck in a detailed 10-card spread, and as a bonus, there are three pages explaining what each Tarot card means for you. This report is also custom made to answer any question you might have. Order this exciting tarot reading today!

**APS03-120** . . . . . . . . . . . . . . . . . . . . . **$10.00**

## Lucky Lotto Report

Do you play the lotteries? Bet on horses? Make trips to the casinos? This reading will determine the best numbers and dates based on specific planets, degrees and other indicators in your own chart. With this information you will know when planetary influences are in your favor, and when you are more likely to win. Learn what numbers are best for you, and begin your journey to financial success today!

**APS03-512 – 3-month report** . . . . . . . . . . . **$10.00**
**APS03-513 – 6-month report** . . . . . . . . . . . **$15.00**
**APS03-514 – 1-year report** . . . . . . . . . . . . **$25.00**

## Numerology Report

Find out which numbers are right for you with this insightful report. This report uses an ancient form of numerology invented by Pythagoras to determine the significant numbers in your life. Using both your given birth name and date of birth, this report will accurately calculate those numbers which stand out as yours. With these numbers, the report can determine certain trends in your life and tell you when the important periods of your life will occur.

**APS03-508 – 3-month report** . . . . . . . . . . . $12.00
**APS03-509 – 6-month report** . . . . . . . . . . . $18.00
**APS03-510 – 1-year report** . . . . . . . . . . . $25.00

## Ultimate Astro-Profile

This report has it all! Receive over 40 pages of fascinating, insightful and uncanny descriptions of your innermost qualities and talents. Read about your burn rate (thirst for change). Explore your personal patterns (inside and outside). Examine the particular pattern of your Houses. The Astro-Profile doesn't repeat what you've already learned from other personality profiles, but considers often the neglected natal influence of the lunar nodes plus much more.

**APS03-505** . . . . . . . . . . . . . . . . . . . . . $40.00

# SPECIAL COMBO OFFER

**Buy both and save!**
**APS03-214** . . **$40.00**

**Personality Profile & Compatibility Profile**
Learn about the real you and discover what the
future holds with that special someone!

# Astrological Services Order Form

Include all birth data plus your full name for all reports.

Service name and number _____

Full name (1st person) _____

Birthtime _____ ☐ a.m. ☐ p.m. Date _____ Year _____

Birthplace (city, county, state, country) _____

_____

Full name (2nd person) _____

Birthtime _____ ☐ a.m. ☐ p.m. Date _____ Year _____

Birthplace (city, county, state, country) _____

_____

Astrological knowledge: ☐ Novice ☐ Student ☐ Advanced

**Include letter with questions on separate sheet of paper.**

Name _____

Address _____

City _____ State _____ Zip _____

Make check or money order payable to Llewellyn Publications, or charge it!

☐ VISA ☐ MasterCard ☐ American Express

Account Number _____

Exp. Date _____ Daytime Phone _____

Signature of Cardholder _____

☐ **Yes!** Send me my **FREE** copy of **New Worlds!**

**Mail this form and payment to:**

Llewellyn's Personal Services, P.O. Box 64383-911,
St. Paul, MN 55164-0383. Allow 4-6 weeks for delivery.

# Find New Meaning in Magical Myths

Myth & Magic
1994

"Laura Simms is one of those rare and indispensible souls who keeps the oral tradition alive for us. She carries within her a tremendous range of material – from all over the world."
—C.G. Jung Foundation

- Behold the brilliance of 12 original full-color paintings

- Learn about symbolic myths that have meaning in our world today

- Keep track of your day-to-day appointments and personal notes

- Explore mythological legends from around the world

- Realize your everyday life is full of myth and magic!

Find new meaning in magical myths with the new 1994 Myth and Magic Calendar. In this premiere calendar come twelve original full-color paintings from Llewellyn artists Hrana Janto and William Giese. Myth comes alive with exciting narrations by renowned story-teller Laura Simms.

Unleash your imagination and find new meaning from the gods and goddesses from around the world including Osiris, Isis and Horus; White Buffalo Woman; Sekhmet; and Pegasus. Order today!

**Llewellyn's 1994 Myth & Magic Calendar**
24 pp. ✦ full-color ✦ 12 x 12 ✦ Order # L-909 ✦ $10.00
Please use order form on last page.

# Make the Most of the Moon in 1994!

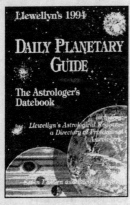

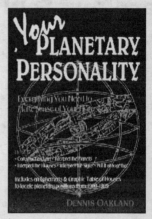

# SUPER DISCOUNTS ON
# LLEWELLYN DATEBOOKS AND CALENDARS!

Llewellyn offers several ways to save money. With a four-year subscription you receive your books as soon as they are published. The price remains the same for four years even if there is a price increase! We pay postage and handling as well. *Buy any 2 subscriptions and take $2 off! Buy 3 and take $3 off! Buy 4 and take an additional $5 off!*

## Subscriptions (4 years, 1995-1998)

| | | |
|---|---|---|
| ❏ | Astrological Calendar | $40.00 |
| ❏ | Sun Sign Book | $19.80 |
| ❏ | Moon Sign Book | $19.80 |
| ❏ | Daily Planetary Guide | $27.80 |
| ❏ | Organic Gardening Almanac | $23.80 |

Order *by the dozen* and save 40%! Sell them to your friends or give them as gifts. Llewellyn pays all postage and handling on quantity orders.

## Quantity Orders: 40% OFF
1994 1995

| | | | |
|---|---|---|---|
| ❏ | ❏ | Astrological Calendar | 12/$72.00 |
| ❏ | ❏ | Sun Sign Book | 12/$35.64 |
| ❏ | ❏ | Moon Sign Book | 12/$35.64 |
| ❏ | ❏ | Daily Planetary Guide | 12/$50.04 |
| ❏ | ❏ | Magical Almanac | 12/$50.04 |
| ❏ | ❏ | Organic Gardening Almanac | 12/$42.84 |

On single copy orders, include $3 p/h for orders under $10 and $4 for orders over $10. We pay postage for all orders over $50.

## Single copies of Llewellyn's Almanacs and Calendars
1994 1995

| | | | |
|---|---|---|---|
| ❏ | ❏ | Astrological Calendar | $10.00 |
| ❏ | ❏ | Sun Sign Book | $4.95 |
| ❏ | ❏ | Moon Sign Book | $4.95 |
| ❏ | ❏ | Daily Planetary Guide | $6.95 |
| ❏ | ❏ | Magical Almanac | $6.95 |
| ❏ | ❏ | Organic Gardening Almanac | $5.95 |
| ❏ | | Myth and Magic Calendar | $10.00 |

**Please use order form on last page.**

# LLEWELLYN ORDER FORM

Llewellyn Publications

P.O. Box 64383-911, St. Paul, MN 55164-0383

You may use this form to order any of the Llewellyn books listed in this publication.

Give Title, Author, Order Number and Price.

_____

_____

_____

_____

_____

_____

_____

**Shipping and Handling:** We ship UPS when possible. Include $3 for orders under $10 and $4 for orders over $10. Llewellyn pays postage for all orders over $50. Please give street address (UPS cannot deliver to P.O. Boxes). Minnesota residents please add 6.5% sales tax.

**Credit Card Orders:** In the U.S. and Canada call 1-800-THE-MOON. In Minnesota call 612-291-1970. Or, send credit card order by mail. Any questions can be directed to customer service 612-291-1970.

❏ Yes! Send me your free catalog!

❏ VISA   ❏ MasterCard   ❏ American Express

Account No. _____

Exp. Date _____ Phone _____

Signature _____

Name _____

Address _____

City _____ State \_\_\_\_\_ Zip _____

*Thank you for your order!*